QUESTION	STATISTICAL TEST	CHAPTER
Equivalency of two methods:		
• Do methods A and B give equivalent results?	Perform F and t tests on data. If both are not significant, the methods are equivalent in precision and average values.	4, 5
Correlation of two variables:		
• Is there a linear relationship between two variables?	Correlation coefficient	6
• If variables X and Y have a linear relationship, what is the best equation for predicting Y from X?	Regression of Y on X	6, 12, 13
• How can I establish the best linear calibration curve for my data?	Regression of Y on X	6, 12, 13
Effect of variables:		
• Does variable A significantly affect my results?	ANOVA, one-way classification	7
• Do variables A and B significantly affect my results?	ANOVA, two-way classification	8
• Which of three variables significantly affect my results?	ANOVA, three-way classification, or Latin square	9
• Which of four variables significantly affect my results?	ANOVA, 2^n factorial	10
• How can I evaluate the results of an interlaboratory study of a method's precision?	ANOVA, nested design	11

PRACTICAL
STATISTICS
FOR
ANALYTICAL
CHEMISTS

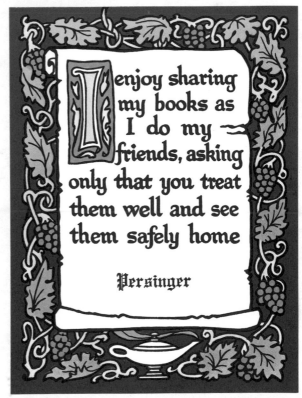

I enjoy sharing my books as I do my friends, asking only that you treat them well and see them safely home

Persinger

PRACTICAL
STATISTICS
FOR
ANALYTICAL
CHEMISTS

Robert L. Anderson

 VAN NOSTRAND REINHOLD COMPANY
——————————————————————— **New York**

Copyright © 1987 by Van Nostrand Reinhold Company Inc.
Library of Congress Catalog Card Number 86–28284
ISBN 0–442–20973–8

Printed in the United States of America

Van Nostrand Reinhold Company Inc.
115 Fifth Avenue
New York, New York 10003

Van Nostrand Reinhold Company Limited
Molly Millars Lane
Wokingham, Berkshire RG11 2PY, England

Van Nostrand Reinhold
480 La Trobe Street
Melbourne, Victoria 3000, Australia

Macmillan of Canada
Division of Canada Publishing Corporation
164 Commander Boulevard
Agincourt, Ontario M1S 3C7, Canada

16 15 14 13 12 11 10 9 8 7 6 5 4 3 2 1

Library of Congress Cataloging-in-Publication Data

Anderson, Robert L., 1927–
    Practical statistics for analytical chemists.

    Includes index.
    1. Chemistry, Analytical—Statistical methods. I. Title.
QD75.4.S8A53   1987   543'.0072   86–28284
ISBN 0–442–20973–8

In memory of HSA and EAA

PREFACE

This book is for analytical chemists who have felt the need for objective ways of evaluating data, but who may have been discouraged from using statistics by the rigorous, theoretical approach of many courses and texts on the subject. My 37 years' experience as an analytical chemist in an industrial research and development department have shown that you can answer the most common questions about analytical data by using simple statistical procedures. Thus, this book emphasizes the practical use of statistics by chemists to help answer questions like "Is method A more precise than method B?", "Is the difference between two results real, or merely due to experimental error?", "Which of several variables play a significant role in my results?", and "How do I establish the best linear calibration curve through my data points?"

Each of the tests and procedures has been found to be useful in the ordinary situations encountered by chemists, but no attempt has been made to include all statistical techniques. My intent has been to include the basic tests you can easily apply, even if you have been unfamiliar with statistics. The usefulness of these techniques has been confirmed by the experience of associates who participated in in-house courses I presented in my employer's R/D department prior to my retirement.

Each technique is illustrated with an example from chemical analysis. A step-by-step solution to the problem is presented. You may follow the mathematics with a scientific model hand calculator, except perhaps in the last two chapters, where matrix algebra is used. Additional problems with answers are provided in Appendices B and C to permit you to practice the principles. The problems are referred to by number in the appropriate chapters. Some of the examples and problems are concerned with strictly analytical problems, such as the precision of a method; others involve aspects, such as production variability, which might appear to be of concern only to process chemists. In industry, the analytical chemist is expected to work closely with other chemists and engineers in process/product development and in production. Thus, these kinds of problems are of concern to the analytical chemist.

You may find that a hand calculator is more convenient than a computer in applying some of the statistical techniques, such as the F and t tests, to small sets of data. Of course, a personal computer with appropriate software is of great help in reducing the tedium of calculation in more involved procedures or

in handling larger sets of data. Because of the great number of statistical programs available, it is not practical to discuss their individual merits. However,
some guidelines are offered in the selection of computer programs.

Essentially no theory of statistics is presented in this book. Theory may be
found in many excellent texts, some of which are listed in Chapter 1. I hope
that your successful use of these more simple statistical procedures will encourage
you to explore wider areas of statistics more thoroughly.

The support of the R/D management of Union Carbide Corporation at South
Charleston, WV, is gratefully acknowledged. This support has included encourag-
ing the application of statistics to analysis, developing and presenting in-house
courses for chemists, enabling consultation with personnel in other departments,
and providing assistance in preparing the material in this book. Special thanks are
due J. L. Hansen and R. A. Lewis of the Applied Mathematics Section of the R/D
Department for their helpful counsel and many discussions. The suggestions of the
anonymous reviewers have resulted in an improved book. The considerable
task of preliminary manuscript preparations was most capably handled by
Stephanie Ball, Linda Christian, Reginia Pauley, Pauline Scott, Gerry Skies, and
Pearl Walker.

ROBERT L. ANDERSON

CONTENTS

Preface / vii

1. WHY BOTHER WITH STATISTICS? / 1

Overview / 1

1.0 Background / 1

1.1 Why Bother With Statistics? / 2

1.2 The Certainty of Uncertainty / 3

1.3 Design of Experiments / 4

1.4 Accuracy and Precision / 5

1.5 The Average / 6

1.6 Abacuses, Hand Calculators, and Computers, or Efficient and Accurate Calculations / 9

1.7 Significant Figures for Chemists / 11

1.8 Coding of Data / 15

1.9 Summary / 17

Resources / 18

Suggested Books for Further Reading / 18

2. SOME BASICS TO HELP YOU GET STARTED / 20

Overview / 20

2.0 Some Assumptions / 20

2.1 Types of Distributions / 21

2.2 Independence / 24

2.3 Effect of Skewed Distribution on Variance / 26

2.4 Transformation of Data / 27

2.5 Outliers / 31

2.6 Summary / 33

2.7 Problems / 33

References / 33

3.   **MEASURES OF PRECISION / 34**

Overview / 34

3.0   Ways of Measuring Precision / 34

3.1   The Best Way — Variance / 35

3.2   Standard Deviation / 40

3.3   Another Measure of Precision — Coefficient of Variation / 42

3.4   Standard Deviation or Coefficient of Variation? / 42

3.5   Sample Sizes in Estimating Precision / 44

3.6   Pooling Precision (Variance) Estimates / 44

3.7   Summary / 45

3.8   Problems / 46

Resources / 46

Reference / 46

4.   **HOW GOOD IS THE ESTIMATED PRECISION? / 47**

Overview / 47

4.0   How Good is the Estimated Variance? (Confidence Intervals For a Variance) / 47

4.1   When Are Two Variances Really Different? / 50

4.2   Comparing More Than Two Variances / 61

4.3   More About Variances / 65

4.4   Summary / 65

4.5   Problems / 66

5.   **AVERAGES / 67**

Overview / 67

5.0   Real Differences / 67

5.1   Does the Average Agree With the Theoretical or An Accepted Value? / 70

5.2   When Are Two Averages Different? / 72

5.3   Sample Size to Detect a Given Difference Between Averages / 83

5.4   How Good is the Estimated Average? (Confidence Intervals for an Average) / 83

5.5   Range of Values Expected for an Average at a Given Confidence Level / 84

5.6   Comparing More Than Two Averages / 85

5.7   Summary / 87

5.8   Problems / 88

6. LINEAR RELATIONSHIPS BETWEEN TWO VARIABLES: CALIBRATION CURVES AND OTHER PREDICTIONS / 89

Overview / 89

6.0 Linear Relationships Between Two Variables / 89

6.1 Regression Lines for Different Kinds of Relationships / 93

6.2 The Calibration Curve and Other Functional Relationships / 94

6.3 Estimating the Calibration Equation With the Curve Forced Through the Origin / 104

6.4 Relationship of Two Methods of Analysis (Linear Association Relationship) / 108

6.5 Correlation Coefficients / 118

6.6 Summary / 120

6.7 Problems / 121

Resources / 121

References / 121

7. COMPARING MORE THAN TWO AVERAGES: ANALYSIS OF VARIANCE / 122

Overview / 122

7.0 Introduction to Analysis of Variance / 122

7.1 Measuring the Effect of One Variable on Averages (One-Way Classification of Variables) / 128

7.2 One-Way Classification With Unequal Observations Per Average / 135

7.3 Summary / 138

7.4 Problems / 139

Resources / 139

8. COMPARING MORE THAN TWO AVERAGES: ANALYSIS OF VARIANCE FOR TWO INDEPENDENT VARIABLES / 140

Overview / 140

8.0 Measuring the Effect of Two Variables on Averages (Two-Way Classification) / 140

8.1 Two-Way Classification With No Replicates / 144

8.2 Two-Way Classification With n Observations Per Combination / 150

8.3 Summary / 156

8.4 Problems / 157

Reference / 157

9. **COMPARING MORE THAN TWO AVERAGES: ANALYSIS OF VARIANCE FOR THREE INDEPENDENT VARIABLES / 158**

Overview / 158

9.0 Measuring the Effect of Different Levels of Three Variables on Averages (Three-Way Classification) / 158

9.1 Latin Squares / 174

9.2 Summary / 179

9.3 Problems / 179

References / 179

10. **COMPARISON OF MORE THAN TWO AVERAGES: ANALYSIS OF VARIANCE FOR FOUR INDEPENDENT VARIABLES / 180**

Overview / 180

10.0 Reducing the Number of Analyses With a Factorial Design / 180

10.1 Measuring the Effect of Two Levels of Four Variables on Averages (2^4 Factorial Design) / 181

10.2 2^n Factorial With Replication / 186

10.3 Summary / 189

10.4 Problems / 189

Resources / 190

Reference / 190

11. **COMPARING MORE THAN TWO AVERAGES: ANALYSIS OF VARIANCE OF NESTED DESIGNS / 191**

Overview / 191

11.0 Interlaboratory Precision Studies Using Nested (or Hierarchical) Designs / 191

11.1 ANOVA of a Nested Design / 193

11.2 General Analysis of a Nested Design / 201

11.3 Summary / 202

11.4 Problems / 203

Resources / 203

References / 203

12. LINEAR RELATIONSHIPS BETWEEN TWO VARIABLES: CALCULATION OF CALIBRATION CURVES USING MATRIX ALGEBRA / 204

Overview / 204

12.0   Linear Relationships Revisited / 204

12.1   Matrix Algebra Principles / 205

12.2   Matrix Operations / 207

12.3   Solving Simultaneous Equations With Matrix Algebra / 213

12.4   Application of Matrices to Calibration Curves (Linear Regression) / 214

12.5   Confidence Intervals / 221

12.6   Correlation Coefficient and Coefficient of Determination / 225

12.7   Summary / 225

12.8   Problems / 226

Resources / 226

References / 226

13. EVALUATION OF THE CALIBRATION EQUATION / 227

Overview / 227

13.0   Evaluation of the Calibration (Linear Regression) Equation / 227

13.1   Analysis of Variance / 227

13.2   Regression Analysis With Replicated Observations / 230

13.3   Testing Our Assumptions: Analysis of Residuals / 236

13.4   Cautions in the Use of Regression Lines / 241

13.5   Summary / 242

13.6   Problems / 243

APPENDICES

A.   Glossary of Some Common Statistical Terms / 245

B.   Problems / 249

C.   Answers to Problems / 263

D.   Table 1: Critical Values of the χ^2 Distribution / 287

Table 2: Critical Values of the F Distribution / 289

Table 3: Critical Values of g / 296

Table 4: Sample Sizes Required for Probability that s^2 Will be Less than $k\sigma^2$ or that s Will be Less than $k\sigma$ / 298

Table 5: Critical Values of Student's t Distribution / 299

Table 6: Sample Size for t Test of Difference Between Two Means / 300

Table 7: Test for Outliers / 302

Table 8: Critical Values of Correlation Coefficient, r / 303

Table 9: Factors for Calculating Range of Two Results
(95% Confidence Level) / 304

Table 10: Duncan's Significant Ranges / 305

Table 11: Runs Test, 5% Level / 307

Table 12: Factors for Calculating Standard Deviation from Range / 308

Table 13: Main Effects and Interactions in Up to a 2^4 Factorial
Design / 309

Index / 311

PRACTICAL
STATISTICS
FOR
ANALYTICAL
CHEMISTS

Chapter 1
WHY BOTHER WITH STATISTICS?

OVERVIEW

The purpose of this chapter is to (a) provide some background information on statistics; (b) show why statistics can be a valuable tool for the analytical chemist in evaluating data; (c) provide a brief introduction to some definitions and concepts we will need in the following chapters; (d) introduce the first statistic, averages; and (e) present rules and guidelines for computation and the use of computers and calculators.

1.0 BACKGROUND

Before we begin exploring how statistics can be a helpful tool to the analytical chemist, we need to take a moment to establish a few definitions so when we use a word everyone will know exactly what we mean. First of all, what do we mean by "statistics?" A dictionary will tell us that "statistics" can mean (1) *the science of inferring generalities from specific observations, (2) systematic procedures for describing data, or (3) the data itself.* However, the root word "statist" goes back to about 1580; it meant a person knowledgeable in state affairs.

The 17th Century French mathematicians Pascal and Fermat did the first theoretical work in statistics in 1654, when they developed the theory of probability as applied to gaming (dice-throwing). This may explain why many courses in statistics begin by discussing how to calculate the odds of getting a tail when a coin is tossed or of getting snake eyes when dice are thrown. The word "statistics," denoting the science of collecting, classifying, and analyzing data of importance in state affairs, appeared about 1785. By early eighteen hundred the term was applied to the data itself.

The early applications of statistics included the enumeration of people, agriculture, and astronomy. Many of the terms used today derive from these uses. Thus, *population* and *individual* reflect measurements of people for state uses, and *universe* and *observation* have an obvious connection with astronomy. Like any science, statistics has developed its own vocabulary. Some of the more common words are listed in the Glossary. Nontechnical terms have been used in defining these words wherever possible. We will be talking about some of these terms later in this chapter, but you should read through the list now and become familiar with the terms. Whenever you have occasion to consult a professional statistician, a working knowledge of the basic vocabulary will greatly facilitate communication.

1.1 WHY BOTHER WITH STATISTICS?

Any chemist who has used a particular method of analysis a few times has a "feel" for how well the values obtained should agree. If this is true, then what benefits does statistics offer the chemist? After all, a causal inspection of a statistics text, or even a course in the subject, can lead one to think that statistics involves a lot of arcane equations and complex calculations, not to mention the vocabulary. Isn't statistics more bother than it's worth?

The fact that you are reading this indicates that you have felt the need for a better way of evaluating data other than a seat-of-the-pants technique which leads you to believe that a given method is more precise than another one, or that the purity of your sample is greater than that of "brand X." Other chemists have shared your feeling. Some very respected statisticians such as W. J. Youden, G. E. P. Box, J. W. Tukey, and Frank Wilcoxon, were chemists before they devoted themselves to statistics.

It is true that statistics can get very involved, and, yes, there are some commonly used technical terms that cannot be avoided. But statistics can be very helpful in providing an objective evaluation of data as well as in extracting the maximum amount of information from a set of experiments. The calculations can be complex, but with electronic pocket calculators and personal computers becoming common laboratory equipment, the drudgery of number crunching is greatly minimized.

1.1.1 Types of Analytical Problems

What are some of the analytical chemist's problems which statistics can help solve?

- A set of data has been obtained using a given method. What is the precision of the method?
- Given average analyses on two or more samples, do the averages really differ?
- Some samples have been analyzed by two methods. Do the two methods give equivalent average results? Is one method more precise than the other?
- All the values in a set of data appear to be consistent except for one. Is it an outlier?
- You supply a certificate of analysis on a shipment to a customer. The customer complains that his analysis shows a water content different from that in the certificate. Are the two water results really different?

● You are developing a method of analysis and think that three variables can affect the results. What is the most efficient way to determine if they influence the results and by how much?

● From your data it appears that variable X varies with variable Y. Is variable X linearly related to Y? If so, what equation best predicts the value of X for a given value of Y? (This is essentially the problem of establishing the best calibration curve.)

● You have been asked about the precision of a method, but all you have are five samples which have been analyzed two to four times by the method. How can you supply a reasonable estimate of the method's precision without obtaining more data?

● You have collected a set of measurements over a period of time. Do the data exhibit a pattern or are they random?

The list of examples could go on. In each of these cases statistics can help solve the problem by the application of rather straightforward techniques.

When we make judgments about data by whatever means, we are making *general inferences* from *specific observations.* Statistics is one means of inferring generalities from specific observations, and it is objective. In addition it enables us to state our conclusion with whatever level of confidence we choose; e.g., we may say the purity of a material is $98.0 \pm 0.32\%$ with 95% certainty. We must make inferences of this nature because if we were to analyze all the material, none would be left for use. Moreover, there is always some degree of uncertainty (the statistician calls it random error) in any measurement.

1.2 THE CERTAINTY OF UNCERTAINTY

It may be disquieting, but we never know the *true* values of anything we measure, although we can get pretty close many times. Most statistical tests and tables were developed from theoretical models in which the true values of certain parameters were known. Parameters are basic properties of a population or a distribution, such as the mean and variance. In real life we can only estimate these properties. An *estimate of a parameter* is called a *statistic.* The statistician uses a different symbol for a parameter and a statistic to avoid confusing the two:

PARAMETER	STATISTIC
Mean, μ	$\bar{X}$
Variance, σ^2	s^2
Standard deviation, σ	s

The *mean* is the average value of a set of numbers. The most familiar mean is what we usually call the average; this is the arithmetical mean. *Variance* and *standard deviation* are measures of the scatter exhibited by data. We will explain these two terms more fully in a later chapter.

1.3 DESIGN OF EXPERIMENTS

Statistical tests may be applied to data which have been collected with little regard to the questions to be answered. This after-the-fact situation usually results in (a) heroic efforts to fit the data to forms amenable to statistical calculations, (b) data not used because it does not fit statistical requirements, or (c) questions only partially answered without running additional experiments, and/or (d) misleading results. Obviously, this approach is not to be recommended. As we examine the various statistical tests, it will become even more obvious that well planned and executed experiments will result in the greatest amount of information from the least amount of data in the easiest manner.

1.3.1 Steps in Designing Experiments

Entire chapters and books have been devoted to the subject of experimental design—that is, how does one go about selecting, collecting, and analyzing data to answer a question. For those who want a detailed discussion of this subject, several good books are listed under Resources at the end of this chapter. However, any good design will include consideration of the following concepts:

1. The first step in the design of an experiment is to define the objectives clearly and in detail. It is not enough to state that the objective is to see if Method A is better than Method B. Just what makes Method A better than Method B? Are the average values obtained by each to be compared? Is the basis for judgment how close each method comes to some reference value? Is the precision of each method to be used as the criterion? If so, is the precision to be measured by replicates performed by one analyst in one laboratory on different days, several analysts in different laboratories on different days, etc.?

2. Another important consideration is the selection of which variables are to be studied and their ranges of values. By use of appropriate statistical techniques several variables can be studied simultaneously with a saving of the number of experiments required over studying one variable at a time. In general, however, the more variables studied, the more experiments will be required. So the variables should be limited to those most likely to influence the results. The chemist will use his knowledge of the chemistry to guide his selection of the variables and their ranges.

3. Once it is decided exactly what questions are to be answered and which variables at what levels are to be included, the best statistical approach can

be selected to provide the needed answers. This, plus the desired level of certainty, will determine how many experiments will be needed to obtain the data required for statistical testing.

4. The careful experimenter will minimize unknown bias and guarantee validity of statistical tests by randomizing the order in which he runs his experiments. In this way the effect of any unsuspected factor or variable will be minimized or cancelled and not be superimposed on one of the variables being studied.

5. The next step is the collection of the experimental data. It is important to carry out the complete schedule of experiments. Missed or skipped determinations will make the straightforward use of statistical tests impossible.

6. Only now can the researcher actually apply the statistical tests selected in step 3.

7. The last step is evaluation of the statistical results. What do the results of the tests signify? If the precision of a method has been determined, is that precision satisfactory for the method's intended use? If not, means of improvement may have to be explored. This in turn can lead to another experimental design. In any event, the conclusions will probably form the basis of a more or less formal report that will inform others of the findings. This report should, of course, include also what was done to arrive at the conclusions.

1.4 ACCURACY AND PRECISION

It should not be necessary here to define the distinction between accuracy and precision, but many people, even those in the scientific world, tend to use these terms interchangeably. *Accuracy is the agreement between an experimentally determined value and the accepted reference value.* Statisticians call this agreement, or lack of it, *bias*. Because *accuracy* is sometimes used in a broader sense that combines the senses of bias and precision, there is a trend to use *bias* in its place. In this book we will use the *accuracy* as defined above.

The accepted reference value may be the theoretical value, or some other agreed upon value. As an analytical chemist, you know that in industry it is often impossible to obtain standards with certified or reliable assays. In such cases, one makes do with a working standard which is assigned an arbitrary value.

Precision is the degree of agreement of repeated measurements of the same property. It is possible for a method to have very good precision (all the results agreeing with one another very closely) and at the same time be very inaccurate (the average value not being very close to the accepted reference value). Conversely, a method may have rather poor precision, but if many repeated measurements are made, their average might be in excellent agreement with the reference value.

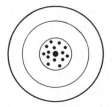

Figure 1.1.   Good accuracy; good precision.

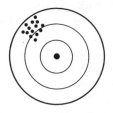

Figure 1.2.   Poor accuracy; good precision.

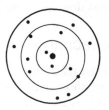

Figure 1.3.   Good accuracy; poor precision.

These concepts of accuracy and precision are often illustrated by considering the patterns of gun shot marks on a bull's-eye target. In Figure 1.1 all the marks are closely grouped near the bull's-eye, corresponding to good accuracy and precision. In Figure 1.2 the marks are still closely grouped (good precision), but the center of the cluster is off the bull's-eye (poor accuracy). In Figure 1.3 the marks are widely scattered over the target (poor precision), but the center of the cluster is close to the bull's-eye (good accuracy).

1.5 THE AVERAGE

The average is the first statistic we will consider. There are several kinds of averages used in statistics. The most common is the one the chemist calls *average* and the statistician, *arithmetic mean* or *mean. It is merely the sum of*

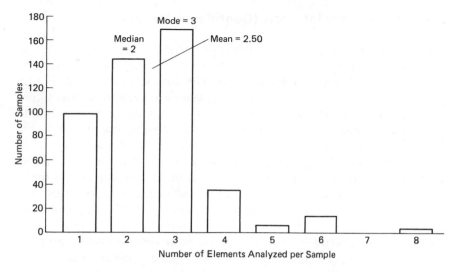

Figure 1.4. Comparison of mean, median, and mode.

the values divided by the number of values. The statistician uses the Greek letter mu, μ, to represent the true but unknown mean and the symbol $\bar{X}$ (read as X-bar) to represent the experimentally determined estimate of the mean. Thus, the equation for the sample mean is

$$\bar{X} = \frac{\sum X}{n} \qquad (1.1)$$

The Greek capital sigma, $\sum$, is widely used to denote the addition of the individual values of the term following it. Thus, Equation (1.1) calls for adding all n values of X and dividing the sum by n. *The mean is the single number which best represents the center of a symmetrically or normally distributed group of values.* In this book we will use *average* to mean *mean* unless otherwise noted.

The *median* is another kind of average and is *the middle item when the values are arranged in order of magnitude.* For symmetrical distributions, the median is an estimate of the mean. Most nonparametric statistical tests use the median instead of the arithmetic average. (A nonparametric test is one which does not require a symmetrical distribution. More will be said about types of distributions in the next chapter.)

The *mode* is another kind of average; it is defined as *the most frequent value* in a frequency distribution. We will make no use of the mode in our discussions, but the chemist should be aware of its existence. Figure 1.4 illustrates these three kinds of averages.

1.5.1 Confidence Intervals (Confidence Ranges)

Suppose we have made five determinations of the purity of a sample and calculated its average to be 99.50%. That average is our best estimate of its purity, but is probably not the true purity. The statistician would say *we have only an estimate of the true average of the population* represented by the sample. By "population" the statistician means a set of observations or objects with one or more common characteristics; e.g., all material produced by a unit in a stated time period, or all analysts in a laboratory, or all assays on a given amount of material. In the example of purity of a bottle of a product, the population is characterized by an average and a standard deviation (a measure of the scatter of the values about the average). *Population* connotes completeness, as opposed to *sample*, which is considered to be a portion of the population.

If we repeated our set of five measurements a second or third time, we would not expect to get exactly the same average value; we would expect the averages to agree within experimental error. Statistics offers us a means of calculating both the experimental error and a range of values about our average which will include the true average a specified percentage of the time. *This range of values is called a confidence interval (or range).* Thus, we might say that the average purity of our sample is $99.50 \pm 0.25\%$ at the 95% confidence level. Such a statement means that although we don't know the true average, and never can know it, 95% of the time the ranges calculated in the same way will include the true value.

One can demonstrate the validity of this concept of confidence intervals by sampling a known population. Imagine a container of 1000 marbles, identical except that each has a number on it. These numbers have been selected so that their frequency of occurrence matches the normal distribution curve. Since we know the numbers on each marble, we know the average value of the 1000 numbers on the marbles. Now if we mix the marbles and withdraw a set of 5, we can calculate the average and confidence interval for that set. If we replace the marbles, mix, and withdraw a second set of 5, we will get a somewhat different average and confidence interval.

If we repeat that process many times and plot our averages of 5 and their confidence intervals, we will get something similar to Figure 1.5. In this figure the averages and intervals are plotted for 10 sets of 5 determinations. In this limited example only the range (the vertical bar) for set number 7 does not include the horizontal line representing the true average.

Of course, the remaining 5% of the time, like set number 7 in Figure 1.5, the confidence limits will not include the true average, but being right 95 times out of 100 is not bad. We could choose to be right some other fraction of the time, say 99% or 90%, and the width of our confidence interval would change accordingly.

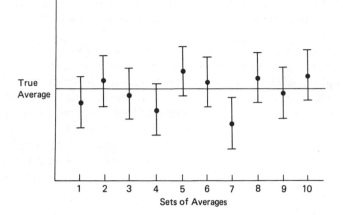

Figure 1.5. Confidence intervals for averages of five determinations.

The calculation of the confidence interval (or range) for an average is not complicated, but it does involve two statistical concepts we have not yet considered. Therefore, we will defer this calculation until we have discussed standard deviations and the t distribution. We shall see also that confidence intervals can be established about other statistics. For example, we can calculate a range which will include the true standard deviation with a stated probability.

1.6 ABACUSES, HAND CALCULATORS, AND COMPUTERS, OR EFFICIENT AND ACCURATE CALCULATIONS

The mechanics of statistical calculations frequently make use of squared terms, logs (natural or base 10), and square roots in addition to the usual operations: addition, subtraction, multiplication, and division. The best ways of performing these operations, including how many significant figures should be used, is the subject of the remainder of this chapter.

1.6.1 Aids to Computation: Calculators and Computers

The arithmetic operations required by most statistical tests can be tedious at best and are time consuming and subject to errors. The use of various calculating devices can remove much of the stress in performing calculations.

Only a few years ago, the mechanical desk calculator (the modern abacus) capable of handling 10 or more digits was the ultimate in efficient computation, and one which was capable of extracting square roots was indeed a marvel. Today most hand calculators, certainly all those of the scientific type, perform all these operations plus log, trigonometric functions, etc., and do them much faster.

All the problems in this book can be solved using a 10-digit hand calculator. The big drawback in using calculators is the labor involved in entering the data as well as the intermediate answers. As a matter of convenience the author prefers the hand calculator with variance and standard deviation functions to a computer for calculating the simplest statistics—variance, standard deviation, average—when small amounts of data are involved.

For more extensive sets of data or more complicated statistical formulas, however, the computer is a godsend. Not only is the computer capable of rapid and accurate calculations, it also can provide a printout of the original data (for verification that they were entered correctly) along with the results of the computations.

Computers come in all sizes (and prices)—from the micro or personal computer to the large mainframes capable of handling the work of many users simultaneously. Commercial statistical programs are available for all types of computers. These programs vary widely in the number of statistical tests they perform and in "user friendliness," that is, their ease of use by the chemist who may not be a computer expert. The best programs are menu driven and guide the user through the program with detailed instructions. The menus enable the user to select which of several functions (data entry, statistical tests, etc.) is to be performed. A good program will include the following features:

- Provides for easy entry and correction of data.
- Is "bullet proof," that is, will not abruptly end or require resetting because of some incorrect response to a request for input.
- Screens inputs (data and responses to questions asked by the program). Incorrect inputs produce an error message indicating why the input was wrong. The user is then permitted to re-enter the input.
- Performs the calculations using procedures (algorithms) with at least 10-digit accuracy.
- Provides the option of having the data and results appear on a printer.

A few examples of commercially available programs are given in the Resources section at the end of this chapter. Note, however, that with the many programs available and with new ones becoming available, it is impossible to offer a comprehensive listing. Most magazines devoted to computers contain advertisements of programs, and these can be consulted for current offerings. There are also directories of statistical programs which may be available in your library.

Those programs designed for use on the larger computers (such as Minitab, and SAS) are likely to offer a comprehensive set of statistical tests, but many of those written for personal computers are reasonably complete for the tests they do cover. Several of these programs, each of limited scope, can take the place of one larger program.

In using any computer program you should thoroughly test it with data for which the answers are known. The test data should represent the extremes expected to be encountered, and all parts of the program should be tested. This is the only way to be sure the program is operating correctly on your computer and that there are no errors in the program.

1.6.2 Computer Accuracy

For most statistical applications, the program should have double precision capability so that data having at least five significant figures can be handled without rounding error. A number handled with double precision requires two machine words of memory as contrasted to one machine word for single precision. If a computer will store up to seven digits in one word, double precision will permit storage of at least 14 digits. Note that in some computer languages some functions such as the square root and power functions may be performed with single precision even though the data and other operations are handled with double precision. This situation can defeat at least to some extent the accuracy obtained by using double precision.

In summary, beware of using a program-computer combination as an infallible "black box." Test to be sure accurate results are obtained by using data with known answers before trusting the results obtained on "real" data.

1.7 SIGNIFICANT FIGURES FOR CHEMISTS

Most chemists already know the rules for how many significant figures (places) to use in calculations and the rules for rounding values to a specified number of places. However, because of the importance of significant places in obtaining accurate values in statistical tests, we now review these rules as applied to statistical calculations.

For the number of significant places to use, the rule *usually* is stated as: *For all mathematical operations (addition, subtraction, multiplication, division, and exponentiation) retain the equivalent of two more places of figures than present in the single observed value.* That is, if the observed values are expressed to the nearest unit (90%), use enough places in the computation to express the numbers to the nearest 0.01 unit (90.01%).

This rule can cause difficulty, however, in squaring operations because when one squares, one can double the number of significant figures: $0.9^2 = 0.81$;

$0.77^2 = 0.5929$; $60.15^2 = 3618.0225$. Therefore, *a safer rule is to retain at least twice the number of significant places as present in the original data*; e.g., if the data consists of values like 60.15, retain at least eight significant places.

Actually, if a computer is used, it is more convenient and better practice to allow the computer to retain the maximum number of places it is capable of. This assumes the computer's capacity will comply with the modified rule just given by using either single or double precision. If this is not the case, the original data should be coded so that the rule is satisfied. We will discuss coding the next section. The same is true for hand calculators. Most scientific calculators will display ten digits, which is usually satisfactory. However, even here, coding can simplify the entering of the data by reducing the number of digits to be entered.

No rounding of calculated values or intermediate results should be done until the final values are obtained. This will prevent the propagation of rounding errors. No precise rule can be given for the number of significant places to be retained in final values. Much depends on whether the final values will be used in other calculations, such as determining confidence intervals for an average. If a further calculation is to be made, it is a good idea to retain at least one more digit than one would otherwise.

Averages are generally expressed to one or two more places than present in the original data. If we average 1.23, 1.40, and 1.16, we get 1.26333. This value should probably be expressed as 1.263, or 1.2633 at the most. Standard deviations are usually expressed to the same number of significant places as the average associated with it. The standard deviation for the three values which averaged 1.263 is 0.123423. This should be rounded to 0.1234 or possibly 0.12342 if additional calculations are to be performed using it.

1.7.1   How Significant Figures Can Affect Results

The importance of using a sufficient number of significant places in calculating statistics can be illustrated by the following example involving the calculation and comparison of two variances to see if they are significantly different. The equations and procedure are explained in a subsequent chapter, so do not worry about the whys of the procedure now; just look at the effect the number of places has on the calculations.

EXAMPLE 1.1.   A chemist was comparing two ways of standardizing $0.5N$ sodium hydroxide: (a) manual titration using phenolphthalein indicator and (b) automatic titration using pH to detect the endpoint. The question to be answered is "Does method (b) have more precision (smaller standard deviation) than method (a)?"

The normalities obtained for 10 runs were:

RUN	MANUAL TITRATION	AUTOMATIC TITRATION
1	0.4986	0.4991
2	0.4984	0.4989
3	0.4988	0.4986
4	0.4988	0.4985
5	0.4985	0.4986
6	0.4985	0.4987
7	0.4990	0.4989
8	0.4988	0.4986
9	0.4990	0.4986
10	0.4988	0.4990
Average	0.49872	0.49875

The standard deviation for each method is calculated using the equation:

$$s = \sqrt{\frac{\sum X^2 - \frac{(\sum X)^2}{n}}{n - 1}}$$

Because there are four decimal places in the original data, the squared terms will have up to eight significant figures. Using a hand calculator with 10-digit capacity and the above equation we obtain:

For the manual method:

$$s = \sqrt{\frac{2.48721678 - (24.87216384/10)}{10 - 1}} = 0.0002097618.$$

For the automatic method:

$$s = \sqrt{\frac{2.48751601 - (24.87515625/10)}{10 - 1}} = 0.0002068279.$$

The F test (discussed in a later chapter) is used to compare the two estimated standard deviations:

$$F = \frac{(0.0002097618)^2}{(0.0002068279)^2} = 1.01.$$

Because the critical value for F is 4.03 at the 95% confidence level and the experimental F value is less than this, we conclude there is no significant difference in the precision of the two methods.

If we use only six digits in the calculations, we obtain:
For the manual method:

$$s = \sqrt{\frac{2.487217 - (24.872164/10)}{10 - 1}} = 0.000000.$$

For the automatic method:

$$s = \sqrt{\frac{2.487516 - (24.87516/10)}{10 - 1}} = 0.000000.$$

Thus, there are insufficient places to retain the variability expressed by the data and we get an unrealistic value of zero for both standard deviations. Not all data sets will be this sensitive to the rounding errors and number of significant places used, but the point is that we want our statistical tests to reflect the variability of our data, not that of the calculations.

1.7.2 Rules for Rounding

As mentioned above, rounding of values should be performed after all computations have been made. The rounding procedure recommended is:

1. When the figure next beyond the last place to be retained is less than 5, the figure in the last place is kept unchanged.
2. When the figure next beyond the last place to be retained is greater than 5, the figure in the last retained place is increased by 1.
3. When the figure next beyond the last place to be retained is 5 and there are only zeroes or no figures beyond the 5, the figure in the last place to be retained is kept unchanged if it is even, or increased by 1 if it is odd. If the 5 next beyond the last figure to be retained is followed by any figure other than zero, the retained figure is increased by 1.

EXAMPLE 1.2. Assume the following values are to be rounded to the nearest 0.01 unit:

37.8346 rounds to 37.83
37.8378 rounds to 37.84
37.8350 rounds to 37.84
37.8355 rounds to 37.84
37.8450 rounds to 37.84

Note that only one rounding operation should be performed on a given value. That is, in the above example one should not round to the nearest 0.001 unit and then round to the nearest 0.01 unit. If one were to do this to 37.8346, rounding to the nearest 0.001 would produce 37.835, and subsequent rounding to the nearest 0.01 unit would produce 37.84 instead of the proper 87.83.

1.8 CODING OF DATA

Sometimes a set of data can be modified to reduce the number of digits in each observation. This can permit a more accurate calculation if the number of digits in the observations is approaching or exceeds the capacity of the calculating device. Reduction in the number of digits also reduces the effort in entering the data. *This modification process is called coding and may be done by three methods:*

Method A. Addition or subtraction of a constant to or from each observation. For example, if all values in a set of data are 99.0% or larger, the data can be coded by subtracting 99.0 from each value so that a 99.52% value becomes 0.52%. This method of coding, of course, affects the average of the coded observations so that 99.0 must be added to it to obtain the average of the uncoded set of data.

The standard deviation and variance are not affected by this kind of coding because they are measures of scatter of the observations about the average. Subtracting or adding a constant from each value does not change the scatter, it merely shifts all the values downward or upward on their scale. Figure 1.6 depicts the effect of subtracting a constant C on the average and standard deviation. When we discuss variance and standard deviation in a subsequent chapter we will have an example which illustrates the effect of coding of data by subtraction of a constant.

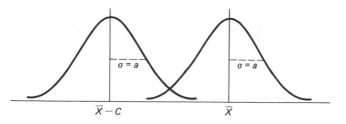

Figure 1.6.   Effect on the average and standard deviation of subtracting a constant C From all data.

Method B. Multiplication or division of each observation by a constant. For example, if all the values are 0.000*xyz*, multiplication by 10,000 will eliminate the zeros so that 0.000546 becomes 5.46. This method of coding affects both the average and the standard deviation. These coded values must be divided or multiplied by the same factor used to code the data (10,000 in this example). The coded value for the variance must be multiplied (or divided) by the square root of the coding factor to obtain the value expressed in the original units. This is because variances are squared terms.

EXAMPLE 1.3.

ORIGINAL DATA	CODED DATA (DIVIDE BY 100)	
2300	23	
2700	27	
2200	22	
Average 2400	24	(Multiply by 100 to get in terms of original data)
Standard deviation 264.58	2.6458	(Multiply by 100 to get in terms of original data)
Variance 70,000.00	7.0000	(Multiply by 10,000 to get in terms of original data.)

Figure 1.7 shows how the average and standard deviation are affected by dividing all values in a set of data by a constant.

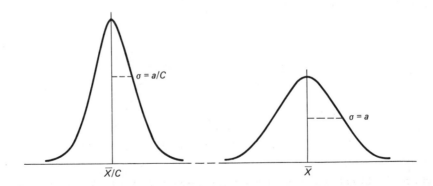

Figure 1.7. **Effect on the average and standard deviation of dividing all data by a constant** *C.*

Method C. The third method of coding is a combination of the first two: addition (or subtraction) accompanied by multiplication (or division). The same corrections to the coded average, standard deviation, and variance described for Methods A and B are applied to obtain the values in the original units of the data.

EXAMPLE 1.4.

ORIGINAL DATA	CODED BY MULTIPLYING BY 100,000	FURTHER CODED BY SUBTRACTING 9900
0.09915	9915	15
0.09920	9920	20
0.09914	9914	14
0.09910	9910	10
———	——	—
Calculated Averages:		
0.099148	9914.8	14.8
Calculated Standard deviations:		
0.00004113	4.113	4.113

To Decode the Average:

$$14.8 + 9900 = 9914.8$$

$$9914.8/100,000 = 0.099148$$

To Decode the Standard Deviation:

$$4.113/100,000 = 0.00004113$$

A word of caution: when coding data, be careful to avoid introducing errors from mathematical mistakes in the coding process. It is a good idea to note on the work sheet exactly how the data were coded so that the coded results can be properly decoded.

1.9   SUMMARY

This introductory chapter attempts to show that statistics is a useful tool to help the analytical chemist solve a wide variety of daily problems. Its use permits an objective evaluation of data and promotes efficient use of experimental resources by extracting the maximum amount of information from the data obtained by planned experiments.

The concepts of precision, accuracy, and confidence intervals were introduced. Suggestions were made regarding the use of calculators and computers in performing calculations. Accurate calculations require that a sufficient number of significant figures be used, with rounding reserved for the final result. Sometimes, the number of digits required can be reduced by coding the data. Three ways to code data were presented, along with the proper method of rounding the final result of calculations.

RESOURCES

EXAMPLES OF COMMERCIALLY AVAILABLE STATISTICAL PROGRAMS

For Large Computers

BMDP Statistical Software, Inc., 1440 Sepulveda Blud., Suite 316, Los Angeles, CA 90025.
COMPSTAT, P. O. Box 268, Gloucester Point, VA 23062.
Minitab. Minitab Project, 215 Pond Laboratory, University Park, PA 16802.
P-STAT. P. O. Box AH, Princeton, NJ 08540.
RS/1. Bolt Beranek and Newman Inc., 50 Moulton St., Cambridge, MA 02238.
SAS. SAS Institute, Inc., Publications Department, Box 8000, Cary, NC 17511.
SPSS. SPSS, Inc., 444 N. Michigan Ave., Suite 3000, Chicago, IL 60611.

For Micro or Personal Computers

ANOVA. Dynacomp, Inc., 1427 Monroe Ave., Rochester, NY 14618.
The Statistician. Quant Systems, P. O. Box 628, Charleston, SC 29402.
Regression I, II, Multilinear Regression. Dynacomp, Inc., 1427 Monroe Ave., Rochester, NY 14618.
STAT. Matrix Software, 315 Marion Avenue, Big Rapids, MI 49307.
STATPAL. Marcel Dekker, Inc., 270 Madison Avenue, New York, 10016.
Statpro. Wadsworth Professional Software, 20 Park Plaza, Boston, MA 02116.
   Note: The appearance of a program in the above list does not necessarily imply a recommendation. This list is intended only to give examples of the variety of computer programs available. The user should determine if a particular program is suitable for his needs.

SUGGESTED BOOKS FOR FURTHER READING

Davies, O. L., and P. Goldsmith, Jr., eds.: *Statistical Methods in Research and Production,* 4th rev. ed. New York: Longman Group Limited, 1980. An excellent general text and one of the few slanted toward chemistry; a cornerstone of modern statistical methods.
Davies, O. L., ed.: *Design and Analysis of Industrial Experiments,* 2nd ed. New York: Longman Group Limited, 1978. A continuation at an advanced level of the subject matter in the book edited by Davies and Goldsmith.
Dixon, W. J., and F. F. Massey, Jr.: *Introduction to Statistical Analysis.* New York: McGraw-Hill Book Co., 1951. Good explanations; slanted toward agricultural applications.
Bowker, A. H., and G. J. Lieberman: *Engineering Statistics,* 2nd ed. Englewood Cliffs, NJ: Prentice-Hall, 1972. Thorough treatment of statistics as applied to engineering problems; rather difficult reading.

Johnson, R. R.: *Elementary Statistics*. North Scituate, MA: Duxbury Press, 1973. An easy to understand introductory book to some basic aspects of statistics for the general reader.

Moroney, M. J.: *Facts From Figures*. Baltimore, MD: Penguin Books, 1956. A very readable paperback on the general uses of statistics; slanted toward the general reader.

Steel, R. G. D., and J. H. Torrie: *Principles and Procedures of Statistics*. New York: McGraw-Hill Book Company, Inc., 1980. A college level text slanted toward biological applications.

Chapter 2
SOME BASICS TO HELP YOU
GET STARTED

OVERVIEW

Statistical tests are designed to yield reliable results with data which meet certain requirements. To make effective use of these tests, we need to know about these requirements: the distribution of the data, the effect of skewed data, and how to reduce it by transforming the data. We will also discuss a test for outliers in a set of data.

2.0 SOME ASSUMPTIONS

Before we start using statistical tests, we need to be aware of certain conditions which our data should meet in order for the tests to give valid results. These conditions are certain assumptions about the nature of the data (observations). If our data do not meet the assumptions, the test may give incorrect answers.

Two assumptions are usually made when statistical tests are being developed: (a) the observations are normally distributed and (b) the errors associated with the observations are independent and random in nature. Observations which are normally distributed will exhibit a pattern approximating those shown in Figure 2.1. There are many types of distributions; we will discuss a few of interest in the next section.

When we make a reading, record a weight, etc., there is always some error associated with the observation. If the error associated with the observation does not affect the other observations, the errors are said to be independent. In the usual course of events some of these errors will be relatively large, some relatively small, some positive, and some negative. If these errors have no particular pattern with respect to size and sign, they are considered to be random. The net result for a series of many repeated measurements is that the sum of these random errors tends to approach zero. We will have more to say on randomness in Section 2.2.

As one might expect, some statistical tests have been developed for those cases where the above assumptions are not met, but these are special cases. An example is *nonparametric tests*, which may be applied regardless for the kind of distribution the data exhibits.

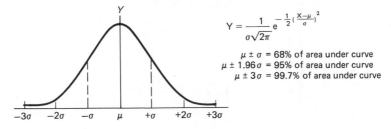

$$Y = \frac{1}{\sigma\sqrt{2\pi}} e^{-\frac{1}{2}(\frac{X-\mu}{\sigma})^2}$$

$\mu \pm \sigma$ = 68% of area under curve
$\mu \pm 1.96\sigma$ = 95% of area under curve
$\mu \pm 3\sigma$ = 99.7% of area under curve

Figure 2.1.   Normal (Gaussian) distribution.

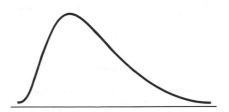

Figure 2.2.   Distribution with positive skewness.

Figure 2.3.   Distribution with negative skewness.

2.1   TYPES OF DISTRIBUTION

There are three types of distribution of particular interest to us. Much of the data collected by chemists have a *normal* (also called *Gaussian*) *distribution*. Data from this type of distribution are well described by the familiar bell-shaped curve shown in Figure 2.1.

Some of our data, however, will have a *skew* distribution; that is, the bell-shape is distorted. Figure 2.2 is an example of a distribution with positive skew; the long tail lies in the direction of the high values of the measurements. When the long tail is toward the low values, as in Figure 2.3, the skew is said to be negative. A skew distribution usually occurs when our measurements are made near a physical limit. For example, if we are measuring iron content,

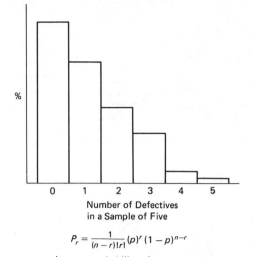

Number of Defectives
in a Sample of Five

$$P_r = \frac{1}{(n-r)!r!} (p)^r (1-p)^{n-r}$$

where p = probability of event occurring
n = number of trials
r = number of events (defectives)
Note: The shape of the histogram will vary with the percentage of defectives in the population sampled, p, and with sample size n.

Figure 2.4.   Binomial distribution.

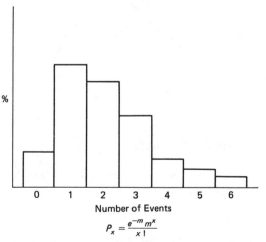

Number of Events

$$P_x = \frac{e^{-m} m^x}{x!}$$

where m = average number of occurrences per unit
x = number of occurrences
Note: The shape of the histogram will vary with m, the average number of occurrences.

Figure 2.5.   Poisson distribution.

we can't have more than 100 percent iron. We will have more to say about skew distributions later in this chapter.

When data are of the two-category type—e.g., a pass or fail test, a qualitative test in which a species is considered present or absent, a reaction carried out in the presence or absence of light, etc.—a *binomial distribution* results. An example of this type of distribution curve is shown in Figure 2.4. If we measure the frequency of occurrence of isolated events in a continuum—e.g., the number of flaws in a stated area of plastic film—a *Poisson distribution* is obtained. Figure 2.5 is an example of the Poisson distribution.

2.1.1   A Test for Normal Distribution

As we said, much of the data collected by chemists has a normal or Gaussian distribution. This is fortunate because most statistical tests assume that the data have this type of distribution. An easy way to determine if a set of data is normally distributed is to plot it on probability graph paper. Normally distributed data will tend to fall on a straight line as shown in Figure 2.6.

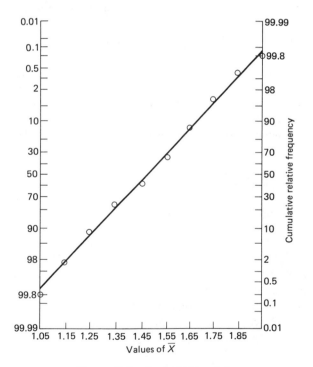

Figure 2.6.   Probability plot.

The data plotted in Figure 2.6 were obtained as follows:

CLASS LIMIT	NUMBER OF VALUES IN CLASS LIMIT	CUMULATIVE RELATIVE FREQUENCY
0.95–1.05	1	$1/501 = 0.0020$
1.05–1.15	8	$9/501 = 0.0180$
1.15–1.25	20	$29/501 = 0.0579$
1.25–1.35	86	$115/501 = 0.230$
1.35–1.45	85	$200/501 = 0.399$
1.45–1.55	130	$330/501 = 0.659$
1.55–1.65	105	$435/501 = 0.868$
1.65–1.75	47	$482/501 = 0.962$
1.75–1.85	15	$487/501 = 0.992$
1.85–1.95	3	$500/501 = 0.998$

Note that the divisor (501) used to calculate the cumulative relative frequencies in column 3 is one unit greater than the total of the values in column 2. This assures that we will be able to plot the last class on the probability graph. Deviations from a straight line near its extremes are not unusual for approximately normal distributions.

There are other types of distributions in statistics. When we discuss various statistical tests, such as the F test and the t test, we will see that these statistics have their own distributions which are sketched at the beginning of many of the tables of critical values in Appendix D. However, we merely need to be aware that these distributions exist. One main concern is whether the distribution of the data is normal, or approximately normal, so that we can use the statistical tests which assume normality.

2.2 INDEPENDENCE

Independence implies a lack of order in the data. If we repeatedly measure some property of our sample, say its moisture content, and our results exhibit a constant upward or downward trend (for example 0.20, 0.18, 0.13, 0.07), we would be highly suspicious that something was wrong. The data lack randomness. We know that the data should consist of higher and lower values with *no* pattern because of the uncertainties of our measurements (random errors). Most of the time, visual inspection of the data will reveal any appreciable lack of randomness. However, there is a simple *runs test* which can be used to check for randomness. This is one of the nonparametric statistical tests we mentioned previously.

2.2.1 The Runs Test for Randomness

This test is used to determine if a set of observations is random or if it shows a pattern; e.g., a steady increase or a cyclical variation. The set of data to be tested should contain 10 to 50 values.

EXAMPLE 2.1. The following concentrations of nickel (ppm) were obtained on samples from a process stream. The samples were taken at hourly intervals. Can this set of data be considered to be random and therefore suitable for use in determining sampling variability, or is there evidence of a concentration trend with time?

ppm Ni: 21.2, 21.8, 21.4, 21.0, 21.3, 21.6, 21.1,
21.7, 22.2, 21.9, 22.3, 22.1, 22.4, 22.2, 22.1

Procedure:
a. Arrange the data in order of magnitude.
b. Select the median value. Remember, this is the middle value. In a set of odd numbered values (like 11), the position of the median will be the number of values divided by two plus 0.5 ($11/2 + 0.5 = 6$). For an even numbered set (like 6), the median is the average of the two middle values.
c. List the data in order of occurrence.
d. Above each value place a $+$ if the value is greater than the median, or a $-$ if it is less. Ignore values equal to the median.
e. Underscore each run. A run is a cluster of one or more like signs.
f. Count the number of runs, the number of $+$'s, and the number of $-$'s. Set n_1 equal to the smaller number of signs, and n_2 equal to the larger number of signs.
g. Compare the number of runs with the critical values in Table 11, Appendix D. If the number of runs is less than, or greater than the range listed for n_1 and n_2, reject the hypothesis that the data are random at the 0.05 level of significance. We will explain "hypothesis," "level of significance," and the testing of hypotheses in the next chapter.

A plot is a useful way to get a picture of what the data look like. The plot may be compared with the results of the statistical test to see if the conclusions are in reasonable agreement with the picture of the data. Figure 2.7 shows the data in this example. Although the plot is pretty jagged, there does appear to be a general trend toward higher values with time. Now we shall see what the runs test shows.

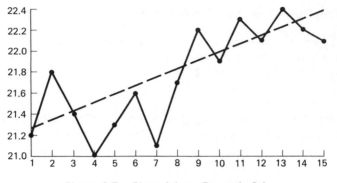

Figure 2.7. Plot of data, Example 2.1.

Steps a and b: Since there are 15 values, we arrange them in increasing order and count in 8 values to find the median value (21.8):

21.0, 21.1, 21.2, 21.3, 21.4, 21.6, 21.7, <u>21.8,</u>
21.9, 22.1, 22.1, 22.2, 22.2, 22.3, 22.4

Steps c, d, and e:

$\overline{21.2}$ $\boxed{21.8}$ $\overline{21.4}$ $\overline{21.0}$ $\overline{21.3}$ $\overline{21.6}$ $\overline{21.1}$ $\overline{21.7}$
$\overset{+}{22.2}$ $\overset{+}{21.9}$ $\overset{+}{22.3}$ $\overset{+}{22.1}$ $\overset{+}{22.4}$ $\overset{+}{22.2}$ $\overset{+}{22.1}$ (The boxed value is the median.)

Step f: Number of values = 15; number of runs = 2 (the −'s beginning just before the median and continuing on to value 21.7 make one run); the number of +'s = 7; number of −'s = 7.

Step g: From Table 11, Appendix D: for $n_1 = 7$, $n_2 = 7$, the number of runs expected is 3 to 13. Since we have 2 runs, the hypothesis that the data are random is rejected, and we conclude there is evidence of a time trend. The conclusion agrees with our appraisal of the plot of the data. Because there is a trend in the data, the set would not be a good one to use to estimate sampling variability.

2.3 EFFECT OF SKEWED DISTRIBUTION ON VARIANCE

Many statistical tests assume the data are normally distributed. Fortunately, this is frequently a valid assumption, but there are instances when the data are badly skewed (their distribution is not symmetrical like the Gaussian curve). Recall that skewness can occur when the values are close to a physical limit.

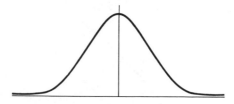

Figure 2.8.   Normal distribution.

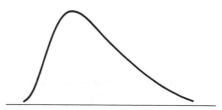

Figure 2.9.   Distribution with positive skewness.

For example, in the determination of trace concentrations of water in a chemical it is physically impossible for the chemical to contain less than 0.0 ppm water, but if the average water content is, say, 2 ppm and the standard deviation of the method is also 2 ppm, normal distribution would demand that about 26% of the values obtained be less than 0.0 ppm. (The standard deviation is a measure of the scatter of results; we will be discussing this statistic in the next chapter.) The distribution of water values, then, would not have a normal (bell-shaped) distribution curve (Figure 2.8). Instead, the distribution curve would be skewed like that shown in Figure 2.9.

This means that the calculated value for the standard deviation may not be an accurate estimate because one of the assumptions on which the calculation is based is not satisfied. We can get around this problem by transforming the data so that the distribution is approximately normal, and then perform the determination of the standard deviation on the transformed data.

2.4   TRANSFORMATION OF DATA

In the preceding section we saw the problem which arose when calculating the standard deviation from data with a skewed distribution. The technique called *transformation of data* may be used to obtain more accurate estimates of the standard deviation from skewed data. Transformation of data is also used to obtain a linear response for correlation purposes and to achieve an equality of variance among subgroups of data for analysis of variance prob-

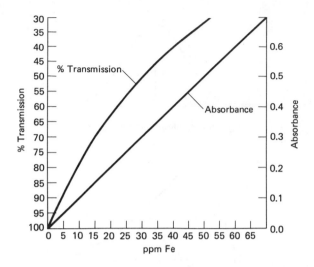

Figure 2.10.   Linearizing effect of transforming percent transmittion to log 100/% T.

lems. *When we transform data we are changing the scale on which our measurements are made.* The appropriate transformation to be used to obtain a more normal distribution, a more linear response, or equality of variance is somewhat a matter of "cut and try," but the following suggestions represent a good starting point.

If the data's distribution is skewed and the data are plentiful, the use of averages of subgroups of data rather than the individual values will tend to produce a normal distribution. The higher the number of observations averaged, the better. This approach is not of much help if the experiment is such that lots of data cannot be obtained.

Other transformations frequently used are those of taking the square root or logarithm (either natural or common) of the original data. The logarithm operation is probably the most familiar one to chemists, who have used this transformation to achieve a linear relationship between percent transmission and analyte concentration in spectrophotometric determinations. These transformed values are called absorbances. Figure 2.10 compares the linearity of percent transmission and of the log $(100/\% T)$ versus concentration.

The general effect of the log transformation on the distribution is illustrated by Figures 2.11 and 2.12.

Generally, the conversion of the data to common logs will result in a normalization of the distribution when a natural limit is responsible for the data being skewed. When normalization is achieved by this means, the data are said to have a *lognormal distribution.* That is, if the logs of the data were

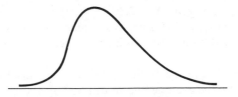

Figure 2.11.   Distribution of original data, $f(X)$.

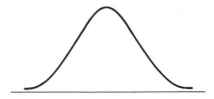

Figure 2.12.   Distribution of transformed data, $f(\log X)$.

plotted on a probability graph, a straight line could be drawn through the points.

The following example of a trace metal analysis will illustrate the procedure to be used. The same procedure would also apply for the opposite case, i.e., for values near the 100% limit.

EXAMPLE 2.2.   The following values were obtained on the cadmium content of a sample taken from a process waste stream.

RUN NO.	CD, PPM	CD, LOG PPM
1	2.0	0.30103
2	1.5	0.17609
3	0.9	−0.04576
4	0.8	−0.09691
5	1.3	0.11394
6	1.1	0.41390
7	0.5	−0.30103
8	2.4	0.38021
9	1.8	0.25527
Average	1.37	0.09158

The estimated standard deviation, s, calculated in the manner described in the next chapter is 0.6164 with 8 degrees of freedom, and the coefficient of variation is 44.99%. The 95% confidence interval for a single determination would be $X \pm t_{0.05,8} \times s$, or $X \pm 2.306 \times 0.6164 = X \pm 1.42$. At the $X = 1$ ppm level this interval includes negative values, which is physically impossible. (Note: the calculation of the confidence interval is explained in the next chapter.)

A useful rule of thumb is: If the coefficient of variation (the standard deviation divided by the average and multiplied by 100) is greater than 33%, the distribution is probably too skewed for accurate estimate. This rule is based on the fact that for a normal distribution, the average plus-and-minus three standard deviation units will include more than 99% of the values under the curve. Thus, if the average minus three times the standard deviation is less than zero, the curve must be skewed.

Now, if we calculate the standard deviation s_L using the common logs of the cadmium concentration instead of parts per million and the same equation for the standard deviation, we find $s_L = 0.21583$. The calculation of the 95% confidence interval about the log average is slightly different. The log of the confidence interval is equal to the log average plus and minus $t_{0.05,8} \times s_L$:

$$\log C.I. = 0.91583 \pm (2.305 \times 0.21583)$$

$$= 0.589287 \text{ to } -0.406121$$

To obtain the confidence interval in terms of the original data, we take the antilogs:

$$C.I. = 3.88 \text{ to } 0.39$$

This range is much more reasonable in that it does not include negative values. The principle used in obtaining the confidence interval applies to other calculations using transformed data; that is, perform the operations on the log values before taking the antilogs.

Note that the log average (0.09158) is not the same as the log of the arithmetic average (0.13672). The antilog of the log average is the *geometric mean*, which better represents the center of data having lognormal distribution than does the arithmetic average. The antilog of 0.09158 is 1.23, as compared with the arithmetic average of 1.37. The geometric mean is always smaller then the arithmetic average. The geometric mean may also be calculated by multiplying each of the n values of data together and taking the nth root of the product.

Now having discussed the correct way of handling data which are close of a natural limit, it must be admitted that many people do not bother with transforming data to achieve a more normal distribution, unless the data are highly skewed. Most of the time they assume normal distribution and if a confidence interval includes a slightly negative value, they cut it off at zero.

2.5   OUTLIERS

All too often the values in a set of observations appear to be in reasonable agreement except for one value that is "off in left field" by being suspiciously high or low.

   EXAMPLE 2.3.   Four gas chromatographic assays on a sample of pentachlorophenol performed under the same conditions are 88.2%, 86.7%, 87.9%, and 87.7%. Using these values, we obtain an average of 87.625% and a standard deviation of 0.65% with three degrees of freedom. The standard deviation makes the method look poor.

   The question is "What do we do with the suspiciously low value of 86.7%?" If we discard it, the average becomes 87.933% and the standard deviation drops to 0.25% which is a nice improvement over the original 0.65%. Are we justified in discarding 86.7% as an outlier?

   If there is a known cause for the "odd" value being too high or low, such as over-titration, wrong sample size, mathematical error, etc., we are justified in discarding the value because it was not obtained under the same conditions as the others. A second justification for discarding the "odd" value is that the value is so different from the others in the set that it probably represents a different population. If we discard a value for any other reason, we will bias our results.

   In the example, assume that we do not know of any reason which would explain the 86.7% value. How do we determine if the 86.7% value is so different from the others that we can attribute it to a different population and therefore discard it? The following test for extreme values gives us an objective means for judging if the suspect value is an outlier at a selected level of confidence. This test should be applied *only once* to a set of values; i.e., only one piece of data may be considered suspect.

2.5.1   Test for Outliers

Arrange the values in order of increasing value and calculate R using the appropriate equation:
   For sets of 3 through 7 values:

$$R = \frac{X_N - X_{N-1}}{X_N - X_1} \tag{2.1}$$

For sets of 8 through 10 values:

$$R = \frac{X_N - X_{N-1}}{X_N - X_2}$$ (2.2)

For sets of 11 through 13 values:

$$R = \frac{X_N - X_{N-2}}{X_N - X_2}$$ (2.3)

where

X_N = the suspected value
X_{N-1} = the value nearest the suspected one
X_{N-2} = the value second nearest the suspected one
X_1 = the value furthest from the suspected one
X_2 = the value second furthest from the suspected one.

The calculated value for R is compared with the critical value in Table 7 in Appendix D. If the critical value is exceeded, the suspected value is considered to be an outlier and may be discarded. The discarded value should be mentioned when the results are reported together with the reason it was discarded.

Using the data from Example 2.3 and Equation (2.1) for a set of 3 through 7 values, we get

$$R = \frac{86.7 - 87.7}{86.7 - 88.2} = \frac{-1.0}{-1.5} = 0.667$$

$R_{95,4} = 0.765$. Thus, the critical value is not exceeded and we are not justified in calling value 86.7% an outlier. If we wish to try to improve the estimated standard deviation, additional runs are in order. After all, four runs are not many on which to base an estimate.

The outlier test described above was selected because the question of a single observation value in a set of data being an outlier is the most common situation. There are, however, other outlier tests which may be applied to other situations, such as two values (a high and a low value) being suspect in one set of data, or two suspiciously high or low values in one set of data. A discussion of these tests may be found in ASTM Practice E 178[1] and in the text by Barnett and Lewis[2] which are listed in the References at the end of this chapter.

2.6 SUMMARY

Most statistical tests are designed to be used with data sets whose values have a normal, or nearly normal, distribution. The errors associated with the values are also assumed to be independent and random. If the data are skewed, the results obtained by the statistical test may be questionable. However, it may be possible to transform the data so that at least an approximately normal distribution is obtained. Taking the logarithm of each observation is one transformation frequently used. The outlier test is useful in determining if an "oddball" value in a set of data may be excluded as representing a population different from that of the other values.

2.7 PROBLEMS

Although examples have been given in the discussions of the tests in this chapter, it is necessary to actually apply the tests to gain a working knowledge of the tests. For this purpose, a set of problems together with their answers has been provided in Appendices B and C.

The following problems (or parts of problems) use the tests discussed in this chapter. Working them will give you the opportunity to apply the tests when the answers are known, and thus will give you greater confidence when you need to apply the tests to real life problems:

SUBJECT	PROBLEM
Randomness of data	2a
Outliers in data	20c

REFERENCES

1. "ASTM Practice for Dealing With Outlying Observations," E 178, Section 14.02, *Annual Book of ASTM Standards*, American Society for Testing and Materials, 1916 Race Street, Philadelphia, PA 19103.
2. Barnett, V., and Lewis, T.: *Outliers In Statistical Data*. New York: John Wiley & Sons, 1978.

Chapter 3
MEASURES OF PRECISION

OVERVIEW

As an analytical chemist one of your major concerns is the precision of your data. In this chapter we will see how statistics can help answer some questions about precision; questions such as:

- What is the best way of expressing the amount of scatter (the precision) in a set of data?
- Precision can be expressed as variance, standard deviation, and coefficient. How are these measures of precision calculated?
- When should precision be expressed as a standard deviation and when as a coefficient of variation?
- How many determinations should be used to obtain a good estimate of precision?
- How can you obtain a better estimate of precision when you have several precision estimates each of which are based on only a few observations?

3.0 WAYS OF MEASURING PRECISION

In Chapter 1 we distinguished between precision and accuracy. We described precision as the degree of agreement of repeated measurements of the same property, or the scatter of results from repeated determinations. There are several ways of measuring this dispersion of results, including the range, average deviation, variance, and standard deviation.

EXAMPLE 3.1. The hydroxyl number of a sample of dodecanol was determined 10 times with the following results[1]

RUN RESULT		$d = X - \bar{X}$	CODED DATA $(X - 280)$
1	293.3	0.33	13.3
2	290.0	2.97	10.0
3	290.7	2.27	10.7
4	297.0	4.03	17.0
5	289.2	3.77	9.2
6	295.4	2.43	15.4
7	296.4	3.43	16.4
8	295.3	2.33	15.3
9	291.8	1.17	11.8
10	290.6	2.37	10.6
$\sum X$	2929.7	$\sum d$ 25.10	$\sum X_c$ 129.7
$\bar{X}$	292.97	$\bar{d}$ 2.51	$\bar{X}_c$ 12.97

The simplest way is merely to use the range of values obtained—the largest minus the smallest value. In the above example, the range is $297.0 - 289.2$, or 7.8. As we will see, the range can be used to estimate the standard deviation of a set of data, if the set is small (less than 15). Use is made of the range in preparing control charts for quality control programs. (A discussion of quality control is beyond the scope of this book. Some of the references listed at the end of this chapter will provide information on this subject for the interested reader.)

The main disadvantages of using the range are (1) the range is very sensitive to extreme values and in fact ignores all the in-between values so that only one extreme value can unduly influence our estimate of the variability; (2) the range is usually size dependent, so that if one takes varying sized groups of random numbers from a population of known dispersion, the value of the range obtained varies with the number of values in the group selected; and (3) it is difficult to make confidence statements about precision based only on the range. We will say more about confidence statements in the next chapter.

Sometimes the average deviation is used as a measure of precision; i.e., the sum of the differences (taken without regard to sign) between the average and each individual observation divided by the number of observations. In Example 3.1 the average deviation is 25.10/10, or 2.51. This method is a better measure than the range because all the values are used in estimating the scatter of results. However, it is difficult to make confidence statements about this measure of precision.

3.1 THE BEST WAY—VARIANCE

The statistician uses variance as the best measure of the dispersion of repeated results (precision). Variance is a bit more complicated to calculate than is the range or average deviation, but it does not have the disadvantages mentioned above. In addition, variances are additive. This is a very important property, as we shall see when we consider the analysis of variance, because it enables us to partition the total variance into its components and thus determine the sources of variability in our data. The symbols, σ^2 and s^2 are generally used to denote this parameter and statistic. There are several forms of the equation used to calculate variance; Equations (3.1a), (3.1b), and (3.1c) are mathematically equivalent, but one form may be easier or more accurate to use than the others, depending on the data and the type of calculating device used:

$$s^2 = \frac{\sum (X - \bar{X})^2}{n - 1} \tag{3.1a}$$

$$= \frac{\sum X^2 - \frac{(\sum X)^2}{n}}{n - 1} \tag{3.1b}$$

$$= \frac{n \sum X^2 - (\sum X)^2}{n(n - 1)} \tag{3.1c}$$

where $\bar{X}$ = arithmetic average of the n individual observations X.

Equation (3.1a) is the easiest form to understand. The variance of a set of data is calculated by squaring the difference between each observation and the average. The squared differences are summed and the total is divided by one less than the number of observations. This form of the equation is the least subject to rounding errors by computers. Some computers may run short of significant figures when numbers with relatively large significant places are squared.

The other two forms of Equation (3.1) are easier to use with calculators because the subtraction operation is performed only once. For these reasons only Equation (3.1a) is recommended for use in computer programs, and either Equation (3.1b) or (3.1c) is recommended for use with calculators. Because most of the examples in this book are designed to permit the reader to follow them with a calculator, Equation (3.1b) will generally be used. Again, any of the three forms of the equation will give the correct answer if sufficient significant places are used.

When all the data are paired—e.g., a series of duplicate determinations, X_1, X_1'; X_2, X_2'; X_3, X_3'; etc.—the variance of the method used to obtain the duplicate values may be calculated by a simplified version of Equation (3.1):

$$s^2 = \frac{\sum d^2}{2n} \tag{3.2}$$

where

$d = X_i - X_1'$, the difference between value 1 and 2 of pair i
n = the number of pairs of data.

Because many methods of analysis call for duplicate determinations, Equation (3.2) provides us an easy way to estimate the variance of such methods.

Before we apply Equations (3.1a), (3.1b), and (3.1c) to Example 3.1, recall that in Chapter 1 the use of coded data was discussed. If, as in Example 3.1, all the values are greater than 280, this amount may be subtracted from each value, resulting in smaller numbers with which to work. The subtraction of a constant from all the data does not affect the variance. This may be seen by comparing Solutions 3.1b and 3.1c.

Solution 3.1a Calculation of s^2 using Equation (3.1a) and the results of Example 3.1:

$$s^2 = \frac{\sum(X - \bar{X})^2}{n - 1} \tag{3.1a}$$

RUN	$x - \bar{X}$	$(X - \bar{X})^2$
1	0.33	0.1089
2	−2.97	8.8209
3	−2.27	5.1529
4	4.03	16.2409
5	−3.77	14.2129
6	2.43	5.9049
7	3.43	11.7649
8	2.33	5.4289
9	−1.17	1.3689
10	−2.37	5.6169

$$\sum(X - \bar{X})^2 = 74.6210$$

$$s^2 = \frac{74.6210}{10 - 1} = 8.29122$$

Solution 3.1b Calculation of s^2 using Equation (3.1b) and the results from Example 3.1:

$$s^2 = \frac{\sum X^2 - \frac{(\sum X)^2}{n}}{n - 1} \qquad (3.1b)$$

The value for $\sum X^2$ is calculated as follows.

RUN	X^2
1	86,024.89
2	84,100.00
3	84,506.49
4	88,209.00
5	83,636.64
6	87,261.16
7	87,852.96
8	87,202.09
9	85,147.24
10	84,448.36

$$\sum X^2 = 858,388.83$$

The value for $\sum X$ from the data in Example 3.1 is 2,929.7. Substituting these values in the equation gives

$$s^2 = \frac{858,388.83 - \frac{2,929.7^2}{10}}{10 - 1}$$

$$= \frac{858,388.83 - 858,314.209}{9}$$

$$= \frac{74.621}{9} = 8.29122$$

Solution 3.1c Calculation of s^2 using Equation (3.1b) and coded data:

$$s^2 = \frac{\sum X^2 - \frac{(\sum X)^2}{n}}{n - 1} \qquad (3.1b)$$

RUN	$(X - 280)^2$
1	176.89
2	100.00
3	114.49
4	289.00
5	84.69
6	237.16
7	268.96
8	234.09
9	139.24
10	112.36

$$\sum X_c^2 = 1,756.83$$

From the listing of the data in Example 3.1, $\sum X_c = 129.7$. Substituting in the equation gives

$$s^2 = \frac{1,756.83 - \dfrac{129.7^2}{10}}{10 - 1} = \frac{1,756.83 - 1,682.209}{9}$$

$$= \frac{74.621}{9} = 8.29122$$

Thus, using the coded values of X gives the same variance as do the original values.

Solution 3.1d Calculation of s^2 using Equation (3.1c) and the coded data:

$$s^2 = \frac{n \sum X^2 - (\sum X)^2}{n(n - 1)} \tag{3.1c}$$

Using the values previously calculated,

$$s^2 = \frac{10(1,756.83) - (129.7)^2}{10(10 - 1)}$$

$$= \frac{17,568.3 - 16,822.09}{90} = \frac{746.21}{90} = 8.29122$$

Thus, we have shown that all three equations for calculating the variance give the same results and that using coded values does not affect the calculated variance.

Now let us try calculating the variance on a set of duplicate values.

EXAMPLE 3.2. Hydroxyl numbers were determined in duplicate on a sample of dodecanol by 12 laboratories using the same method.[1] Calculate the variance of the method.

LAB	RUN A	RUN B	d	d^2
1	292.0	294.6	2.6	6.76
2	291.2	293.4	2.2	4.84
3	292.1	288.0	4.1	16.81
4	287.2	287.2	0.0	0.00
5	290.3	291.1	0.8	0.64
6	291.6	289.2	2.4	5.76
7	297.1	296.9	0.2	0.04
8	298.6	301.4	2.8	7.84
9	309.0	311.0	2.0	4.00
10	305.0	303.0	2.0	4.00
11	289.8	288.7	1.1	1.21
12	289.4	289.6	0.2	0.04

$$\sum d^2 = 51.94$$

$$s^2 = \frac{\sum d^2}{2n} \tag{3.2}$$

$$s^2 = \frac{51.94}{2(12)} = 2.1642$$

3.2   STANDARD DEVIATION

As has been mentioned, the variance is considered the best measure of the scatter or spread of a set of data. However, as you have undoubtedly noticed from the previous examples, the variance is a squared term which does not have the same units as the data from which it is calculated. This makes it difficult to compare this measure of scatter with the data. In Example 3.1 the average hydroxyl number was 292.7 (mg KOH/g sample), and the variance was 8.29122 ((mg KOH/g)^2). Therefore, precision is usually expressed as the positive square root of the variance. This square root is called the *standard deviation*. It is represented by the symbol s and has the same dimensions as the data. Going back to Example 3.1 again, the standard deviation is equal to $\sqrt{8.29122}$, or 2.879 (mg KOH/g sample), with $n-1$ or 9 degrees of freedom.

Degrees of freedom is a term which indicates the amount of data on which the statistic is calculated. Usually, the degrees of freedom is equal to the number of observations minus one. Refer to the Glossary for a more detailed description of how degrees of freedom are calculated. The more data on which a statistic is based, the more confidence we are inclined to place in it. Thus, the degrees of freedom should be stated along side the statistic so the reader will know the size of the data set used in calculating the statistic.

3.2.1 Estimating the Standard Deviation Using the Range

Earlier in this chapter we said the range of a small set of observations could be used to estimate the standard deviation of the observations. This estimate is not as accurate as that obtained by taking the square root of the variance [calculated using Equation (3.1)]. However, it often agrees remarkably well with it and is very useful in checking the mathematical calculations of the latter. This method is designed for normally distributed values, but it is useful even when this condition is not satisfied. It should be used only on small sets of observations—5 to 10 values, or some authorities say a maximum of 15. The equation used is

$$s = \frac{X_L - X_S}{d_2} \tag{3.3}$$

where

X_L = the largest value in the set
X_S = the smallest value in the set
d_2 = the value from Table 12, Appendix D

EXAMPLE 3.3. Using the set of 10 hydroxyl numbers from Example 3.1, and the value for d_2 for 10 observations from Table 12 in Equation (3.3) we have

$$s = \frac{297.0 - 289.2}{3.078} = \frac{7.8}{3.078} = 2.534$$

This value is close to standard deviation obtained by taking the square root of the variance calculated in Example (3.1): $\sqrt{8.29122} = 2.879$.

EXAMPLE **3.4.** Our observed values are 4.2, 4.5, 4.2, and 4.4. Using Equation 3.3 we estimate the standard deviation to be

$$s = \frac{4.5 - 4.2}{2.059} = 0.146$$

Using Equation (3.1) and taking the square root of the variance gives $s = 0.150$.

Note: For a quick rough estimate, mentally divide the range of the set by the square root of the number of values in the set. For Examples 3.1 and 3.4 this gives 2.5 and 0.15, respectively.

3.3. ANOTHER MEASURE OF PRECISION—COEFFICIENT OF VARIATION

Precision can also be expressed as the *coefficient of variation* which is the standard deviation divided by the average and multiplied by 100. Since the standard deviation and the average have the same dimensions, the coefficient of variation (abbreviated C.V.) is a dimensionless, relative measure of precision. It is sometimes called the *relative standard deviation*. In Example 3.1 we had a standard deviation of 2.879 and an average of 292.97. The corresponding coefficient of variation is calculated to be

$$\text{C.V.} = s/\bar{X} \times 100 \tag{3.4}$$

$$= 2.879/292.97 \times 100$$

$$= 0.9827\%$$

3.4 STANDARD DEVIATION OR COEFFICIENT OF VARIATION?

We have seen that precision can be expressed by the standard deviation (s) or by the coefficient of variation (C.V.). Why have two different measures of the same property? When should each be used? Having two measures of precision is useful when it is desired to describe the precision over a relatively broad range of levels. We might for example be interested in the precision of a method for 0 to 50% of the analyte. In some cases it will be found that the standard deviation is essentially constant over the concentration range. In such cases the standard deviation is the term which best describes the precision.

In other cases the coefficient of variation will be found to be essentially constant over the concentration range of interest. In other words, the standard deviation is proportional to the average. In these cases the coefficient of variation should be used to describe the precision. The following examples illustrate these uses of the standard deviation and coefficient of variation.

EXAMPLE 3.5. Eleven runs were made on each of three samples representing three levels of concentration. The average, standard deviation, and coefficient of variation were calculated for each sample as listed below.[1] Which is the better way of expressing the precision of the method over this concentration range?

$\bar{X}$	DF	s	C.V.
24.5%	10	0.16	0.65
12.1	10	0.20	1.65
0.2	10	0.14	70.00

Because the values of the standard deviation show little variation, the standard deviation is the better unit for expressing the precision.

EXAMPLE 3.6. The following statistics were obtained on a set of samples analyzed by a specified method.[1] Which is the better way of expressing the method's precision?

$\bar{X}$	DF	s	C.V.
247.0	10	1.32	0.53
292.9	10	1.46	0.50
1543.0	8	9.76	0.63
1752.5	10	7.68	0.43

In this set of data, the coefficient of variation shows good agreement over the range and should be used to express the precision.

The remaining possibility is that neither the standard deviation nor the coefficient of variation is constant over the range of interest. In this event one can try transforming the data to obtain a uniform standard deviation. Transforming the data means to change the measurement scale by any of several means such as using the reciprocals of the observations. (Using logarithms of the observations is equivalent to using the coefficient of variation, so this transformation is not appropriate.) Alternately, the chemist can state the precision estimates separately for each level in terms of the standard deviation, or divide the range of levels into smaller segments over which either the standard deviation or coefficient of variation is approximately constant.

3.5   SAMPLE SIZES IN ESTIMATING PRECISION

We have said that we are more confident of a statistic, such as a variance or a standard deviation, which is calculated from many observations than in a statistic based on only a few. But how many observations should be made? The number will depend on how closely we wish to estimate the true variance, σ^2, or true standard deviation, σ, and how confident we wish to be about our estimate. Table 4A (Appendix D) shows the minimum sample size required so that the estimate of the variance, s^2, will be less than a given multiple k of the true variance with a stated probability. For example, if we wish to be 95% certain that s^2 will be less than twice the value of σ^2, we enter the k column of Table 4A, read down to the row with 2 and over to the column headed by 95% to find that a sample size of 9 is required.

Table 4B (Appendix D) shows the minimum sample size required in order that the estimate of the standard deviation, s, will be less than a given multiple k of the true standard deviation with a stated probability. If we wish to be 99% certain that s will be less than 1.50 times the value of σ, we enter the k column of Table 4B, read down to the row marked 1.50 and over to the column headed by 99% to find that a sample size of 12 is needed.

3.6   POOLING PRECISION (VARIANCE) ESTIMATES

Often our only estimates of variance are based on a few degrees of freedom for each estimate. We may have analyzed eight samples of a material in triplicate by a method and wish to estimate the variance, standard deviation, or coefficient of variation for the method. We have from the eight sets of data eight estimates of the precision, but each has only 2 degrees of freedom.

Providing there are no significant differences among the eight sample estimates of the variance (the variances are homogeneous), they can be combined by a statistical operation termed *pooling* to give one estimate in which we can place considerably more confidence because it would be based on the sum of the degrees of freedom for each of the estimates, in this case 16. In the next chapter we will discuss how to determine if variances are homogeneous. Let's take a simple example to see how variances are pooled.

EXAMPLE 3.7.   We have three estimates of the standard deviation of a method, each with 10 degrees of freedom: $s_1 = 0.16$, $s_2 = 0.20$, and $s_3 = 0.14$. Accept for now that these estimates are homogeneous by the test we will get to in the next chapter.

The equation for pooling variances is

$$s_p = \sqrt{\frac{(s_1^2 \times df_1) + (s_2^2 \times df_2) + \cdots + (s_n^2 \times df_n)}{df_1 + df_2 + \cdots + df_n}} \qquad (3.5)$$

$$df_p = df_1 + df_2 + \cdots + df_n$$

where

s_1^2, s_2^2, s_n^2 = variance for data set 1, 2, ..., n
df_1, df_2, df_n = degrees of freedom for data set 1, 2, ..., n

The same equation is used for pooling coefficients of variation by substituting C.V. values in place of s values.

Substituting our values in this equation gives

$$s_p = \sqrt{\frac{(0.16^2 \times 10) + (0.20^2 \times 10) + (0.14^2 \times 10)}{10 + 10 + 10}}$$

$$= \sqrt{\frac{0.8520}{30}} = \sqrt{0.2840} = 0.1685, \quad 30 \text{ df}$$

EXAMPLE 3.8. Using the data from Example 3.2, calculate the variance for each of the 12 pairs of laboratory data and pool them.

LAB	s^2	LAB	s^2	LAB	s^2
1	3.38	5	0.32	9	2.00
2	2.42	6	2.88	10	2.00
3	8.405	7	0.02	11	0.605
4	0.00	8	3.92	12	0.02
$\sum s^2 = 25.97$					

$$s_{pooled}^2 = \frac{1(25.97)}{12} = 2.1642$$

Note that the value for the pooled variance obtained by pooling is the same as that obtained in Example 3.2 using Equation 3.2.

3.7 SUMMARY

In this chapter we have discussed the general topic of precision which is the amount of scatter in data.

Precision is best measured by variance; it may be expressed as the standard deviation or coefficient of variation. The standard deviation is the preferred way of expressing precision when the standard deviation is independent of the average. The coefficient of variation is appropriate when the standard deviation is proportional to the average.

Guidance was given in determining how many observations are needed to obtain a good estimate of the precision.

Finally, we learned how to combine or pool several small sets of data to provide a better estimate of the precision.

Now, try your hand at applying these techniques to the problems listed in the next section.

3.8 PROBLEMS

The following problems (or parts of problems) use the tests discussed in this chapter:

SUBJECT	PROBLEMS
Calculation of variance, standard deviation, and coefficient of variation	1a, 2b, 2c, 3a, 6a, 7a, 14, 15a, 16a, 17a, 18a, 20a
Pooling variances	6b, 7b, 15, 16b, 17e, 18e, 19, 20d (Assume that the variances in these problems are homogeneous.)

RESOURCES

ASTM Manual on Presentation of Data and Control Chart Analysis, STP 15D. Philadelphia, PA: American Society for Testing and Materials, 1976. This publication is written for the practical user and includes detailed examples.

Grant, E. L., and Leavenworth, R.: *Statistical Quality Control*, 5th ed. New York, NY: McGraw-Hill Book Company, 1979. This book is broader in coverage and presents a good balance of theory and application.

REFERENCES

1. The data are from ASTM Recommended Practice E180. Reprinted with permission from the *Annual Book of Standards*, Volume 15.05. Copyright, ASTM, 1916 Race Street, Philadelphia, PA 19103.

Chapter 4
HOW GOOD IS THE ESTIMATED PRECISION?

OVERVIEW

In Chapter 3 we learned how to estimate precision based on one set of measurements from a population of all possible measurements. If we repeat the work using additional sets of measurements, our subsequent estimates of the population variance (or standard deviation) will not agree *exactly* with the first estimate. In this chapter we will see how statistics can help answer some questions related to this situation:

- How much spread about our "point" estimate of the variance is required to include the true but unknown population variance? This spread is called the confidence limits.
- How to decide if the estimated precision values based on two sets of data are significantly different.
- How to decide if the precision based on one set of measurements is consistent with the known or established precision of a method.
- How to decide if more than two estimates of precision are equivalent.

In answering such questions we will learn about the reasoning process used in performing statistical tests of significance.

4.0 HOW GOOD IS THE ESTIMATED VARIANCE? (CONFIDENCE INTERVALS FOR A VARIANCE)

When the variance is calculated from a random set of data, a *point estimate* s^2 is obtained, which is the best estimate of the variance of the population represented by that set of data. For example, we make 11 replicated analyses and calculate the sample variance s^2 to be 0.09 with 10 degrees of freedom. If other sets of data were taken at random from the same population, their calculated point estimates of the variance would differ from the first estimate of 0.09 and would tend to concentrate about the true variance, σ^2. Therefore, we are frequently interested in predicting the maximum and minimum values for our calculated variance that will include the true variance with a stated level of confidence. *The interval included by these minimum and maximum values is known as the confidence interval or confidence range.*

EXAMPLE 4.1.   Assume we wish to calculate a 95% confidence interval for σ^2, based on our point estimate of $s^2 = 0.09$ with 10 degrees of freedom. The 95% confidence interval means that if we were to repeat the process of taking sets of 11 observations and calculating the confidence range for each set a large number of times, 95% of those ranges would include the true variance.

How do we calculate confidence intervals? This is done by making use of the *Chi square distribution function.* The Chi square distribution function relates the experimental variance s^2 to the true variance σ^2 for normally distributed data:

$$\chi^2 = \frac{(n-1)s^2}{\sigma^2} \tag{4.1}$$

where

s^2 = experimental variance with $n - 1$ degrees of freedom
σ^2 = the true variance.

The values of Chi square can be obtained by establishing a large population of known variance, σ^2. From that population many repeated samples of size n are taken and the variance for each sampling is calculated. Using Equation (4.1), the corresponding values of Chi square are calculated. The distribution of the values of Chi square is then obtained. A plot of the distribution curve for the Chi square function resembles Figure 4.1. Table 1 (Appendix D) lists the critical values for the Chi square distribution for various $n - 1$ degrees of freedom and confidence levels α.

These critical values represent the value of Chi square that corresponds to the area under the curve to the right of that value for Chi square that is equal

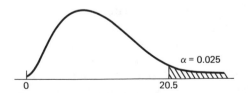

Figure 4.1.   Chi-square distribution for $\alpha = 0.025$ and 10 degrees of freedom.

to various proportions α of the total area under the curve. The statistician calls α the *level of significance.*

For 10 degrees of freedom and α equal to 0.025 the critical value for Chi square is found to be 20.5. This means that for Chi square equal to 20.5, the fraction of the area under the curve to the right of 20.5 on the Chi square axis is equal to 0.025, as shown in Figure 4.1. Conversely the fraction of the area under the curve to the left is equal to $1.0 - 0.025 = 0.975$. Stated another way, 97.5% of the values for Chi square will be equal to or less than 20.5, and 2.5% the values will be greater than 20.5.

Thus, if the calculated value for Chi square is equal to or less than 20.5, these values could result from normal variation in the estimate of σ^2 by the statistic s^2 97.5% of the time. This limit on the value of s^2, as measured by Chi square, represents one of the limits for the 95% confidence interval.

The other limit is calculated in a similar fashion using 10 degrees of freedom, and α equal to 0.975 probability. For these values, Table 1 shows Chi square to be 3.25. See Figure 4.2. Thus, the limits for Chi square for our example are 3.25 and 20.5, as shown in Figure 4.3. How can they be related to our estimated variance of 0.09?

Equation (4.1) can be rearranged by solving it for σ^2:

$$\sigma^2 = \frac{(n - 1)s^2}{\chi^2} \quad \text{or} \quad \sigma^2 = \frac{(\text{df})s^2}{\chi^2} \tag{4.2}$$

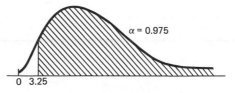

Figure 4.2.   Chi-square distribution for $\alpha = 0.975$ and 10 degrees of freedom.

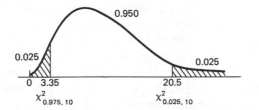

Figure 4.3.   Chi-square distribution for $\alpha = 0.975$ and 0.025 and 10 degrees of freedom.

And we can set up the following inequality:

$$\frac{(df)s^2}{\chi^2_\alpha} < \sigma^2 < \frac{(df)s^2}{\chi^2_{1-\alpha}} \tag{4.3}$$

Substituting our values into this inequality gives:

$$\frac{(10)\,0.09}{20.5} < \sigma^2 < \frac{(10)\,0.09}{3.25}$$

or

$$0.0439 < \sigma^2 < 0.2769$$

Stated in words, the above says that the true variance σ^2 will be between 0.0439 and 0.2769 95% of the time. Note that although we use our estimated variance to calculate the confidence interval, the confidence interval is for the true variance σ^2. In this example our best estimate of the true variance is 0.09, but we are saying that the confidence interval of 0.04 to 0.28 includes the true variance with a probability of 0.95.

If we are interested in the standard deviation's confidence interval, we do exactly the same thing except in addition we would take the square roots of 0.0439 and 0.2769 to get the interval for the standard deviation, or 0.2095 to 0.5262.

Other confidence intervals may be calculated by choosing the appropriate probability columns from Table 1 so that their difference corresponds to the interval desired. For example, to obtain the 99% confidence interval, select probabilities of 0.995 and 0.005.

4.1 WHEN ARE TWO VARIANCES REALLY DIFFERENT?

One type of question frequently asked by the chemist concerns comparing the precision associated with two sets of experimental conditions: is method A more (or less) precise than method B, or are the results obtained by one analyst more precise than those by a second analyst? We saw in our discussion of confidence limits for the variance that repeated measurements of the variance of a single population may be expected to give different numerical values. In this case we are concerned with comparing precision estimates of two different populations.

4.1.1 Philosophy of Statistical Testing

This is a good point to introduce the philosophy of statistical testing, because we will make use of it in deciding if our two estimates of precision (variance) of two different populations are really different. The idea is to state the problem in a form which can be answered by applying the appropriate statistical test. The form is called a *null hypothesis* and its opposite, the *alternative hypothesis*. Although this may appear a little strange, the process is really not much different from the one chemists use.

Given the need to decide if two experimental estimates of variances of two populations (two sets of data) are really different, a chemist would probably go through the following steps:

a. *Formulate a hypothesis:* The precision of population *A* is equal to that of population *B*, or (depending on how much the estimates differ), the precision of population *A* is not equal to that of *B*.

b. *Define the boundaries:* We are interested in comparing the precision of two sets of data obtained by the analysis of a selected sample. The sets of data will be the values obtained on n_A and n_B runs using methods *A* and *B*. All observations will be made under the same conditions on the same material; only the methods M_A and M_B, will be different.

c. *Plan the experiment:* Select a typical sample of material to be analyzed and make ten runs on the sample by each of the two methods using the same analyst. All analyses will be made on the same day. The precision of each method will be calculated from the set of ten runs, using the total range (largest value minus the smallest) as a measure of the precision.

d. *Basis for decision:* Evaluate the size of any difference between the two ranges.

e. *Run the experiment* according to plan to obtain data.

f. *Evaluate the data:* Calculate the range for each set of data and compare the two ranges.

g. *State the conclusion:* If the difference in the two ranges is equal to or less than the experimental error, conclude that the two methods do not differ in precision. If the difference is greater than experimental error, conclude that the method with the smaller range is more precise.

Now, let us take a look at how the statistician might approach the same problem.

a. *Formulate a null hypothesis:* Assume that the precision (variance) of population *A*, σ_A^2, as measured by its variance s_A^2, is equal to that of population *B*, σ_B^2, as measured by its variance s_B^2. This null hypothesis is usually written as $H_0: \sigma_A^2 = \sigma_B^2$. The assumption of equality of variances is required because the statistical test is based on this assumption. In other words, we can test to see if the two variances are equal, but we cannot directly test the assumption that they are unequal. The statistician, therefore, would rephrase the question "Are my two variances really different?" as "Are the two variances equally precise?"

a'. *Formulate an alternative hypothesis:* If the two variances are not equal, the nonequality may be stated in three ways: $H_A: \sigma_A^2 \neq \sigma_B^2$, $\sigma_A^2 < \sigma_B^2$, and $\sigma_A^2 > \sigma_B^2$. The first way of stating the inequality merely says the two values are different, whereas the last two ways specify that one or the other value is greater. If we are not interested in specifying which variance is the greater, we would use the first statement (equation).

If we were interested in a true difference only if variance B were greater, we would use the second statement, and if we were interested in a true difference only if variance A were greater, we would use the last statement. This may seem to be rather picky, but the choice of the alternative hypothesis determines which form of the F test we use. If we are merely interested in deciding that a real difference exists, the two-tailed form of the F test is used in testing for significance. If we are interested in a real difference only if variance A (or variance B) is greater, the one-tailed form of the F test is used.

b. *Define the population (or universe) and state any assumptions:* We are interested in deciding whether the variances for two populations are equal. The variances will be estimated for ten random subsamples analyzed by each method, with each subsample coming from the same typical sample of material. The errors in the measurement process are random and have a normal distribution.

c. *Plan the experiment:* The same analyst will analyze a typical sample ten times by each of the two methods on the same day. The variance for each set of data will be calculated using Equation (3.1).

d. *Basis for decision:* Compare the calculated variances using the F test and the single-tailed critical value corresponding to $\alpha = 0.05$ (95% confidence level), and 9 degrees of freedom for the numerator and denominator.

e. *Run the experiment as planned.*

f. *Evaluate the data:* Calculate the variance for each method, s_A^2 and s_B^2; perform the F test; and compare with the critical value of F.

g. *State the conclusion:* If the value of F is less than or equal to the critical value, accept the null hypothesis and conclude that no significant difference between the two variances has been demonstrated. Note: This is not quite the same as saying that there is no difference, which would be overstating the case. There may be a difference, but it was not detected. Also note that we have used an objective basis (the result of the F text) for drawing our conclusion. In the previous approach the conclusion depended on how we defined the magnitude of experimental error, which might be pretty subjective.

If the critical F value is exceeded, reject the null hypothesis. This implies acceptance of the alternative hypothesis. Conclude that there is a real difference in the precisions of the two methods when tested at $\alpha = 0.05$ (95% confidence level).

In the above statistical approach to the problem we wanted to determine if there was a real difference in the true variances σ_A^2 and σ_B^2. We don't know what these values are, so we estimated them with s_A^2 and s_B^2, and the F test was run using these estimates.

Our decision to accept or reject a null hypothesis may be a correct one, i.e., we may accept a true null hypothesis or reject a false null hypothesis. On the other hand, our decision may be wrong. We may reject the true null hypothesis, i.e., commit a *Type I error*. Or we may accept as true a false hypothesis, in which case we have committed a *Type II error*. These possibilities can be summarized in the following *truth table*:

	Real Situation	
Decision	H_0 is true	H_0 is false
H_0 is true	Correct $p = 1 - \alpha$	Type II error $p = \beta$
H_0 is false	Type I error $p = \alpha$	Correct $p = 1 - \beta$

The probability p of making a Type I error is α and thus the probability of making a correct decision when the null hypothesis is true is $1 - \alpha$. Similarly, the probability of making a Type II error when the null hypothesis is false is β and the probability of making a correct decision is $1 - \beta$.

We may select the probability we desire for α. Generally, probabilities of 0.01, 0.05, and 0.10 are used. These correspond to probabilities of 0.99, 0.95, and 0.90, or 99%, 95%, and 90%, of making a correct decision when the null hypothesis is true.

The probability associated with β is set by the number of observations in the data set; the more observations, the lower the value of β. It is possible to estimate how many observations would be required for a desired value of β or vice versa. This is usually done by reference to graphs called operating characteristic curves. We will not discuss these curves in this book. The interested reader can refer to nearly any text on general statistics for a description of them.

Thus, the statistical decision making process is a logical series of steps that permits us to make an objective decision based on the given data. Moreover, we can be confident that in the long run these decisions will be correct a certain percentage of the time. Note that we are not claiming and cannot claim that any one decision is, say, 95% correct. Any single decision is either 100% correct or wrong. Rather, if we continue to make decisions in this fashion, 95% (or some other selected value) of many such decisions will be correct.

4.1.2 Where Do the Critical Values for Statistical Tests Come From?

In steps d and g of the statistical decision making process we blithely said we would compare our experimental F value with the critical value for F. But where do these wonderful values for statistical tests come from? In brief, they are derived from the evaluation of populations of known standard deviations. Let us use the F test as an example. As will be seen in the next section, the F test is used to determine if two variances are significantly different. The F value is defined as the ratio of two variances:

$$F = \frac{s_A^2}{s_B^2} \qquad (4.4)$$

where

$s_A^2 = $ the first estimated variance with $n_A - 1$
   degrees of freedom for population A
$s_B^2 = $ the second estimated variance with $n_B - 1$
   degrees of freedom for population B.

Populations A and B are known to have equal variances, i.e., $\sigma_A^2 = \sigma_B^2$. Samples of size n_A and n_B are taken, the sample variances s_A^2 and s_B^2 are calculated, and their F values determined. If this process is repeated a great many times, the distribution of the F values will resemble Figure 4.4. The exact

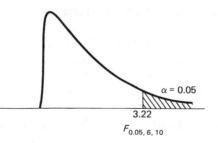

$\alpha = 0.05$

3.22

$F_{0.05, 6, 10}$

Figure 4.4. F distribution, one-tailed.

shape of the curve will vary with the degrees of freedom associated with the variances in the numerator and denominator.

The area under the curve represents the probability that F will have the values shown on the F axis. The total area under the curve represents $p = 1$; that is, since all possible values of F are covered by the curve, the probability that a value of F falls within the range of values on the F axis is unity or 100%. Since populations A and B have equal variances, the estimates of their variances will tend to be close to each other and thus the values of F will tend to be close to unity.

Of course, the exact curve obtained from these repeated observations will differ for different sample sizes n_A and n_B, so we are talking about a family of many curves. But for a given pair of values for n_A and n_B, their curve could be used to determine the probability of obtaining any given value of F. As you probably have guessed, such curves are not used for this purpose. It is much easier and more accurate to use tables of values obtained by integration of the areas under this family of curves. To keep the tables as compact as possible, it has been agreed that in applying the F test, the variance with the larger value will always be the numerator and the one smaller one the denominator, resulting in F values of unity or greater. Thus, the tables need represent only half of the mathematical symmetry of the F distribution.

Examples of such tables are Tables 2A, 2B, and 2C at the back of this book. These tables give the critical values for F for stated values of $\alpha = 0.50$, 0.025, and 0.10, which correspond to confidence levels ($1 - \alpha$ expressed as percentages) of 95%, 97.5% and 99%. These are the most frequently used confidence levels. Tables for other values of α may be found in collections of statistical tables, such as W. H. Byer, ed., *Handbook of Tables for Probability and Statistics*, 2nd Ed., The Chemical Rubber Co., Cleveland, OH, 1982.

Within each confidence level we enter the table on the row corresponding to the degrees of freedom associated with the denominator and move over to the intersection of that row and the column corresponding to the degrees of freedom associated with the numerator. The value at that intersection is the critical value for F. For example, to find the critical value for $\alpha = 0.05$ for 6 df in the numerator and 10 df in the denominator, enter Table 2A at the column labeled 6 and the row labeled 10 to find the critical value of 3.22.

The values listed in most tables of the critical F values are for the one-tailed F test. In Figure 4.4 the area to the right of the critical value of 3.22 represents $\alpha = 0.05$ or 5% of the total area. This is the probability in which we are interested for the one-tailed test. The one-tailed test is used when our alternative hypothesis is that the variance of A is greater than the variance of B, or that the variance of B is greater than the variance of A.

If our alternative hypothesis is merely that the variance of A is not equal to the variance of B, then we use the two-tailed test and we are interested in

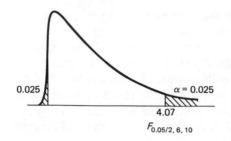

Figure 4.5. *F* distribution, two-tailed.

both the left and right ends of the distribution curve, each containing 0.025 of the total area under the curve, as shown in Figure 4.5.

The shaded area on the right-hand side represents 2.5% of the total area, which is the proportion corresponding to the critical *F* value at $\alpha = 0.025$. Therefore, the critical *F* values for the two-tailed *F* test can be obtained by using the one-tailed table for $\frac{1}{2}\alpha$. Thus, for *F* at $\alpha = 0.05$, one-tailed, 6 degrees of freedom for the numerator, and 10 degrees of freedom for the denominator, Table 2A lists the critical value for $\alpha = 0.05$ as 3.22. If we wanted the same value for a two-tailed test, we would go to Table 2B, which gives the critical value at $\alpha = 0.025$ as $F_{0.05/2,6,10} = 4.07$.

In this discussion of statistical decision making and the use of tables of critical values we used the *F* test as an example. However, the concepts are the same for all the statistical tests we will be using.

4.1.3 Comparison of Two Variances—The *F* Test

The *F* test, so named by George Snedecor in honor of R. A. Fisher (both gentlemen being distinguished statisticians), is used to answer this problem. To use the *F* test, we assume that variances of the two normal populations (*A* and *B*) being considered are equal, i.e., $\sigma_A^2 = \sigma_B^2$. This assumption is called the *null hypothesis*. The alternative, that the variances are not equal ($\sigma_A^2 \neq \sigma_B^2$) is called the *alternative hypothesis*.

If n_A and n_B samples are taken from populations *A* and *B* and the sample variances are calculated, *F* is defined as the ratio of these estimates:

$$F = \frac{s_A^2}{s_B^2} \tag{4.3}$$

where

$s_A^2 =$ the larger variance estimate
$s_B^2 =$ the smaller variance estimate.

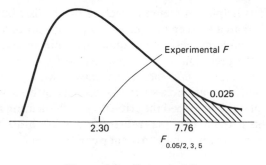

Experimental F

0.025

2.30

7.76

$F_{0.05/2, 3, 5}$

Figure 4.6.   Example 4.2.

The actual testing of two variances by the F test is very straightforward, as illustrated by the following examples. Note that one of the assumptions for this test is that of normal distributions in the populations. If this condition is not met, the results of the test should be interpreted with caution.

EXAMPLE 4.2.   Two analysts determined the purity of a crude sample of ethyl acetate. Analyst G made 6 determinations whose variance was 0.00428; Analyst K made 4 determinations with a variance of 0.00983. Do these two analysts differ in the precision of their determinations at $\alpha = 0.05$?

Here we are interested in whether the two sets of measurements differ in precision. The precision of Analyst G may be either greater or smaller than that of Analyst K. Therefore, we use a two-tailed test. Our null hypothesis is $H_0: \sigma_G^2 = \sigma_K^2$, and the alternative hypothesis is $H_A: \sigma_G^2 \neq \sigma_K^2$.

$$F = 0.00983/0.00428 = 2.30$$

Since we are using a two-tailed test, we obtain the critical value of F from Table 2B of Appendix D for the 0.025 level of significance: $F_{0.05/2, 3, 5} = 7.76$. Figure 4.6 illustrates the situation: the shaded area of the right-hand tail corresponds to the 5% of F values which exceed the critical value of 7.76 for this example. The unshaded portion of the curve between $F = 1$ and 7.76 is the 95% of the F values less than 7.76.

Our experimental value is 2.30, which lies in the unshaded area of the curve; we would expect to get such a value (or even one as large as 7.76) 95% of the time due to chance alone. Therefore, we accept the null hypothesis that $\sigma_G^2 = \sigma_K^2$.

Usually, we shorten our thinking process a bit from the above and just compare the experimental F value with its critical value, as in the next example. But it is helpful to mentally picture the F distribution curve and the shaded critical area to keep our reasoning process straight.

Accepting the null hypothesis is not quite the same as saying that there is no difference in the precision of the two analysts. *It is more accurate to say that our test has detected no difference.* If the analysts were to continue to make measurements and the variances of the larger sets of data were tested, the observed value of F might exceed the critical value, indicating a real difference in precision. This is the reason the statistician would phrase the problem as "Is there a difference" rather than "Are they equally precise?"

EXAMPLE 4.3. A sample of water has been analyzed for silicon content by two methods, one of which represents a modification of the other in an attempt to improve the precision of the determination. As shown by the data below, the five measurements made by the regular method have a variance of 66.8, and five measurements by the modified method have a variance of 8.5. Is the modified method more precise at $\alpha = 0.05$?

	ORIGINAL METHOD	MODIFIED METHOD
	149 ppm	150 ppm
	139	147
	135	152
	140	151
	155	145
Average =	143.6	149.0
Std. dev. =	8.173	7.915
Variance =	66.8	8.50

This time we are interested in learning only if the modified method is more precise than the original method. Therefore we will use the one-tailed test. Our null hypothesis is $H_0: \sigma_0^2 = \sigma_M^2$, and our alternative hypothesis is $H_A: \sigma_M^2 < \sigma_0^2$.

$$F = 66.8/8.5 = 7.86$$

The critical value for F for the one-tailed F test is obtained from Table 2A, Appendix D, which gives the values at the 0.05 level of significance: $F_{0.05,4,4} = 6.39$. Refer to Figure 4.7.

Since our observed value of F lies in the shaded rejection area (exceeds the critical value), we reject the null hypothesis and conclude that there is a real difference (improvement) in the precision of the modified method over the original one at $\alpha = 0.05$ (the 95% confidence level).

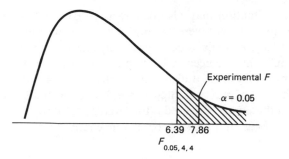

Figure 4.7. Example 4.3.

Let us look now at the critical value of F at $\alpha = 0.01$: $F_{0.01,4,4} = 15.98$ for the preceding example. This critical value is far greater than our observed value, indicating that no difference has been established.

This is not an example of how one can prove anything by statistics. It merely reflects the logical situation that the more confident we want to be about judging if differences exist, the larger those differences must be. If we were interested in measuring the lengths of two lines with a ruler graduated in 1/8 inch increments we would be hard pressed to detect with confidence differences of the order of 1/64 inch. This is somewhat the type of situation we have with our 4 degrees of freedom in the above example. If we switched to a ruler graduated in 1/64 inch increments or 1/128 inch increments, we would be much more confident of detecting differences of 1/64 inch. In our example, obtaining more data (and therewith more degrees of freedom) is like switching to the finer graduated ruler to permit us to make finer distinctions.

4.1.4 Statistically and Practically Significant Differences

In Example 4.3 the experimental variances of 66.8 and 8.5 (corresponding to standard deviations of 8.12 and 2.9) were concluded to be statistically different with $\alpha = 0.05$. The averages associated with this pair of data were 143.6 and 149.0. Because of the magnitudes of the standard deviations in comparison to their averages, I think we would agree that the difference in the variances is also significant from a practical point of view.

However, this is not always the case. Had the averages been 14,360 and 14,900, the differences between the standard deviations and their averages would be relatively small. We might well decide that from a practical standpoint it makes no difference whether the variance is 66.8 or 8.5 when we are dealing with values of 14,000. If the unmodified method were easier or faster to perform, we might elect to conclude there is no significant difference, based on practical considerations.

The obverse situation may also occur, as in Example 4.3 when we used $\alpha = 0.01$ and the averages were 143.6 and 149.0. Here the differences in the variances are large enough to be of practical importance, but they were not statistically different. We need to be careful not to conclude such differences are significant if they are not also statistically significant. If the difference is large enough to be of practical importance, but is not statistically significant, it is likely that the sample size used is too small, or that the method being used is not precise enough to pick up the difference reliably.

4.1.5   Comparison of an Experimental Variance with a Reference

If we wish to compare an experimental variance with an accepted or reference variance, we can use either the Chi square test [Equation (4.1)] or the equivalent F test with infinite degrees of freedom for the reference variance.

EXAMPLE 4.4.   A change in the indicator used in a method was expected to improve its precision—a known standard deviation of $\sigma = 0.3317$. Based on 20 determinations, the modified method had an estimated standard deviation of $s = 0.2490$. Does this lower value represent a significant improvement in precision at $\alpha = 0.05$?

Using the Chi square test [Equation (4.1)]:

$$\chi^2 = \frac{(n-1)s^2}{\sigma^2}$$

$$= \frac{(19)0.2490^2}{0.3317^2} = 10.71$$

$\chi^2_{0.95,19} = 10.1$, i.e., the probability that a value *greater* than 10.1 would be observed is 0.95 or 95%. The probability that a value less than 10.1 would occur by chance is $1 - 0.95$ or 0.05. See Figure 4.8. Thus, 10.71 is not significant at the 95% confidence level, and we conclude no improvement has been shown in the precision and the original indicator should be used. Thus, either indicator could be used without affecting the method's precision. Selection of which should be used would depend on other factors, such as toxicity, relative costs, availability, etc.

If the claim had been that the new indicator would make the method less precise, and we obtained the above data, the critical value for χ^2 would be $\chi^2_{0.05,19} = 30.1$. That is, the probability of a value at least as large as 30.1 is 0.05 (a confidence level of 95%). Since the observed value is less than the critical

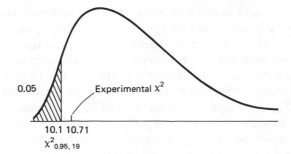

Figure 4.8. Example 4.4 using Chi-square test.

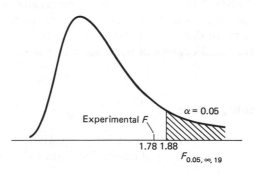

Figure 4.9. Example 4.4 using F test.

value, we would again conclude that no significant difference in precision had been shown.

Using the F test [Equation (4.4)]:

$$F = s^2 \text{ (larger)}/s^2 \text{ (smaller)}$$

$$= 0.3317^2/0.2490^2 = 1.775$$

$$F_{0.05,\infty,19} = 1.88$$

Because the observed F ratio is less than the critical value of F (Figure 4.9), we again conclude that no significant difference (no improvement) in the precision has been demonstrated.

4.2 COMPARING MORE THAN TWO VARIANCES

When we wish to compare more than two variances to see if they differ significantly, we could apply the F test repeatedly to all possible pairs of the set of variances. For example, if we had a set of four variances, the F test could be applied to variances s_A^2 and s_B^2, s_A^2 and s_C^2, s_A^2 and s_D^2, s_B^2 and s_C^2, s_B^2 and s_D^2, and s_C^2 and s_D^2. However, the confidence level for the results would drop drastically. If we select the 95% confidence level for all comparisons, we would expect to make the correct decision 95% of the time for the first comparison, but we could expect to make the correct decision for the first plus the second one 95% of 95% of the time, and so on for each of the six comparisons so that by the time the sixth pair were compared, the confidence level for making the correct decision on all six pairs would have dropped to only 70%. Note, however, that the confidence level for each comparison is still 95%.

To avoid this situation, there are two tests for comparing more than two variances (the statistical term is testing for *homogeneity of variances*). The Cochran test is a simple one, but it requires that all the variances have the same degrees of freedom. The Bartlett test is applicable whether or not all variances have equal degrees of freedom, but it is more complicated to perform.

4.2.1   The Cochran Test

Like the F test, the Cochran test uses a ratio of variances, but in a different manner. The ratio is called the g statistic. The g statistic is calculated using the following equation:

$$g = \frac{\text{largest } s^2}{s_1^2 + s_2^2 + s_3^2 + \cdots + s_k^2} \tag{4.5}$$

Compare the calculated g value with the critical value from the table for the 0.05 or 0.01 level of significance (95 or 99% confidence level), Table 3A or 3B (Appendix D). Enter the table with n, the number of observations associated with each variance, and k, the number of variances being compared. Accept the null hypothesis that the variances are equal if the critical value is not exceeded.

EXAMPLE 4.5.   One sample each of three different ketones has been analyzed 11 times by a general method for determining purity. The calculated standard deviations, each with 10 degrees of freedom, are $s_1 = 0.16$, $s_2 = 0.20$, and $s_3 = 0.14$. Does the method exhibit the same precision for these ketones?

$$g = \frac{0.20^2}{0.16^2 + 0.20^2 + 0.14^2} = 0.4695$$

$g_{0.05,11,3} = 0.6025$. Thus, we conclude the three variances are equal at $\alpha = 0.05$, and that there is no evidence of differences in the precision obtained for the three ketones. We could pool these three estimates to obtain an estimated precision of the method as applied to the three ketones with 30 degrees of freedom as opposed to only 10.

4.2.2 The Bartlett Test

The Bartlett test is similar to the F test in that an F ratio is obtained and compared with the usual critical values for F. It differs in the manner in which the variances are handled and in how the degrees of freedom are calculated. In applying the Bartlett test, the following equations are used:

$$s_p^2 = \sum (n_i - 1)s_i^2/(N - k)$$

$$M = (N - k)\ln s_p^2 - (n_i - 1)\ln s_i^2$$

$$df_1 = k - 1$$

$$A = \frac{1}{3(k-1)}\left(\sum\left(\frac{1}{n_i - 1}\right) - \frac{1}{N - k}\right)$$

$$df_2 = (k + 1)/A^2$$

$$b = \frac{df_2}{1 - A + \dfrac{2}{df_2}}$$

$$F = \frac{df_2 M}{df_1(b - M)}$$

(4.6)

where

n_i = number of observations associated with each variance s_i^2
N = sum of all n's
k = number of variances being compared
df_1 = degrees of freedom of numerator
df_2 = degrees of freedom for denominator.

Warning: When applied to data whose distributions are *not* normal, this test may give an erroneous verdict of nonhomogeneity. Because of this sensitivity to distribution, some statisticians recommend it not be used. It is included in this text because other statisticians do use it when the distributions are at least approximately normal and because there is no other test for homogeneity of more than two variances whose degrees of freedom are not equal.

EXAMPLE 4.6. Using the same data as in Example 4.5, use the Bartlett test to compare the three standard deviations. (*Note:* One would not ordinarily use the Bartlett test on these data, since all three variances have 10 degrees of freedom. However, we are using these data so that the results can be compared with those obtained from using the Cochran test.)

$$s_1 = 0.16, 10 \text{ df}; \quad s_2 = 0.20, 10 \text{ df}; \quad s_3 = 0.14, 10 \text{ df}$$

$$n_1 = n_2 = n_3 = 11$$

$$N = 33$$

$$k = 3$$

$$s_p^2 = \frac{((11 - 1)0.16^2) + ((11 - 1)0.20^2) + ((11 - 1)0.14^2)}{33 - 3}$$

$$= \frac{0.8520}{30} = 0.0284$$

$$M = (33 - 3)\ln 0.02840 - ((11 - 1)\ln 0.16^2 + (11 - 1)\ln 0.20^2$$

$$+ (11 - 1)\ln 0.14^2)$$

$$= -106.840984 - (-36.651629 - 32.18876 - 39.3226)$$

$$= 1.3217$$

$$A = \frac{1}{3(3 - 1)}\left(\frac{1}{11 - 1} + \frac{1}{11 - 1} + \frac{1}{11 - 1} - \frac{1}{33 - 3}\right) = 0.0444$$

$$df_1 = 3 - 1 = 2$$

$$df_2 = \frac{3 + 1}{0.0444^2} = 2029$$

$$b = \frac{2029}{1 - 0.0444 + \dfrac{2}{2029}} = 2121.0854$$

$$F = \frac{2029(1.3217)}{2(2121.0848 - 1.3217)} = 0.6326$$

$F_{0.05, 2, 2029} = 3.00$. Therefore, the standard deviations do not differ significantly, which is the same conclusion as reached by the Cochran test. (*Note:* The table of critical values was entered on the row for infinite degrees of freedom for the denominator because 2029 lies between the rows for 1000 and infinity.)

4.3 MORE ABOUT VARIANCES

We have now covered the basic operations concerning variances. We will have more to say about the additive properties of variances in Chapter 7 on analysis of variance, but first we need to consider some operations involving averages. This is the subject of the next chapter.

4.4 SUMMARY

In this chapter we discussed several ways of evaluating our estimates of variances. We learned how to establish confidence limits about our estimate to help us see how good the estimate was. We saw how the F test is used to help us decide when two variances are significantly different. In applying the F test the statistical concepts of hypotheses and alternative hypotheses were introduced and used to state our problem in a form which could be answered by the test. We discovered that sometimes variances which are significantly different by a statistical test, may not be viewed as different from a practical viewpoint. We learned how to compare a sample variance with a reference value. We also learned how to determine if more than two sample variances are significantly different.

Now try your hand at applying these techniques to the problems listed in the next section.

4.5   PROBLEMS

The following problems (or parts of problems) use the tests discussed in this chapter.

SUBJECT	PROBLEMS
Confidence intervals	1c, 2d, 3b, 15b, 17b, 18b, 20b
Comparing two variances	1e, 2g, 20d
Comparing more than two variances	6b, 7b, 14, 16b, 17e, 18e, 20d

Chapter 5
AVERAGES

OVERVIEW

In this chapter we will be concerned with questions about averages (arithmetic means) and the statistical tests used to answer them.

- Probably the most frequent question is, Are two (or more) averages really different, or are their numerical differences merely the reflection of the lack of precision of our measurements?

Other questions include:

- Does the average agree with the theoretical or an accepted value?
- How confident can we be of an average based on a given number of determinations (can we establish limits of confidence on it)?
- How closely should we expect two averages to agree when they are obtained under the same conditions?
- Given a set of three or more averages, which ones differ significantly from the others?

5.0 REAL DIFFERENCES

In the previous chapters we talked about the precision of our measurements. This chapter is devoted to their arithmetic mean or average and to how statistics can help us decide when differences between averages are "real." We will begin by considering five similar situations involving averages:

1. Comparison of an average with a theoretical or reference value. *Example:* Our average of three measurements of the molecular weight of a product is 102.03. Does the population represented by our average differ significantly from the theoretical 101.11?
2. Comparison of two averages based on different samples when the precision (variance) of each average is known. *Example:* A sample from each of two tank cars of an ester is analyzed by a standard method with

established precision. Do the populations represented by the two averages differ significantly?

3. Comparison of two averages based on different samples when the precision of each average is unknown but equal. "Unknown" means that the precision of each average must be estimated from the data used to calculate the average. *Example:* The same as situation 2, except the precision of the method has not been established.

4. Comparison of two averages based on different samples when the precision of each average is unknown and unequal. *Example:* The same as situation 3 except the precision estimates for the two averages are unequal.

5. Comparison of two averages based on the same sample, or samples. *Example:* Two analysts use the same method to determine the viscosity in triplicate of the same sample. Are the analysts' results in agreement?

We will then discuss confidence limits for averages, the range of values which can be expected for an average, and finally, one approach to comparing more than two averages. However, before we consider the comparison of an average with a theoretical value, we need to understand something of the principles involved in the statistical tests for the situations listed above.

All the statistical tests for differences of averages (really different versions of one test) are based on the null hypothesis that there is no difference between the populations represented by the averages. You will recall from Chapter 4 that the null hypothesis is written in the form, $H_0: \mu_1 = \mu_2$. Along with the null hypothesis, we have the alternative hypothesis, which is written in the form $H_A: \mu_1 \neq \mu_2$ or $H_A: \mu_1 < \mu_2$, $H_A: \mu_1 > \mu_2$, etc.

The null hypothesis is accepted (considered to be true) until the test statistic exceeds the critical value, at which time, it is rejected and the alternative hypothesis is accepted. If the critical value is not exceeded, the decision is that the equality of the null hypothesis has not been proved false and therefore it appears to be true. We should not go so far as to say the null hypothesis has been proven true, although this is sometimes done, for this would be overstating the conclusion.

In determining the critical value of the statistic we must decide upon several things. The first decision is the degree of risk we will accept of making a Type 1 error, i.e., the risk of rejecting a true statement, or of rejecting the null hypothesis when it should not be rejected. The probability of making this kind of error is called α and becomes the significance level of the test. A commonly used significance level is $\alpha = 0.05$, which is also called the 5% level of significance. There is of course the risk of making a Type 2 error, of failing to reject a false statement; e.g., if two methods truly have different variances and we conclude that the variances are not different, we have made a Type 2 error.

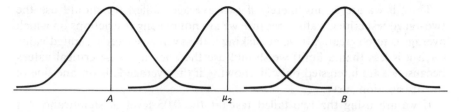

Figure 5.1.   Distributions of μ_1 and μ_2 for H_A: $\mu_1 \neq \mu_2$. μ_1 can be either in position A or B.

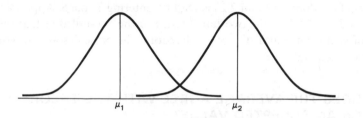

Figure 5.2.   Distributions of μ_1 and μ_2 for H_A: $\mu_1 < \mu_2$.

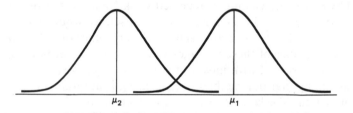

Figure 5.3.   Distributions of μ_1 and μ_2 for H_A: $\mu_1 > \mu_2$.

The probability of making a Type 2 error is β. This type of error is controlled by selecting an appropriate number of observations to be made.

The next decision depends on how the alternative hypothesis is stated. If we select the form H_A: $\mu_1 \neq \mu_2$, when we accept H_A we are merely stating that μ_1 is so different from μ_2 (without stating which is the larger) that only a small part of the two distribution curves overlap, as shown in Figure 5.1. This is the two-tailed test condition we discussed in Chapter 4.

If we select the form H_A: $\mu_1 < \mu_2$, when we adopt H_A we are stating that μ_1 is so much smaller than μ_2 that its distribution curve falls near the left-hand extremity of that of μ_2, and it is very unlikely that they are equal, as shown in Figure 5.2. Just the reverse is true for H_A: $\mu_1 > \mu_2$ as shown in Figure 5.3. Both of these cases are the one-tailed test condition.

Thus, if we are asking merely if two averages differ, we should use the two-tailed test critical values because we are not placing restrictions on which average is to be greater. If we are asking if the average exceeds a stated value (or if it is less than a limit) we should use the one-tailed test critical values because we are interested only in knowing if the average falls on one side of the distribution curve.

If we are using the two-tailed test (at the 0.05 level of significance for example), the critical region under the curve is divided into two equal parts (each corresponding to 0.025 probability in this example), and the critical statistic is usually subscripted 0.05/2, as $t_{0.05/2, 10} = 2.23$, where 10 is the degrees of freedom for t and 2.23 is read by entering Table 5, Appendix D for 10 dF and $\alpha = 0.05$ for the two-tailed test. For the one-tailed test, at the same level of significance and degrees of freedom, the critical statistic would be written as $t_{0.05, 10} = 1.81$.

5.1 DOES THE AVERAGE AGREE WITH THE THEORETICAL OR AN ACCEPTED VALUE?

If we have a population whose true average, μ, and normal distribution (defined by σ) are known and we repeatedly take random sets of a given size from it and determine the average $\bar{X}$ for each set, we would not expect the calculated values for $\bar{X}$ to agree exactly with each other or with the value of μ. If a large number of these averages were graphed a normal distribution curve would be formed with most of the values being close to μ. (We are of course assuming that our method of measuring is accurate, or in statistical jargon, unbiased.) The larger the number of averages obtained, the closer this sample distribution curve approaches a normal distribution curve.

Now compare the $\bar{X}$ for one of our sets of observations with the true average of the population, μ. If we knew the standard deviation σ for the population, the standard deviation for $\bar{X}$ would be $\sigma/\sqrt{n}$, where n is the number of observations. Moreover, we know that approximately 95% of the estimates of μ will fall in the range $\mu \pm 2\sigma/\sqrt{n}$. So if $\bar{X}$ differed from the theoretical or accepted value by more than $\pm 2\sigma/\sqrt{n}$, we would be pretty confident that μ really differed significantly from theory. If $\bar{X}$ differed by more than $\pm 3\sigma/\sqrt{n}$, we would be even more confident of the reality of the difference.

Unfortunately, we do not know the true standard deviation of our set; we have only an estimate s based on n observations. Thus, the distribution curve for $\bar{X}$ is an estimate of the true distribution curve. A research chemist, W. S. Gosset, worked out the relationship between these estimates of the distribution curve and the true one so that we can use s in place of σ. Gosset was employed by a well-known Irish brewery which did not want its competitors to know it was using statistical methods. However, he was permitted to publish his work under the pen name "Student," and the test for differences in averages based on his work is known as Student's t test. Student's t test assumes that the average is based on data from a normal population. The basic equation used for the t test distribution may be expressed mathematically as

$$t = \frac{\bar{X} - \mu}{s/\sqrt{n}}; \quad df = n - 1 \tag{5.1}$$

where

$s =$ the standard deviation of the n observations whose average is $\bar{X}$. Thus, $s/\sqrt{n}$ is the estimate of the standard deviation of $\bar{X}$.
$df =$ degrees of freedom.

Note: Generally, the absolute difference of $\bar{X}$ is used so that only positive values of t are obtained. This simplifies comparison with the tables of critical values, which list only positive values.

EXAMPLE 5.1. Six determinations were made of the hydrogen content of a compound whose theoretical composition is 9.55% H. Does the average value differ significantly from theory? Use the 0.05 level of significance.

$H_0: \mu = 9.55$

$H_A: \mu \neq 9.55$ (Results in the 2-tailed test)

$\alpha = 0.05$

% H
9.17
9.09
9.14
9.10
9.13
9.27

$\bar{X} = 9.15, \quad s = 0.0654$ [by Equation (3.1)]

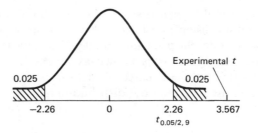

Figure 5.4. Example 5.1, two-tailed t test.

Using Equation (5.1):

$$t = \frac{9.15 - 9.55}{0.0654/\sqrt{6}} = \frac{0.40}{0.0267} = 14.98; \quad df = 5$$

Referring to the critical values for t in Table 5 in Appendix D for a significance level of 0.05 and 5 degrees of freedom for the two-tailed test, we find $t_{0.05/2,\,5} = 2.57$. Refer to Figure 5.4. Since our calculated value of 14.98 exceeds the critical value, we reject the null hypothesis and conclude that the population average is significantly different from the theoretical value for $\alpha = 0.05$.

5.2 WHEN ARE TWO AVERAGES REALLY DIFFERENT?

The comparison of two averages for a significant difference is a logical extension of comparing an average with a reference value. Whereas in the latter case we had to consider the variance of the average in judging if the average differed from the reference, in comparing two averages, each has its own variance which must be taken into account. What we are doing is determining if the tails of the two distributions of the averages overlap enough to consider the averages to be the same or different. This is done by a modified pooling of the two variances. The kind of pooling used depends upon whether the averages are independent or dependent and whether the variances are known, unknown and equal, or unknown and unequal.

What determines whether the averages are independent or dependent? If the same samples are used in determining both averages, the averages are said to be dependent. For example, if the same set of samples is analyzed by two methods, or by two analysts, the averages obtained are dependent. If separate samples are used in determining the averages, the averages are classed as independent. For example, if two tank cars representing perhaps different plants' production of a product are sampled to determine if the cars differ in purity, the samples obviously come from different populations, and since different samples are used in obtaining the average value for each car, the averages are independent.

5.2.1 Comparing Two Independent Averages With Known Variances

Most of the time in analytical chemistry we do not know the variances of the averages, but when they are known, such as might be true in comparing averages by an established method, the following equation is used to calculate the t value:

$$t = \frac{\bar{X}_1 - \bar{X}_2}{\sqrt{\dfrac{\sigma_1^2}{n_1} + \dfrac{\sigma_2^2}{n_2}}}; \quad \mathrm{df} = \infty \tag{5.2}$$

where

n_1 = number of observations comprising X_1 with variance σ_1^2
n_2 = number of observations comprising X_2 with variance σ_2^2
df = degrees of freedom associated with the t value.

Note 1: The numerator of the t equation really should be $(\bar{X}_1 - \bar{X}_2) - (\mu_1 - \mu_2)$, but when the hypothesis of the t test is $\mu_1 = \mu_2$, the last term always equals zero and is omitted from this equation and the other equations for t in this book.

Note 2: Most statistical texts call for the use of the Z test to compare two averages with known variances. Except for the substitution of Z for t, the equation is identical to Equation (5.2). The critical values are obtained from a Z table. The Z test may be considered to be a special case of the t test where the degrees of freedom are large. In fact, the critical values for Z are the same as those in the t table for the same level of significance with infinite degrees of freedom. Thus, for our purposes we will use the t test with infinite degrees of freedom to compare two means with known variances.

Note 3: As indicated for Equation (5.1), the absolute difference of $\bar{X}_1$ and $\bar{X}_2$ generally is used so that only positive t values are obtained.

EXAMPLE 5.2. Two batches of a product are analyzed for water content by a standard Karl Fischer method which has a standard deviation of $\sigma = 0.025$. Based on the data, do the two batches differ significantly in water content? Use 0.05 level of significance and the 2-tailed test.

% WATER

BATCH A	BATCH B
0.50	0.53
0.53	0.56
0.47	0.51
	0.53
	0.50
$\bar{X} = 0.500$	$\bar{X} = 0.526$
$n = 3$	$n = 5$

$$H_0: \mu_1 = \mu_2$$

$$H_A: \mu_1 \neq \mu_2$$

$$\alpha = 0.05/2$$

$$t = \frac{0.500 - 0.526}{\sqrt{\dfrac{0.025^2}{3} + \dfrac{0.025^2}{5}}} = \frac{0.026}{\sqrt{0.0003333}} = 1.424; \quad df = \infty$$

$t_{0.05/2, \infty} = 1.96$. Therefore, the null hypothesis is not rejected, and we conclude there is no evidence of a significant difference in the water content of the two batches for $\alpha = 0.05/2$. Refer to Figure 5.5.

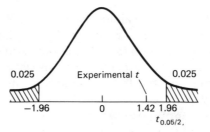

Figure 5.5.   Example 5.2, two-tailed t test.

5.2.2   Comparing Two Independent Averages with Unknown and Equal Variances

Most likely, we do not know the variances associated with the two averages of interest, and the variances must be calculated from the same data used to determine the averages. The two variances are first subjected to the F test. If they appear to be homogeneous (i.e., not significantly different) by the F test, then Equation (5.3), below, is used to test the two averages. If the variances are significantly different, another test, discussed in the next section, is used.

$$t = \frac{\bar{X}_1 - \bar{X}_2}{s_p\sqrt{1/n_1 + 1/n_2}} = \frac{\bar{X}_1 - \bar{X}_2}{s_p}\sqrt{\frac{n_1 n_2}{n_1 + n_2}}; \quad df = n_1 + n_2 - 2 \quad (5.3)$$

where

$$s_p = \sqrt{\frac{(n_1 - 1)s_1^2 + (n_2 - 1)s_2^2}{n_1 - 1 + n_2 - 1}}$$

n_1 = number of observations comprising the first average $\bar{X}_1$
n_2 = number of observations comprising the second average $\bar{X}_2$
s_p = pooled standard deviation of the standard deviations s_1 and s_2 for the first and second sets of data.

Note 1: When $n_1 = n_2$, the square root term in the second form of Equation (5.3) reduces to $\sqrt{n/2}$.

Note 2: As mentioned for Equation (5.1), the absolute difference of $\bar{X}_1$ and $\bar{X}_2$ is generally used.

EXAMPLE 5.3. Two samples, one each from two batches of a product, were analyzed for trace iron content by the same method with the following results. Do the batches differ significantly in iron content? Test at $\alpha = 0.05$ significance level of the 2-tailed test.

	Fe, ppm	
RUN	BATCH A	BATCH B
1	6.1	5.9
2	5.8	5.7
3	7.0	6.1
	$\bar{X} = 6.30$	$\bar{X} = 5.90$
	$s = 0.6245$	$s = 0.2000$

$$F = 0.6245^2/0.2000^2 = 9.75$$

$F_{0.05/2, 2, 2} = 39.00$. Thus, the variances appear to be equal and can be pooled for use in Equation (5.3).

$$s_p = \sqrt{\frac{(3-1)0.6245^2 + (3-1)0.2000^2}{3-1+3-1}} = \sqrt{\frac{0.8600005}{4}} = 0.4637, \quad 4\text{ df}$$

$$H_0: \mu_A = \mu_B, \qquad H_A: \mu_A \neq \mu_B$$

$$t = \frac{6.30 - 5.90}{0.4637}\sqrt{\frac{3 \times 3}{3 + 3}} = 1.056$$

$t_{0.05/2, 4} = 2.78$. As shown in Figure 5.6, the critical value is not exceeded. We accept the null hypothesis and conclude there is no significant difference between the population averages. Thus, the iron content of the two batches has not been shown to be significantly different at $\alpha = 0.05$.

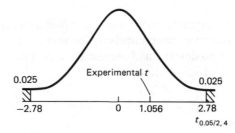

Figure 5.6.   Example 5.3, two-tailed t test.

5.2.3   Comparing Two Independent Averages with Unknown and Unequal Variances

This situation is similar to the preceeding one, except that when we apply the F test to our estimates of the variances, they are found to be significantly different. Note that Equation (5.4), below, used for calculating the t value, is the same as Equation (5.2) except that s is substituted for σ, and that the degrees of freedom are calculated differently.

$$t = \frac{\bar{X}_1 - \bar{X}_2}{\sqrt{\dfrac{s_1^2}{n_1} + \dfrac{s_2^2}{n_2}}} \tag{5.4}$$

$$\mathrm{df} = \frac{\left(\dfrac{s_1^2}{n_1} + \dfrac{s_2^2}{n_2}\right)^2}{\dfrac{\left(\dfrac{s_1^2}{n_1}\right)^2}{n_1 + 1} + \dfrac{\left(\dfrac{s_2^2}{n_2}\right)^2}{n_2 + 1}} - 2 \tag{5.4a}$$

where

n_1 = number of observations comprising the first average $\bar{X}_1$
n_2 = number of observations comprising the second average $\bar{X}_2$
s_1 = standard deviation for the first set of data
s_2 = standard deviation for the second set of data
df = degrees of freedom associated with t.

Note 1: The degrees of freedom will always be between the smaller of $(n_1 - 1)$ and $(n_2 - 1)$ and the sum of $(n_1 + n_2 - 2)$.

Note 2: As with the other equations for the t test, the absolute difference between the two averages is generally used.

EXAMPLE 5.4. In Example 5.3 we had only three determinations on each sample, giving us a total of 4 degrees of freedom for the t test. This meant that the critical value of t was higher than it would have been had we had more degrees of freedom. Let us obtain additional analyses on the two samples from Example 5.3 and see if the new averages are different, using $\alpha = 0.05$ and the 2-tailed test.

	Fe, ppm	
RUN	BATCH A	BATCH B
1	6.1	5.9
2	5.8	5.7
3	7.0	6.1
4	6.1	5.8
5	5.8	5.9
6	6.4	5.6
7	6.1	5.6
8	6.0	5.9
9	5.9	5.7
10	5.8	5.6
	$\bar{X} = 6.10$	$\bar{X} = 5.78$
	$s = 0.3682$	$s = 0.1686$
	$n = 10$	$n = 10$

$$F = 0.3682^2/0.1686^2 = 4.77$$

$F_{0.05/2,9,9} = 4.03$. We reject the null hypothesis that $\sigma_A^2 = \sigma_B^2$ and conclude that the variances are *not* equal at $\alpha = 0.05$. Therefore, we need to use Equation (5.4) to calculate the t statistic and Equation (5.4a) to calculate df.

$$H_0: \mu_A = \mu_B. \qquad H_A: \mu_A \neq \mu_B$$

$$t = \frac{6.10 - 5.78}{\sqrt{\dfrac{0.3682^2}{10} + \dfrac{0.1686^2}{10}}} = \frac{0.32}{\sqrt{0.01355712 + 0.00284260}}$$

$$= \frac{3.2}{\sqrt{0.01639972}} = 2.50$$

$$\mathrm{df} = \left[\frac{0.01639972^2}{\dfrac{0.01355712^2}{11} + \dfrac{0.0284260^2}{11}} \right] - 2 = 15.4 - 2$$

$$= 13, \text{ rounded to the nearest whole number}$$

$t_{0.05/2,13} = 2.16$. As shown in Figure 5.7, the critical t value is exceeded. We therefore reject the null hypothesis and conclude that the two population averages differ significantly at $\alpha = 0.05$.

Note: The values of 0.01639972, 0.01355712, and 0.02842620 used in calculating the degrees of freedom can be obtained from the terms in the denominator in the t equation.

If we had wanted to test the alternative hypothesis that $\mu_B < \mu_A$, we would have used the one-tailed value of $t_{0.05,13} = 1.77$ in comparing our experimental t. Since this critical value is exceeded, we would reject this alternative hypothesis and conclude that Batch B contains significantly less iron.

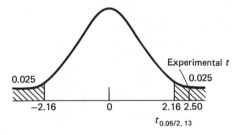

Figure 5.7. Example 5.4, two-tailed t test.

5.2.4 Comparing Two Dependent Averages (Paired Data)

Comparison of two dependent averages is a common situation in analytical chemistry. We may be interested in knowing if two different methods give the same average value for a given sample, or if two analysts obtain the same result on a common sample. In this kind of situation we are dealing with paired data.

Paired data are used in situations where it is difficult to control some factors which may affect our results. For example, when two methods for determining percent active ingredient in a product are being compared, the results might be affected by variation in the concentration of active ingredient, the analyst, variation in concentrations of minor components, etc. We want to keep all conditions constant so the results will reflect only differences between the methods. Factors like the analyst can be held constant, but factors like the concentrations of active ingredients and minor components are difficult to hold constant if more than one sample is involved.

If we analyze each of a series of samples by the two methods, we will obtain a pair of results for each sample. The difference between these two results for each pair will reflect only the difference in the methods; the effects of concentrations of active ingredient and minor components have been virtually eliminated. There is an additional benefit to using paired data. In an industrial environment it is frequently more cost effective to evaluate two methods by analyzing a series of routine production samples once by each method rather than by replicating the analysis of one sample by each method.

The following equation is used for the t test on paired data:

$$t = \frac{\bar{d}}{s_d}\sqrt{n}; \quad df = n - 1 \tag{5.5}$$

where

$$s_d = \sqrt{\frac{\sum d^2 - \frac{(\sum d)^2}{n}}{n - 1}}$$

d = the difference in each pair of values
$\bar{d}$ = the average difference in the pairs of values. As in the previous t equations, the absolute value is generally used.
n = the number of pairs of values
df = degrees of freedom associated with t
s_d = standard deviation of the differences between the pairs of observations.

EXAMPLE 5.5. Assume that the data presented in Example 5.4 were obtained under different conditions than those stated: that batch B is batch

A after treatment to remove an interfering impurity. Is the average iron content of batch A equivalent to that of batch B?

Subtracting the values for batch B from batch A gives the following differences and squares of differences:

RUN	d	d^2
1	0.2	0.04
2	0.1	0.01
3	0.9	0.81
4	0.3	0.09
5	−0.1	0.01
6	0.8	0.64
7	0.5	0.25
8	0.1	0.01
9	0.2	0.04
10	0.2	0.04
Total	3.2	1.94
$\bar{d}$	0.32	

$$H_0: \mu_A = \mu_B; \qquad H_A: \mu_A \neq \mu_B$$

$$s_d = \sqrt{\frac{1.94 - \dfrac{(3.2)^2}{10}}{10 - 1}} = \sqrt{0.1017778} = 0.3190, \quad 9 \text{ df}$$

$$t = \frac{0.32}{0.3190}\sqrt{10} = 3.172, \quad 9 \text{ df}$$

$t_{0.05/2,9} = 2.262$. Figure 5.8 illustrates the results. Since the critical value is exceeded, we reject the null hypothesis and conclude that the populations represented by the average values are significantly different at $\alpha = 0.05$. The treatment of batch A significantly reduces the measured iron content.

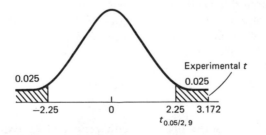

Figure 5.8.   Example 5.5, two-tailed t test.

EXAMPLE 5.6.   Ten production samples are analyzed for water content by the standard Karl Fischer method and by a coulometric version of the KF method. Is there a real difference in the precision and water values due to the methods? Test at $\alpha = 0.05$ significance level of the two-tailed test.

SAMPLE	COUL. KF	REGULAR KF	DIF.
1	12.1%	14.7%	2.6
2	10.9	14.0	3.1
3	13.1	12.9	−0.2
4	14.5	16.2	1.7
5	9.6	10.2	0.6
6	11.2	12.4	1.2
7	9.8	12.0	2.2
8	13.7	14.8	1.1
9	12.0	11.8	−0.2
10	9.1	9.7	0.6
Avg.	11.60	12.87	1.27
s	1.814	2.075	1.126

Compare method variances: Note that with only one observation per sample by each method, there is no way to calculate the variance of the methods. The standard deviation values listed for each method includes variation due to sample differences in addition to the method's variance.

Compare averages (paired data t equation):

$$H_0: \mu_C = \mu_R; \qquad H_A: \mu_C \neq \mu_R$$

$$t = \frac{\bar{d}}{s_d}\sqrt{n} = \frac{1.27}{1.126}\sqrt{10} = \frac{1.27}{1.126} \times 3.162 = 3.567*$$

(an asterisk is frequently used to mark significant test results.)

$$df = n - 1 = 9$$

$t_{0.05/2,9} = 2.26$. Thus, as illustrated in Figure 5.9, there is a significant difference between the average values when tested at $\alpha = 0.05$. We conclude that the two methods give different average water contents.

If we had elected to test the alternate hypothesis that $\mu_C < \mu_R$, we would have used the critical value of $F_{0.05,9} = 1.83$ in testing the null hypothesis as shown in Figure 5.10. We would have rejected the null hypothesis and concluded that the coulometric method tends to give significantly lower water values.

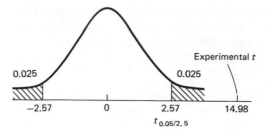

Figure 5.9.   Example 5.6, two-tailed t test.

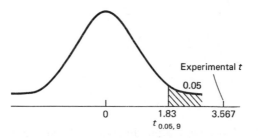

Figure 5.10.   Example 5.6, one-tailed t test.

Now, let us calculate the t test using the equation for variances unknown and equal (*an incorrect test*):

$$t = \frac{\bar{X}_1 - \bar{X}_2}{s_p}\sqrt{\frac{n_1 n_2}{n_1 + n_2}} = \frac{|11.60 - 12.87|}{1.9488}\sqrt{\frac{10 \times 10}{10 + 10}} = 1.457 \text{ NS}$$

(The value of s_p was obtained by pooling the standard deviations of 1.814 and 2.075.)

$$df = n_1 + n_2 - 2 = 18$$

$t_{0.05/2,18} = 2.10$. The critical value is not exceeded. Thus, we accept the null hypothesis and conclude there is *no* significant difference between the two averages!

Why the difference in results of the t tests? (Note that the first t test is the proper one for paired data.)

Look at the value for s for the difference values; it is less than those for either method. This indicates the variation between samples is large enough to obscure the variation between the methods. In cases like this, where extraneous variation is large compared to the difference of interest, the t test on the differences is the more sensitive and correct procedure.

5.3 SAMPLE SIZE TO DETECT A GIVEN DIFFERENCE BETWEEN AVERAGES

We have seen how the t test is used to test for significant differences between two averages. However, in planning experiments it is important to know how many observations will be needed in order for the t test to be able to detect the difference of interest. For example, if it is important to know if two methods give average results which differ by no more than 0.05%, we should plan to run enough analyses so that with the precision of the methods the t test will be able to pick up differences this great with probabilities of types I and II error at acceptable levels. Recall that a type I error is deciding there is a difference when in fact there is none, and a type II error is deciding there is not a difference when in fact there is. The probability of a type I error is α, of a type II error, β.

Table 6 in Appendix D gives the number of samples required for various combinations of the above conditions. The numbers in the table assume that $n_1 = n_2 = n$, since this is the most commonly used arrangement of data for the t test. It also gives the smallest β error for any given α and fixed total number of observations $(n_1 + n_2)$.

Assume that we wish to detect a real difference of 0.32, we estimate the standard deviation to be 0.289, and we wish α and β to each be at 0.05. First we calculate $D = d/\sigma = 0.32/0.289 = 1.11$. We enter Table 6 at the $D = 1.1$ row and go over the set of columns headed $\alpha = 0.05$ for the double tailed t test, and the column headed 0.05 for β to find that we should use 23 samples. This may sound like a lot of samples, but consider that we want to detect a difference of 0.32 with 95% certainty for both types of errors and the standard deviation is almost as large as the difference to be detected.

Let us take another example where the standard deviation is smaller than the difference to be detected: Assume we want to detect a difference of 0.05, the standard deviation is estimated to be 0.02, and α and β are again at the 0.05 level. $D = 0.05/0.02 = 2.50$. This time we see that the number of pairs of samples is 6.

5.4. HOW GOOD IS THE ESTIMATED AVERAGE? (CONFIDENCE INTERVALS FOR AN AVERAGE)

Recalling the plot of the normal distribution curve, we said that the true mean μ plus-or-minus 1σ included about 68% of the area under the curve, that

$\mu \pm 1.96\sigma$ included about 95% of the area, and the $\mu \pm 3\sigma$ included about 99.7% of the area. Another way of stating this would be that the interval $\mu \pm 1.96\sigma$ includes 95% of the values obtained in an infinite number of observations. Thus, this interval of $\mu \pm 1.96\sigma$ is called the 95% confidence interval. However, in real life things are a bit more complicated.

Assume $\bar{X} = 24.5$, $s = 0.26$, and df = 5. It is *not* correct to say that the 95% confidence interval for the average is $\mu = 24.5 \pm 1.96\,(0.26/\sqrt{6})$, or 24.5 ± 0.11. Why not? Because $\bar{X}$ and s are merely estimates of μ and σ and as such have uncertainties associated with their values. We can use the t function to correct for the uncertainty in s. The correct calculation is $\mu = \bar{X} \pm ts/\sqrt{n}$, or $\mu = 24.5 \pm 2.571 \times 0.26/\sqrt{6} = 24.5 \pm 0.27$. The value of 2.571 for t is obtained from the two-tailed t table at the 0.05 level of significance and 5 degrees of freedom.

Note: The degrees of freedom for t (5 in this example) are those associated with the estimated standard deviation s, not with the sample size n. Therefore, in the above example if we wanted to calculate the confidence interval for the averages of duplicates instead of averages of six determinations, the equation would become: confidence interval for $\mu = \bar{X} \pm 2.571 \times 0.26/\sqrt{2} = \bar{X} \pm 0.47$. The plus-or-minus term is much larger for the average of duplicates than for the average of 6 determinations. This is reasonable because we are more confident about the average of a larger number of observations.

5.5   RANGE OF VALUES EXPECTED FOR AN AVERAGE AT A GIVEN CONFIDENCE LEVEL

Many times we are not as interested in the confidence interval for an average as we are in how closely we can expect two such values to agree. For the previous example of $\bar{X} = 24.5$, $s = 0.26$, and df = 5, some authors suggest calculating this range by multiplying the estimated standard deviation by a factor ($\sqrt{2} \times t_{0.05/2,\,df}$) whose value depends on the degrees of freedom associated with the s value. For 5 degrees of freedom, the factor from Table 9 in Appendix D is 3.64. Thus, $0.26/\sqrt{6} \times 3.64 = 0.39$, which is the maximum difference we might expect between two averages of six observations (obtained under the conditions which lead to the quoted average and standard deviation) 95 times out of 100. If two such averages differ by more than 0.39, we would conclude that the difference is significant when tested at $\propto = 0.05$.

However, Mandell and Lashof[1] have shown that using a multiplier of $\sqrt{2} \times 1.96$ or 2.77 in place of the values in Table 9 results in ranges which more closely meet the 95% confidence level. Regardless of the multiplier used, the likelihood of the confidence level being exactly 95% is small unless the degrees of freedom are greater than about 30. They recommend using the 2.77

multiplier to obtain the range for two results at approximately the 95% confidence level. This text will follow their suggestion. Thus, for $\bar{X} = 24.5$ and $s = 0.26$, the better estimate of the maximum difference expected between two averages of six observations is $0.26/\sqrt{6} \times 2.77$ or 0.29 instead of the 0.39 we previously calculated.

5.6 COMPARING MORE THAN TWO AVERAGES

So far we have discussed comparing one average with a reference value or another average value. There are times when we have more than two averages which we wish to compare with each other and determine if any are significantly different. For example, we may have prepared 6 batches of a product and analyzed several samples from each batch. Are the averages which differ numerically really different? This situation is analogous to the comparison of more than two variances in Chapter 4.2. We would, of course, repeatedly apply the t test to all possible pairs of the 6 batches, but the confidence level for the aggregate comparison would rapidly decrease in the same manner explained in Chapter 4.2.

Duncan's test for separation of means offers us a way of telling with a stated probability which averages differ significantly from the others. The analysis of variance of the data (discussed in a later chapter) will tell us if there are significant differences among the averages, but not which ones differ.

5.6.1 Duncan's Separation of Means Procedure

The use of Duncan's separation of means procedure to determine which average value or values differ significantly from a set of averages is best explained by going through an example. A pilot plant made 5 batches of a new product. Each batch was analyzed for saponification number in triplicate, making a total of 15 results. The average saponification number for each batch (A, B, C, D, and E) is listed below in order of increasing value. The pooled standard deviation estimate for the five sets of triplicate results is 4.420 with 10 degrees of freedom.

BATCH	D	A	B	C	E
Avg. sap. #	99.6	101.0	105.6	112.8	120.0

In brief what we will do is to decide which of the 10 differences, $E - D$, $E - A, E - B, \ldots, C - D, C - A, \ldots, B - D, B - A, \ldots,$ and $A - D$, between the 5 averages considered one pair at a time are significant. We shall use a 5% level of significance in making these decisions.

First, a table of significant ranges for a 5% level test (Table 10A in Appendix D) is entered at the row for df = 10, and the significant ranges are read for samples of sizes $p = 2, 3, 4,$ and 5 since these are the numbers of averages we are comparing. Table 10B in Appendix D gives the significant ranges we would use if we wished to use a 1% level of significance.

These significant ranges are then multiplied by the pooled standard deviation, $s_p = 4.420$, to form a set of least significant ranges which are listed together with the averages below:

Least significant ranges:

For samples of		2	3	4	5
Significant ranges		3.15	3.30	3.37	3.43
Least significant ranges		13.9	14.6	14.9	15.2
Averages	D	A	B	C	E
	99.6	101.0	105.6	112.8	120.0

The procedure for the underscoring shown will be explained in a moment, but its significance is this: Any averages underscored by the same line are *not* significantly different.

We now proceed to test the differences in this order: the largest average minus the smallest, the largest minus the second smallest, and so on up to the largest minus the second largest. Then, the second largest minus the smallest, the second largest minus the second smallest, etc., finally finishing with the second smallest minus the smallest. In this example the order is $E - D, E - A,$ $E - B, E - C; C - D, C - A, C - B; B - D, B - A;$ and $A - D.$

With only one exception, each difference is significant if it exceeds the corresponding least significant range; otherwise it is not significant. Because $E - D$ is the range of 5 averages, it must exceed 15.2, the least significant range for 5 averages, to be significant, etc. The exception to this rule is that no difference between two averages can be declared significant if the two averages in question are both contained in a subset with a nonsignificant range.

Because of this exception, as soon as a nonsignificant difference is found between two averages, it is convenient to group these two averages and all the intervening averages together by underscoring them with a line as shown for averages $B, C,$ and $E.$ The remaining differences between all members of a subset so underscored are not significant according to the exception rule, and they should not be tested against the least significant ranges.

For our example the stepwise comparison of the 5 averages is:

$E - D = 20.4$ vs. 15.2; thus $E - D$ is significant
$E - A = 19.0$ vs. 14.9; thus $E - A$ is significant
$E - B = 14.4$ vs. 14.6; thus $E - B$ is not significant; denote
                                 by underscoring B, C, and E. ($E - C$
                                 is not tested.)
$C - D = 13.2$ vs. 14.9; thus $C - D$ is not significant; denote
                                 by underscoring D, A, B, and C.
                                 ($C - A$, $C - B$, $B - D$, $B - A$, and $A - D$
                                 are not tested.)

Now, what do these results mean? The Duncan separation of means test tells us that given the five averages and the standard deviation, we cannot distinguish between four batches having averages of 99.6 to 112.8 nor between three batches with averages between 105.6 and 120.0 at the 0.05 level of significance. This situation may not be very gratifying, but that is what our data tells us. If we need to be able to distinguish more finely between these averages, we can perhaps improve the method of analysis so that it has better precision, or we could make additional determinations so that we have averages of a greater number of determinations. Either of these approaches would lead to a smaller value of s_w and thus smaller least significant ranges.

If in our example s_w had equaled 4.000 instead of 4.420, the least significant ranges would be 12.6, 13.2, 13.5, and 13.7 for samples of 2, 3, 4, and 5. This would result in only averages D, A, B, and C being underscored. In other words, in this case we could not distinguish between batches A, B, C, and D, but average E is different.

5.7 SUMMARY

This chapter was devoted to averages and some of the more common questions we ask about them.

In deciding whether an average value is in agreement with the theoretical or accepted value, or whether two averages agree, we saw how one of five forms of the t test could be used to help us decide.

We learned how to calculate how much data to use in order to detect a given difference with a stated degree of confidence.

We saw how to establish confidence limits about an average so that the interval would include the true average a stated percentage of the time.

Given an estimate of the precision of a method, we learned how to calculate how closely two averages obtained by that method should be expected to agree a stated percentage of the time.

We also learned how to determine which averages in a set of averages differed significantly from each other.

5.8 PROBLEMS

The following problems (or parts of problems) make use of the tests discussed in this chapter. Answers are given in the answer section in the back of the book.

SUBJECT	PROBLEMS
Comparison of average with a reference	3e
Comparison of two averages	1f, 2h, 26, 27
Confidence intervals for averages	1b, 2e, 3c, 15c, 17c, 18d
Range of two results	1d, 2f, 3d, 15d, 16c, 17d, 18c, 20c
Comparing more than two averages	9 (use $s_p = 0.03507$, 6 df for the analysts and $s_p = 0.03038$, 6 df for the drums)

REFERENCE

1. Mandell, John, and Lashof, Theodore W., *J. Qual. Tech.*, *19*, No. 1, Jan. 1987, pp. 29–36.

Chapter 6
LINEAR RELATIONSHIPS BETWEEN TWO VARIABLES: CALIBRATION CURVES AND OTHER PREDICTIONS

OVERVIEW

Every chemist has observed that sometimes two variables of an experiment appear to be related to each other:

- The yield of a polymer seems to increase with increasing time.
- The rate of hydrolysis of a compound appears to be associated with pH.
- The absorbance of a solution is proportional to the concentration of a colored solute (a basis for a calibration curve).
- Similar hydroxyl numbers are obtained for a series of samples when measured using two different reagents.

When two variables exhibit such relationships we may be interested in quantifying the relationship so that values of one variable may be estimated from values of the other. A common example for analytical chemists is the calibration curve (usually a straight line) which relates the concentration of the analyte to absorbance or some other measurable property. In this chapter we will learn how a statistical technique called regression can give us the best line through our data points, whether for a calibration curve or other linear relationship. In addition we will be able to establish confidence limits around our line and predicted values.

6.0   LINEAR RELATIONSHIPS BETWEEN TWO VARIABLES

Based on our observations, two or more variables may appear to be related to each other. The relationship may be linear or nonlinear, but our discussion will be limited to two variables and linear relationships. If you are interested in the relationship of more than two variables or in nonlinear relationships, Chapter 12 will provide an introduction to linear regression. Some books on

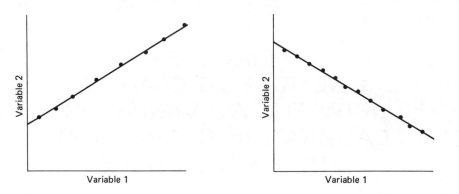

Figure 6.1.   High and positive correlation.   Figure 6.2.   High and negative correlation.

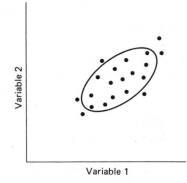

Figure 6.3.   Moderate and positive correlation.

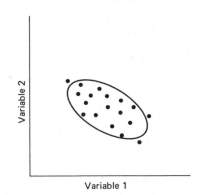

Figure 6.4.   Moderate and negative correlation.

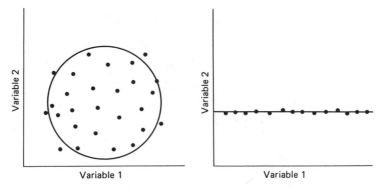

Figure 6.5.   No correlation.   Figure 6.6.   No correlation.

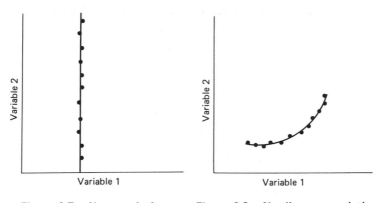

Figure 6.7.   No correlation.   Figure 6.8.   Nonlinear correlation.

general regression and correlation are suggested under Resources at the end of this chapter.

In considering the relationship of two variables the first step should be to plot the values of one variable versus those of the second. The plot will usually form one of several patterns similar to those shown in Figures 6.1 through 6.8.

If the plot resembles Figure 6.5, there is obviously no significant relationship, and no calculations are required. If the plot shows very little scatter, as in Figures 6.1 and 6.2, there is little doubt that a significant relationship exists, and a straight line positioned by eye is probably precise enough for use even though such a line might miss the optimum location by a small amount. Again, no calculation may be needed to establish the best line, but we will not be able to make quantitative statements about how good our estimates are.

Frequently the plot will resemble Figures 6.3 or 6.4. In these cases, there is

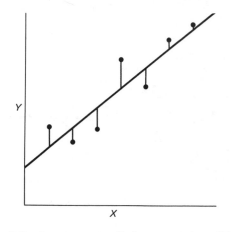

Figure 6.9.   Least squares fit for regression of Y on X.

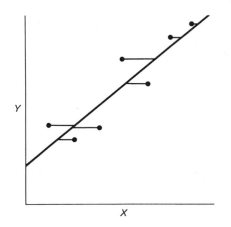

Figure 6.10.   Least squares fit for regression of X on Y.

little doubt that a relationship exists, but some mathematics is required to locate the line which best describes the relationship. One such mathematical procedure is called the *least squares* technique and is generally accepted as the best objective way of estimating the location of the line.

The equation derived by this technique produces a line whose position is such that the sum of the squares of the vertical distances of each data point to the line is a minimum if the line is to be used to predict Y from values of X (Figure 6.9), or the sum of the squares of the horizontal distances is a minimum if X is to be predicted from Y (Figure 6.10).

If the plot suggests a nonlinear relationship, such as in Figure 6.8, techniques for dealing with nonlinear data may be used. (For such procedures refer to the texts in the Resource section at the end of this chapter.) Sometimes the data may be transformed so that the relationship becomes linear. A familiar example is the relationship of percent transmission to concentration of a colored solute. Transformation (a change of the scale used) of the percent T values to log 100/percent T produces a linear relationship, as illustrated in Figure 2.9 of Chapter 2. Logarithms may also be used in other cases, as indicated in the following list, which suggests several linearizing transformations, depending on the type of nonlinearity:[1]

	TRANSFORMATION OF:	
FORM OF RELATIONSHIP	Y	X
$Y = a + b/X$	Y	$1/X$
$Y = 1/(a + bX)$, or		
$\quad 1/Y = a + bX$	$1/Y$	X
$Y = X/(a + bX)$	X/Y	X
$Y = ab^X$	log Y	X
$Y = ae^{bX}$	log Y	X
$Y = aX^b$	log Y	log X
$Y = a + bX^n$, where n is known	Y	X^n

Obviously, the regression technique may be applied to the fitting of analytical calibration curves, although often the scatter of the points is so small that a line visually positioned through the points is sufficiently accurate.

It should be noted that differences of opinion exist among statisticians about the best way of expressing the relationship between variables. Various classification schemes with differing calculations have been proposed. We will consider two situations, each with its own set of equations for calculating the line which best fits the data. Our approach has the approval of a substantial number of statisticians, but do not be surprised to see other approaches used in other texts.

6.1 REGRESSION LINES FOR DIFFERENT KINDS OF RELATIONSHIPS

The idea of regression began with Sir Francis Galton, a 19th Century British explorer, anthropologist, and eugenicist. When he studied the heights of fathers and their grown sons, he found that fathers taller than the average by a certain amount had sons whose average height was also above average, but by only one-half this amount. Similarly, fathers below average height by a certain amount had sons whose average height was also below average, but by one-half this amount. This tendency for sons to regress, i.e., go back toward the average, is the origin of the term "regression." Galton's idea of regression and of predicting the heights of sons from their fathers' height is applied in many areas today.

Our first application of regression will be for cases where the two variables have an underlying principle; that is, a *functional relationship*. This situation is exemplified by the problem of fitting the best line to calibration data. Typically, we will have a series of standards of known values covering the range of interest, the independent variable (X), and corresponding measurements of the second or dependent variable (Y). The values of X are considered constants because their values are accurately known, whereas the values of Y have random errors associated with them.

The second application of regression will be for cases where the two variables do *not* have an underlying principle; that is, the *association relationship*. This type of relationship is illustrated by the results obtained by two laboratories which analyze the same series of samples for a property whose magnitude is not accurately known. Here *both* the X and Y values have random errors associated with them.

In both applications we are interested in being able to predict a value of the dependent variable (Y) from a given value of the independent value (X). In order to do this, we will perform a regression of Y on X. We could of course reverse things and calculate the equation for a line to be used to predict X from a value of Y (regression of X on Y). It should be noted that these two regression lines will usually have different slopes, but both will pass through the point representing the grand averages of X and Y. The only time these curves will superimpose is when there is a perfect fit of the data points to the line.

6.2 THE CALIBRATION CURVE AND OTHER FUNCTIONAL RELATIONSHIPS

As noted previously, when the values of variables X and Y have an underlying physical relationship, a functional relationship is said to exist. Laboratory calibration curves fit this description. Measurements such as absorbance are made of the dependent random variable Y. There will be error associated with these measurements. The corresponding values of the independent variable X, however, are considered constants because they are accurately known, or at least the error associated with their values is much less than that associated with the Y values. Experiments dealing with the effect of time usually fit this functional relationship. Time can generally be measured accurately enough that it may be considered to be without error.

The assumptions made for this kind of relationship are:

1. Y is linearly related to X, i.e. $Y = a + bX$.
2. The X values have no error associated with them, or at least the errors are much smaller than those associated with the Y values.
3. The errors associated with the Y values are independent, homogeneous over the range of Y values (belong to the same population), and have an average value of zero.

EXAMPLE 6.1.   A nephelometer is to be calibrated so that its scale readings can be converted to ppm solids. The calibration solutions are prepared by appropriately diluting a standard stock suspension of very fine silica particles with distilled water. The stock suspension has a known ppm solids content as determined by a gravimetric method. The following data were obtained from the standard suspensions:

X, PPM SOLIDS	Y, SCALE READING
0.00	0
0.15	23
0.30	38
0.40	45
0.50	61
0.60	76
0.70	82

A plot of the data (Figure 6.11) suggests a linear relationship of the two variables, i.e.

$$Y = a + bX$$

where

$a =$ the intercept of the line
$b =$ the slope of the line.

We will calculate the following:

1. The least squares estimates of a and b (A and B) for the regression equation.
2. The 95% confidence intervals for a and b.
3. A point estimate of the average scale reading for a suspension containing 0.5 ppm solids.

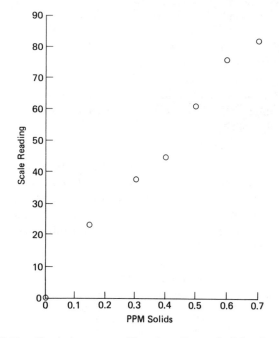

Figure 6.11. Nephelometer calibration, Example 6.1—data points.

4. A 95% confidence interval for the average scale reading for 0.5 ppm solids.
5. A 95% confidence interval for an individual value of the scale reading at 0.5 ppm.
6. A 95% confidence interval for the ppm of solids present for a scale reading of 60.
7. A test for significance of the relationship of the two variables. Null hypothesis: that the slope of the calibration line is zero ($b = 0$), i.e., there is no relationship between scale readings and solids concentration.
8. A test of the hypothesis that the intercept passes through the origin ($a = 0$).

The following format is suggested for ease of calculating if a desk calculator is used:

$n = 7$, the number of pairs of X, Y values

$df = n - 1 = 6$, degrees of freedom

$$\sum X = 2.65, \qquad \sum Y = 325$$

$$\sum X^2 = 1.3725, \qquad \sum Y^2 = 20{,}219$$

$$\sum XY = 166.35$$

$$\frac{(\sum X)^2}{n} = 1.00321429, \qquad \frac{(\sum Y)^2}{n} = 15{,}089.28571$$

$$\frac{\sum X \sum Y}{n} = 123.0357143$$

$$\bar{X} = \frac{\sum X}{n} = 0.3785714286, \qquad \bar{Y} = \frac{\sum Y}{n} = 46.42857143$$

$$s_X^2 = \frac{\sum X^2 - \dfrac{(\sum X)^2}{n}}{n-1} = 0.061547619, \qquad s_Y^2 = \frac{\sum Y^2 - \dfrac{(\sum Y)^2}{n}}{n-1} = 854.952381$$

$$s_X = \sqrt{s_X^2} = 0.24808793, \qquad s_Y = \sqrt{s_Y^2} = 29.23956875$$

6.2.1   Estimating the Calibration Equation

The least squares estimate of a and b uses the following equations:

$$B = \frac{\sum XY - \dfrac{\sum X \sum Y}{n}}{\sum X^2 - \dfrac{(\sum X)^2}{n}} \tag{6.1}$$

$$A = \bar{Y} - B\bar{X} \tag{6.2}$$

Substituting the values from Example 6.1 gives

$$B = \frac{166.35 - 123.0357143}{1.3725 - 1.003214286} = 117.292071$$

$$A = 46.42857143 - (117.292071 \cdot 0.37857143)$$

$$= 2.025145$$

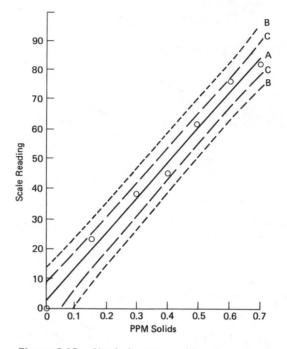

Figure 6.12. Nephelometer calibration curve:
A: regression line of *Y* on *X*
B: 95% confidence limits on an individual *Y*
C: 95% confidence limits to include true *y*

Thus the regression equation is

$$Y = 2.025144 + 117.292071X$$

The line generated by this equation is shown as the solid line in Figure 6.12. This least squares line is the best fit for our data.

Having established the regression line, we will use it to estimate the ppm solids contents of samples from their measured scale readings on the nephelometer. We can read the ppm value value corresponding to a scale reading from the calibration curve, or we can calculate it by solving the regression equation for X:

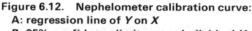

$$Y = 2.025144 + 117.29071X$$

or

$$X = \frac{(Y - 2.025144)}{117.292071}$$

For example, a scale reading of 60 substituted for Y in the above equation gives $X = 0.49$ ppm silica.

6.2.2 Confidence Intervals for the Intercept and Slope

The confidence intervals for the intercept a and the slope b are calculated using Equations (6.3) and (6.4):

$$a = A \pm t_{\alpha/2, n-2} s_{Y \cdot X} \sqrt{\frac{1}{n} + \frac{\bar{X}^2}{\sum X^2 - \frac{(\sum X)^2}{n}}} \qquad (6.3)$$

where

$$s_{Y \cdot X} = \sqrt{\frac{n-1}{n-2}(s_Y^2 - b^2 s_X^2)}$$

the standard deviation of Y on X, and

$$b = B \pm t_{\alpha/2, n-2} \frac{s_{Y \cdot X}}{\sqrt{\sum X^2 - \frac{(\sum X)^2}{n}}} \qquad (6.4)$$

Substituting the values from Example 6.1 and using the value for $t_{0.05/2, 5}$ gives the following 95% confidence limits:

$$s_{Y \cdot X} = \sqrt{\frac{7-1}{7-2}(854.952381 - (117.292071^2 \times 0.061547619))}$$

$$= 3.139807491$$

$$a = 2.205 \pm 2.57 \times 3.1398 \sqrt{\frac{1}{7} + \frac{0.37857142^2}{0.36928571}}$$

$$= 2.205 \pm 5.880 = -3.675 \text{ to } 8.085$$

$$b = 117.292070 \pm 2.01 \frac{3.13980493}{\sqrt{0.36928571}}$$

$$= 117.29207 \pm 10.27867 = 104.0134 \text{ to } 130.5708$$

Note that the confidence interval for a includes zero. This suggests that the curve passes through the origin, which is what we would expect from the way the experiment was run. The absorbance for zero solids content was obtained using distilled water as the standard referenced to distilled water and so should be zero. We will have more to say about curves which pass through the origin Section 6.3.

6.2.3 A Point Estimate for the Average Y

The point estimate for the average scale reading Y for 0.5 ppm solids (or any other value for X) is obtained by substituting the value of X in the regression equation or by reading the value of Y from a graph. For $X = 0.5$,

$$Y = 2.025 + (117.292 \times 0.5) = 60.7$$

You will note that the calculated value $Y = 60.7$ differs slightly from the 61 scale units obtained when the 0.5 ppm standard was measured. The difference is due to the fact that the 0.5 ppm point does not lie exactly on the calibration curve. This estimate of the scale reading is probably closer to the true scale reading because it represents the combined effects of seven readings of the various standards, whereas the value of 61 represents only a single observation.

We can estimate similar values of Y for other values of X in the same manner. However, the values of X used should not exceed the range used to establish the calibration curve because we cannot be certain of the position of the extrapolated curve—it may not be linear at higher concentrations, for example.

6.2.4 Confidence Intervals for y

In Section 6.2.3 we calculated a point estimate for Y at 0.5 ppm solids. Now we shall calculate a 95% confidence interval for the *true mean* value of y for this same level of solids. We will use Equation (6.5):

$$y = A + Bx \pm t_{\alpha/2, n-2} s_{Y \cdot X} \sqrt{\frac{1}{n} + \frac{(X - \bar{X})^2}{\sum X^2 - \frac{(\sum X)^2}{n}}} \qquad (6.5)$$

For $X = 0.5$,

$$y = 2.025 + (117.292 \times 0.5) \pm 2.57 \times 3.13981 \sqrt{\frac{1}{7} + \frac{(0.5 - 0.37857143)^2}{1.3725 - 1.00321429}}$$

$$= 60.7 \pm 3.45 = 57.2 \text{ to } 64.1$$

If we substitute other values for X in the above equation covering the range of $X = 0.0$ to 0.8 ppm and plot these limits, we obtain the pair of slightly curved lines labeled C in Figure 6.12. This envelope is the 95% confidence interval for the regression line. The confidence interval has a minimum value at the average value for X and increases as we move in either direction from the midpoint.

These confidence limits can be useful in judging if our estimates of y are suffficiently precise for our application. If the 95% confidence interval for y had been 50 scale units, but we needed to be sure of the value for y within 5 scale units, the regression equation would be of little use to us. In such a case we should consider ways to reduce the variance or perhaps find another way to calibrate the nephelometer.

6.2.5 Confidence Interval for an Individual Value of y

If we wish to calculate a 95% confidence interval for an *individual* value of the scale reading, Y, corresponding to a solids content of 0.5 ppm, the following equation is used:

$$y = A + BX \pm t_{\alpha/2,n-2} s_{Y \cdot X} \sqrt{1 + \frac{1}{n} + \frac{(X - \bar{X})^2}{\sum X^2 - \frac{(\sum X)^2}{n}}} \qquad (6.6)$$

where $s_{Y \cdot X}$ is calculated in the same manner as for Equation (6.3). The equation is valid for only one prediction and should not be used to make repeated predictions on the same sample. Assume we made four observations of Y at 0.5 ppm solids content, calculated the 95% interval, and then made a fifth observation at 0.5 ppm. If we repeated this whole sequence many times, on the average 95% of these intervals will contain the additional observation. Of course, other confidence levels may be calculated by using the appropriate t value.

Using our data from Example 6.1

$$s_{Y \cdot X} = 3.13980493$$

$$y = 2.025 + (117.292071 \times 0.05)$$

$$\pm \left(2.57 \times 3.13980493 \sqrt{1 + \frac{1}{7} + \frac{(0.5 - 0.37857143)^2}{1.3725 - 1.00321429}} \right)$$

$$= 60.7 \pm 8.78 = 51.9 \text{ to } 69.5$$

6.2.6   Confidence Intervals for *X* Predicted from *Y*

In Section 6.2.1 we used the regression equation to estimate that $X = 0.49$ ppm for a scale reading of 60. This is a point estimate for the solids content. However, we can establish confidence limits about x, the true solids content, by use of this equation:

$$x = \frac{Y - A}{B} \pm \left(\frac{t_{\alpha/2,\,n-2}\, s_{Y \cdot X}}{B} \sqrt{1 + \frac{1}{n} + \frac{\left(\dfrac{X - A}{B} - \bar{X} \right)^2}{\sum X^2 - \dfrac{(\sum X)^2}{n}}} \right) \tag{6.7}$$

Using our data for $Y = 60$ in Equation 6.7:

$$x = \frac{60 - 2.025145}{117.292071}$$

$$\pm \left(\frac{2.57 \times 3.139805}{117.292071} \sqrt{1 + \frac{1}{7} + \frac{\left(\dfrac{60 - 2.025145}{117.292071} - 0.37857143 \right)^2}{1.3725 - 1.00321429}} \right)$$

$$= 0.49 \pm 0.075 = 0.42 \text{ to } 0.56 \text{ ppm solids}$$

6.2.7   Test for Significance of Relationship Between Variables

This is really a test of the hypothesis that the slope b of the calibration curve is zero. If $b = 0$, changing values of one variable are not related to changes in the other. The following t test is used to test the null hypothesis $H_0: b = 0$. In the present example, the estimated slope of 117.29 is high enough that it is unlikely that in reality the true slope is zero, but we will test it to illustrate the use of this equation:

$$t = \frac{|b - B|}{s_{Y \cdot X} \sqrt{1 / \left(\sum X^2 - \dfrac{(\sum X)^2}{n} \right)}} \tag{6.8}$$

The vertical bars in the numerator mean we will use the absolute value of $b - B$. Substituting the values of our example in Equation (6.8) and using the $\alpha = 0.05$ level of significance, we have:

$$t = \frac{|0 - 117.29|}{3.3198\sqrt{\dfrac{1}{0.3692857}}} = 117.29/5.1668 = 22.70$$

$$t_{0.05/2, 5} = 2.57$$

Since the critical value for t is exceeded, we reject the null hypothesis $H_0: b = 0$ and accept the alternative hypothesis that $b \neq 0$, or stated another way, the absorbance and solids content are related.

6.2.8 Test for Zero Intercept

When we calculated the confidence interval for the intercept of our calibration curve in Section 6.2.2, we noted that the interval included zero and we stated that this suggested the calibration passed through the origin. There is another test for the hypothesis $H_0: a = 0$; it makes use of the following equation:

$$t = \frac{|a - A|}{s_{Y \cdot X}\sqrt{\dfrac{1}{n} + \dfrac{\sum X^2}{\sum X^2 - \dfrac{(\sum X)^2}{n}}}} \tag{6.9}$$

This is essentially the same as the confidence interval in Section 6.2.2.

Again, using the data from Example 6.1 and $\alpha = 0.05$:

$$t = \frac{|0 - 2.02515|}{3.1398\sqrt{\dfrac{1}{7} + \dfrac{0.37857^2}{0.36928571}}}$$

$$= 2.02515/2.287845 = 0.8852$$

$$t_{0.05/2, 5} = 2.57$$

Since the critical value for t is not exceeded, we accept the null hypothesis that $a = 0$, i.e., the curve does pass through the origin. This conclusion as well as the theory of our experiment justifies recalculating the calibration curve with the restriction that it must pass through the origin. This is the subject of the next section.

6.3   ESTIMATING THE CALIBRATION EQUATION WITH THE CURVE FORCED THROUGH THE ORIGIN

This type of regression is a special case of the one we have just discussed. The equations are similar, but are more simple because the a term of the regression equation is zero. The equation for the regression line is

$$y = bX \tag{6.10}$$

6.3.1   Estimating the Equation

The equation for the least squares estimate of b is

$$B = \frac{\sum XY}{\sum X^2} \tag{6.11}$$

Using the data from Example 6.1

$$B = 166.35/1.3725 = 121.2021858$$

In this example the value of B is close to the 117.29 value obtained without the constraint of the curve passing through the origin. This is not surprising, because the intercept A was only 2.02.

Thus, the equation for the regression line is

$$Y = 121.2022X$$

and the calibration curve is shown in Figure 6.13.

6.3.2   Confidence Intervals for the Slope

The 95% confidence interval for b is calculated using the equation

$$b = B \pm \frac{t_{\alpha/2,n-1} s_{Y\cdot X}}{\sqrt{X^2}} \tag{6.12}$$

where

$$s_{Y\cdot X} = \sqrt{\frac{Y^2 - ((\sum XY)^2/\sum X^2)}{n-1}}$$

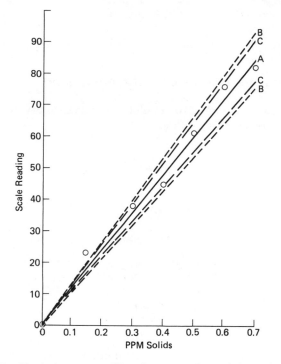

Figure 6.13. Nephelometer calibration curve forced through the origin:
A: regression line of Y on X
B: 95% confidence limits on an individual Y
C: 95% confidence limits to include true y

Again, using the data from Example 6.1

$$s_{Y \cdot X} = \sqrt{\frac{20.219 - (166.35/1.3725)}{7 - 1}} = 3.082650$$

$$b = 121.2022 \pm \frac{2.45 \times 3.082650}{\sqrt{1.3725}} = 121.20 \pm 6.45$$

$$= 114.74 \text{ to } 127.65$$

6.3.3   A Point Estimate for the Average Y

To calculate a point estimate for the average scale reading for 0.5 ppm solids
we merely substitute the value of 0.5 for X into the regression equation or

read the scale value from the calibration curve.

$$Y = 121.2022X = 121.2022 \times 0.5 = 60.6$$

6.3.4 Confidence Intervals for the Average y

The following equation is used to calculate confidence intervals for the average scale reading corresponding to a given X:

$$y = BX \pm t_{\alpha/2, n-1} s_{Y \cdot X} \sqrt{\frac{X^2}{\sum X^2}} \tag{6.13}$$

Again, using the data from Example 6.1, the 95% confidence interval for $X = 0.5$ ppm solids is

$$y = 121.2022 \times 0.5 \pm 2.45 \times 3.08265 \sqrt{\frac{0.5^2}{1.3725}}$$

$$= 60.6 \pm 3.22 = 57.4 \text{ to } 63.8$$

As before, substitution of other values for X in the above equation and plotting the intervals results in the 95% confidence interval for the regression line as shown by lines C in Figure 6.13. Note that these lines show that the interval is zero for $X = 0$ and increases linearly with increasing values of X.

6.3.5 Confidence Limits for an Individual Value of y

The confidence intervals for an *individual* scale reading Y for a given value of X obtained by the following equation.

$$y = BX \pm t_{\alpha/2, n-1} s_{Y \cdot X} \sqrt{1 + \frac{(X)^2}{\sum X^2}} \tag{6.14}$$

For $X = 0.5$, the 95% confidence interval is

$$y = 121.2022 \times 0.5 \pm 2.45 \times 3.08265 \sqrt{1 + \frac{0.5^2}{1.3725}}$$

$$= 60.5 \pm 8.21 = 52.4 \text{ to } 68.8$$

By substituting other values for X into the equation, the limits shown as lines

B in Figure 6.13 are obtained. Note that these limits for one additional observation are broader than those for the average y (Section 6.3.4).

6.3.6   Confidence Intervals for x Predicted from Y

The following equation is used to calculate the confidence intervals for a value of x, the ppm solids, predicted from a given Y, the scale reading:

$$x = Y/B \pm \left(\frac{t_{\alpha/2, n-1} s_{Y \cdot X}}{B} \sqrt{1 + \frac{(Y/B)^2}{\sum X^2}} \right) \qquad (6.15)$$

Using our Example 6.1, for a scale reading B of 60 the 95% confidence interval is

$$x = 60/121.2022 \pm \frac{2.45 \times 3.08265}{121.2022} \sqrt{1 + \frac{(60/121.2022)^2}{1.3725}}$$

$$= 0.4950 \pm 0.068 = 0.43 \text{ to } 0.56$$

6.3.7   Test for Significance of Relationship Between Variables

To test the hypothesis that $b = 0$, i.e., there is no relationship between Y, the scale reading, and X, the ppm solids, we use this equation:

$$t = \frac{|B - b|}{\sqrt{s^2_{Y \cdot X} / \sum X^2}} \qquad (6.16)$$

Using the data from Example 6.1 and $\alpha = 0.05$:

$$t = \frac{|121.2022 - 0|}{\sqrt{\dfrac{3.08265^2}{1.3725}}} = 46.1$$

$$t_{0.05/2, 6} = 2.45$$

Since the critical t value is exceeded, we reject the null hypothesis $H_0: b = 0$ at the $\alpha = 0.05$ level, and conclude that the slope of the curve is not zero, i.e., there is a statistical relationship between scale readings and solids content.

6.4 RELATIONSHIP OF TWO METHODS OF ANALYSIS (LINEAR ASSOCIATION RELATIONSHIP)

Earlier in this chapter we said that association relationships have no known principle to explain the relationship between two variables. We also said that a characteristic of this type of relationship was that error was present in the measurement of both variables rather than in just one of the two variables. This type of relationship can occur when a set of randomly selected samples are analyzed for a property by two laboratories, each laboratory using a different method. Another example might be the situation where two different properties, such as total carbonyl content and color stability, are measured on a set of randomly selected samples. In this situation we still would like to be able to predict values for one variable from values obtained on the second variable.

   We will still use a regression equation, but it will differ from that used in the preceding sections because we now have to take into account the error present in the measurements of the independent variable X. However, the linear regression equation is still $y = a + bx$.

   EXAMPLE 6.2. Sulfuric acid color tests are run by a producer of a poly-ethylene glycol. A customer also runs the same type of tests on his purchases

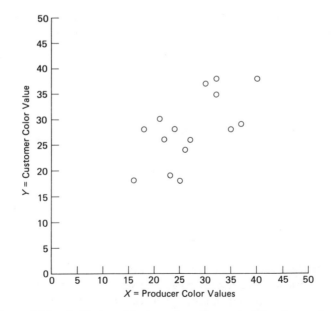

Figure 6.14. Sulfuric acid test colors, Example 6.2—data points.

of the product, but the customer uses slightly different test conditions which results in a different amount of color being produced. Neither laboratory wanted to change its test conditions; therefore, the question to be answered is "Can the results obtained by the producer's laboratory be used to predict the results obtained by the customer's laboratory?" Samples of a series of randomly selected batches were exchanged, and each laboratory reported its duplicate results. The colors are reported as a sum of red and yellow Lovibond color scales, and the following data are plotted in Figure 6.14:

BATCH NO.	PRODUCER COLOR (X)			CUSTOMER COLOR (Y)		
	RUN 1	RUN 2	AVG.	RUN 1	RUN 2	AVG.
1	22	24	23	19	19	19
2	24	20	22	24	28	26
3	15	17	16	20	16	18
4	25	27	26	28	20	24
5	38	42	40	35	41	38
6	26	28	27	28	24	26
7	20	22	21	29	31	30
8	39	35	37	27	31	29
9	18	18	18	31	25	28
10	33	37	35	26	30	28
11	31	32	32	37	33	35
12	29	31	30	39	35	37
13	24	26	25	17	19	18
14	25	23	24	31	25	28
15	31	33	32	40	36	38

The pattern in Figure 6.14 suggests a reasonable linear relationship. We will estimate the values of the slope b and the intercept a in the regression equation, and we will calculate the 95% confidence interval for the slope. The following preliminary calculations are made directly on the above data.

$$n = 15, \text{ the number of pairs of data}$$

The variance of each method is calculated using Equation (3.2) and the two runs made on each batch:

$$s^2 = \frac{\sum d^2}{2n}$$

where

$d = $ run 1 $-$ run 2 for batch i
$n = $ number of batches.

Producer's Method: Customer's Method:

$$s_P^2 = 101/30 = 3.366667 \qquad s_C^2 = 308/30 = 10.266667$$

$$\lambda = s_C^2/s_P^2 = 10.266667/3.366667 = 3.049505$$

The following calculations use the average values for X and Y for each batch:

$$\Sigma X = 408.0 \qquad\qquad \Sigma Y = 422.0$$

$$\sum X^2 = 11{,}782.0 \qquad\qquad \sum Y^2 = 12{,}512.0$$

$$\bar{X} = \sum X/n = 408.0/15 \qquad \bar{Y} = \sum Y/n = 422.0/15$$

$$= 27.2 \qquad\qquad = 28.1333$$

The sums of squares for the producer and customer data:

$$\text{SS}_X = \sum X^2 - ((\textstyle\sum X)^2/n) \qquad \text{SS}_Y = \sum Y^2 - ((\textstyle\sum Y)^2/n)$$

$$= 11{,}782 - (408^2/15) \qquad = 12{,}512 - (422^2/15)$$

$$= 684.40 \qquad\qquad = 639.7340$$

$$\sum XY = 11{,}898.0$$

$$\sum X \sum Y/n = (408 \times 422)/15 = 11{,}478.40$$

$$\text{SS}_{XY} = \sum XY - \frac{(\sum X \sum Y)}{n}$$

$$= 11{,}898.0 - 11{,}478.40 = 419.60$$

$$s_X^2 = \text{SS}_X/(n-1) \qquad s_Y^2 = \text{SS}_Y/(n-1)$$

$$= 684.4/14 \qquad\qquad = 639.7333/14$$

$$= 48.885714 \qquad\qquad = 45.695238$$

$$s_X = \sqrt{s_X^2} = 6.9918 \qquad s_Y = \sqrt{s_Y^2} = 6.7598$$

6.4.1 Estimating the Regression Equation

The estimate of the slope b in the regression equation

$$y = a + bx$$

is made using the following Equation:[2]

$$B = \frac{SS_Y - \lambda SS_X + \sqrt{((SS_Y - \lambda SS_X)^2 + 4\lambda SS_Y^2)}}{2SS_{XY}} \qquad (6.17)$$

where

$$SS_Y = \sum Y^2 - \frac{(\sum Y)^2}{n}$$

$$\lambda = s_Y^2 / s_X^2$$

$$SS_X = \sum X^2 - \frac{(\sum X)^2}{n}$$

$$SS_{XY} = \sum XY - \frac{\sum X \sum Y}{n}$$

Note: The sign of B is the same as the sign of SS_{XY}.

The estimate of the intercept a is made using Equation (6.2):

$$A = \bar{Y} - B\bar{X}$$

Substituting the values from Example 6.2 into Equation (6.17), we have

$$SS_Y = 639.7333$$

$$\lambda = 3.049505$$

$$SS_X = 684.40$$

$$SS_{XY} = 419.20$$

$$SS_{XY}^2 = 419.60^2 = 176,064.1600$$

and

$$B = 612.37297/839.20 = 0.7297$$

Substituting $X = 27.20$, $Y = 28.1333$, and $B = 0.7297$ into Equation (6.2) gives

$$A = 28.1333 - (0.7297 \times 27.20) = 8.2852$$

Thus, the regression equation is

$$Y = 8.2852 + 0.7297X$$

The curve representing this equation is shown in Figure 6.15. This equation or the regression curve may be used to estimate values of Y from values of X.

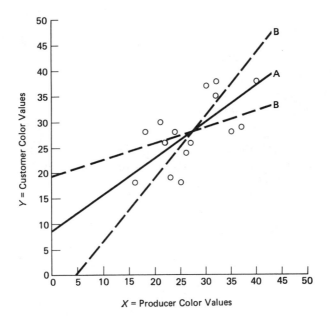

A = Regression line
B = 95% Confidence interval of slope

Figure 6.15.   Sulfuric acid test colors, Example 6.2:
A: regression line
B: 95% confidence interval on slope

6.4.2   Confidence Intervals for the Slope

The confidence intervals for the slope b may be calculated using the following equation:[3]

$$b = \sqrt{\lambda}\,\tan(\tan^{-1}(B/\sqrt{\lambda}) \pm 0.5\sin^{-1}(R)) \tag{6.18}$$

where

$$R = 2t_{\alpha,n-2}\sqrt{\frac{\lambda(SS_X SS_Y - SS_{XY}^2)}{(n-2)((SS_Y - \lambda SS_X)^2 + 4\lambda SS_{XY}^2)}}$$

Note: If the argument of $\sin^{-1}$ in Equation (6.18) is greater than unity, no real angle exists. That is, no limits exist on the slope for the confidence level selected.

Using the data from Example 6.2 to calculate the 95% confidence interval, we have:

$$\lambda = 3.049505$$

$$B = 0.7297$$

$$t_{0.05,13} = 1.77$$

$$SS_X = 684.40$$

$$SS_Y = 639.7333$$

$$SS_{XY}^2 = 176{,}064.1600$$

Substituting these values in Equation (6.18) gives

$$b = 0.310269 \text{ to } 1.23561$$

These 95% confidence limits are shown as dashed lines B in Figure 6.15.

6.4.3   Estimating the Regression Equation when Error Variances Are Not Available

Equation (6.17) for estimating B includes a term, λ, which is the ratio of the error variances for the dependent and independent variables. These variances are usually estimated from replicated measurements of the variables, either from current experiments or previous data. If these variances are not available, the following procedure[4,5] can be used to estimate a and b in the regression equation:

(a) One point on the regression line is located at the average values of X and Y. Now only the slope of the line is needed to define the line.

(b) Plot the data on a graph and divide the points into three groups along the X-axis. The two end groups must have the same number of points, m, and the number should be as close to $n/3$ as possible, where n is the total number of points. In addition, the three groups must not overlap in the X-direction.

(c) Calculate the averages of each end group, X_1, Y_1, X_3, Y_3.

(d) Calculate the slope using

$$B = \frac{\bar{Y}_3 - \bar{Y}_1}{\bar{X}_3 - \bar{X}_1} \tag{6.19}$$

(e) Calculate the intercept using Equation (6.2):

$$A = \bar{Y} + B\bar{X}$$

EXAMPLE 6.3.   Assume that in Example 6.2 the average sulfuric acid color values given are single determinations per batch. Also assume that we have no precision data on the two methods. We will use these data and the above procedure to estimate the regression equation.

(a) The grand averages are $\bar{X} = 27.2$ and $\bar{Y} = 28.1333$.

(b, c) The data points are plotted in Figure 6.14. Since there are 15 points, we divide them into three groups of five each, and arrange the data as follows:

Group 1:

BATCH NO.	X	Y
3	16	18
9	18	28
7	21	30
2	22	26
1	23	19
Total	100	121
Average	20.0	24.2

Group 2:

BATCH NO.	X	Y
14	24	28
13	25	18
4	26	24
6	27	26
12	30	37
Total	132	133

Group 3:

BATCH NO.	X	Y
11	32	35
15	32	38
10	35	28
8	37	29
5	40	38
Total	176	168
Average	35.2	33.6

(d) Calculate *B*:

$$B = \frac{\bar{Y}_3 - \bar{Y}_1}{\bar{X}_3 - \bar{X}_1} = \frac{33.6 - 24.2}{35.2 - 20.0} = 0.6184$$

(e) Calculate *A*:

$$A = \bar{Y} - B\bar{X} = 28.1333 - 0.6184 \times 27.2 = 11.3128$$

The equation for the regression line is

$$Y = 11.3128 + 0.6184X$$

This regression line is plotted as line *A* in Figure 6.16. This equation is slightly different from that obtained in Section 6.4.1 ($Y = 8.2819 + 0.7297X$). We should not expect exact agreement between the two equations because only the equation calculated in Section 6.4.1 makes use of the variances of the two methods. However, the value of *B* falls within the 95% confidence interval calculated in Section 6.4.2.

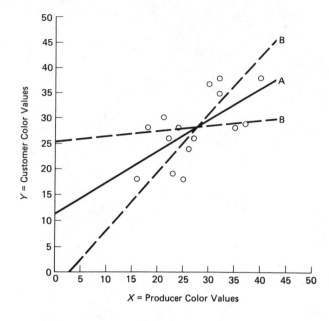

A = Regression line
B = 95% Confidence interval of slope

Figure 6.16.   Sulfuric acid test colors, Example 6.3:
A: regression line
B: 95% confidence interval on slope

6.4.4   Confidence Interval for the Slope

The following equation[4,5] is used to calculate confidence intervals for the slope b:

$$0.5m(\bar{X}_3 - \bar{X}_1)^2(B - b)^2 = t^2_{\alpha/2, n-2}(SS_Y - 2bSS_{XY} + b^2SS_X)/(n - 3) \quad (6.20)$$

where

m = number of points in each outer groups

n = total number of points

B = estimate of slope from Equation (6.19)

$\bar{X}_1, \bar{X}_3$ = averages of outer groups.

$$SS_X = \sum X_{1i}^2 - \frac{\sum(X_{1i})^2}{m} + \sum X_{2i} - \frac{\sum(X_{2i})^2}{n-2m} + \sum X_{3i} - \frac{\sum(X_{3i})^2}{m}$$

$$SS_{XY} = \sum X_{1i}Y_{1i} - \frac{\sum X_{1i}\sum Y_{1i}}{m} + \sum X_{2i}Y_{2i} - \frac{\sum X_{2i}\sum Y_{2i}}{n-2m} + \sum X_{3i}Y_{3i}$$

$$- \frac{\sum X_{3i}\sum Y_{3i}}{m}$$

$$SS_Y = \sum Y_{1i}^2 - \frac{\sum(Y_{1i})^2}{m} + \sum Y_{2i}^2 - \frac{\sum(Y_{2i})^2}{n-2m} + \sum Y_{3i}^2 - \frac{\sum(Y_{3i})^2}{m}$$

After substituting the values into Equation (6.20) and combining terms, we have a quadratic equation of the form:

$$Cb^2 + Db + E = 0$$

This equation can be solved using the usual quadratic root formula,

$$b = \frac{-D \pm \sqrt{D^2 - 4CE}}{2C}$$

Using the data from Example 6.3 to calculate the terms in Equation (6.20) gives

$$SS_X = 16^2 + 18^2 + 21^2 + 22^2 + 23^2 - (100^2/5) + 24^2 + 25^2$$

$$+ 26^2 + 27^2 + 30^2 - (132^2/5) + 32^2$$

$$+ 32^2 + 35^2 + 37^2 + 40^2 - (176^2/5)$$

$$= 102.0$$

Similarly,

$$SS_{XY} = 53.2$$

$$SS_Y = 401.2$$

$$n = 15$$

$$m = 5$$

$$t_{0.05/2,13} = 21.8$$

Substituting them into Equation (6.20) gives:

$$0.5(5)(35.2 - 20)^2(0.6184 - b)^2 = 2.18^2(401.2 - (2b \times 53.2)$$

$$+ (b^2 102.0))/(15 - 3)$$

Combining terms gives the quadratic equation:

$$537.20460b^2 - 672.23774b + 61.996387 = 0$$

and

$$b = \frac{672.23774 \pm 564.52157}{1{,}074.4092}$$

$$= 0.1003 \text{ to } 1.1511$$

These confidence limits are shown in Figure 6.16 as lines B.

6.5 CORRELATION COEFFICIENTS

The *correlation coefficient* is another measure of the linear relationship between two variables. It is a measure of the degree of association between the variables. The correlation coefficient ρ may have values between $+1$ and -1. When $\rho = +1$, there is a perfect positive correlation, i.e. an increase in one variable is associated with an increase in the other. When $\rho = -1$, there is a perfect negative correlation, i.e., when one variable increases, there is a decrease in the other. When $\rho = 0$, there is no correlation; one variable has no linear relationship to the other. Other values of ρ represent less than perfect correlation. Note that unlike linear regression equations, the correlation coefficient does not enable us to predict the value of one variable from the value of the second one. It provides an overall measure of degree of linear relationship.

If both variables are randomly selected, the calculated correlation coefficient r estimates ρ for the population represented by the variables, and the degree of relationship is applicable to that population. If the variables are not randomly selected, the relationship measured by r applies only to the selected values of the variables. For example, in the functional relationship of a calibration curve the values of concentration X are chosen by the chemist, and the corresponding values of absorbance Y are observed. Here, r measures the overall degree of linear relationship for the selected values of X. Usually there is a theoretical basis for the relationship, and the value of r can be considered as applying also to the intermediate values of X. However, regardless of how the values are chosen, the relationship measured by r should not be extrapolated beyond the range of values of X and Y used in calculating r.

The estimate of the correlation coefficient r is calculated by the equation:

$$r = \frac{\sum XY - \dfrac{\sum X \sum Y}{n}}{\sqrt{\left(\sum X^2 - \dfrac{(\sum X)^2}{n}\right)\left(\sum Y^2 - \dfrac{(\sum Y)^2}{n}\right)}}; \qquad df = n - 2 \quad (6.22)$$

where

X = individual values for independent variable
Y = individual values for dependent variable
n = number of pairs of data.

As usual in statistical tests, the null hypothesis is that no relationship exists ($\rho = 0$). The calculated value r is compared with the critical value obtained by entering Table 8 in Appendix D at the desired level of significance, α, and $n - 2$ degrees of freedom. If the calculated value exceeds the critical value, the null hypothesis is rejected, and we accept the alternative hypothesis that $\rho \neq 0$, i.e., there is a significant relationship between the two variables.

Caution: The fact that two variables show a significant relationship does *not* establish a causal relationship. A cause-and-effect relationship must be established on theoretical or other grounds. For example, it was reported that a study showed a high correlation between the incidence of goiter and altitude. Goiter is known to be caused by iodine deficiency, not altitude. The explanation for the correlation lies in the fact that soils at higher elevations tend to be poor in iodine content.

The square of the correlation coefficient is called the *coefficient of determination* r^2. The coefficient of determination is a measure of the amount of variation in the dependent variable that is accounted for by the independent variable. If our set of data has a correlation coefficient of $+1.0$, then $1.0^2 = 1.0$ or 100% of the variation is accounted for by the independent variable. If the correlation coefficient were 0.90, then the coefficient of determination would be $0.90^2 = 0.81$, and 81% of the variation would be explained by the independent variable.

Now we shall go through the calculation of the correlation coefficient using Equation (6.22) and the data from Example 6.2. Substituting the values in the equation gives:

$$r = \frac{11,898 - 11,478.40}{\sqrt{(11,781.0 - 11,097.6)(12,512.0 - 11,872.2667)}}$$

$$= 0.6341; \quad 13 \text{ df}$$

$$r_{0.05,13} = 0.514$$

Thus, the calculated value exceeds the critical value, and we reject the null hypothesis H_0: $\rho = 0$ at $\alpha = 0.05$ and conclude that the producer and customer sulfuric acid colors do correlate significantly.

The coefficient of determination is

$$r^2 = 0.6341^2 = 0.4021$$

This means that 40.2% of the variation in the customer's colors is accounted for by the producer's colors. This may not seem very high, but reference to Figure 6.15 shows that there is considerable scatter in the points, an appreciable amount of which is due to the poor precision of the methods used to determine the color.

6.6   SUMMARY

In this chapter we looked at linear relationships between two variables. We considered two types of relationships: (1) the functional relationship, where the two variables are related by a known principle, theory, or law and where only one of the variables has error associated with its values, and (2) the association relationship, where the two variables have no known principle which connects them and where both variables have error associated with their values. For both types of relationships we learned how to estimate a regression line based on least squares which best estimates the linear relationship and which enables us to estimate one variable for given values of the other. We also were able to estimate various confidence intervals about the regression line and about predicted values of the variables. Great caution must be used if regression lines (or their equations) are used for predictions beyond the limits of the data used to establish them.

The correlation coefficient and the coefficient of determination are measures of the degree of association between two variables. They are properly applied only in cases where both variables are randomly selected. A significant correlation coefficient does not establish a cause-and-effect relationship. Such a relationship must be based on theoretical or other grounds.

6.7   PROBLEMS

The following problems make use of the tests discussed in this chapter:

SUBJECT	PROBLEMS
Linear functional relationships	4, 5
Linear association relationships	2j, 2k
Correlation coefficients	2i, 4b, 5a

RESOURCES

Draper, N. R., and Smith, H., *Applied Regression Analysis*, 2nd ed. New York, NY: John Wiley & Sons, 1981. Covers various types of regression analysis.

Freund, R., and Minton, P., *Regression Methods—A Tool for Data Analysis*. New York, NY: Marcel Dekker, 1979. Covers various types of regression analysis.

Younger, M. S., *Handbook for Linear Regression*. New York, NY: Duxbury, 1979. A good book; starts with the fundamentals of regression.

Neter, J., Wasserman, W., *Applied Linear Statistical Models*. Homewood, Ill: Richard D. Irwin, Inc., 1974. A more advanced book than Younger's.

REFERENCES

1. Suggested transformations from M. G. Natrella, *Experimental Statistics*, p. 5–31, National Bureau of Standards Handbook 91, 1966. U.S. Government Printing Office, Washington, D.C. 20402.
2. Williams, *Regression Analysis*, New York, NY: John Wiley & Sons, 1959.
3. Creasy, M. A., "Confidence Limits for the Gradient in Linear Functional Relationships," *J. Roy. Statist. Soc., B*, **18**, 65–69 (1956).
4. Bartlett, M. S., "Fitting a Straight Line When Both Variables Are Subject to Error," *Biometrics*, **5**, 201–212 (1949).
5. Wald, A., "The Fitting of Straight Lines If Both Variables Are Subject to Error," *Ann. Math. Statist.*, **11**, 284–300 (1940).

Chapter 7
COMPARING MORE THAN TWO AVERAGES: ANALYSIS OF VARIANCE

OVERVIEW

In Chapter 5 we saw how the t test is used to determine if two averages are really different. We also saw how Duncan's test for separation of means enabled us to tell which of five average yields differed significantly from the others. In this chapter we will learn how to apply the ANOVA technique to determine whether there is a significant difference among a set of averages for one independent variable. ANOVA also provides a way to determine if the independent variable(s) has a significant effect on the dependent variable. In subsequent chapters we will consider ANOVA for cases where we are interested in more than one independent variable.

7.0 INTRODUCTION TO ANALYSIS OF VARIANCE

In analytical chemistry we often face certain categories of problems that are not amenable to solution by any of the methods covered until now. One type of problem is that of determining which variables in a method of analysis have a significant effect on the results obtained. For example, the reagent concentration, reaction time, reaction temperature, and pH might affect the parts per million iron found using a method for determining trace iron.

Another type of problem concerns the precision and accuracy of methods of analysis used in more than one laboratory. For example, if a sample is analyzed in the producer's laboratory and later in the customer's laboratory, how well should the two analyses agree? If either laboratory repeats the analysis, how well should it agree with itself?

These problems have certain characteristics in common; there is more than one source of variability in the data. Fortunately, the analysis of variance (ANOVA) technique enables us to partition the total variability in a set of determinations into the variability attributable to each source.

If we have five samples which we have analyzed repeatedly by the same method, we may wish to determine if the five average values differ significantly, i.e., do the five samples differ in respect to the property we have measured?

We could compare the averages two at a time using the t test. This means we would have to apply the test 10 times. If we selected the 0.05% level of significance, the probability of our making the correct decision would be 0.95 or 95% for the first pair of averages. The probability of making the correct decision for the second pair would also be 95%, but the probability of making both decisions correctly would be 95% of 95%, so that by the time we applied the t test to the tenth pair, our probability would be only 60%! Fortunately, the ANOVA technique enables us to make comparisons for any number of averages without this loss of assurance.

7.0.1   Using Variances to Compare Averages

Let's look at a simplified example in which we have analyzed two drums of a material. Each drum was analyzed by five analysts:

Case A:

ANALYST	DRUM 1	DRUM 2	SUM
1	4	13	17
2	5	0	5
3	3	2	5
4	4	1	5
5	4	4	8
Sum	20	20	40
Average	4	4	
Variance	0.50	27.5	

The values in Case A result in the same sum for Drums 1 and 2 and thus the same average values. However, the sums of the rows (Analysts) vary from 5 to 17. In this set of data all the variability is in the rows.

Case B:

ANALYST	DRUM 1	DRUM 2	SUM
1	8	0	8
2	5	3	8
3	8	0	8
4	7	1	8
5	2	6	8
Sum	30	10	40
Average	6	2	

The values in Case B show a difference between the totals for the two drums and thus between their averages. The sums of the rows, however, are identical. In this set of data all the variability is in the drums.

In real life, it is rare to see an example like either Case A or B. In the usual situation there is variability in both the analysts and drums, as shown below.

Case C:

ANALYST	DRUM 1	DRUM 2	SUM
1	6	1	7
2	4	5	9
3	3	3	6
4	7	4	11
5	5	2	7
Sum	25	15	40
Average	5	3	

Here variability is evident in both the sums of the rows and the columns.

Up to now we have used the F test to compare two variances and the t test to compare two averages to see if they differed significantly. The title of this chapter implies that an analysis of variance can be used to compare averages. How can variances be used to compare averages?

The principle behind this technique is that if two normal populations having equal averages and variances ($\mu_1 = \mu_2$, and $\sigma_1^2 = \sigma_2^2$) are combined, the resulting population will have the same average and variance ($\mu_{1+2} = \mu_1 = \mu_2$, and $\sigma_{1+2}^2 = \sigma_1^2 = \sigma_2^2$). On the other hand if population 1 has a true average of $\mu_1 = 0$ and population 2 has a true average of $\mu_2 = 10$ with both populations having a variance of 1, the combined population will have an average of 5, but a variance much greater than unity. This situation is illustrated by the data in Table 7.1.

In Table 7.1 the 60 values for Sample A were taken from a table of random normal deviates having a true average of 0 and a variance of 1. A table of random normal deviates is a random listing of values which are all numbers from a normally distributed population characterized by the stated average and standard deviation. Entering such a table at random enables us to obtain samples of values from a known population.

The values for Sample B are the same values used in Sample A, each increased by 10.0. The calculated average and variance for Sample A are reasonably close to the expected values of 0 and 1. If we had used a larger sample size, we would expect to get values even closer to 0 and 1. The calculated average for Sample B is exactly 10.0 greater than that for Sample

TABLE 7.1 Comparison of the Averages and Variances of a Sample of 60 Numbers from a Table of Random Normal Deviates With $\mu = 0$ and $\sigma^2 = 1$ with the Same Numbers Incremented by 10.0.

Sample A—From Population A (Original Values From Table)

−0.597	0.496	−0.561	−1.033	−0.578	−0.378	0.074	0.261	−0.766	−1.046
0.361	−0.043	−1.927	1.527	0.605	1.475	0.230	0.046	0.978	−1.901
1.162	−0.545	0.697	1.151	2.033	0.080	2.162	−0.562	1.190	0.925
0.092	0.126	−2.039	−0.182	0.578	0.417	−0.671	1.076	−1.101	0.469
−1.615	−1.549	0.239	−0.202	1.282	−2.437	0.527	0.808	0.039	−0.691
0.305	1.214	−0.433	0.429	−0.592	−1.180	1.382	−0.602	0.302	−0.812

Average = 0.0116   Variance = 1.0335

Sample B—From Population B (Original Values From Population A + 10.000)

9.403	10.496	9.439	8.967	9.422	9.622	10.074	10.261	9.234	8.954
10.361	9.957	8.073	11.527	10.605	11.475	10.230	10.046	10.978	8.099
11.162	9.455	10.697	11.151	12.033	10.080	12.162	9.438	11.190	10.925
10.092	10.126	7.961	9.818	10.578	10.417	9.329	11.076	8.899	10.469
8.385	8.451	10.239	9.798	11.282	7.562	10.527	10.808	10.039	9.309
10.305	11.214	9.567	10.429	9.408	8.820	11.382	9.398	10.302	9.188

Average = 10.0116   Variance = 1.0336

Combined Samples A + B

Average = 5.0116   Variance = 26.2348

A, and the variance is the same as for Sample A within rounding error. This is as expected, because you remember we said in our discussion of coding of values in a set of data, that the addition of a constant to all values in a set of data did not change its variance. The calculated average for the combined Samples A and B is the average of the two, 5.0116. But the variance is approximately 25 times greater!

Therefore, if we can figure out a way of calculating the averages and variances of each subset of our data (we already know how to calculate these for the whole set), we should be able to use this increase in variance to tell us when the averages of the subsets of data differ significantly.

Now, we shall go back to Case A where all the variability is in the analysts and see if we can figure out a way of separating the total variance of the set of data into the part due to the drums and that due to the runs.

We already know how to calculate the total variance of the whole set of data by using one of the forms of Equation (3.1):

$$s^2 = \frac{\sum X^2 - \frac{(\sum X)^2}{n}}{n - 1}$$

Let us calculate just the numerator of that equation to get what is known as the *total sum of squares*, SS_t:

$$SS_t = 4^2 + 5^2 + 3^2 + \cdots + 4^2 - (40^2/10)$$

$$= 272 - 160 = 112$$

The last term $(40^2/10)$ in the above equation is the grand total squared and divided by the total number of values. It is sometimes called the correction factor because it adjusts the sum of squares for the average level of the measurements.

Next, let's look at the totals of the two columns. If we perform a similar calculation using these totals and the grand total, the resulting sum of squares for the columns, SS_c, should give us a measure of the variance between the columns:

$$SS_c = 20^2/5 + 20^2/5 - (40^2/10) = 160 - 160 = 0$$

In the above equation we divided the square of each column total by 5 because there were 5 values comprising each total. The value of SS_c is zero, which agrees with our original observation that there was no variability between the drums (columns).

Finally, let us estimate the variability within the drums (columns). We calculate the sum of squares for within columns, SS_w, as follows:

$$SS_w = 4^2 + 5^2 + 3^2 + 4^2 + 4^2 - (20^2/5) + 13^2 + 0^2$$

$$+ 2^2 + 1^2 + 4^2 - (20^2/5)$$

$$= 82 - 80 + 190 - 80 = 112$$

In the above equation we (a) squared each value in the first column, added the squares together, and subtracted the square of the sum of the column divided by the number of values in the sum; (b) repeated these operations for the second column; and (c) added all the terms together to obtain 112. This is also the value we got for the total sum of squares, SS_t. This is reasonable because the total sum of squares is equal to the sum of the sum of squares within columns and the sum of squares between columns, i.e., $SS_t = SS_w + SS_c$.

We can summarize our results in a tabular form called an analysis of variance table:

SOURCE	SUM OF SQUARES	DEGREES OF FREEDOM	MEAN SQUARE	EXPECTED MEAN SQUARES
Between columns	(SS_c) 0	1	0	$\sigma^2 + 5\sigma^2$
Within columns	(SS_w) 112	8	14	σ^2
Total	(SS_t) 112	9		

The values for the degrees of freedom are obtained as follows: Since we have two columns, we have $2 - 1$ or 1 degree of freedom for the between-columns sum of squares; we have a set of 5 observations within each of the two columns, so there are $(5 - 1)2$ or 8 degrees of freedom for the within-columns sum of squares; we have a total of 10 values in our data set, so $10 - 1$ or 9 for the total degrees of freedom.

The mean square values are simply each sum of squares divided by its degrees of freedom. These mean square values may be considered estimates of the variances for the sources given in the expected mean square column. In our example the variance for within columns is estimated to be 14, and the square root of 14 is 3.742. Try pooling the variances listed for Drums 1 and 2 in Case A. You should get 3.742 as the pooled standard deviation.

The above has not been a rigorous derivation of the ANOVA process; we just wanted to get a feel for the approach. We will look at a more realistic example in the next section.

7.1 MEASURING THE EFFECT OF ONE VARIABLE ON AVERAGES (ONE-WAY CLASSIFICATION OF VARIABLES)

The simplest type of ANOVA concerns only one independent variable and the comparison of two means. In this type of problem we have one independent variable, hence a one-way classification. The following example will show how the technique works.

EXAMPLE 7.1. Two samples, one from each of two drums were analyzed five times for an impurity by a given method. The data obtained are given below. Do the drums differ in impurity concentration?

DRUM A	DRUM B
49 ppm	44 ppm
44	57
70	34
50	48
58	50

Total, $T_A = 271$ $T_B = 233$ Grand Total, $T = 504$
Runs, $n_A = 5$ $n_B = 5$
Average, $\bar{X}_A = 54.2$ $\bar{X}_B = 46.6$
$s_A = 10.1587$ $s_B = 8.4735$, both with 4 df

First, we will use the t test that we learned in Chapter 5 to compare the two drum averages. To select the proper t test, we will apply the F test to determine if the variances are equal (we will use $\alpha = 0.05$):

$$F = 10.1587^2/8.4735^2 = 1.437 \text{ N.S. (not significant)}$$

$$F_{0.05/2,4,4} = 9.60$$

Therefore, the variances are equal, and we apply the t test for variances unknown, but equal [Equation (5.3)]:

$$s_P = \sqrt{\frac{(n_A - 1)s_A^2 + (n_B - 1)s_B^2}{n_A - 1 + n_B - 1}} = 9.3541$$

$$t = \frac{\bar{X}_A - \bar{X}_B}{s_P}\sqrt{\frac{n_A \times n_B}{n_A + n_B}} = \frac{54.2 - 46.6}{9.3541}\sqrt{\frac{5 \times 5}{5 + 5}} = 1.285$$

$$df = n_A + n_B - 2 = 8$$

$$t_{0.05/2,8} = 2.306$$

Thus, the averages are not significantly different when tested against the critical value for $\alpha = 0.05$.

Now examine the same data using ANOVA. Using the same approach we used in Section 7.0.1, we calculate the following sums of squares:

(a) Total sum of squares:

$$SS_t = 49^2 + 44^2 + 70^2 + \cdots + 48^2 + 50^2 - (504^2/10)$$

$$= 26,246.00 - 25,401.60 = 844.40$$

(b) Sum of squares for columns:

$$SS_c = \frac{T_A^2}{n_A} + \frac{T_B^2}{n_B} - \frac{T^2}{N} = \frac{271^2}{5} + \frac{233^2}{5} - \frac{504^2}{10}$$

$$= 14,688.2 + 10,857.8 - 25,401.6 = 144.40$$

(c) Sum of squares for within columns:

$$SS_w = \sum X_{iA}^2 - \frac{T_A^2}{nA} + \sum X_{iB}^2 - \frac{T_B^2}{nB} = 49^2 + 44^2 + \cdots + 58^2 - \frac{271^2}{5}$$

$$+ 44^2 + 57^2 + \cdots + 50^2 - \frac{233^2}{5}$$

$$= 15,101 - 14,688.2 + 11,145 - 10,857.8$$

$$= 700.00$$

Note: Since we saw previously that $SS_t = SS_c + SS_w$, it is a lot easier to calculate SS_w by subtracting SS_c from SS_t: $SS_w = SS_t - SS_c = 844.40 - 144.40 = 700.00$

In the equation for step c, the $\sum X_{iA}^2$ and $\sum X_{iB}^2$ terms mean that we square each value in column A and add them together and, similarly, we square each value in column B and add them together.

We are now ready to prepare an analysis of variance table using our values for SS_c, SS_w, and SS_t:

ANOVA Table

SOURCE	SS		DF	MEAN SQUARES	EXPECTED MEAN SQUARES
Between methods	(SS_c)	144.40	1	144.40	$\sigma^2 + n\sigma^2$
Within methods	(SS_w)	700.00	8	87.50	σ^2
Total	(SS_t)	844.40	9		

The values in the degrees of freedom column were obtained as follows: Since there are two methods, the degrees of freedom for between methods is $2 - 1$ or 1. There are five observations by each method, so the degrees of freedom for each is 4, giving a total of 8 for the two methods. There are a total of 10 observations, so the degrees of freedom for the set of data is $10 - 1$ or 9. The figures in the mean squares column are obtained by dividing each sum of squares by its degrees of freedom.

From the column of expected mean squares we see that the mean square for within methods, 87.50, is an estimate of σ^2. Therefore $s^2 = 87.50$, and $s = 9.3541$, which is the same value we obtained for s_P in the t test above.

We also note that the expected mean for between methods is $\sigma^2 + n\sigma_c^2$, where $n = 5$ for the five replicate values and σ_c^2 is the variance associated with the methods. Now if there is a real difference between the methods, the mean square for between methods (144.40) will tend to be significantly greater than the mean square for within methods. If there is no real difference between the methods, i.e., $\sigma_c^2 = 0$, then the mean squares for between methods and within methods will both be estimates of only σ^2 and these mean squares should not be significantly different.

We already know that we can use the F test to see if two variances are significantly different, and that is what we do here:

$$F = 144.40/87.50 = 1.65 \text{ N.S. (not significant)}$$

$$F_{0.05, 1, 8} = 5.3$$

Therefore, we conclude the two variances do not differ significantly, and thus, there is no significant difference between the two methods for $\alpha = 0.05$. This is the same conclusion we reached by the t test. In fact, it is the same as the t test because F with one degree of freedom in the numerator is equal to t^2: $1.65 = 1.285^2$.

Note that we used the critical value for one-tailed F test because we are

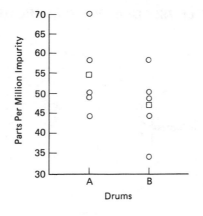

O Individual value
□ Average value

Figure 7.1.   Data from Example 7.1.

interested only in testing to see if 144.40 is significantly greater than 87.50. The mean square for between methods cannot be significantly less than the mean square for within methods.

Our conclusion that the two drums do not differ significantly in impurity concentration is consistent with the plot of the data in Figure 7.1.

So far there does not seem to be any advantage in using ANOVA over the t test. To see the advantage, let us apply ANOVA to a case involving more than two means. Before we do that, however, we should take a look at the general equations used for one-way classifications. Refer to Table 7.2. These equations will help us recall the mathematical steps used. In addition you will want to compare this summary of the steps with those we will use when we are interested in two variables.

The expressions in the ANOVA table are mathematical shorthand for the operations we performed in the previous example. To calculate the sum of squares for between columns, SS_c, we squared each column total, summed the squares, and divided by the number of values in the column. These operations are represented by $\sum T_{cj}^2/n$ in the table. We then squared the grand total T and divided it by the total number of values comprising the total. This is the T^2/N in the table. Finally, we subtracted these two results to obtain SS_c. The expression $\sum\sum X_{ij}^2$ in the sum of squares for within columns SS_w is merely the summation of the squares of each observation.

Now we shall use this general model for one-way classification (one independent variable) on another example. This time, instead of comparing two

TABLE 7.2 One-Way Classification

Data Format:

	VARIABLE			
	A	B	C	j
Replicates $\{$	X_{11}	X_{12}	X_{13}	X_{1j}
	X_{21}	X_{22}	X_{23}	X_{2j}
	X_{31}	X_{32}	X_{33}	X_{3j}
	X_{i1}	X_{i2}	X_{i3}	X_{ij}
Column Totals:	$T_{c1}\ +$	$T_{c2}\ +$	$T_{c3}\ +$	$T_{cj} = T$

Analysis of Variance Table, One-Way Classification:

SOURCE	SUM OF SQUARES	DEGREES OF FREEDOM	MEAN SQUARES	EXPECTED MEAN SQUARES
Between variables (columns)	$SS_c = \dfrac{\sum T_{cj}^2}{n} - \dfrac{T^2}{N}$	$j - 1$	$SS_c/(j-1)$	$\sigma^2 + n\sigma_c^2$
Within variables (rows)	$SS_w = \sum\sum X_{ij}^2 - \dfrac{\sum T_{cj}^2}{n}$	$N - j$	$SS_w/(N-j)$	σ^2
Total:	$SS_t = \sum\sum X_{ij}^2 - \dfrac{T^2}{N}$	$N - 1$		

j = number of categories (columns)
n = number of values in each column (number of replicates)
N = total number of values, $n \times j$
T_{cj} = total of values in the jth category (column)
T = grand total of values, or $\sum T_{cj}$
SS_w = also, $SS_t - SS_m$

drums of a material, we will compare results from four laboratories. Note that the independent variable is laboratories. Since we have four of them, there are four levels of the independent variable.

EXAMPLE 7.2. Four laboratories made five determinations of ethyl acetate content on samples from the same drum of material. Care was taken that the material in the drum was homogeneous and that identical samples were sent to each laboratory. The results obtained by the laboratories are listed below. The questions to be answered are (a) are the average values obtained by the four laboratories significantly different, and (b) how much of the total variance is due to differences between the laboratories and how much is due to within laboratory differences?

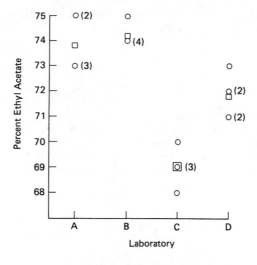

O Individual values; number of
  determinations with same value
  in parentheses
□ Average for laboratory

Figure 7.2.   Data from Example 7.2.

	LAB A	LAB B	LAB C	LAB D
	73%	74%	68%	71%
	75	74	69	72
	73	75	69	72
	75	74	70	71
	73	74	69	73
	—	—	—	—
T_{cj}:	369	371	345	359 $T = 1,444$
$\bar{X}$	73.8	74.2	69.0	71.8

A plot of these data is shown in Figure 7.2.

(a)
$$SS_c = \frac{369^2}{5} + \frac{371^2}{5} + \frac{359^2}{5} - \frac{1,444^2}{20}$$

$$= 104,341.60 - 104,256.80 = 84.80$$

(b)
$$SS_t = 73^2 + 75^2 + 73^2 + \cdots + 73^2 - \frac{1,444^2}{20}$$

$$= 104,352.0 - 104,256.80 = 95.20$$

(c)
$$SS_w = 95.20 - 84.80 = 10.40$$

(*Note:* From the general equations for one-way classifications, $SS_t - SS_c$ is equivalent to the equation for SS_w.

ANOVA Table

SOURCE	SS	DF	MS	EXPECTED MEAN SQUARES
Between labs	(SS_c) 84.80	3	28.270	$\sigma^2 + 5\sigma_c^2$
Within labs	(SS_w) 10.40	16	0.650	σ^2
Total	(SS_t) 95.20	19		

$$F = 28.270/0.650 = 43.49$$

$$F_{0.05, 3, 16} = 3.24$$

Thus, the variance for between labs is significant at the $\alpha = 0.05$ significance level. This conclusion is consistent with the data plotted in Figure 7.2. Because of additional potential sources of variance, we would generally expect data from several laboratories to have greater variability than data from a single laboratory. These sources might include apparatus, analysts, reagents, ambient temperature, etc.—all of which might be constant within one laboratory but different in other laboratories.

Figure 7.2 suggests that there might be significant differences in the results obtained by the laboratories. If you apply Duncan's procedure for separation of means, you will find that only laboratories A and B are not significantly different. This suggests that an additional investigation might be in order to determine why laboratories C and D tend to report lower values than the other two.

The standard deviation for the variability within the laboratories is the square root of 0.650 or $s = 0.806$ with 16 degrees of freedom.

The standard deviation for the variability between the laboratories is calculated as follows:

$$s^2 = 0.650$$

$$s^2 + 5s_c^2 = 28.270$$

Substituting the value of s^2 from the first equation into the second equation gives

$$0.650 + 5s^2 = 28.270$$

or

$$s_c^2 = (28.270 - 0.650)/5 = 5.524$$

and

$$s_c = \sqrt{5.524} = 2.350 \text{ with 3 DF}$$

Assuming that the above laboratories represent a random sampling of competent laboratories, we may now make some precision statements regarding analyses of samples of the type used to obtain the above data by all competent laboratories. Based on the estimated standard deviation for within laboratories of 0.806 with 16 degrees of freedom, we should expect that two analyses performed by the same laboratory should agree within 0.806 × 2.77 or 2.2% at the $\alpha = 0.05$ significance level. (Refer to Chapter 5 to refresh your memory on how this range is obtained.)

If we are also interested in how well we should expect two single determinations by two laboratories to agree, we must take into consideration both the within and between laboratory variances.

$$s_b^2 = s^2 + s_c^2 = 0.806^2 + 2.350^2 = 6.172$$

$$s_b = 2.484 \text{ with 3 DF}$$

Based on 2.484 with 3 DF, we should expect that two single determinations by two laboratories will agree within 2.484 × 2.77 or 6.88% at the 0.05 significance level. This may seem like a very large difference, but remember that the standard deviation for between labs is rather large and that we have only three degrees of freedom upon which to predict a range that will include the true value 95 percent of the time.

7.2 ONE-WAY CLASSIFICATION WITH UNEQUAL OBSERVATIONS PER AVERAGE

In Example 7.2 there were an equal number of analyses by each laboratory. However, it is not essential that there be an equal number of replicates for each category of the variable in order to perform an analysis of variance and determine if the different categories of the variable are significantly different.

The calculations are the same as those summarized in Table 7.2 with these exceptions: (1) the value of n in the term $\sum T_{cj}^2/n$ for calculating SS_c will change to reflect the different numbers of replicates in each category; (2) the expected mean square for between variables becomes $\sigma^2 + n'\sigma_c^2$ (n' is defined below); and (3) SS_w is calculated as the difference $SS_T - SS_C$.

$$n' = (N^2 - \sum n_i^2)/(j - 1)N$$

where

N = total number of values

j = number of categories (columns)

$\sum n_i^2$ = sum of the squares of the number of replicates in each column.

(*Note:* n' is approximately equal to the average number of replications per category.)

The following example illustrates the situation where there are unequal numbers of replicates:

Example 7.3.   Five different analysts ran hydroxyl numbers on a sample. Each was told to run enough replicates to get a "good" average value. As might be expected, the analysts performed different numbers of replicates. Based on these values, is there a difference among the analysts? Which ones differ significantly?

ANALYST

RUN	A	B	C	D	E	
1	30.0	29.3	29.6	32.5	31.0	
2	31.3	30.7	28.3	32.0	32.0	
3	31.2	30.3	29.9	29.8	31.5	
4	30.5	31.2		30.5	33.0	
5		28.7		30.9		
6		30.0				
T_{cj}:	123.0	180.2	87.8	155.7	127.5	$T = 674.2$
n	4	6	3	5	4	$N = 22$
$\bar{X}$	30.75	30.03	29.27	31.14	31.88	$\bar{\bar{X}} = 30.64$

(a) $$SS_c = \frac{123.0^2}{4} + \frac{180.2^2}{6} + \frac{87.8^2}{3} + \frac{155.7^2}{5} + \frac{127.5^2}{4} - \frac{674.2^2}{22}$$

$$= 20{,}676.4305 - 20{,}661.1654 = 15.2651$$

(b) $SS_t = 30.0^2 + 31.3^2 + 31.2^2 + \cdots + 33.0^2 - (674.2^2/22)$

$= 20{,}690.24 - 20{,}661.1654 = 29.0746$

(c) $SS_w = SS_t - SS_c = 29.0746 - 15.2651 = 13.8095$

$n' = (22^2 - (4^2 + 6^2 + 3^2 + 5^2 + 4^2))/(5-1)22 = 4.34$

ANOVA Table

SOURCE	SS	DF	MS	EXPECTED MEAN SQUARES
Between analysts	(SS_c) 15.2651	4	3.8163	$\sigma^2 + 4.34\sigma_c^2$
Within analysts	(SS_w) 13.8095	17	0.8123	σ^2
Total	(SS_t) 29.0746	21		

$$F = 3.8163/0.8123 = 4.698$$

$$F_{0.05,4,17} = 2.96$$

$$F_{0.01,4,17} = 4.67$$

Thus, the variance due to analysts is significant even at the 0.01 level of significance. This conclusion is not surprising because we usually would expect data from several analysts to have greater variability than data from a single analyst.

The standard deviation within analysts, s, equals $\sqrt{0.8123} = 0.9013$, 17 DF. This is considered a measure of the precision of the method.

The standard deviation for between analysts is:

$$s_c = \sqrt{\frac{3.8163 - 0.8123}{4.34}} = 0.8230, \quad 4\,\text{DF}$$

Because Duncan's procedure requires equal sample sizes, we cannot use it to determine which analysts, if any, differ. However, the large amount of overlap in the data as shown in Figure 7.3 suggests that no one analyst differs appreciably from the others.

Based on our analysis of the data in this example, we can conclude that (1) there is a significant effect on the average hydroxyl numbers due to analysts; (2) we are unable to say that any one analyst differs significantly from the

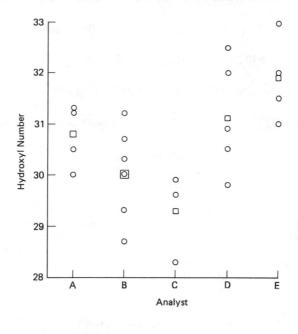

Analyst

○ Individual values
□ Average for analyst

Figure 7.3.   Data from Example 7.3.

others; and (3) the standard deviation for the analysts ($s_c = 0.8320$) does not differ greatly from that for the method ($s = 0.9013$).

7.3   SUMMARY

In this chapter you were introduced to the technique called analysis of variance (ANOVA). This technique assumes that the populations being compared have at least approximately normal distributions and equal variances. We have seen how to use it on sets of data in which we were interested in only one independent variable. The ANOVA technique enables us to determine if the variable has a significant effect on the results of the experiment, and this conclusion enables us to say whether the average values of the dependent variable differ significantly among themselves. The ANOVA technique will not tell us which of the averages are different; we must make use of Duncan's separation of means procedure to find this out.

In the following several chapters we will see how ANOVA can be applied to cases in which we are interested in more than one independent variable.

7.4   PROBLEMS

Problems 6c, 7c, and 8 make use of the one-way analysis of variance technique. Try your hand at them and see if your answers agree with those in the "back of the book".

RESOURCES

Davies, O. L., ed. *Design and Analysis of Industrial Experiments*, 2nd ed. New York: Longman Group Limited, 1978.

Dixon, W. J., and Massey, Jr., F. F. *Introduction to Statistical Analysis*. New York: McGraw-Hill Co., 1951.

Johnson, R. R. *Elementary Statistics*, 2nd ed. North Scituate, MA: Duxbury Press, 1976.

Chapter 8
COMPARING MORE THAN TWO AVERAGES: ANALYSIS OF VARIANCE FOR TWO INDEPENDENT VARIABLES

OVERVIEW

Chapter 7 introduced the concept of analysis of variance (ANOVA), and we learned how this technique is used when only one variable is of interest. In this chapter we will see how ANOVA is used with two variables, both with and without replication of the observations.

8.0 MEASURING THE EFFECT OF TWO VARIABLES ON AVERAGES (TWO-WAY CLASSIFICATION)

The analysis of variance technique also permits testing for significant differences when two variables are of interest. Each variable may have several different levels (average values). One would measure an appropriate property for various combinations of the two variables. In the case of a colorimetric reaction, one might measure the absorbance as a function of various times and temperatures. Another example is described below.

EXAMPLE 8.1.   The wetting ability of a surfactant is measured by an empirical test in which the time in seconds to wet a standard fiber is measured for a fixed concentration of the surfactant. We wish to estimate the variance due to analysts and batches of surfactant if either has a significant effect on the wetting ability. The following data were obtained by three analysts who analyzed the same sample of each of four batches of the surfactant. The data have been coded by subtracting a constant from each observation to simplify the calculations.

	VARIABLE I: ANALYST			
VARIABLE II: BATCH	A	B	C	ROW TOTAL
1	20	27	25	72
2	1	7	15	23
3	16	28	30	74
4	14	27	29	70
Column Total	51	89	99	239

When there are two (or more) independent variables, *interaction* may exist between the variables, i.e., their combined effect is greater (or less) than that expected for the straight addition of the effects. Consider the case of two variables, each at two levels. The responses may be represented as:

Variable I

		Low	High
Variable II	Low	a	b
	High	c	d

The differences between responses a and b and between c and d are both measures of the effect of changing the level of variable I. Likewise the differences between a and c and between b and d are measures of the effect of variable II. If variable II has no effect on variable I, $b - a$ and $d - c$ will be equal (within experimental error), and therefore $(b - a) - (d - c)$, which is a measure of interaction, should equal zero. If these differences are not zero (within experimental error), interaction is said to exist.

Suppose the values for a, b, c, and d are

Variable I

		Low	High
Variable II	Low	5	15
	High	20	30

These values are plotted in Figure 8.1. Here $b - a = 15 - 5$ or 10 and $d - c = 30 - 20$ or 10, and $(d - c) - (b - a) = 0$. Figure 8.1 shows two parallel lines.

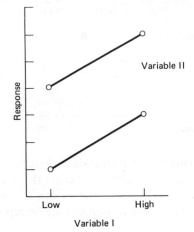

Figure 8.1.   Two variables; no interaction.

The effect of changing variable I from its low to high level is 10 units for both levels of variable II. Thus, there is no evidence of interaction.

If the values for *a*, *b*, *c*, and *d* are

Variable I

Variable II		Low	High
	Low	6	15
	High	10	30

Here $b - a = 15 - 5 = 10$; $d - c = 30 - 10 = 20$; and $(d - c) - (b - a) = 10$. Figure 8.2 shows the plot of these values, which result in nonparallel lines. In this instance the effect produced by changing the level of variable I is influenced by the level of variable II; that is, there is interaction between the two variables.

With only one observation per combination of the two variables, no measure of the significance of the interaction, if it exists, is possible. If it is desired to test for the significance of interaction, replicate measurements must be made for each combination of the two variables.

Note: Generally, two-way classification is *not* the best way to analyze interlaboratory precision studies because the estimates of standard deviation for different levels of the variables are usually dependent upon the level, and

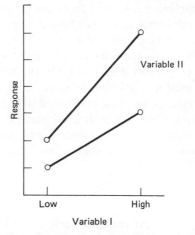

Figure 8.2. Two variables; interaction present.

the estimate obtained is an average effect. Of course, if the data can be transformed so that the estimated standard deviations are independent of the level, this technique is suitable.

In addition to the possibility of interaction when we have two or more variables, we also need to consider whether each variable (also called an effect) is *random* or *fixed*. The mathematics in the analysis of variance is the same up through the calculation of the mean squares regardless of whether the variables are random or fixed. However, the quantities estimated by the mean squares do differ according to whether the variables are random or fixed. The next sections will help us decide in which type our variables belong.

8.0.1 Random Effects

If the values or levels of a variable are selected at random from a large number of possible values, the variable is said to be random. If all the variables are randomly selected, the mathematical model representing the response is said to be a random model. For example, three analysts selected at random from twenty, two days from a month, etc., would be random effects. The conclusions drawn from the analysis of a random effect are considered to be applicable to all members of the population represented by the random sample.

8.0.2 Fixed Effects

If the values or levels of a variable selected are the only ones available or of interest, the variable is said to be fixed. For example, your laboratory may have only two spectrophotometers and these are the only ones of interest to you, or there may be only three analysts who would perform an analysis. *The mathematical model describing only such variables is called a fixed model.* The conclusions drawn from the analysis of a fixed variable apply only to the particular set of conditions used to obtain the data. In effect all of the population has been used in obtaining the data. Some texts use a term other than variance to describe the variance associated with a fixed variable, but we will use the same terminology for both fixed and random variables. But it must be emphasized that *the values obtained for the variance of fixed effects are not applicable beyond the values or range of values used in obtaining the data.*

8.0.3 Mixed Effects

When some of the variables are randomly selected and some are of the fixed type, the model describing the response is said to be *mixed*.

The decision of whether a variable is fixed or random effect is the chemist's, not the statistician's. If the chemist considers a variable to be a random effect and wants the results to apply to the population of levels represented by those selected for the experiment, then the chemist must make sure the levels are really chosen at random from a large number of available levels.

Now that we are aware of some of the conditions affecting the analysis of variance with two or more variables, we shall show how to apply the technique for the case in which there is only one observation per combination of variables. Later in the chapter we will consider the application to cases with replicate observations.

8.1 TWO-WAY CLASSIFICATION WITH NO REPLICATES

Example 8.1 fits the situation of one observation per combination. The general equations for a two-way classification are very similar to those for the one-way, as shown in Table 8.1.

In the data format the usual matrix notation is used for subscripting the values. The first subscript designates the number of the row in which the value appears, and the second designates the number of the column. Thus, X_{23} denotes the value in the second row and third column. For totals of the columns, the first subscript is c for column total, and for row totals the second subscript r is used. The grand total is an unsubscripted T.

In Table 8.1 the formula for the sum of squares for the first source (between columns) is the same as for that in the one-way classification we discussed in Chapter 7, and the mathematical operations are also the same. The formula for the sum of squares for between rows is the same as that for between columns except that the total for rows is used in place of the total for columns.

TABLE 8.1. Two-Way Classification, No Replicates.

Data format:

VARIABLE II	VARIABLE I					TOTAL
	A	B	C	D	i	
a	X_{11}	X_{12}	X_{13}	X_{14}	X_{1j}	T_{1r}
b	X_{21}	X_{22}	X_{23}	X_{24}	X_{2j}	T_{2r}
c	X_{31}	X_{32}	X_{33}	X_{34}	X_{3j}	T_{3r}
i	X_{i1}	X_{i2}	X_{i3}	X_{i4}	X_{ij}	T_{ir}
Column Totals:	T_{c1}	T_{c2}	T_{c3}	T_{c4}	T_{cj}	T

ANOVA Table:

SOURCE	SS	DF	MS
Between columns	$SS_c = \dfrac{\sum T_{cj}^2}{r} - \dfrac{T^2}{rc}$	$c - 1$	SS_c/DF
Between rows	$SS_r = \dfrac{\sum T_{ir}^2}{c} - \dfrac{T^2}{rc}$	$r - 1$	SS_r/DF
Residual	$SS = SS_t - SS_c - SS_r$	$(c - 1)(r - 1)$	SS/DF
Total	$SS_t = \sum \sum X_{ij}^2 - \dfrac{T^2}{rc}$	$rc - 1$	

r = number of rows
c = number of columns
T_{cj} = total of values in column i
T_{ir} = total of values in row i
T = grand total of all values

With two (or more) variables there is the possibility of interaction between the variables. In the case of a two-way classification with no replication of results for each combination of conditions, we cannot test the significance of this effect. Thus, we have the third source in the ANOVA table: Residual. This source includes any variability other than that attributable to variables I and II, and the formula indicates that the residual sum of squares is obtained as the difference between the total sum of squares and the sums due to variables I and II. The formula for the total sum of squares is the same as for the one-way classification.

Table 8.1 does not include an expected mean square column. This information appears in Table 8.2. We will discuss its contents in connection with Example 8.1.

Now let us use the data from Example 8.1 to illustrate the use of ANOVA in analyzing data obtained with two independent variables.

TABLE 8.2.   Expected Mean Squares: Two-Way Classification, No Replicates.

SOURCE	RANDOM EFFECTS	FIXED EFFECTS	MIXED EFFECTS
Between columns	$\sigma^2 + \sigma_i^2 + r\sigma_c^2$	$\sigma^2 + r\sigma_c^2$	—
Between rows	$\sigma^2 + \sigma_i^2 + c\sigma_r^2$	$\sigma^2 + c\sigma_r^2$	—
Residual	$\sigma^2 + \sigma_i^2$	$\sigma^2 + \sigma_i^2$	—
Between columns (F)	—	—	$\sigma^2 + \sigma_i^2 + r\sigma_c^2$
Between rows (R)	—	—	$\sigma^2 + c\sigma_r^2$
Residual (R)	—	—	$\sigma^2 + \sigma_i^2$
Between columns (R)	—	—	$\sigma^2 + r\sigma_c^2$
Between rows (F)	—	—	$\sigma^2 + \sigma_i^2 + c\sigma_r^2$
Residual (R)	—	—	$\sigma^2 + \sigma_i^2$

i = interaction
r = number of rows (levels of row variable)
c = number of columns (levels of column variable)
(F) = fixed variable
(R) = random variable

a: $$SS_c = \frac{51^2 + 89^2 + 99^2}{4} - \frac{239^2}{12}$$

$$= 5{,}080.75 - 4{,}760.0833 = 320.6667$$

b: $$SS_r = \frac{72^2 + 23^2 + 74^2 + 70^2}{3} - \frac{239^2}{12}$$

$$= 5{,}363.0 - 4{,}760.0833 = 602.9167$$

c: $$SS_t = 20^2 + 1^2 + 16^2 + \cdots + 30^2 + 29^2 - (239^2/12)$$

$$= 5{,}735.0 - 4{,}760.0833 = 947.9167$$

d: $$SS = SS_t - SS_r - SS_c$$

$$= 974.9167 - 602.9167 - 320.6667 = 51.3333$$

ANOVA Table

SOURCE	SUM OF SQUARES	DF	MS	EMS
Between analysts	(SS_c) 320.6667	2	160.3334	$\sigma^2 + 4\sigma_c^2$
Between batches	(SS_r) 602.9167	3	200.9722	$\sigma^2 + 3\sigma_r^2$
Residual	(SS) 51.3333	6	8.5556	σ^2
Total	(SS_t) 974.9167	11		

8.1.1 Evaluation of the Random Effects Model

If we assume that the three analysts in Example 8.1 were randomly selected from a large group of possible analysts and that the four batches were also randomly chosen from a large number of production batches, then we have a random effects model.

Inspection of the expected mean square terms in Table 8.2 shows that for the random effects model we do not have to make any assumptions about the presence of interaction. If you are interested in how the terms in the expected mean square table were derived, Hicks has described very clearly a simple method for determining them.[1]

To determine if the batch (row) variable is significant, we will use the F test to compare the mean square for the batch (row) effect with the mean square for the residual. Likewise, we will compare the mean square for the analyst effect with that for the residual. Notice that in each case the terms in the expected mean squares column of Table 8.2 tells us that the mean square for each variable is a measure of the variances for the residual and the interaction plus only one other variance, that of the variable in question. Thus, if the mean square for the variable is not significantly greater than that for the residual term, the variable has not been shown to have any effect.

First, we will test the batch mean square:

$$F = 200.9722/8.5556 = 23.49$$

$$F_{0.05, 3, 6} = 4.36$$

Since the critical value is exceeded, we conclude that the batch averages are not equal, that is, they exert a significant effect on the wetting time.

Next, we will test the analyst mean square:

$$F = 160.3334/8.5556 = 18.74$$

$$F_{0.05, 2, 6} = 5.14$$

Again, the critical value is exceeded, and we conclude that the analyst averages are not equal; thus, the analysts have a significant effect on the wetting time.

Having determined that both variables are significant factors, we now calculate how much of the total variability is due to each variable.

The standard deviation for the residual effect is merely the square root of the residual mean square:

$$s_{(residual)} = \sqrt{8.5556} = 2.9250 \text{ with 6 DF}$$

The standard deviation for the batch effect is:

$$s_{r(\text{batch})} = \sqrt{(200.9722 - 8.5556)/3} = \sqrt{64.1389}$$

$$= 8.0087 \text{ with 3 DF}$$

The standard deviation for the analyst effect is:

$$s_{c(\text{analyst})} = \sqrt{(160.3334 - 8.5556)/4} = \sqrt{37.9444}$$

$$= 6.1599 \text{ with 2 DF}$$

The variance due to analysts is about 34% of the total variance; that due to batches (production variation) about 58% of the total; and about 8% is residual, not explained by either of the two variables. The residual variance value includes any interaction variance if interaction is present. If we assume that no interaction is present, the residual variance (or standard deviation) may be considered a measure of the precision of the method used.

Having obtained estimates of the variances, we can use them to calculate how well two analyses by the same or different analysts should agree. Based on the estimated standard deviation for the method of 2.9250 with 6 degrees of freedom, we can expect two analyses performed by the same analyst to agree within $2.9250 \times 2.77 = 8.1$ seconds at the 0.05 level of significance.

If we are interested in analyses by two analysts, we must include the standard deviation for between analysts of 6.1599 with 2 degrees of freedom. The total variance of interest is $2.9250^2 + 6.1599^2 = 46.5000$, and the standard deviation is $\sqrt{46.5000} = 6.8191$ with 2 degrees of freedom. Thus, analyses of the same sample by two analysts should agree within $6.8191 \times 2.77 = 18.9$ seconds at the 0.05 significance level. This appears to be a large difference, but the estimate is based on only three analysts. In addition the variability between analysts is appreciable. On batch 4 there is a range of 15 seconds. In view of these factors, a predicted difference of 18.9 seconds is reasonable.

8.1.2 Evaluation of the Fixed Effects Model

In Example 8.1 if the three analysts were the only ones who would perform the analysis and the four batches of surfactant represented a special production run, then neither variable was randomly selected. Therefore, in evaluating the mean square values listed in the previous section we need to look at the expected mean squares for the fixed effect model in Table 8.2.

The residual mean square is seen to estimate the residual variance σ^2 plus the interaction variance σ_i^2. The interaction variance does not appear in the terms estimated by the mean squares for rows and columns. Thus, to make

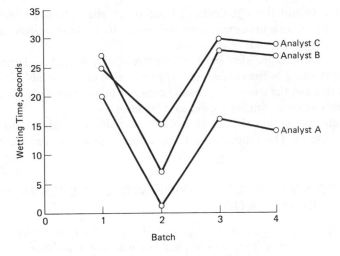

Figure 8.3.   Plot of Example 8.1 data.

valid tests of significance for the row and column mean squares we must assume that no interaction is present. That is, the residual mean square of 8.5556 estimates only σ^2. For the assumed conditions in our example, it is unlikely that interaction would exist between the analysts and batches. A plot of the data in Figure 8.3 does not suggest appreciable interaction. Therefore, we can test the mean squares for rows and columns against the residual mean square in the same fashion as when both variables were considered random. The calculations for the standard deviations are the same as in Section 8.1.1. However, the results are applicable to only the three analysts and the four batches used in the experiment.

8.1.3   Evaluation of the Mixed Effects Model

If either variable in Example 8.1 is considered fixed and the other variable random, we have a *mixed effects model*. A reasonable situation might be that there were only three analysts available (a fixed variable), but that the four batches were randomly selected from a large population of production.

Look at the expected mean squares in Table 8.2 for the mixed effects model with between columns (analysts) fixed and between rows (batches) random. Under these conditions we can test the significance of the columns (analyst) effect without making assumptions about interaction. However, the expected mean square for rows (batches) does not contain the interaction term which is present in the residual expected mean square. Thus, we must assume no interaction to test the significance of the batch effect. In our example it is unlikely that interaction exists and therefore the σ_i^2 term equals zero. This makes the F test for significance valid.

The calculations are identical to those previously described. However, the results pertaining to the column (analyst) variable are applicable only to the three analysts in the study. The results concerning the row variable (batches) are applicable to all similarly produced batches.

A similar situation exists if the column variable is random and the row variable is fixed. The conditions for the columns and rows are merely interchanged.

8.2 TWO-WAY CLASSIFICATION WITH n OBSERVATIONS PER COMBINATION

In the preceding section we said that with only one observation per combination of variables there was no way to measure the significance of any interaction. Many times interaction between variables is probable, and we need to be able to measure it. This is done by repeating the observations for each combination of the two variables. In the following example duplicate observations are made.

EXAMPLE 8.2. An experimental design to investigate the effects of time and temperature on the percent residual monomer in a polymerization reaction gave the following data. Test the effect of time and temperature and the possible time-temperature interaction for the 0.05 level of significance. Estimate the variability of each "real" effect. The data are plotted in Figure 8.4.

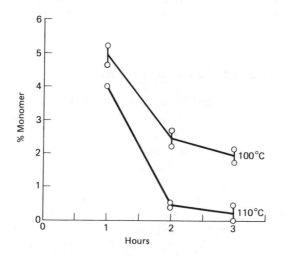

Figure 8.4. Plot of Example 8.2 data.

TEMP.	TIME, HRS			REPLICATE TOTALS			TOTAL
	1	2	3				
100 C	5.4	2.7	2.1	10.2	5.0	4.0	19.2
	4.8	2.3	1.9				
110 C	4.2	0.4	0.4				
	4.2	0.5	0.0	8.4	0.9	0.4	9.7
	18.6	5.9	4.4				28.9

The general equations (see Table 8.3) for the two-way classification with n observations per combination are similar to the two-way classification with only one observation per combination. One of the differences is in the matrix notation for the data. Each data element will have three subscripts instead of two. The first two subscripts, i and j, indicate the row and column position, just as previously. The third subscript, k, indicates the replication of the observation within the specified row and column variables. Table 8.3 does not include the expected mean squares column. This information is given later, in Table 8.4.

The equations in Table 8.3 will be used to prepare the analysis of variance table for this example:

$$T^2/rcn = 28.9^2/12 = 69.6008$$

$$SS_c = \frac{18.6^2}{4} + \frac{5.9^2}{4} + \frac{4.4^2}{4} - 69.6008 = 100.0325 - 69.6008 = 30.4317$$

$$SS_r = \frac{19.2^2}{6} + \frac{9.7^2}{6} - 69.6008 = 77.1217 - 69.6008 = 7.5209$$

$$SS_s = \frac{10.2^2}{2} + \frac{8.4^2}{2} + \frac{5.0^2}{2} + \frac{0.9^2}{2} + \frac{4.0^2}{2} + \frac{0.4^2}{2} - 69.6008$$

$$= 108.2850 - 69.6008 = 38.6842$$

$$SS_i = SS_s - SS_c - SS_r = 38.6842 - 30.4317 - 7.5209 = 0.7316$$

$$SS = 5.4^2 + 4.8^2 + 4.2^2 + \cdots + 0.0^2 - 69.6008$$

$$= 108.6500 - 69.6008 = 39.0492$$

$$SS_w = SS_t - SS_s = 39.0492 - 38.6842 = 0.3650$$

TABLE 8.3. Two-Way Classification: n Observations per Combination Data Format:

Data Format:

VARIABLE II	VARIABLE I				REPLICATE TOTALS				ROW TOTAL
	A	B	C	j					
a	X_{111} X_{112} X_{113} X_{11k}	X_{121} X_{122} X_{123} X_{12k}	X_{131} X_{132} X_{133} X_{13k}	X_{1j1} X_{1j2} X_{1j3} X_{1jk}	T_{11e}	T_{12e}	T_{13e}	T_{1je}	T_{1re}
b	X_{211} X_{212} X_{213} X_{21k}	X_{221} X_{222} X_{223} X_{22k}	X_{231} X_{232} X_{233} X_{23k}	X_{2j1} X_{2j2} X_{2j3} X_{2jk}	T_{21e}	T_{22e}	T_{23e}	T_{2je}	T_{2re}
i	X_{i11} X_{i12} X_{i13} X_{i1k}	X_{i21} X_{i22} X_{i23} X_{i2k}	X_{i31} X_{i32} X_{i33} X_{i3k}	X_{ij1} X_{ij2} X_{ij3} X_{ijk}	T_{i1e}	T_{i2e}	T_{i3e}	T_{ije}	T_{ire}
Column Totals:					T_{c1e}	T_{c2e}	T_{c3e}	T_{cje}	T

ANOVA Table:

SOURCE	SS	DF	MS
Between columns	$SS_c = \dfrac{\sum T_{cje}^2}{rn} - \dfrac{T^2}{rcn}$	$c - 1$	SS_c/DF
Between rows	$SS_r = \dfrac{\sum T_{ire}^2}{cn} - \dfrac{T^2}{rcn}$	$r - 1$	SS_r/DF
Column × row interaction	$SS_i = SS_s - SS_c - SS_r$	$(c - 1)(r - 1)$	SS_i/DF
Subtotal	$SS_s = \dfrac{\sum T_{ije}^2}{n} - \dfrac{T^2}{rcn}$	$rc - 1$	SS_s/DF
Within combination	$SS_w = SS_t - SS_s$	$rc(n - 1)$	SS_w/DF
Total	$SS_t = \sum\sum X_{ijk}^2 - \dfrac{T^2}{rcn}$	$rcn - 1$	

r = number of rows
c = number of columns
n = number of replicates for each combination
T_{cje} = total of values in column j
T_{ire} = total of values in row i
T_{ije} = total of values in combination ij
T = grand total of all values

TABLE 8.4. Expected Mean Squares, Two-Way Classification: n Observations per Combination

SOURCE	RANDOM EFFECTS	FIXED EFFECTS	MIXED EFFECTS
Between columns	$\sigma^2 + n\sigma_i^2 + rn\sigma_c^2$	$\sigma^2 + rn\sigma_c^2$	—
Between rows	$\sigma^2 + n\sigma_i^2 + cn\sigma_r^2$	$\sigma^2 + n\sigma_r^2$	—
C × R interaction	$\sigma^2 + n\sigma_i^2$	$\sigma^2 + n\sigma_i^2$	—
Within combination	σ^2	σ^2	—
Between columns (F)	—	—	$\sigma^2 + n\sigma_i^2 + rn\sigma_c^2$
Between rows (R)	—	—	$\sigma^2 + cn\sigma_r^2$
C × R interaction	—	—	$\sigma^2 + n\sigma_r^2$
Within combination	—	—	σ^2
Between columns (R)	—	—	$\sigma^2 + rn\sigma_c^2$
Between rows (F)	—	—	$\sigma^2 + n\sigma_i^2 + cn\sigma_r^2$
C × R interaction	—	—	$\sigma^2 + n\sigma_i^2$
Within combination	—	—	σ^2

n = number of replicates
r = number of rows (levels of row variable)
c = number of columns (levels of column variable)

(F) = fixed effect
(R) = random effect

C × R interaction and within-combination sources are always random variables

ANOVA Table.

SOURCE	SS	DF	MS	EXPECTED MEAN SQUARE
Between columns (hrs)	30.4317	2	15.2158	$\sigma^2 + 4\sigma_c^2$
Between rows (C)	7.5209	1	7.5209	$\sigma^2 + 2\sigma_c^2$
Column × row interaction	0.7316	2	0.3658	$\sigma^2 + 2\sigma_i^2$
Subtotal	38.6842	5		
Within combination	0.3650	6	0.0608	σ^2
Total	39.0492	11		

In the next section we will discuss the expected mean squares portion of the above ANOVA table.

8.2.1 Quantities Estimated by the Mean Squares (Two-Way Classification With n Replicates)

The procedures used to calculate the sums of squares, etc., are exactly the same for all three types of effects and were summarized in Example 8.2. However, the expected mean squares can be quite different, as indicated in Table 8.4,

Expected Mean Squares, Two-way Classification With n Observations Per Combination. We will use Example 8.2 to illustrate the use of the the expected mean square terms for a two-way classification problem.

The terms in the expected mean squares column of our ANOVA table for Example 8.2 are those for a fixed effects model as given in Table 8.4, because the time and temperature variables are both considered to be fixed variables.

In testing the effects (sources) for significance we first test the interaction mean squares versus the within-combination mean square because the terms in the expected mean squares indicate that these mean squares differ in the components being measured only with respect to twice the variance of the interaction. Therefore, if the mean square for the interaction is not significantly greater than that for within combination, the variance of the interaction is not significant (equals zero). The ratio of these mean squares is 0.3658/0.0608 or 6.02. The critical value for $F_{0.05, 2, 6} = 5.14$; therefore, we conclude the interaction effect is significant at the 0.05 significance level.

We next test the significance of the mean square for between rows (temperature). According to the expected mean square column, the quantity estimated by this mean square is the sum of the variance due to interaction and twice the variance due to rows. Therefore, our F test is the ratio of the mean square for rows to that for interaction: $F = 7.5209/0.0608 = 123.69$. The critical value $F_{0.05, 1, 6} = 5.99$ is exceeded, indicating that the row averages are not equal. We conclude the row (temperature) effect is significant at $\alpha = 0.05$.

Finally, we test the significance of the between columns (hours) mean square. We compare this mean square with that for the interaction in accordance with the components of variance given in the expected mean square column: $F = 15.21585/0.0608 = 250.26$. Because this value is greater than the critical value for $F_{0.05, 2, 6} = 5.14$, we conclude that the column (hours) effect is also significant at $\alpha = 0.05$.

Had the interaction term been found to be not significant, we would have followed the procedure described in Section 8.2.2 to test the significance of the row and column effects.

We are now ready to estimate the variability of the sources of variance. The within-combination variance is $s_w^2 = 0.0608$, and the standard deviation is $s_w = 0.2466$ with 6 degrees of freedom.

The interaction (time-temperature) variance is calculated as follows:

$$s_i^2 = \frac{0.3658 - 0.0608}{2} = 0.152500$$

$$s_i = 0.3905, \ 2 \ \text{DF}$$

The between rows (temperature) and the between columns (time) variances and standard deviations are calculated in the same manner:

$$s_r^2 = \frac{7.5209 - 0.0608}{2} = 3.73005$$

$$s_r = 1.9313, 1 \text{ DF}$$

$$s_c^2 = \frac{15.2158 - 0.0608}{4} = 3.78875$$

$$s_c = 1.9465, 2 \text{ DF}$$

Summarizing the results of our analysis, we have found that both time and temperature have a significant effect on the amount of residual monomer and that there is significant interaction between these variables. Quantitatively, we have:

SOURCE	VARIANCE	STANDARD DEVIATION
Hours (columns)	3.78875	1.9465, 2 DF
Temperature (rows)	3.73005	1.9318, 1 DF
Interaction	0.15250	0.3905, 2 DF
Within combination	0.06080	0.2466, 6 DF
	7.73210	

Time and temperature exert almost the same amount of influence on the monomer content (49.0% and 48.2% of the total variance). The interaction of these two variables is relatively small (about 2% of the total variance). Interaction effects are usually much smaller than their corresponding main effects. The within combination effect may be considered to be the analytical method's precision. These findings regarding the main effects and interaction confirm the plot of the data in Figure 8.4.

Note that in this example both variables are considered to be fixed variables. If our model had been either the random or mixed effects model, and if the interaction mean square were significant, we would consult Table 8.4 to select the correct mean squares to use in calculating the row and column variances. For example, the row variance for the random effects model would be calculated using

$$s_r^2 = \frac{MS_r - MS_i}{cn}$$

In this example interaction was found to be significant. It may well be that time and temperature are interacting and we correctly recognized this fact.

However, the presence of an uncontrolled and unmeasured variable (such as days in our example) could cause the interaction effect to be significant. Not randomizing the order in which the experiments are carried out is a likely cause of this situation. Of course, there is a chance equal to α that there is really no interaction, but we obtain a F value which exceeded the critical value (a type I error).

8.2.2   Interpretation of Mean Squares When the Interaction Is Not Significant

In Example 8.2, if the interaction mean square had tested not significant in the F test, we would proceed to test the between rows (temperature) mean square for significance in the following manner.

First, we would add the sums of squares for interaction and within combination and divide the total by the sum of their respective degrees of freedom to obtain a new within combination mean square. This is justified on the basis that since the interaction mean square is not significant, it and the within combination mean square are both estimates of the within combination mean square. Some statistical texts do not approve of this method, while others do. The present author sides with those that do approve. Using the data from Example 8.2, the new estimate for within combination variance is $(0.7316 + 0.3650)/(2 + 6) = 0.1371$.

Having obtained the new estimate for within combination variance, we use it as the denominator in the F test on the mean square for rows: $F = 7.5209/0.1371 = 54.85$. The critical value for $F_{0.05, 1, 8}$ is 5.32. Therefore, we conclude the row effect is real at the 0.05 significance level. Similarly, we would test the between columns mean square: $F = 15.2158/0.1371 = 111.0$. The critical value for $F_{0.05, 2, 8}$ is 4.46, and we conclude that the columns (hours) effect is also real at the 0.05 significance level.

The rest of the analysis is similar to that used when the interaction mean square is significant except σ_i^2 is set equal to zero in the expected mean square terms.

8.3   SUMMARY

In this chapter we have learned how to extend the use of ANOVA to problems in which we test two independent variables for significant effects (two-way classification). The inclusion of replicate determinations for each combination of the two variables enables us to measure the amount of interaction of the two variables, if present. We were introduced to the concept of fixed and random variables and saw how to calculate the components of variance for various combinations of fixed and random variables. In Chapter 9 we will extend the use of ANOVA to three independent variables.

8.4 PROBLEMS

To test your understanding of the concepts in this chapter, try working problems 9, 10, 11, and 12.

REFERENCE

1. Hicks, C. R., "Fundamentals of Analysis of Variance," *Industrial Quality Control*, August 1956, pp. 17–20; September 1956, pp. 5–8; October 1956, pp. 13–16.

Chapter 9
COMPARING MORE THAN TWO AVERAGES: ANALYSIS OF VARIANCE FOR THREE INDEPENDENT VARIABLES

OVERVIEW

This chapter continues the discussion of analysis of variance with its application to problems with three independent variables (three-way classification). The advantages and limitations of the Latin square design are also presented as applied to the three-way classification.

9.0 MEASURING THE EFFECT OF DIFFERENT LEVELS OF THREE VARIABLES ON AVERAGES (THREE-WAY CLASSIFICATION)

The analysis of variance may also be used when three independent variables are of interest (three-way classification). The procedure is similar in principle to that already discussed in the preceding chapters, but the mechanics of handling the data differs. This is most easily explained with an example.

EXAMPLE 9.1.   A viscous liquid chemical is produced in a batch operation. Each batch produces enough product to fill 1000 drums. The assay of the product is determined by infrared analysis performed in duplicate by one of 20 analysts in the plant laboratory. In an effort to improve product quality a study was made to determine which of three sources of variability were significant and the magnitude of variability of each significant source. The sources selected were: variable A, batches—three batches selected at random from a month's production; variable B, analysts—two selected at random; and variable C, samples—two drums selected at random from each batch. The assay values obtained are summarized in Table 9.1 together with the coded values which were obtained by subtracting 90.0 from each value.

Table 9.1a is formed by summing the replicate values in Table 9.1. Thus, each entry in Table 9.1a is based on two observations, as indicated by a [2](superscript) to the left of each entry. These data are plotted in Figure 9.1.

TABLE 9.1. Data for Example 9.1.

		Assay, %				Coded Assay $(X - 90.0)$			
		C, Drum No.				C, Drum No.			
A, Batch No.		I		II		I		II	
		B, Analyst		B, Analyst		B, Analyst		B, Analyst	
	Run	M	P	M	P	M	P	M	P
23	1	94.6	95.8	97.7	97.8	4.6	5.8	7.7	7.8
	2	95.2	95.8	98.1	98.6	5.2	5.8	8.1	8.6
Subtotal		189.8	191.6	195.8	196.4	9.8	11.6	15.8	16.4
35	1	96.2	96.5	98.0	99.0	6.2	6.5	8.0	9.0
	2	96.4	96.9	98.4	99.0	6.4	6.9	8.4	9.0
Subtotal		192.6	193.4	196.4	198.0	12.6	13.4	16.4	18.0
2	1	97.9	98.4	99.2	99.6	7.9	8.4	9.2	9.6
	2	98.1	98.6	99.4	100.0	8.1	8.6	9.4	10.0
Subtotal		196.0	187.0	198.6	199.6	16.0	17.0	18.6	19.6

TABLE 9.1a. Coded Assay.

	C, Drum No.			
A, Batch No.	I		II	
	B, Analyst		B, Analyst	
	M	P	M	P
23	^{2}9.8	^{2}11.6	^{2}15.8	^{2}16.4
35	^{2}12.6	^{2}13.4	^{2}16.4	^{2}18.0
2	^{2}16.0	^{2}17.0	^{2}18.6	^{2}19.6

Table 9.1b is formed by summing the *same* levels of variable B (analyst) for each combination of variable A (batch) and variable C (drum) in Table 9.1a; e.g., for batch 23 and analyst M, add 9.8 and 15.8 to get 25.6, which is based on four observations. The data are shown in Figure 9.2.

Table 9.1c is formed by summing the *different* levels of variable B (analyst)

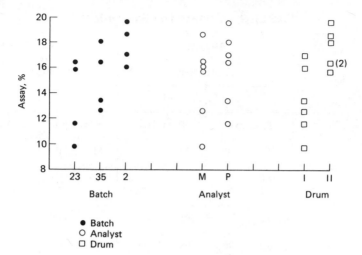

Figure 9.1. Data from Example 9.1, Table 9.1A.

TABLE 9.1b. Batch × Analyst.

A, Batch No.	B, Analyst M	B, Analyst P	Total
23	[4]25.6	[4]28.0	[8]53.6
35	[4]29.0	[4]31.4	[8]60.4
2	[4]34.6	[4]36.6	[8]71.2
Total	[12]89.2	[12]96.0	[24]185.2

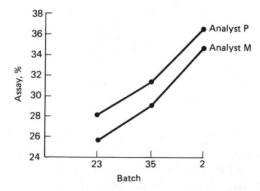

Figure 9.2. Data from Example 9.1, Table 9.1B. Batch and analyst vs. assay.

TABLE 9.1c.   Batch × Drum.

A, Batch No.	C, Drum No.		Total
	I	II	
23	[4]21.4	[4]32.2	[8]53.6
35	[4]26.0	[4]34.4	[8]60.4
2	[4]33.0	[4]38.2	[8]71.2
Total	[12]80.4	[12]104.8	[24]185.2

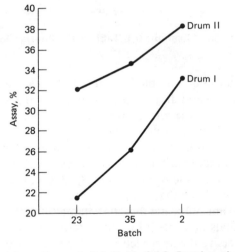

Figure 9.3.   Data from Example 9.1, Table 9.1C. Batch and drum vs. assay.

TABLE 9.1d.   Analyst × Drum.

B, Analyst	C, Drum No.		Total
	I	II	
M	[6]38.4	[6]50.8	[12]89.2
P	[6]42.0	[6]54.0	[12]96.0
Total	[12]80.4	[12]104.8	[24]185.2

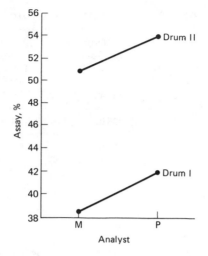

Figure 9.4. Data from Example 9.1, Table 9.1D. Analyst and drum vs. assay.

for each combination of variable A (batch) and variable C (drum) in Table 9.1a; e.g., for batch 23 and drum I, add 9.8 and 11.6 to get 21.4, based on four observations. Note that the row totals in Table 9.1c are equal to the row totals in Table 9.1b. Figure 9.3 is a plot of these data.

Table 9.1d is formed by summing the *different* levels of variable A (batch) for each combination of variable B (analyst) and variable C (drum) in Table 9.1a; e.g., for analyst M and drum I, add 9.8, 12.6, and 16.0 to get 38.4, based on six observations. Note that the row totals in Table 9.1d are equal to the column totals in Table 9.1b, and that the column totals in Table 9.1d are equal to the column totals in Table 9.1c. These data are shown in Figure 9.4. As noted, the numbers to the upper left of each entry in Tables 9.1a, 9.1b, 9.1c, and 9.1d are the number of observations summed in obtaining that entry. These numbers will be used in the calculations of the sums of squares. In this example we have three levels of variable A, two levels each of variables B and C, and duplicate determinations for each combination of the variables; obviously, these levels may be changed by appropriate expansion of the tables.

In the following calculations some of the same symbols are used for each table, and while they have the same value within each table, they may differ between tables.

Calculations based on Table 9.1, Coded Values: Total crude sum of squares, $CSS_T = \sum X_i^2$ where $X_i^2 =$ each entry in Table 9.1, squared:

$$CSS_T = 4.6^2 + 5.2^2 + 6.2^2 + \cdots + 10.0^2 = 1,478.700000$$

Correction factor, $CF = (grand\ total)^2/N$:

$$CF = 185.2^2/24 = 1{,}429.126667$$

Total sum of squares, $SS_T = CSS_T - CF$:

$$SS_T = 1{,}478.700000 - 1{,}429.126667 = 49.573333$$

Calculations based on Table 9.1a: Sum of squares for replicates,

$$SS_R = CSS_T - \frac{\sum X_i^2}{n}$$

where

X_i^2 = each entry in Table 9.1a squared
n = the number of observations comprising X_i

$$SS_R = 1{,}478.700000 - \frac{9.8^2 + 12.6^2 + \cdots + 19.6^2}{2} = 0.900000$$

Calculations based on Table 9.1b: Sum of squares, variable A (batch):

$$SS_A = \frac{r_1^2 + r_2^2 + \cdots}{n_r} - CF$$

where

r_i^2 = the square of the total of row r_i
n_r = the number of observations comprising r_i

$$SS_A = \frac{53.6^2 + 60.4^2 + 71.2^2}{8} - 1{,}429.12667$$

$$= 1{,}448.820000 - 1{,}429.126667 = 19.693333$$

Sum of squares, variable B (temperature):

$$SS_B = \frac{c_1^2 + c_2^2 + \cdots}{n_c} - CF$$

where

c_i^2 = the square of the total of column c_i
n_c = the number of observations comprising c_i

$$SS_B = \frac{89.2^2 + 96.0^2}{12} - 1,429.12667$$

$$= 1,431.053333 - 1,429.126666 = 1.926667$$

Sum of squares, interaction of variables A and B:

$$SS_{AB} = \frac{\sum X_i^2}{n_i} - CF - SS_A - SS_B$$

where

X_i^2 = each entry in Table 9.1b squared
n_i = the number of observations comprising X_i

$$SS_{AB} = \frac{25.6^2 + 29.0^2 + \cdots + 36.6^2}{4} - CF - SS_A - SS_B$$

$$= 1,450.760000 - 1,429.126667 - 19.693334 - 1.926666 = 0.013333$$

Calculations based on Table 9.1c: Sum of squares, variable C (catalyst concentration):

$$SS_C = \frac{c_1^2 + c_2^2 + \cdots}{n_c} - CF = \frac{80.4^2 + 104.8^2}{12} - CF$$

where

c_i^2 = the square of the total of values in column i
n_c = the number of observations comprising c_i

$$SS_C = 1,453.933333 - 1,429.126667 = 24.806666$$

Sum of squares, interaction of variables A and C:

$$SS_{AC} = \frac{\sum X_i^2}{n_i} - CF - SS_A - SS_C$$

where

X_i^2 = each entry in Table 9.1c squared
n_i = the number of observations comprising X_i

$$SS_{AC} = \frac{21.4^2 + 26.0^2 + 33.0^2 + \cdots + 36.2^2}{4} - CF - SS_A - SS_C$$

$$= 1{,}475.600000 - 1{,}429.12667 - 19.693334 - 24.806666 = 1.973333$$

Calculations based on Table 9.1d: Sum of squares, interaction of variables B and C:

$$SS_{BC} = \frac{\sum X_i^2}{n_i} - CF - SS_B - SS_C$$

where

X_i^2 = each entry in Table 9.1d squared
n_i = the number of observations comprising X_i

$$SS_{BC} = \frac{38.4^2 + 42.0^2 + 50.8^2 + 54.0^2}{6} - CF - SS_B - SS_C$$

$$= 1{,}455.866667 - 1{,}429.126667 - 1.926666 - 24.806666 = 0.00668$$

The last calculation, the sum of squares for the interaction of variables A, B, and C makes use of the previously calculated sum of squares:

$$SS_{ABC} = SS_T - SS_A - SS_B - SS_C - SS_{AB} - SS_{AC} - SS_{BC} - SS_R$$

$$= 49.573333 - 19.693333 - 1.926666 - 24.806666$$

$$- 0.013333 - 1.973333 - 0.006668 - 0.900000$$

$$= 0.253337$$

These sums of squares are used to form the analysis of variance table.

The general forms of the analysis of variance tables for random effects (all variables random), fixed effects (all variables except replicates fixed), and mixed effects models are given in Table 9.2. Inspection of the expected mean squares for the appropriate model will tell us which mean squares should be used in the F test to test each variable for significance. The expected mean

TABLE 9.2.   Expected Mean Square: Three-Way Classification.

SOURCE	SUM OF SQUARES	DF	MEAN SQUARE	EXPECTED MEAN SQUARE
1. All Fixed Variables:				
A	SS_A	$a - 1$	SS_A/DF	$bcr\sigma_A^2 + \sigma^2$
B	SS_B	$b - 1$	SS_B/DF	$acr\sigma_B^2 + \sigma^2$
C	SS_C	$c - 1$	SS_C/DF	$abr\sigma_C^2 + \sigma^2$
AB	SS_{AB}	$(a-1) \times (b-1)$	SS_{AB}/DF	$cr\sigma_{AB}^2 + \sigma^2$
BC	SS_{BC}	$(b-1) \times (c-1)$	SS_{BC}/DF	$ar\sigma_{BC}^2 + \sigma^2$
AC	SS_{AC}	$(a-1) \times (c-1)$	SS_{AC}/DF	$br\sigma_{AC}^2 + \sigma^2$
ABC	SS_{ABC}	$(a-1) \times (b-1) \times (c-1)$	SS_{ABC}/DF	$r\sigma_{ABC}^2 + \sigma^2$
Replicates	SS_R	$(r-1) \times abc$	SS_R/DF	σ^2
Total	SS_T	$(abcr) - 1$		
2. Variables B and C Fixed; Variable A Random:				
A	SS_A	$a - 1$	SS_A/DF	$bcr\sigma_A^2 + \sigma^2$
B	SS_B	$b - 1$	SS_B/DF	$acr\sigma_B^2 + cr\sigma_{AB}^2 + \sigma^2$
C	SS_C	$c - 1$	SS_C/DF	$abr\sigma_C^2 + br\sigma_{AC}^2 + \sigma^2$
AB	SS_{AB}	$(a-1) \times (b-1)$	SS_{AB}/DF	$cr\sigma_{AB}^2 + \sigma^2$
BC	SS_{BC}	$(b-1) \times (c-1)$	SS_{BC}/DF	$ar\sigma_{BC}^2 + r\sigma_{ABC}^2 + \sigma^2$
AC	SS_{AC}	$(a-1) \times (c-1)$	SS_{AC}/DF	$br\sigma_{AC}^2 + \sigma^2$
ABC	SS_{ABC}	$(a-1) \times (b-1) \times (c-1)$	SS_{ABC}/DF	$r\sigma_{ABC}^2 + \sigma^2$
Replicates	SS_R	$(r-1) \times abc$	SS_R/DF	σ^2
Total	SS_T	$(abcr) - 1$		
3. Variables C Fixed; Variables A and B Random:				
A	SS_A	$a - 1$	SS_A/DF	$bcr\sigma_A^2 + cr\sigma_{AB}^2 + \sigma^2$
B	SS_B	$b - 1$	SS_B/DF	$acr\sigma_B^2 + cr\sigma_{AB}^2 + \sigma^2$
C	SS_C	$c - 1$	SS_C/DF	$abr\sigma_C^2 + br\sigma_{AC}^2 + ar\sigma_{BC}^2 + r\sigma_{ABC}^2 + \sigma^2$
AB	SS_{AB}	$(a-1) \times (b-1)$	SS_{AB}/DF	$cr\sigma_{AB}^2 + \sigma^2$
AC	SS_{AC}	$(b-1) \times (c-1)$	SS_{AC}/DF	$br\sigma_{AC}^2 + r\sigma_{ABC}^2 + \sigma^2$

TABLE 9.2 (continued)

SOURCE	SUM OF SQUARES	DF	MEAN SQUARE	EXPECTED MEAN SQUARE
ABC	SS_{ABC}	$(a-1) \times$ $(b-1) \times$ $(c-1)$	SS_{ABC}/DF	$r\sigma^2_{ABC} + \sigma^2$
Replicates	SS_R	$(r-1) \times$ abc	SS_R/DF	σ^2
Total	SS_T	$(abcr) - 1$		

4. No Variables Fixed; All Variables Random:

A	SS_A	$a-1$	SS_A/DF	$bcr\sigma^2_A + cr\sigma^2_{AB} + br\sigma^2_{AC} + r\sigma^2_{ABC} + \sigma^2$
B	SS_B	$b-1$	SS_B/DF	$acr\sigma^2_B + cr\sigma^2_{AB} + ar\sigma^2_{BC} + r\sigma^2_{ABC} + \sigma^2$
C	SS_C	$c-1$	SS_C/DF	$abr\sigma^2_C + br\sigma^2_{AC} + ar\sigma^2_{BC} + r\sigma^2_{ABC} + \sigma^2$
AB	SS_{AB}	$(a-1) \times$ $(b-1)$	SS_{AB}/DF	$cr\sigma^2_{AB} + r\sigma^2_{ABC} + \sigma^2$
BC	SS_{BC}	$(b-1) \times$ $(c-1)$	SS_{BC}/DF	$ar\sigma^2_{BC} + r\sigma^2_{ABC} + \sigma^2$
AC	SS_{AC}	$(a-1) \times$ $(c-1)$	SS_{AC}/DF	$br\sigma^2_{AC} + r\sigma^2_{ABC} + \sigma^2$
ABC	SS_{ABC}	$(a-1) \times$ $(b-1) \times$ $(c-1)$	SS_{ABC}/DF	$r\sigma^2_{ABC} + \sigma^2$
Replicates	SS_R	$(r-1) \times$ abc	SS_R/DF	σ^2
Total	SS_T	$(abcr) - 1$		

5. Variable A Fixed; Variables B and C Random:

A	SS_A	$a-1$	SS_A/DF	$bcr\sigma^2_A + cr\sigma^2_{AB} + r\sigma^2_{ABC} + \sigma^2$
B	SS_B	$b-1$	SS_B/DF	$acr\sigma^2_B + ar\sigma^2_{BC} + \sigma^2$
C	SS_C	$c-1$	SS_C/DF	$abr\sigma^2_C + ar\sigma^2_{BC} + \sigma^2$
AB	SS_{AB}	$(a-1) \times$ $(b-1)$	SS_{AB}/DF	$cr\sigma^2_{AB} + r\sigma^2_{ABC} + \sigma^2$
AC	SS_{AC}	$(a-1) \times$ $(c-1)$	SS_{AC}/DF	$br\sigma^2_{AC} + r\sigma^2_{ABC} + \sigma^2$
ABC	SS_{ABC}	$(a-1) \times$ $(b-1) \times$ $(c-1)$	SS_{ABC}/DF	$r\sigma^2_{ABC} + \sigma^2$
Replicates	SS_R	$(r-1) \, abc$	SS_R/DF	σ^2
Total	SS_T	$(abcr) - 1$		

6. Variables A and B Fixed; Variable C Random:

A	SS_A	$a-1$	SS_A/DF	$bcr\sigma^2_A + br\sigma^2_{AC} + \sigma^2$
B	SS_B	$b-1$	SS_B/DF	$acr\sigma^2_B + ar\sigma^2_{BC} + \sigma^2$

TABLE 9.2 (continued)

SOURCE	SUM OF SQUARES	DF	MEAN SQUARE	EXPECTED MEAN SQUARE
C	SS_C	$c - 1$	SS_C/DF	$abr\sigma_C^2 + \sigma^2$
AB	SS_{AB}	$(a - 1) \times (b - 1)$	SS_{AB}/DF	$cr\sigma_{AB}^2 + r\sigma_{ABC}^2 + \sigma^2$
AC	SS_{AC}	$(a - 1) \times (c - 1)$	SS_{AC}/DF	$br\sigma_{AC}^2 + \sigma^2$
ABC	SS_{ABC}	$(a - 1) \times (b - 1) \times (c - 1)$	SS_{ABC}/DF	$r\sigma_{ABC}^2 + \sigma^2$
Replicates	SS_R	$(r - 1)\,abc$	SS_R/DF	σ^2
Total	SS_T	$(abcr) - 1$		

7. *Variables A and C Fixed; Variable B Random:*

A	SS_A	$a - 1$	SS_A/DF	$bcr\sigma_A^2 + cr\sigma_{AB}^2 + \sigma^2$
B	SS_B	$b - 1$	SS_B/DF	$acr\sigma_B^2 + \sigma^2$
C	SS_C	$c - 1$	SS_C/DF	$abr\sigma_C^2 + ar\sigma_{BC}^2 + \sigma^2$
AB	SS_{AB}	$(a - 1) \times (b - 1)$	SS_{AB}/DF	$cr\sigma_{AB}^2 + \sigma^2$
AC	SS_{AC}	$(a - 1) \times (c - 1)$	SS_{AC}/DF	$br\sigma_{AC}^2 + r\sigma_{ABC}^2 + \sigma^2$
ABC	SS_{ABC}	$(a - 1) \times (b - 1) \times (c - 1)$	SS_{ABC}/DF	$r\sigma_{ABC}^2 + \sigma^2$
Replicates	SS_R	$(r - 1)\,abc$	SS_R/DF	σ^2
Total	SS_T	$(abcr) - 1$		

8. *Variable B Fixed; Variables A and C Random:*

A	SS_A	$a - 1$	SS_A/DF	$bcr\sigma_A^2 + br\sigma_{AC}^2 + \sigma^2$
B	SS_B	$b - 1$	SS_B/DF	$acr\sigma_B^2 + cr\sigma_{AB}^2 + ar\sigma_{BC}^2 + r\sigma_{ABC}^2 + \sigma^2$
C	SS_C	$c - 1$	SS_C/DF	$abr\sigma_C^2 + br\sigma_{AC}^2 + \sigma^2$
AB	SS_{AB}	$(a - 1) \times (b - 1)$	SS_{AB}/DF	$cr\sigma_{AB}^2 + r\sigma_{ABC}^2 + \sigma^2$
AC	SS_{AC}	$(a - 1) \times (c - 1)$	SS_{AC}/DF	$br\sigma_{AC}^2 + \sigma^2$
ABC	SS_{ABC}	$(a - 1) \times (b - 1) \times (c - 1)$	SS_{ABC}/DF	$r\sigma_{ABC}^2 + \sigma^2$
Replicates	SS_R	$(r - 1)\,abc$	SS_R/DF	σ^2
Total	SS_T	$(abcr) - 1$		

a = number of levels of variable A
b = number of levels of variable B
c = number of levels of variable C
r = number of replicate determinations

squares for the fixed effects model are quite simple, consisting solely of the variance of the effect plus that for replicates. Therefore, each source's mean square is divided by the mean square for replicates to obtain the F value, which is compared with the critical value for F with the appropriate degrees of freedom. If there is no replication ($r = 1$), the third-order interaction term, ABC, is used as a measure of the analytical error.

In the case of the random effects model things get a bit more complicated if all the variables and their interactions are significant. We begin testing for significance by comparing the mean squares of ABC with that for replicates. The second-order interaction terms AB, BC, and AC are tested against ABC.

When we get ready to test the main variables, A, B, and C, for significance we find that the terms in the expected mean squares column of Table 9.2 for these variables contain combinations which are not found in any one expected mean square for the interactions or replicates. We must, therefore, use a combination of mean squares to test for significance of the main variables. Satterthwaite's procedure[1] is used to arrive at the proper combinations of mean squares for each test. For variable C:

$$F = \frac{\text{MS}_C + \text{MS}_{ABC}}{\text{MS}_{BC} + \text{MS}_{AC}}$$

The above equation for F, variable C, is obtained as follows: If we write out the terms of the expected mean squares used in the above F test, we get

$$\text{MS}_C = 12\sigma_C^2 + 6\sigma_{BC}^2 + 4\sigma_{AC}^2 + 2\sigma_{ABC}^2 + \sigma^2$$

$$\text{MS}_{ABC} = 2\sigma_{ABC}^2 + \sigma^2$$

$$\text{Sum} = 12\sigma_C^2 + 6\sigma_{BC}^2 + 4\sigma_{AC}^2 + 4\sigma_{ABC}^2 + \sigma^2$$

$$\text{MS}_{BC} = 6\sigma_{BC}^2 + 2\sigma_{ABC}^2 + \sigma^2$$

$$\text{MS}_{AC} = 4\sigma_{AC}^2 + 2\sigma_{ABC}^2 + \sigma^2$$

$$\text{Sum} = 4\sigma_{AC}^2 + 2\sigma_{ABC}^2 + 2\sigma^2$$

The terms in the expression for the sum of $\text{MS}_C + \text{MS}_{ABC}$ differ from those for the sum of $\text{MS}_{ABC} + \text{MS}_{AC}$ only in the term $12\sigma_C^2$. Thus, the ratio of these two sums will provide the proper F value for testing the significance of variable C. Similar sums for variables B and A are given below. The degrees of freedom for the numerator (p) and the denominator (q) are calculated as follows:

$$p = \frac{(MS_C + MS_{ABC})^2}{\dfrac{MS_C^2}{DF_C} + \dfrac{MS_{ABC}^2}{DF_{ABC}}}, \qquad q = \frac{(MS_{BC} + MS_{AC})^2}{\dfrac{MS_{BC}^2}{DF_{BC}} + \dfrac{MS_{AC}^2}{DF_{AC}}}$$

For variable B:

$$F = \frac{MS_B + MS_{ABC}}{MS_{AB} + MS_{BC}}$$

The degrees of freedom, p and q, are calculated by the following equations:

$$p = \frac{(MS_B + MS_{ABC})^2}{\dfrac{MS_B^2}{DF_B} + \dfrac{MS_{ABC}^2}{DF_{ABC}}}, \qquad q = \frac{(MS_{AB} + MS_{BC})^2}{\dfrac{MS_{AB}^2}{DF_{AB}} + \dfrac{MS_{BC}^2}{DF_{BC}}}$$

For variable A:

$$F = \frac{MS_A + MS_{ABC}}{MS_{AB} + MS_{AC}}$$

The degrees of freedom, p and q, are calculated by the following equations:

$$p = \frac{(MS_A + MS_{ABC})^2}{\dfrac{MS_A^2}{DF_A} + \dfrac{MS_{ABC}^2}{DF_{ABC}}}, \qquad q = \frac{(MS_{AB} + MS_{AC})^2}{\dfrac{MS_{AB}^2}{DF_{AB}} + \dfrac{MS_{AC}^2}{DF_{AC}}}$$

Since the testing of the variables for significance and determining their standard deviations for the fixed effects model is straight forward, we will proceed with our example in which all the variables are random. The analysis of variance table would then look like this:

Analysis of Variance.

SOURCE	SS		DF	MS	EXPECTED MEAN SQUARE
A (Batch)	SS_A	19.6933	2	9.8466	$8\sigma_A^2 + 4\sigma_{AC}^2 + 4\sigma_{AB}^2 + 2\sigma_{ABC}^2 + \sigma^2$
B (Analyst)	SS_B	1.9267	1	1.9267*	$12\sigma_B^2 + 6\sigma_{BC}^2 + 4\sigma_{AB}^2 + 2\sigma_{ABC}^2 + \sigma^2$
C (Drum)	SS_C	24.8067	1	24.8067*	$12\sigma_C^2 + 6\sigma_{BC}^2 + 4\sigma_{AB}^2 + 2\sigma_{ABC}^2 + \sigma^2$
AB	SS_{AB}	0.0133	2	0.0066	$4\sigma_{AB}^2 + 2\sigma_{ABC}^2 + \sigma^2$
BC	SS_{BC}	0.0067	1	0.0067	$6\sigma_{BC}^2 + 2\sigma_{ABC}^2 + \sigma^2$
AC	SS_{AC}	1.9733	2	0.9866*	$4\sigma_{AC}^2 + 2\sigma_{ABC}^2 + \sigma^2$
ABC	SS_{ABC}	0.2533	2	0.1266	$2\sigma_{ABC}^2 + \sigma^2$
Replicates	SS_R	0.9000	12	0.750	σ^2
Total	SS_T	49.5733	23		

First we test the third-order interaction, ABC, for significance:

$$F = 0.1266/0.0750 = 1.69, \qquad F_{0.05, 2, 12} = 3.89$$

Therefore, ABC is not shown to be significant.

Next we test the second-order interactions against ABC; however, since ABC was not shown to be significant, we combine the sum of squares and degrees of freedom for ABC and Replicates to obtain a new mean square for replicates: $(0.2533 + 0.9000)/14 = 0.08238$ and use it to test the significance of the other sources.

Interaction AC (Batch $\times$ Drum):

$$F = 0.9866/0.08238 = 11.98, \qquad F_{0.05, 2, 14} = 3.74$$

Therefore, AC is significant. This is consistent with Figure 9.3, in which the slopes for drums suggests an interaction.

Interaction BC (Analyst $\times$ Drum):

$$F = 0.0067/0.8238 = 0.08, \qquad F_{0.05, 1, 14} = 4.60$$

Thus, BC is not shown to be significant. The parallel lines for drums in Figure 9.4 support this conclusion.

Interaction AB (Batch $\times$ Analyst):

$$F = 0.0066/0.8238 = 0.08, \qquad F_{0.05, 2, 14} = 3.74$$

Thus, AB is not shown to be significant. In Figure 9.2 the nearly parallel lines for analysts suggest lack of interaction.

We next combine the sums of squares of the interactions not found to be significant with that for replicates to get a better estimate of the replicate variability: ABC, BC, AB, and Replicates.

$$MS_R = \frac{0.2533 + 0.0067 + 0.0133 + 0.0133 + 0.9000}{2 + 1 + 2 + 12} = 0.0690$$

We are now ready to test the main variables A, B, and C for significance. For variable C we use the equation for F based on Satterthwaithe's procedure:

$$F = \frac{MS_C + MS_{ABC}}{MS_{BC} + MS_{AC}} = \frac{24.8067 + 0.1266}{0.0067 + 0.9866} = 23.57$$

$$p = \frac{(MS_C + MS_{ABC})^2}{\dfrac{MS_C^2}{DF_C} + \dfrac{MS_{ABC}^2}{DF_{ABC}}} = \frac{(24.8067 + 0.1266)^2}{\dfrac{24.8067^2}{1} + \dfrac{0.1266^2}{2}} = \frac{621.6694}{615.3799}$$

$$= 1.01 \text{ or } 1$$

$$q = \frac{(MS_{BC} + MS_{AC})^2}{\dfrac{MS_{BC}^2}{DF_{BC}} + \dfrac{MS_{AC}^2}{DF_{AC}}} = \frac{(0.0067 + 0.9866)^2}{\dfrac{0.0067^2}{1} + \dfrac{0.9866^2}{2}} = \frac{0.98664}{0.48710}$$

$$= 2.02, \text{ or } 2$$

$F_{0.05,1,2} = 18.5$. Thus variable C is significant at $\alpha = 0.05$.

In the above equations, the values of MS_{ABC} and MS_{BC} from the ANOVA table are used even though they were not found to be significant. Using the pooled MS_R (0.0690) in their place would cause the same MS to appear in both the numerator and denominator of the Satterthwaithe F test. This would destroy the basis of the test, i.e., the independence of the numerator and denominator.

In a similar manner we test variable B for significance:

$$F = \frac{MS_B + MS_{ABC}}{MS_{AB} + MS_{BC}} = \frac{1.9267 + 0.1266}{0.0066 + 0.0067} = 154.4$$

$$p = \frac{(MS_B + MS_{ABC})^2}{\dfrac{MS_B^2}{DF_B} + \dfrac{MS_{BC}^2}{DF_{BC}}} = \frac{2.0533^2}{\dfrac{1.9267^2}{1} + \dfrac{0.1266^2}{2}} = 1.13, \text{ or } 1$$

$$q = \frac{(MS_{AB} + MS_{BC})^2}{\dfrac{MS_{AB}^2}{DF_{AB}} + \dfrac{MS_{BC}^2}{DF_{BC}}} = \frac{0.0133^2}{\dfrac{0.0066^2}{2} + \dfrac{0.0067^2}{1}} = 2.65, \text{ or } 3$$

$F_{0.05,1,3} = 10.1$. Thus, variable B is significant at $\alpha = 0.05$.

Likewise, variable A is tested for significance:

$$F = \frac{MS_A + MS_{ABC}}{MS_{AB} + MS_{AC}} = \frac{9.8466 + 0.1266}{0.0066 + 0.9866} = 10.04$$

$$p = \frac{(MS_A + MS_{ABC})^2}{\dfrac{MS_A^2}{DF_A} + \dfrac{MS_{ABC}^2}{DF_{ABC}}} = \frac{9.9743^2}{\dfrac{9.8466^2}{2} + \dfrac{0.1266^2}{2}} = 2.05, \text{ or } 2$$

$$q = \frac{(MS_{AB} + MS_{AC})^2}{\dfrac{MS_{AB}^2}{DF_{AB}} + \dfrac{MS_{AC}^2}{DF_{AC}}} = \frac{0.9932^2}{\dfrac{0.0066^2}{2} + \dfrac{0.9866^2}{2}} = 2.03, \text{ or } 2$$

$F_{0.05,2,2} = 19.00$. Thus, variable A is not shown to be significant.

We may also calculate the standard deviations for each of the significant variables. Here we use the pooled $MS_R = 0.0690$ (which is composed of the sum of squares for replicates, ABC, BC, and AB) to obtain the best estimates of the standard deviations:

$$s_R = \sqrt{0.0690} = 0.2627, \ 17 \ DF$$

$$s_{AC} = \sqrt{(MS_{AC} - MS_{ABC})/br} = \sqrt{(MS_{AC} - MS_R)/br}$$

$$= \sqrt{\frac{0.9866 - 0.0690}{4}} = \sqrt{0.22940} = 0.4790, \ 2 \ DF$$

$$s_C = \sqrt{\frac{MS_C + MS_{ABC} - MS_{BC} - MS_{AC}}{abr}} = \sqrt{\frac{MS_C + MS_R - MS_R - MS_{AC}}{abr}}$$

$$= \sqrt{\frac{24.8067 + 0.0690 - 0.0690 - 0.9866}{12}} = \sqrt{1.985008}$$

$$= 1.4089, \ 1 \ DF$$

$$s_B = \sqrt{\frac{MS_B + MS_{ABC} - MS_{AB} - MS_{BC}}{acr}} = \sqrt{\frac{MS_B + MS_R - MS_R - MS_R}{acr}}$$

$$= \sqrt{\frac{1.9267 + 0.0690 - 0.0690 - 0.0690}{12}} = \sqrt{0.154808}$$

$$= 0.3935, \ 1 \ DF$$

Thus, based on the 24 yields, we have established that for the levels covered, variables B (analysts), C (drums), and the AC interaction are significant at $\alpha = 0.05$. In addition to identifying the significant variables, we have obtained estimates of their standard deviations and of the analytical procedure:

SIGNIFICANT SOURCES	VARIANCE	% OF TOTAL VARIANCE	STANDARD DEVIATION	DEGREES OF FREEDOM
B (Analysts)	0.154808	6.4	0.3935	1
C (Drums)	1.985008	81.4	1.4089	1
AC (Interaction)	0.229400	9.4	0.4790	2
Replication	0.069000	2.8	0.2627	17
	2.438216	100.0		

The variability between drums accounts for most of the total variance (81.4%), followed by interaction (9.4%). The replication variance, which is a measure of the analytical variability, is the smallest at 2.8% of the total. The variance due to analysts is also relatively small (6.4%). These results indicate that perhaps more thorough mixing of the product is needed before filling the drums. Little would be gained by trying to improve the analytical method or providing better training for the analysts. The significant batch-drum inter-action effect suggests that an unidentified variable may be affecting the results. A review of the process might identify other potentially significant variables. These could then be tested with another set of experiments.

9.1   LATIN SQUARES

The Latin square experimental design is a special form of the block (or crossed) design by which three variables may be evaluated. All of the examples we have discussed so far in the analysis of variance have been of this type, in which each level of each variable is crossed with, or has a corresponding value at, each level of every other variable. In Example 9.1, for each batch number there is a corresponding level for analyst and for drum number. The second primary type of design, the hierarchical, will be discussed in Chapter 11. The usual assumption that the variables are independent applies to Latin squares also.

Another way of saying this is that any interaction of the variables is small in comparison to the main effects. In a Latin square there are the same number of levels for each variable. The responses form a square with one variable being assigned to the columns, the second variable to the rows, and the third variable being assigned to a lettered position within the square:

Variable	Variable 1		
2	1	2	3
I	aA	bB	cC
II	dB	eC	fA
III	gC	hA	iB

In the above square the three levels of the third variable are indicated by the capital letters; the lower case letters denote the values of the response. The assignment of the capital letters is subject to the restriction that each level of the third variable must appear once, and only once, in each row and each column. The arrangement shown above is one of twelve which satisfies this restriction for a 3×3 Latin square. The use of Latin letters in the square is the origin of the name "Latin squares". Although the example above is a 3×3

square, a Latin square design may have any reasonable dimension. In any Latin square there must be the same number of levels for each variable as the dimension; thus a 6×6 square will have six levels for each of the three variables.

The interaction of variables 1 and 2 in the 3×3 square provides an estimate of the variance of the measurements, or experimental error. This is the reason for the earlier statement that interactions must be small. If there is a high degree of interaction, the estimate of error is inflated. The variables usually studied in a chemical process (concentrations, temperatures, flow rates, etc.) may not be independent of each other, and if there is a significant amount of dependency, the Latin square design is not well suited to detect any but the largest effects. Latin squares are generally suited to evaluating variables in test methods where interactions of the variables are usually small. Latin square designs are also useful when we have two sources over which we have little or no control, but which affect our results. An example is the crucibles in Example 9.2 below; other examples might include apparatus, positions of a machine, operators, runs, days, etc.

The procedure used in analyzing a Latin square design is similar to that already discussed and is most easily explained by an example.

EXAMPLE 9.2. A study of the effect of the drying oven temperature on the results of a gravimetric determination of chlorides as silver chloride was made. The length of time the precipitated silver chloride was allowed to coagulate, and the variability of the Gooch crucibles used to collect and weigh the precipitate were the other two variables of interest. Three drying oven temperatures, three coagulation times, and three crucibles were selected. The same size aliquot was used for all samples and all other known factors were kept as constant as possible during the runs. The data, which consist of the weights of precipitated silver chloride in milligrams, are given in the following table. The capital letters A, B, and C, beside each weight refer to the level of oven temperature used. The data are plotted in Figure 9.5.

LATIN SQUARE.

COAGULATION TIME	CRUCIBLE NUMBER		
	1	2	3
I	A 380	B 392	C 411
II	B 400	C 400	A 380
III	C 424	A 384	B 404

The Latin square design is analyzed in the following steps.

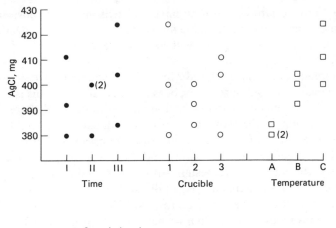

● Coagulation time
○ Crucible number
□ Oven Temperature

Figure 9.5. Data from Example 9.2.

First, we perform the following additions:

Sum of values for crucible 1 = 1,204 (C_1)
Sum of values for crucible 2 = 1,176 (C_2)
Sum of values for crucible 3 = 1,195 (C_3)

Total of column values   = 3,575 (grand total)

Sum of values for coagulation time I   = 1,183 (R_1)
Sum of values for coagulation time II = 1,180 (R_2)
Sum of values for coagulation time III = 1,212 (R_3)

Total of row values   = 3,575

Sum of values for oven temperature A = 1,144 (T_1)
Sum of values for oven temperature B = 1,196 (T_2)
Sum of values for oven temperature C = 1,235 (T_3)

Total of treatment values   = 3,575

Next, the above totals are used in obtaining the sums of squares:
Correction factor, CF = (grand total)^2/N = 3,575^2/9 = 1,420,069.4440

Sum of squares for columns (crucibles):

$$SS_c = \frac{C_1^2 + C_2^2 + C_3^2}{n_c} - CF = \frac{1204^2 + 1176^2 + 1195^2}{3} - CF$$

$$= 1{,}420{,}205.6670 - 1{,}420{,}069.4440 = 136.2227$$

Sum of squares for rows (coagulation time):

$$SS_r = \frac{R_1^2 + R_2^2 + R_3^2}{n_r} - CF = \frac{1183^2 + 1180^2 + 1212^2}{3} - CF$$

$$= 1{,}420{,}277.6670 - 1{,}420{,}069.4440 = 208.2227$$

Sum of squares for treatment (oven temperature), SS_t:

$$SS_t = \frac{T_1^2 + T_2^2 + T_3^2}{n_t} - CF = \frac{1144^2 + 1196^2 + 1235^2}{3} - CF$$

$$= 1{,}421{,}459.0000 - 1{,}420{,}069.4440 = 1{,}389.5560$$

Total sum of squares:

$$SS_{tt} = \sum X^2 - CF \text{ (where } X^2 = \text{each individual value squared)}$$

$$= 380^2 + 400^2 + \cdots + 404^2 - CF$$

$$= 1{,}421{,}833.0000 - 1{,}420{,}069.4440 = 1{,}763.5560$$

Sum of squares for residual (error) or interaction:

$$SS_e = SS_{tt} - SS_c - SS_r - SS_t$$

$$= 1{,}763.5560 - 136.2227 - 208.2227 - 1{,}389.5560$$

$$= 29.5545$$

The above sums of squares are used in the analysis of variance table. The general form for Latin squares is:

Analysis of Variance

SOURCE	SS	DF	MS	EXPECTED MEAN SQUARE
Between columns	SS_c	$m - 1$	$SS_c/m - 1$	$\sigma^2 + m\sigma_c^2$
Between rows	SS_r	$m - 1$	$SS_r/m - 1$	$\sigma^2 + m\sigma_r^2$
Between treatment	SS_t	$m - 1$	$SS_t/m - 1$	$\sigma^2 + m\sigma_t^2$
Residual (error)	SS_e	$(m - 1)(m - 2)$	$SS_e/(m - 1)(m - 2)$	σ^2
Total	SS_{tt}	$m^2 - 1$		

where m is the number of levels of the variables. For our example the table would be:

Analysis of Variance

SOURCE	SS	DF	MS	F RATIO	EMS
Between crucibles	136.2227	2	68.1114	4.61 NS	$\sigma^2 + 3\sigma_c^2$
Between coagulation times	208.2227	2	104.1114	7.05 NS	$\sigma^2 + 3\sigma_r^2$
Between oven temperatures	1,389.5560	2	694.7780	47.04*	$\sigma^2 + 3\sigma_t^2$
Residual (error)	29.5545	2	14.7772		σ^2
Total	1,763.5560	8		$F_{0.05,2,2} = 19.00$	

The values in the F ratio column indicate that only the drying oven temperature has a significant effect. We may, therefore, combine the sums of squares for the other effects with the residual to obtain a better estimate of the mean square error:

$$\frac{136.2227 + 208.2227 + 29.5545}{2 + 2 + 2} = 62.3333$$

The standard deviation for the error is

$$s_e = \sqrt{62.3333} = 7.90 \text{ with 6 DF}$$

The standard deviation for the oven temperature effect is

$$s_t = \sqrt{\frac{694.7780 - 62.3333}{3}} = \sqrt{210.8149} = 14.52 \text{ with 2 DF}$$

Note that with only nine analyses we have been able to determine which of three variables were significant and to estimate the effects (their standard deviations or variances) of the significant variables. This represents a considerable saving in effort, time, and costs as compared with a regular full scale block design which for three levels each of three variables would require $3 \times 3 \times 3$ or 27 analyses without any replication. Of course we pay a price for the savings: (1) We have no measure of the significance of any interaction; indeed, recall that one of the assumptions of the Latin square design is that interaction is absent or very small. (2) With only three levels we have only two degrees of freedom associated with each variable.

9.2. SUMMARY

In this chapter we have learned how to use ANOVA on problems in which we have three independent variables. We also learned how to use the Latin square design on three-way classification problems in which no or limited interaction was expected between the variables. We saw how use of the Latin square reduced the number of analyses requiring for an ANOVA. In the next chapter we will explore ways of handling problems with four variables.

9.3. PROBLEMS

Problems 13, 23, and 24 will enable you to try your hand at applying ANOVA to three-way classifications.

REFERENCE

1. Searle, S. R., *Linear Models*, pp. 411–413. New York, NY: John Wiley and Sons, 1971.

Chapter 10
COMPARISON OF MORE THAN TWO AVERAGES: ANALYSIS OF VARIANCE FOR FOUR INDEPENDENT VARIABLES

OVERVIEW

You may have noticed that the use of block experimental designs, such as we have considered thus far, requires a rapid increase in the number of analyses as we increase the number of variables being studied. One answer to this situation is to restrict each variable to only two levels. This type of design, called the 2^n factorial, is the subject of this chapter. The 2^n factorial, where n is the number of variables, is particularly suited to screening studies where we desire to see which of a relatively large number of variables exert a major influence on the dependent variables.

10.0 REDUCING THE NUMBER OF ANALYSES WITH A FACTORIAL DESIGN

Theoretically, any number of variables can be studied for their effects by the analysis of variance. However, the block (or crossed) design of experiments, such as we have been considering, results in an exponential increase in the number of experiments with the number of variables and their levels. In Chapter 9 we saw that if we had three variables at three levels each, 3^3 or 27 experiments were required, although some information might be gained from only nine if the Latin square design were used. If we wish to consider four variables at four levels, 4^4 or 256 experiments would be needed.

To reduce the number of experiments when more than three variables are of interest, it is common to investigate only two levels of each variable. This type of experimental design is known as a 2^n factorial, where n is the number of independent variables. In the case of four variables, this requires only 2^4 or 16 experiments—a much more manageable number.

Another way of reducing the number of experiments when many variables are of interest is to use fractional factorial designs. This technique is beyond the scope of this text, but there are excellent texts which treat the design of experiments at greater length than is possible here. A few such texts are listed under Resources at the end of this chapter. Computer programs are frequently used to reduce the effort of analyzing the data. Consultation with a statistician is always a good idea, and it is highly advised *before* undertaking the considerable time and effort required for the larger studies. By now the reason for stressing "before" should be obvious.

A disadvantage of the 2^n factorial design is that with only two levels for each factor, we cannot detect nonlinearity in the response.

The analysis of variance technique is used to decide which effects are significant in a 2^n factorial design. The mechanics of the technique are different from those we have used up to now, and they can be explained most easily by an example which is given in the next section.

10.1 MEASURING THE EFFECT OF TWO LEVELS OF FOUR VARIABLES ON AVERAGES (2^4 FACTORIAL DESIGN)

The following example illustrates the ANOVA procedure for a design of four variables at two levels, a 2^4 factorial design. The procedure is easily adaptable to other values of n, as illustrated in the next section.

EXAMPLE 10.1. In an investigation of the thiocyanate colorimetric method for determining iron, the chemist was interested in the effects of the following variables on the amount of color developed for a fixed amount of iron:

A = Concentration of nitric acid at $0.1N$ and $0.5N$
B = Reaction time of 5 and 15 minutes
C = Reaction temperatures of 20 and 30 C
D = Concentration of KCNS reagent at $0.1M$ and $0.3M$

Each combination was tested only once, and the tests were performed in a random order to minimize or eliminate any effects of other variables which might change with time. The data obtained are summarized in Table 10.1.

In the table the lower case letters indicate values obtained with the high level of that variable. Absence of a lower case letter indicates the low level of the variable, and "(l)" indicates that all variables are at the low level.

The data are entered in column II of Table 10.2, alongside their treatment combinations in column I, lines 1 through 16. The total of the absorbances is entered in column II of line 17.

The values in column III are obtained by adding and subtracting the absorbances in column II as indicated by the signs given in Table 13 (Appendix

TABLE 10.1.   Absorbances, Example 10.1.

Time	B, 5 min.				b, B, 15 min.			
Temp.	C, 20 C		c, C, 30 C		C, 20 C		c, C, 30 C	
KCNS	D, 0.1M	d, D, 0.3M	D, 0.1M	d, D, 0.3M	D, 0.1M	d, D, 0.3M	D, 0.1M	d, D, 0.3M
A, HNO₃, 0.1N,	(l), 0.140	d, 0.150	c, 0.135	cd, 0.153	b, 0.126	bd, 0.137	bc, 0.122	bcd, 0.138
a, A, HNO₃, 0.5N,	a, 0.135	ad, 0.146	ac, 0.141	acd, 0.142	ab, 0.120	abd, 0.131	abc, 0.127	abcd, 0.128

TABLE 10.2.   Calculations for Example 10.1.

I TREATMENT COMBINATION	II ABS.	III SUM	IV EFFECT: COL. III/8	V SUM OF SQUARES: $(\text{COL. III})^2/16$
1 (l)	0.140	2.171 = total		
2 a (HNO$_3$)	0.135	−0.031 = 8A	−0.003875	0.0000600625
3 b (time)	0.126	−0.113 = 8B	−0.014125	0.0007980625
4 ab	0.120	−0.003 = 8AB	−0.000375	0.0000005625
5 c (temp.)	0.135	0.001 = 8C	0.000125	0.0000000625
6 ac	0.141	0.011 = 8AC	0.001375	0.0000075625
7 bc	0.122	0.001 = 8BC	0.000125	0.0000000625
8 abc	0.127	0.003 = 8ABC	0.000375	0.0000005625
9 d (KCNS)	0.150	0.079 = 8D	0.009875	0.0003900625
10 ad	0.146	−0.031 = 8AD	−0.003875	0.0000600625
11 bd	0.137	−0.001 = 8BD	−0.000125	0.0000000625
12 abd	0.131	0.001 = 8ABD	0.000125	0.0000000625
13 cd	0.153	−0.007 = 8CD	−0.000875	0.0000030625
14 acd	0.142	−0.033 = 8ACD	−0.114125	0.0000680625
15 bcd	0.138	−0.003 = 8BCD	−0.000375	0.0000005625
16 $abcd$	0.128	0.003 = 8$ABCD$	0.000375	0.0000005625
17 Total	2.171			0.0013894375

D). The value in column III for treatment combination (l) is merely the total sum of the absorbances because all the signs in column T of Table 13 are +'s. The value in column III for treatment combination a is calculated as follows, using the signs in column A of Table 13:

Sum A $= -0.140 + 0.135 - 0.126 + 0.120 - 0.135 + 0.141 - 0.122 + 0.127$

$- 0.150 + 0.146 - 0.137 + 0.131 - 0.153 + 0.142 - 0.138 + 0.128$

$= -0.031$

Likewise, the value for treatment combination b is calculated using the signs in column B of Table 13:

Sum B $= -0.140 - 0.135 + 0.126 + 0.120 - 0.135 - 0.141 + 0.122 + 0.127$

$- 0.150 - 0.146 + 0.137 + 0.131 - 0.153 - 0.142 + 0.138 + 0.128$

$= -0.113$

The remaining values in column III are calculated in like manner.

TABLE 10.3.   Analysis of Variance for Example 10.1.

	SOURCE	DF	MEAN SQUARE	F RATIO	$F_{0.05,15} = 6.61$ $F_{0.01,1,5} = 16.3$
A	HNO$_3$ concentration	1	0.0000600625	4.30	Not significant
B	Reaction time	1	0.0007980625	57.16	Significant
C	Reaction temp.	1	0.0000000625	0.004	Not significant
D	KCNS concentration	1	0.0003900625	27.94	Significant
	Interaction AB	1	0.0000005625	0.04	Not significant
	Interaction AC	1	0.0000075625	0.54	Not significant
	Interaction AD	1	0.0000600625	4.30	Not significant
	Interaction BC	1	0.0000000625	0.004	Not significant
	Interaction BD	1	0.0000000625	0.004	Not significant
	Interaction CD	1	0.0000030625	0.22	Not significant
	Error[a]	5	0.0000139625		
Total		15			

[a] The error term is composed of the third- and fourth-order interactions:

ABC	0.0000005625
ABD	0.0000000625
ACD	0.0000680625
BCD	0.0000005625
ABCD	0.0000005625

Error	0.0000698125/5 = 0.0000139625

The values in column IV, effect, are obtained by dividing each corresponding value in column III by 8 which is the number of times each variable is represented at one level in the set of data. For example, variable A appears at its high level in half of the 16 values in Table 10.1 (those marked a, ad, ac, acd, ab, abd, abc, and $abcd$).

The values in column V, sum of squares, are obtained by squaring each value in column III and then dividing by 16, the number of values in the set of data.

The ANOVA table, Table 10.3, is prepared using columns I and V of Table 10.2 for the source and mean square columns. Note that, except for the error term, the mean square in this case equals the sum of squares because the degrees of freedom is one.

Since each combination of variables was tested only once (no replicates), there is no direct estimate of experimental error variance by which the significance of the effects may be judged. It is common in non-replicated experiments to use some or all of the interaction mean squares as an estimate of the error variance, as was done in the error entry in Table 10.3. The decision as to which interaction terms are likely to be small enough to be used for estimating the error should be made before the experiment is done, based on the order of the interaction and a theoretical knowledge of the factors involved.

The values for the degrees of freedom given in Table 10.3 are calculated in the usual manner: For each main effect (variables A, B, and C) the degrees of freedom is the number of levels of the variable minus one, or $2 - 1 = 1$. The degrees of freedom for each interaction is the product of the degrees of freedom for each variable represented; e.g., for interaction AB the degrees of freedom equals the degrees of freedom for variable A multiplied by that for variable B, or $1 \times 1 = 1$.

In this design all the variables are considered to be fixed because their levels represent arbitrary choices rather than random selections. The expected mean square for each source (except error) consists of the error variance plus a second term. This term is a sum of squares divided by the degrees of freedom and is similar to a variance. Thus, the ratio of the mean square for each variable and interaction to the error mean square is used in the F-test for significance.

When we test the significance of all 15 mean squares in a 2^4 experiment at $\alpha = 0.05$, there is a chance of about one in two that one or two of the F-tests will be significant even if none of the factors have any real effect. Therefore, Davies[1] has suggested that if only one out of six or more F values just reaches the critical value at $\alpha = 0.05$, that factor should be regarded only as tentatively significant. A larger, more sensitive experiment can be performed to confirm that factor's significance. If a mean square is significant at $\alpha = 0.01$, the factor may be considered to have a real effect.

The ANOVA table's F values indicate that only variables B (reaction time) and D (KCNS concentration) are significant at the $\alpha = 0.01$ significance level. None of second-order interactions are significant. The magnitudes and signs of the significant variables in the effect column (column IV) of Table 10.2 indicate that the amount of color fades (decreased absorbance values) with time and increases with increasing concentration of potassium thiocyanate over the ranges studied.

The absorbance for any of the combinations of conditions used in the study may be estimated. For example, the best estimate of the absorbance using the high level of the thiocyanate ($0.3M$) and the low level of reaction time (5 minutes) is obtained by substituting the values for d and b in column III of Table 10.2 in the following equation (the values of the other terms in the equation are taken to be zero because their effects were not found to be significant):

$$\text{Absorbance} = (\text{total} - a - b + ab - c + ac + bc - abc + d$$

$$- ad - bd + abd - cd + acd + bcd - abcd)/16$$

$$= (2.171 - 0 + 0.113 + 0 - 0 + 0 + 0 - 0$$

$$+ 0.079 - 0 - 0 + 0 - 0 + 0 - 0)/16$$

$$= 0.148$$

The terms and their signs used in the equation are obtained from row d of the table for main effects and interactions in up to a 2^4 factorial design (Table 13, Appendix D).

In the above example, if we had found all the variables to be significant, and consequently had used all of the values from column III of Table 10.2 in the above equation, the absorbance would have been calculated to be 0.150, which is the same value recorded for d in column II, row 9 of Table 10.2.

If further optimization of the two significant variables is desired, additional experiments at other levels of just these two variables can be performed.

10.2 2^n FACTORIAL WITH REPLICATION

The analysis of a 2^n factorial with m replicates is not complicated. First, we determine the sum of the replicate observations for each combination. This gives us a 2^n factorial design in which each result is the sum of the replicated observations. These summed values are then arranged in the same fashion as was done in the preceding section for the 2^4 factorial. If there are m replicates, the effects are divided by m. The same is true for the mean squares.

An additional mean square is obtained from the repeats for each combination of conditions. This is easily calculated as the difference between the sum of squares for the $2^n - 1$ variables and the total sum of squares of all $m \times n^2$ individual observations. If duplicate determinations are made, the sum of squares of these differences can be used, just as was done in calculating the variance of paired values.

EXAMPLE 10.2. If in Example 10.1 we consider variable C (reaction temperature) as a replication because its effect was not significant, and add the duplicate values together, we get the absorbance values shown in Table 10.4. The lower case letters in Table 10.4 have the same meaning that they had in Table 10.1 for Example 10.1.

TABLE 10.4. Absorbances, Example 10.2.

	(1), B, 5 min.		b, B, 15 min	
	(1), D, 0.1M KCNS	d, D, 0.3M KCNS	(1), D, 0.1M KCNS	d, D, 0.3M KCNS
HNO_3, 0.1N, A	(1), 0.275	d, 0.303	b, 0.248	bd, 0.275
HNO_3, 0.5N, A	a, 0.276	ad, 0.288	ab, 0.247	abd, 0.259

TABLE 10.5. Calculations for Example 10.2.

I TREATMENT COMBINATION	II ABS.	III SUM	IV EFFECT: COL. III/8	V SUM OF SQUARES: (COL. III)^2/16
1 (1)	0.275	2.171 = total		
2 a (HNO_3)	0.276	−0.031 = 4A	−0.003875	0.0000600625
3 b (time)	0.248	−0.113 = 4B	−0.014125	0.0007980625
4 ab	0.247	−0.003 = 4AB	−0.000375	0.0000005625
5 d (KCNS)	0.303	0.079 = 4D	0.009875	0.0003900625
6 ad	0.288	−0.031 = 4AD	0.003875	0.0000600625
7 bd	0.275	−0.001 = 4BD	−0.000125	0.0000000625
8 abd	0.259	0.001 = 4ABD	0.000125	0.0000000625
9 Total	2.171			0.0013089375

Since we have eliminated one variable (reaction time) by making it a duplicate set of measurements, we now have a 2^3 factorial, and we proceed to analyze the data in the same fashion as we did in Example 10.1. This information is summarized in Table 10.5.

Note: The demoninators 8 and 16 in columns IV and V of Table 10.5 would be expected to be 4 and 8, based on the number of times each variable is represented at one level and the number of values in the set of data in Table 10.4. However, each value in Table 10.4 is the sum of duplicates, and thus represents two values. Therefore, we double 4 and 8 and arrive at the denominators used in Table 10.5.

Using the results from Table 10.5, we form an analysis of variance table (Table 10.6) in the same fashion as previously.

TABLE 10.6.   Analysis of Variance, Example 10.2.

	SOURCE	SS	DF	MEAN SQUARE	F RATIO
A	HNO$_3$ concentration	0.0000600625	1	0.0000600625	5.97 *
B	Reaction time	0.0007980625	1	0.0007980625	79.31 **
D	KCNS concentration	0.0003900625	1	0.0003900625	38.76 **
	Interaction AB	0.0000005625	1	0.0000005625	0.06 NS
	Interaction AD	0.0000600625	1	0.0000600625	5.96 *
	Interaction BD	0.0000000625	1	0.0000000625	0.01 NS
	Interaction ABD	0.0000000625	1	0.0000000625	0.01 NS
Subtotal		0.0013089375	7		
Duplicates		0.0000805000	8	0.0000100625	
Total		0.0013894375	15	$F_{0.05,1,8} = 5.32$	
				$F_{0.01,1,8} = 11.26$	

The sums of squares (SS) for all entries except the duplicates and total are taken directly from Table 10.5. The total sum of squares is obtained by squaring each individual observation (each value in Table 10.1), summing, and subtracting from the sum the grand total squared and divided by the number of observations:

$$(0.140^2 + 0.135^2 + \cdots + 0.128^2) - (2.171^2/16)$$

$$= 0.295967 - 0.2945775625 = 0.0013894375$$

The sum of squares for duplicates is most easily obtained by taking the difference between the total and subtotal sums of squares. However, it may be calculated by determining the sums of squares for each set of replicates and summing these. In the case of duplicate determinations, this calculation reduces to taking the difference between each pair of results, squaring each difference, summing the squared values, and dividing by 2:

$$\frac{(0.140 - 0.135)^2 + (0.135 - 0.141)^2 + \cdots + (0.131 - 0.128)^2}{2} = 0.000080500$$

The F ratios are obtained by dividing each mean square by the mean square for duplicates. The critical values are $F_{0.05,1,8} = 5.32$ and $F_{0.01,1,8} = 11.26$. As indicated by the double asterisk, the reaction time and thiocyanate concentration are significant variables at the $\alpha = 0.01$ significance level, and the nitric acid concentration and the interaction of nitric acid and thiocyanate are significant at the $\alpha = 0.05$ significance level.

The effect column in Table 10.5 indicates:

- Lower concentration of nitric acid and shorter reaction time produces a higher absorbance,
- The interaction of nitric acid and time indicates the combined effect of these variables is greater at their lower values, and
- Higher concentration of thiocyanate produces a higher absorbance.

The best estimate of the absorbance using the high level of thiocyanate and the low level of nitric acid and time is given by the following equation, whose terms are obtained from line c of Table 13 of Appendix D (line c is used instead of line d because when we eliminated the c effect by making it a duplicate, the d effect actually became the new c effect):

$$\text{Absorbance} = (\text{total} -a - b + ab + d - ad - bd + abd)/8$$

(The d's in the equation are c's in Table 13, for the reason just given.)

Substituting the corresponding values from column III of Table 10.5 for total, nitric acid, time, thiocyanate, and the nitric acid-thiocyanate interaction, we get

$$\text{Absorbance} = (2.171 - (-0.031) - (-0.113) + 0 + 0.079$$

$$- (-0.031) - 0 + 0)/8$$

$$= 0.3031$$

The other effects are set equal to zero because they were not found to be significant.

10.3 SUMMARY

We have learned how to apply ANOVA to 2^n factorial designs. These designs do not require as many experiments per variable as the block designs we have previously used. Therefore, they are frequently used to screen a relatively large number of variables for significance.

10.4 PROBLEMS

Problem 25 will enable you to practice applying ANOVA to a 2^n factorial situation.

RESOURCES

Box, G. E. P., Hunter, W. G., and Hunter, J. S., *Statistics for Experimenters.* New York, NY: John Wiley & Sons, 1978.

Daniel, C., *Applications of Statistics to Industrial Experimentation.* New York, NY: John Wiley and Sons, 1976.

Davies, O. L., ed., *Design and Analysis of Industrial Experiments,* 2nd. ed. New York, NY: Longman, 1978.

Natrella, M. G., *NBS Handbook 91, Experimental Statistics.* Washington, DC: U. S. Government Printing Office, 1963.

REFERENCE

1. Davies, O. L., ed., *Design and Analysis of Industrial Experiments.* New York, NY: Hafner Publishing Company, 1956, p. 285.

Chapter 11
COMPARING MORE THAN TWO AVERAGES: ANALYSIS OF VARIANCE OF NESTED DESIGNS

OVERVIEW

This chapter introduces a different type of experimental design: the nested (or hierarchical) design. The differences between cross and nested designs are discussed as are the resulting consequences. The use of analysis of variance for the nested design is described for a typical application—an interlaboratory study of a method of analysis for precision.

11.0 INTERLABORATORY PRECISION STUDIES USING NESTED (OR HIERARCHICAL) DESIGNS

Up to now we have been considering one type of experimental design: the crossed or factorial design. The following table illustrates this type of design:

SAMPLE	INSTRUMENT	RUN	ANALYST 1	ANALYST 2	ANALYST 3	ANALYST 4
A	Spectrophotometer	1				
		2				
	Colorimeter	1				
		2				
B	Spectrophotometer	1				
		2				
	Colorimeter	1				
		2				

Note that in the crossed design each level of each factor is crossed with each level of every other factor, i.e., each of the four analysts uses the spectrophotometer on samples *A* and *B* to make two runs, and each of the two instruments is used by each analyst. As a consequence of this crossing of effects there is the possibility of interaction, for example, between analysts and instruments.

Now let us consider a different arrangement of the above factors:

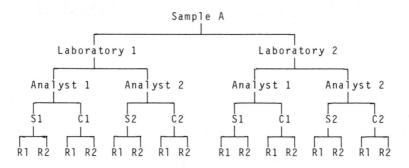

In the above diagram each factor is not crossed with each other factor; i.e., although each analyst uses a spectrometer *S* and a colorimeter *C* and makes duplicate measurements on the sample, analyst 1 in laboratory 1 does not use the same instruments used by analyst 2 in that laboratory nor by analysts 1 and 2 in laboratory 2. Analysts 1 and 2 are said to be nested in laboratory 1. Also, analysts 1 and 2 of laboratory 1 are not the same as analysts 1 and 2 of laboratory 2. The instruments are considered to be nested in analysts, and the runs nested in instruments.

Under these conditions, there can be no interaction between the variables. Another consequence of the nested design is a slight change in the method of calculating the sums of squares for the analysis of variance table which we will describe with an example. It is, of course, possible to have a design in which both crossed (factorial) and nested elements are present. In this case the design is called a nested factorial. For example, if both analysts in each laboratory used the same instruments, analysts and instruments would be crossed and interaction between these variables would be possible. We will consider only the simple nested design. More complicated designs are treated in texts such as those listed under Resources.

The definition of the problem and how the experiments are planned determines whether a nested, factorial, or a nested factorial design is used. As suggested by the above diagram, the nested design is generally used in interlaboratory studies, although its use is not restricted to this application. Considerable thought, planning and effort is required for a successful interlaboratory study. References 1 and 2 provide helpful information on these aspects as well as details on calculation and interpretation of the results.

11.1   ANOVA OF A NESTED DESIGN

The difference in the method for calculating the sums of squares lies in the correction factor applied to each sum of squares. In the crossed design the same correction factor is used for all sums of squares. In a nested design the correction factor is the square of the total of the observations of the nested group divided by the number of observations in that group. This is easier to see in an example.

EXAMPLE 11.1.   An acetic anhydride-pyridine method was developed for determining the hydroxyl number of a product. Since the method was to be used routinely by many different laboratories, the precision of the method both within and between laboratories needed to be determined. Based on these, the expected agreement within and between laboratories could be calculated. A typical homogeneous sample was sent to each of four randomly selected laboratories. Within each laboratory three analysts were randomly selected (one from each shift). Each analyst ran the sample in duplicate on each of two randomly selected days. From the data obtained, we want to calculate the precision between laboratories, between analysts, between days, and between runs. With this information we will be able to calculate how well duplicate determinations, results within a laboratory, and results between laboratories should agree.

The coded data are shown in Table 11.1 on lines I and II. The values on lines III, IV, V, and VI are obtained by addition. The following sums of squares calculations will be used in the ANOVA table.

SS_T, Total Sum of Squares. Square each individual observation (in lines I and II), sum the squares, and subtract the square of the grand total (line VI) which has been divided by the total number of observations:

$$SS_T = 5.1^2 + 1.0^2 + 0.2^2 + \cdots + 10.6^2 + 6.4^2 - \frac{302.3^2}{48}$$

$$= 2{,}394.890000 - 1{,}903.860208 = 491.029792$$

SS_B, Sum of Squares for Labs Within Sample. Square the total for each lab (line V), sum these squares, divide by the number of observations in each lab total, and subtract the square of the grand total (line VI) which has been

TABLE 11.1.   Data for Example 11.1.

Sample: S1

	L1						L2						L3						L4					
Analysts	A1		A2		A3		A1		A2		A3		A1		A2		A3		A1		A2		A3	
Days	D1	D2	D1	D2	D1	D2	D1	D2	D1	D2	D1	D2	D1	D2	D1	D2	D1	D2	D1	D2	D1	D2	D1	D2
(I) Run 1	5.1	0.2	3.3	4.6	4.2	2.5	10.1	11.6	8.9	7.2	6.8	8.2	8.8	7.2	5.0	4.2	7.8	9.3	9.2	5.3	2.8	2.4	4.4	10.6
(II) Run 2	1.0	0.2	4.1	2.2	2.9	3.6	9.9	14.4	7.9	6.5	7.7	10.7	10.0	8.3	7.6	6.4	8.8	7.0	9.7	7.8	1.7	2.6	5.2	6.4
(III) Day Total	6.1	0.4	7.4	6.8	7.1	6.1	20.0	26.0	16.8	13.7	14.5	18.9	18.8	15.5	12.6	10.6	16.6	16.3	18.9	13.1	4.5	5.0	9.6	17.0
(IV) Analyst Total	6.5		14.2		13.2		46.0		30.5		33.4		34.3		23.2		32.9		32.0		9.5		26.6	
(V) Lab Total	33.9						109.9						90.4						68.1					
(VI) Grand Total	302.3																							

divided by the total number of observations:

$$SS_B = \frac{33.9^2 + 109.9^2 + 90.4^2 + 68.1^2}{12} - \frac{302.3^2}{48}$$

$$= 2,169.74167 - 1,903.860208 = 265.888959$$

SS_C, Sum of Squares for Analysts Within Labs. Square the total for each analyst (line IV) in the first laboratory, sum the squares, divide by the number of observations in the analyst total, and subtract the square of the lab total (line V) which has been divided by the number of observations in the lab total. Repeat for each laboratory, and sum these values. Note that since the lab total is different for each laboratory, the correction factor is different for each and is also different from that used in calculating SS_T and SS_B:

$$SS_C = \frac{6.5^2 + 14.2^2 + 13.2^2}{4} - \frac{33.9^2}{12} + \frac{46.0^2 + 30.5^2 + 33.4^2}{4} - \frac{109.9^2}{12}$$

$$+ \frac{34.3^2 + 23.2^2 + 32.9^2}{4} - \frac{90.4^2}{12} + \frac{32.0^2 + 9.5^2 + 26.6^2}{4} - \frac{68.1^2}{12}$$

$$= 8.765000 + 33.9511667 + 18.271667 + 68.985000$$

$$= 129.973333$$

SS_D, Sum of Squares for Days Within Labs. Square the total for each day for the first analyst (line III), sum the squares, divide by the number of observations in each day total, and subtract the square of the analyst total (line IV) which has been divided by the number of observations in that total. Repeat for each analyst, and sum the values. Note again the different correction factors for each analyst.

$$SS_D = \frac{6.1^2 + 0.4^2}{2} - \frac{6.5^2}{4} + \frac{7.4^2 + 6.8^2}{2} - \frac{14.2^2}{4} + \cdots$$

$$+ \frac{9.6^2 + 17.0^2}{2} - \frac{26.6^2}{4}$$

$$= 8.122500 + 0.090000 + 13.690000$$

$$= 50.612500$$

SS_E, Sum of Squares for Replicates Within Days (Error). The following equation is general for two or more replicates. If there are only two replicates, there is an easier equation which will be given after the general one.

Square each observation within the first day column (lines I and II), sum the squares and subtract the square of the day total (line III) which has been divided by the number of observations in the day. Repeat for each of the day columns, and sum the values. Again, the correction factors are different for each day.

$$SS_E = 5.1^2 + 1.0^2 - \frac{6.1^2}{2} + 0.2^2 + 0.2^2 - \frac{0.4^2}{2} + \cdots + 10.6^2 + 6.4^2 - \frac{17.0^2}{2}$$

$$= 8.405000 + 0.000000 + \cdots + 8.820000$$

$$= 44.555000$$

If there are only two replicates per day, it is easier to obtain the SS_E by taking the differences for each day (value on line I minus line II), square each difference, sum the squares, and divide by two:

$$SS_E = \frac{(5.1 - 1.0)^2 + (0.2 - 0.2)^2 + \cdots + (10.6 - 6.4)^2}{2}$$

$$= 44.555000$$

The above five sums of squares are used in the analysis of variance table in Table 11.2.

The terms given under the expected mean square column provide the means for (a) testing the mean square values for significance and (b) calculating the standard deviation for each source.

The between-days mean square is tested against that for replicates to see if it is significantly different. According to the terms in the expected mean square column, the only difference between the mean squares for days and replicates is that the former includes the day component. If the F test shows that the between days mean square is significantly larger than that for replicates, the days effect is "real;" otherwise, the days effect has not been demonstrated to be significant at the selected level of the F test.

$$F = \frac{4.217708}{1.856458} = 2.27, \qquad F_{0.05, 12, 24} = 2.18$$

Since the critical F value is exceeded at the $\alpha = 0.05$ significance level, the presence of the days effect is demonstrated.

TABLE 11.2.   ANOVA, Example 11.1.

SOURCE	SUM OF SQUARES	DEGREES OF FREEDOM	MEAN SQUARE	EXPECTED MEAN SQUARE (RANDOM EFFECTS)
Between labs within samples	$SS_B = 265.888959$	$b - 1 = 3$	88.629653	$\sigma^2 + e\sigma_D^2 + de\sigma_A^2 + cde\sigma_L^2$
Between analysts within labs	$SS_C = 129.973333$	$b(c - 1) = 8$	16.246667	$\sigma^2 + e\sigma_D^2 + de\sigma_A^2$
Between days within analysts	$SS_D = 50.612500$	$bc(d - 1) = 12$	4.217708	$\sigma^2 + e\sigma_D^2$
Between replications within days (Error)	$SS_E = 44.555000$	$bcd(e - 1) = 24$	1.856458	σ^2
Total	$SS_T = 491.029792$	$(bcde) - 1 = 47$		

b = number of labs $\qquad$ σ_L^2 = variance for labs
c = number of analysts $\qquad$ σ_A^2 = variance for analysts
d = number of days $\qquad$ σ_D^2 = variance for days
e = number of replicates $\qquad$ σ^2 = variance for replicates

The standard deviation for replicates is merely the square root of the mean square for replicates:

$$s_E = \sqrt{1.856458} = 1.3625 \text{ with 24 DF}$$

The standard deviation for days is calculated as follows, since the days mean square, 4.217708, includes the variance for replicates plus the number of replicates times the days variance:

$$s_D^2 = (4.217708 - 1.856458)/2 = 1.180625$$

and

$$s_D = \sqrt{1.180625} = 1.080625 \text{ with 12 DF}$$

Next, the analysts mean square is tested for significance by comparing it with that for days because the only difference between these two mean squares is the term due to analysts:

$$F = \frac{16.246667}{4.217708} = 3.85, \qquad F_{0.05,8,12} = 2.85$$

Again, the critical value is exceeded, and the presence of the analysts effect has been demonstrated. The standard deviation for analysts is calculated in a similar manner to that for days. In this case, the denominator is the product of the number of days and the number of replicates, as indicated by the entry in the expected mean square column of Table 11.2:

$$S_C = \sqrt{\frac{16.246667 - 4.217708}{2 \times 2}} = \sqrt{3.007240} = 1.7341 \text{ with 8 DF}$$

Finally, the labs mean square is tested for significance by comparing it with that for analysts because the only difference between these two is the lab variance term:

$$F = \frac{88.629653}{16.246667} = 5.46, \qquad F_{0.05,3,8} = 4.07$$

Since the critical value of F is exceeded, the standard deviation is calculated in the same manner previously used. The denominator is the product of the number of analysts, the number of days, and the number of replicates.

$$s_B = \sqrt{\frac{88.629653 - 16.246667}{3 \times 2 \times 2}} = \sqrt{6.031916}$$

$$= 2.4560 \text{ with 3 DF}$$

Note that if any of the F tests had not demonstrated the presence of one of the effects, the variance for that effect is assumed to be zero and, therefore, its standard deviation is also zero, and the variance is dropped from subsequent calculations. For example, if the mean square for days had been 2.418 in the example instead of 4.218, the F test would have given $2.418/1.856 = 1.30$ which is less than the critical value of 2.18. In that case σ_D^2 would have been set equal to zero. In other words the mean squares of 2.41 and 1.856 would have been considered to be two estimates of only one variance, that for replicates. The mean square for replicates would have been re-calculated by summing the sums of squares 29.016000 and 44.555000 to give 73.5710 which would have been divided by the summed degrees of freedom 12 plus 24, or 36, to give a new mean square of 2.0436. (The value of 29.016000 is the sum of squares for between days which would have given the assumed value of 2.418 for days mean square.) The σ_d^2 terms in the expected means squares column would have been set equal to zero, and the mean square for between analysts would have been compared with 2.0436 to test for its significance. Note that the mean square for between labs would still be compared with that for between analysts, assuming that the between analysts value were found to be significant.

The standard deviation for results obtained within a laboratory includes the variability due to runs, days, and analysts effects:

$$s_W = \sqrt{\frac{s_E^2}{e} + s_D^2 + s_C^2}$$

where $e = $ number of replicates. The degrees of freedom associated with the within-laboratory standard deviation is conservatively considered to be that for either s_D or s_C, whichever is the lesser. (Special case: If only one analyst per laboratory is used in the interlaboratory study, the degrees of freedom for s_D is used for s_W.)

In the example,

$$s_W = \sqrt{\frac{1.856458}{2} + 1.180625 + 3.00723975}$$

$$= \sqrt{5.11609375}$$

$$= 2.2619 \text{ with approx. 8 DF}$$

In the above equation for s_W the s_E^2 term is divided by the number of replicates used, $e = 2$, because the method being tested called for reporting the average of duplicate determinations in comparing results within a laboratory. Had the method specified reporting the average of triplicates or quaduplicates, the s_R^2 term would have been divided by the number of replicates used in the average.

The standard deviation for results obtained by two laboratories includes the variability due to runs, days, analysts, and labs effects:

$$s_{Bet} = \sqrt{\frac{s_E^2}{e} + s_D^2 + s_C^2 + s_B^2}$$

The degrees of freedom associated with the between lab standard deviation is conservatively considered to be that for s_B.

In the example,

$$s_{Bet} = \sqrt{\frac{1.856458}{2} + 1.180625 + 3.00723975 + 6.031916}$$

$$= \sqrt{11.14800975}$$

$$= 3.3389 \text{ with 3 DF}$$

Having obtained the standard deviations for replicates, for within lab, and for between labs, we can calculate how much two runs, two averages within a lab, and two averages between labs may be expected to agree at the 95% confidence level. This is done as described in Chapter 5.

In Example 11.1 the standard deviation for replicates, s_E, is 1.3625 with 24 degrees of freedom. Therefore, two runs should be considered suspect at the 95% confidence level if they differ by more than 1.3625×2.77 or 3.77. Similarly, two results obtained within a laboratory on different days, each the average of two runs, should be considered suspect at the 95% confidence level if they differ by more than 2.2619×2.77 or 6.26. The results obtained by two laboratories, each the average of two runs, should be considered suspect at the 95% confidence level if they differ by more than 3.3389×2.77 or 9.25.

Our analysis of variance shows that the between-laboratory variance of 6.031916 accounts for about 50% of the total variance, and the between analysts variance of 3.007240 accounts for about 25%. The between days and replicates variances account for only about 10% and 15%, respectively. If the standard deviations (or the ranges we just calculated) for within or between laboratories are considered too large, an investigation to find causes of the differences between laboratories and between analysts would be in order. Common causes for differences include clerical errors in recording, calculating, and reporting data; differences in interpreting the analytical method; and the presence of one or more uninvestigated variables which are not sufficiently controlled by the experimental conditions.

11.2 GENERAL ANALYSIS OF A NESTED DESIGN

After having gone through a specific example for a nested design with three variables, let us look at the analysis of variance in a general form for a nested design with three variables, B, C, D, and the error term, E:

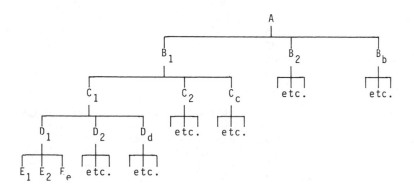

In this design there are b levels of variable B nested within A, c levels of variable C within each level of variable B, d levels of variable D within C, and e levels of E (usually replicates to provide an estimate of measurement error) within variable D. The first part of the analysis of variance table is given in Table 11.3.

TABLE 11.3. General ANOVA Table for a Nested Design.

SOURCE	SS	DF	MS
Between variable B within A	SS_B	$b - 1$	MS_B
Between variable C within B	SS_C	$b(c - 1)$	MS_C
Between variable D within C	SS_D	$bc(d - 1)$	MS_D
Between replicates within variable D (error)	SS_E	$bcd(e - 1)$	MS_E
Total	SS_T	$(bcde) - 1$	

b = number of levels of variable B
c = number of levels of variable C
d = number of levels of variable D
e = number of levels of replication

TABLE 11.4. Expected Mean Squares for a Nested Design.

SOURCE	MS	RANDOM EFFECTS MODEL	FIXED EFFECTS MODEL
Between B within A	MS_B	$\sigma^2 + e\sigma_D^2 + e\sigma_C^2 + cde\sigma_B^2$	$\sigma^2 + cde\sigma_B^2$
Between C within B	MS_C	$\sigma^2 + e\sigma_D^2 + de\sigma_C^2$	$\sigma^2 + de\sigma_C^2$
Between D within C	MS_D	$\sigma^2 + e\sigma_D^2$	$\sigma^2 + e\sigma_D^2$
Between replicates within D (error)	MS_E	σ^2	σ^2

SOURCE		B, C RANDOM; D FIXED	B, D RANDOM; C FIXED
Between B within A	MS_B	$\sigma^2 + de\sigma_C^2 + cde\sigma_B^2$	$\sigma^2 + e\sigma_D^2 + cde\sigma_B^2$
Between C within B	MS_C	$\sigma^2 + de\sigma_C^2$	$\sigma^2 + e\sigma_D^2 + de\sigma_C^2$
Between D within C	MS_D	$\sigma^2 + e\sigma_D^2$	$\sigma^2 + e\sigma_D^2$
Between replicates within D (error)	MS_E	σ^2	σ^2

SOURCE		C, D RANDOM; B FIXED	B RANDOM; C, D FIXED
Between B within A	MS_B	$\sigma^2 + e\sigma_D^2 + de\sigma_C^2 + cde\sigma_B^2$	$\sigma^2 + cde\sigma_B^2$
Between C within B	MS_C	$\sigma^2 + e\sigma_D^2 + de\sigma_C^2$	$\sigma^2 + de\sigma_C^2$
Between D within C	MS_D	$\sigma^2 + e\sigma_D^2$	$\sigma^2 + e\sigma_D^2$
Between replicates within D (error)	MS_E	σ^2	σ^2

SOURCE		C RANDOM; B, D FIXED	D RANDOM; B, C FIXED
Between B within A	MS_B	$\sigma^2 + de\sigma_C^2 + cde\sigma_B^2$	$\sigma^2 + e\sigma_D^2 + cde\sigma_B^2$
Between C within B	MS_C	$\sigma^2 + de\sigma_C^2$	$\sigma^2 + e\sigma_D^2 + de\sigma_C^2$
Between D within C	MS_D	$\sigma^2 + e\sigma_D^2$	$\sigma^2 + e\sigma_D^2$
Between replicates within D (error)	MS_E	σ^2	σ^2

c = number of levels of variable C
d = number of levels of variable D
e = number of levels of replication

The mean square (MS) for each source is of course obtained by dividing the source's sum of squares by its degrees of freedom. The expected mean squares for each source is shown in Table 11.4 for the random, fixed, and mixed effects models. This table can of course be expanded to include any desired number of variables.

11.3 SUMMARY

In this chapter we discussed yet another application of the analysis of variance: to nested designs. In nested designs the levels of a variable are nested within another variable instead of being crossed at all levels with each level of all the other variables. A common example of the nested design is the interlaboratory study.

11.4   PROBLEMS

Problems 21 and 22 will enable you to practice ANOVA on nested designs.

RESOURCES

Davies, O. L., ed., *Design and Analysis of Industrial Experiments*, 2nd ed. New York: Longman, 1978.

Dixon, W. J., and Massey, Jr., F. J., *Introduction to Statistical Analysis*, 3rd ed. New York, NY: McGraw-Hill Book Co., 1969.

Diamond, W. J., *Practical Experimental Designs for Engineers and Scientists*. Belmont, CA: Lifetime Learning Publications, 1981.

REFERENCES

1. ASTM Standard Practice E 180, "Determining the Precision of ASTM Methods for Analysis and Testing of Industrial Chemicals," *Annual Book of Standards*, Volume 15.05, American Society for Testing and Materials, Philadelphia, PA.
2. ASTM Standard Practice E 691, "Conducting an Interlaboratory Study to Determine the Precision of a Test Method," *Annual Book of Standards*, Volume 14.02, American Society for Testing and Materials, Philadelphia, PA.

Chapter 12
LINEAR RELATIONSHIPS BETWEEN TWO VARIABLES: CALCULATION OF CALIBRATION CURVES USING MATRIX ALGEBRA

OVERVIEW

In Chapter 6 we saw that if two variables (such as absorbance and concentration) were related in a linear fashion, we could quantify this relationship and predict the value of one (concentration) for given values of the other (absorbance). The technique of least squares and simple algebra were used to estimate the regression line which best described the linear relationship. Another approach to calculating the regression line is to use matrix algebra. Matrix algebra enables us to use the same equations regardless of the number of independent variables. In this chapter we will see how matrix algebra is used when one independent variable is of interest and verify that the regression line obtained is the same as that obtained using simple algebra.

12.0 LINEAR RELATIONSHIPS REVISITED

In Chapter 6 we learned how to establish the best calibration curve to describe the linear relationship between one independent variable and one dependent variable which were functionally related. Simple algebra was used in the calculations.

If we are interested in predicting or estimating the value of a dependent variable (such as yield) when two or more independent variables (such as time and temperature) are involved, the algebraic equations for the regression lines become complicated. Moreover, we must use different equations for each number of independent variables. Another technique which is widely used to calculate regression lines makes use of matrix algebra. Matrix algebra enables us to use the same equations for any number of independent variables. However, even matrix algebra becomes tedious if we have to perform the calculations manually. Fortunately, computers don't mind tedious operations, and today almost all matrix calculations are made quickly and accurately by appropriate computer programs.

There are many computer programs or packages of programs which include regression capabilities. Some, such as SAS, SPSS, and BMDP, are written for the large mainframe computer; others, such as SPM, FLURP, MLR, CRISP, STATPRO PC, and SPSS PC, are for use on mini or personal computers.[1] These programs vary considerably in memory requirements and in the format of their outputs, but all reduce the drudgery of manual calculations and their attendant calculation errors. Some excellent suggestions on using regression programs are given by Hendrix.[2]

Much of the time the analytical chemist is concerned with the linear relationship of a dependent variable and only one independent variable. Examples include establishment of calibration curves and comparison of results by two methods. In this chapter we will see how matrix algebra is applied to the calibration example of Chapter 6 and verify that we obtain the same regression line that we calculated using simple algebra.

More details on regression can be found in standard texts on matrix algebra and regression statistics. The texts by Younger and by Draper and Smith are especially recommended for beginners (see Resources). Draper and Smith also discuss nonlinear regression, which is not considered in this book.

Once we have calculated the regression equation we will want to confirm that there is a real relationship between the variables and to see how useful the equation is. This topic will be considered in the next chapter.

The application of matrix techniques to cases where there is appreciable error in both X and Y and to cases of association relationships is beyond the scope of this book. Although theoretical statisticians will not approve, it should be noted that some statisticians apply the techniques designed for cases with error only in Y to problems in which both X and Y contain error.

12.1 MATRIX ALGEBRA PRINCIPLES

In this section we will review the principles of matrix algebra as they are applied to regression analysis. If you are already familiar with matrix algebra, you may wish to skip to Section 12.4 where we will apply matrix algebra to regression analysis.

12.1.1 Some Definitions Used in Matrix Algebra

Matrix: A rectangular array of numbers or variables enclosed by brackets; e.g.,

$$\begin{bmatrix} 1 & 3 & 5 \\ 4 & 9 & 2 \end{bmatrix} \quad \begin{bmatrix} a & b & c \\ d & e & f \\ g & h & i \end{bmatrix}$$

A matrix is usually designated by a boldface capital letter:

$$\mathbf{A} = \begin{bmatrix} 7 & 3 & 1 \\ 2 & 1 & 3 \end{bmatrix}$$

Elements: The components or individual values in a matrix, designated by lower case letters.

Dimension: The size of a matrix, expressed by the number of rows r and the number of columns c. Matrix **A** above is a 2×3 matrix.

Vector: A matrix with only one row or column. A row vector has only one row, and a column vector has only one column. Vectors are designated by a boldface lowercase letter:

$$\mathbf{d} = \begin{bmatrix} 40 & 23 & 5 & 54 \end{bmatrix}$$

Scalar: A matrix with only one row and one column; that is, it has only one element: $[\mathbf{x}]$.

Transpose: The transpose of a $r \times c$ matrix is a $c \times r$ matrix with the row and column elements switched. A transpose is designated by a prime boldface letter. If

$$\mathbf{A} = \begin{bmatrix} 1 & 3 & 5 \\ 4 & 9 & 2 \end{bmatrix}$$

then its transpose is

$$\mathbf{A'} = \begin{bmatrix} 1 & 4 \\ 3 & 9 \\ 5 & 2 \end{bmatrix}$$

Diagonal matrix: A matrix in which all the elements are zero except those on the principal diagonal:

$$\begin{bmatrix} d & 0 & 0 & 0 \\ 0 & d & 0 & 0 \\ 0 & 0 & d & 0 \\ 0 & 0 & 0 & d \end{bmatrix}$$

Identity matrix: A diagonal matrix whose diagonal elements are all 1's. It is sometimes designated as **I**.

Symmetric matrix: A square matrix whose *ij* and *ji* elements are equal:

$$\mathbf{B} = \begin{bmatrix} a & d & e \\ d & b & f \\ e & f & c \end{bmatrix}$$

Equality of matrices: Two matrices are equal if two conditions are satisfied: (a) the two matrices have the same dimensions, and (b) they contain the same elements in the same positions.

12.2   MATRIX OPERATIONS

Matrices may be added, subtracted, and multiplied. However, these operations are not carried out in the same fashion as in algebra. There are also some unique operations for matrices we will be using and which will be discussed. Since we will not need to add or subtract matrices, these operations will not be discussed.

12.2.1   Scalar Multiplication

The product of a scalar and a matrix is a matrix containing the products of the scalar and each element:

$$2 \begin{bmatrix} 3 & -1 \\ 3 & 0 \\ 1 & 5 \end{bmatrix} = \begin{bmatrix} 6 & -2 \\ 6 & 0 \\ 2 & 10 \end{bmatrix}$$

12.2.2   Matrix Multiplication

Two matrices can be multiplied only if their dimensions are conformable: that is, the number of columns of the first matrix must equal the number of rows of the second matrix. If matrix **X** has dimensions of 2×3 and matrix **Y** has dimensions of 3×4, the product **XY** can be formed. The product is a matrix with the number of rows of the first matrix and the number of columns of the second. In our example $\mathbf{X}_{2 \times 3} \mathbf{Y}_{3 \times 4} = \mathbf{XY}_{2 \times 4}$.

An easy way of remembering the above conditions is that for two matrices to be conformable, their "inside" subscripts (3 and 3 in the example) must be equal; the dimensions of their product are the same as the "outside" subscripts (2 and 4 in the example).

Matrix multiplication appears a bit complicated until one gets familiar with the process. The operations are illustrated with the following example and are the same for any dimensions:

$$\begin{bmatrix} a & b & c \\ d & e & f \end{bmatrix}_{2 \times 3} \begin{bmatrix} g & j \\ h & k \\ i & l \end{bmatrix}_{3 \times 2} \begin{bmatrix} ag + bh + ci & aj + bk + cl \\ dg + eh + fi & dj + ek + fl \end{bmatrix}_{2 \times 2}$$

In words, to get the first row–first column element of the product, we multiply each element of the first row of the first matrix by the corresponding element of the first column of the second matrix, reading the row from left to right and the column from top to bottom, and we add the products. This gives us $ag + bh + ci$ in the example. This is repeated for each successive column of the second matrix. In our example, since there are only two columns, we are finished with the first row of the product after the second column of the second matrix: $aj + bk + cl$.

To get the first column of the next row of the product matrix, we multiply each element of the next row of the first matrix by the corresponding element of the first column of the second matrix, and obtain the sum. This gives us $dg + eh + fi$ in our example. Similarly, to get the elements of the next column we multiply the elements of the same row of the first matrix by the elements of the next column of the second matrix, and add. This gives us $dj + ek + fl$ in the example. We continue this process until all the rows and columns of the two matrices have been used.

Using numbers in place of letters, we have

$$\begin{bmatrix} 2 & 1 & 3 \\ 5 & 2 & 1 \end{bmatrix}_{2 \times 3} \begin{bmatrix} 1 & 3 \\ 4 & 2 \\ 1 & 1 \end{bmatrix}_{3 \times 2} = \begin{bmatrix} 2(1) + 1(4) + 3(1) & 2(3) + 1(2) + 3(1) \\ 5(1) + 2(4) + 1(1) & 5(3) + 2(2) + 1(1) \end{bmatrix}_{2 \times 2}$$

$$= \begin{bmatrix} 9 & 11 \\ 14 & 20 \end{bmatrix}_{2 \times 2}$$

Note that, unlike ordinary multiplication where $A \times B = B \times A$, in matrix multiplication **AB** is usually not equal to **BA**. For example, if

$$A = \begin{bmatrix} 1 & 3 \\ 4 & 2 \end{bmatrix} \quad \text{and} \quad B = \begin{bmatrix} -1 & 2 \\ 2 & -3 \end{bmatrix}$$

then

$$AB = \begin{bmatrix} 1 & 3 \\ 4 & 2 \end{bmatrix}\begin{bmatrix} -1 & 2 \\ 2 & -3 \end{bmatrix} = \begin{bmatrix} 1(-1)+3(2) & 1(2)+3(-3) \\ 4(-1)+2(2) & 4(2)+2(-3) \end{bmatrix} = \begin{bmatrix} 5 & -7 \\ 0 & 2 \end{bmatrix}$$

but

$$BA = \begin{bmatrix} -1 & 2 \\ 2 & -3 \end{bmatrix}\begin{bmatrix} 1 & 3 \\ 4 & 2 \end{bmatrix} = \begin{bmatrix} -1(1)+2(4) & -1(3)+2(2) \\ 2(1)-3(4) & 2(3)-3(2) \end{bmatrix}$$

$$= \begin{bmatrix} 7 & 1 \\ -10 & 0 \end{bmatrix}$$

12.2.3   Determinant of a Matrix

The determinant of a matrix is a number that represents the matrix. It is determined by all the elements of the matrix. A determinant is denoted by vertical bars on each side of the letter representing the matrix; e.g. $|A|$.

The determinant of a 2×2 matrix is easily calculated. If

$$A = \begin{bmatrix} a & b \\ c & d \end{bmatrix}$$

its determinant is $|A| = ad - bc$. For

$$A = \begin{bmatrix} 1 & 2 \\ 3 & 4 \end{bmatrix}, \qquad |A| = 1(4) - 2(3) = -2$$

Calculating the determinant of larger sized matrices is more complicated. For a 3×3 matrix;

$$A = \begin{bmatrix} a_{11} & a_{12} & a_{13} \\ a_{21} & a_{22} & a_{23} \\ a_{31} & a_{32} & a_{33} \end{bmatrix}$$

the procedure is as follows:

(a) For matrix A select an element, say a_{11}, and strike out of A the row and column in which a_{11} appears. This results in a 2×2 matrix:

$$\begin{bmatrix} a_{22} & a_{23} \\ a_{32} & a_{33} \end{bmatrix}$$

(b) The determinant of this 2×2 submatrix is $a_{22}a_{33} - a_{23}a_{32}$, and it is called the *minor* of the element a_{11}. There is a minor corresponding to each element in the matrix.

A *cofactor* is a minor that has been multiplied by either $+1$ or -1. The sign is determined by the subscripts on the element whose minor is being calculated. If the sum of the subscripts is even the sign is positive $(+1)$; if the sum is odd, the sign is negative (-1). A cofactor is denoted by a subscripted capital letter: A_{11}, A_{23}, etc. The matrix whose elements are the cofactors of the corresponding elements of **A** (i.e., A_{ij} in place of a_{ij}) is called the *cofactor matrix* of **A**. This matrix will come in handy later, where we are calculating the inverse of **A**.

(c) Having determined the cofactors, select any single row or column in the original matrix, multiply each element by its cofactor, and sum the products. This gives the determinant.

Selecting row 1 of **A**, we have

$$|A| = a_{11}A_{11} + a_{12}A_{12} + a_{13}A_{13}$$

Let us follow the above steps using a numerical example:

$$A = \begin{bmatrix} 2 & 1 & 2 \\ 1 & 3 & 2 \\ 1 & 0 & 1 \end{bmatrix}$$

(a) Select the first row to work with and determine the minors for each element of that row. The calculations can be summarized in the following table:

ELEMENT	MINOR	COFACTOR
$a_{11} = 2$	$\begin{bmatrix} 3 & 2 \\ 0 & 1 \end{bmatrix} = 3 - 0 = 3$	$+1(3) = 3 = A_{11}$
$a_{12} = 1$	$\begin{bmatrix} 1 & 2 \\ 1 & 1 \end{bmatrix} = 1 - 2 = -1$	$-1(-1) = 1 = A_{12}$
$a_{13} = 2$	$\begin{bmatrix} 1 & 3 \\ 1 & 0 \end{bmatrix} = 0 - 3 = -3$	$+1(-3) = -3 = A_{13}$

The determinant, $|A| = 2(3) + 1(1) + 2(-3) = 1$

Note: Determinants are used in finding the inverse of a matrix, in case you are wondering why we are going through these steps.

12.2.4 Inverse of a Matrix

The inverse of a (square) matrix **A** is another matrix, A^{-1}, such that the products AA^{-1} and $A^{-1}A$ are both equal to **I**, the identity matrix. We shall show how the inverse of a matrix is calculated by finding the inverse of a 3×3 matrix:

$$\mathbf{A} = \begin{bmatrix} a_{11} & a_{12} & a_{13} \\ a_{21} & a_{22} & a_{23} \\ a_{31} & a_{32} & a_{33} \end{bmatrix}$$

For this matrix let A_{ij} = cofactor of element a_{ij}. Then, the inverse is

$$\mathbf{A}^{-1} = \frac{1}{|\mathbf{A}|} \begin{bmatrix} A_{11} & A_{21} & A_{31} \\ A_{12} & A_{22} & A_{32} \\ A_{13} & A_{23} & A_{33} \end{bmatrix}$$

Note that this matrix is the transpose of the cofactor matrix, divided by the determinant. Note also that presence of the determinant of matrix $\mathbf{A}$ in the denominator means that the determinant must not be zero.

Now we shall run through a numerical example in which we find the inverse of the matrix

$$\mathbf{A} = \begin{bmatrix} 2 & 1 & 2 \\ 1 & 3 & 2 \\ 1 & 0 & 1 \end{bmatrix}$$

The first step is to calculate the cofactor of every element:

ELEMENT	MINOR	SIGN	COFACTOR
$a_{11} = 2$	$\begin{bmatrix} 3 & 2 \\ 0 & 1 \end{bmatrix} = 3 - 0 = 3$	$+$	$3 = A_{11}$
$a_{12} = 1$	$\begin{bmatrix} 1 & 2 \\ 1 & 1 \end{bmatrix} = 1 - 2 = -1$	$-$	$1 = A_{12}$
$a_{13} = 2$	$\begin{bmatrix} 1 & 3 \\ 1 & 0 \end{bmatrix} = 0 - 3 = -3$	$+$	$-3 = A_{13}$
$a_{21} = 1$	$\begin{bmatrix} 1 & 2 \\ 0 & 1 \end{bmatrix} = 1 - 0 = 1$	$-$	$-1 = A_{21}$
$a_{22} = 3$	$\begin{bmatrix} 2 & 2 \\ 1 & 1 \end{bmatrix} = 2 - 2 = 0$	$+$	$0 = A_{22}$
$a_{23} = 2$	$\begin{bmatrix} 2 & 1 \\ 1 & 0 \end{bmatrix} = 0 - 1 = -1$	$-$	$1 = A_{23}$
$a_{31} = 1$	$\begin{bmatrix} 1 & 2 \\ 3 & 2 \end{bmatrix} = 2 - 6 = -4$	$+$	$-4 = A_{31}$
$a_{32} = 0$	$\begin{bmatrix} 2 & 2 \\ 1 & 2 \end{bmatrix} = 4 - 2 = 2$	$-$	$-2 = A_{32}$
$a_{33} = 1$	$\begin{bmatrix} 2 & 1 \\ 1 & 3 \end{bmatrix} = 6 - 1 = 5$	$+$	$5 = A_{33}$

Then, using the first row, $|\mathbf{A}| = 2(3) + 1(-1) + 1(-4) = 1$. The cofactor matrix is

$$\begin{bmatrix} A_{11} & A_{12} & A_{13} \\ A_{21} & A_{22} & A_{23} \\ A_{31} & A_{32} & A_{33} \end{bmatrix} = \begin{bmatrix} 3 & 1 & -3 \\ -1 & 0 & 1 \\ -4 & -2 & 5 \end{bmatrix}$$

and its transpose is

$$\begin{bmatrix} A_{11} & A_{21} & A_{31} \\ A_{12} & A_{22} & A_{32} \\ A_{13} & A_{23} & A_{33} \end{bmatrix} = \begin{bmatrix} 3 & -1 & -4 \\ 1 & 0 & -2 \\ -3 & 1 & 5 \end{bmatrix}$$

Therefore, the inverse of $\mathbf{A}$ is

$$\mathbf{A}^{-1} = \frac{1}{+1} \begin{bmatrix} 3 & -1 & -4 \\ 1 & 0 & -2 \\ -3 & -1 & 5 \end{bmatrix} = \begin{bmatrix} 3 & -1 & -4 \\ 1 & 0 & -2 \\ -3 & -1 & 5 \end{bmatrix}$$

A check of the products $\mathbf{AA}^{-1}$ and $\mathbf{A}^{-1}\mathbf{A}$ shows each equals $\mathbf{I}$:

$$\mathbf{AA}^{-1} = \begin{bmatrix} 2 & 1 & 2 \\ 1 & 3 & 2 \\ 1 & 0 & 1 \end{bmatrix} \begin{bmatrix} 3 & -1 & -4 \\ 1 & 0 & -2 \\ -3 & 1 & 5 \end{bmatrix}$$

$$= \begin{bmatrix} 6+1-6 & -2+0+2 & -8-2+10 \\ 3+3-6 & -1+0+2 & -4-6+10 \\ 3+0-3 & -1+0+1 & -4+0+5 \end{bmatrix}$$

$$= \begin{bmatrix} 1 & 0 & 0 \\ 0 & 1 & 0 \\ 0 & 0 & 1 \end{bmatrix} = \mathbf{I}$$

$$\mathbf{A}^{-1}\mathbf{A} = \begin{bmatrix} 3 & -1 & -4 \\ 1 & 0 & -2 \\ -3 & 1 & 5 \end{bmatrix} \begin{bmatrix} 2 & 1 & 2 \\ 1 & 3 & 2 \\ 1 & 0 & 1 \end{bmatrix}$$

$$= \begin{bmatrix} 6-1-4 & 3-3+0 & 6-2-4 \\ 2+0-2 & 1+0+0 & 2+0-2 \\ -6+1+5 & -3+3+0 & -6+2+5 \end{bmatrix}$$

$$= \begin{bmatrix} 1 & 0 & 0 \\ 0 & 1 & 0 \\ 0 & 0 & 1 \end{bmatrix} = \mathbf{I}$$

The method for calculating the determinant of the 3×3 matrix can be directly extended to a 4×4 or higher dimension matrix. The calculations, however, become increasingly involved with increasing dimensions. For a 4×4 matrix the minor associated with each element is the determinant of a 3×3 matrix, and this minor must be evaluated. Therefore, to find the determinant of a 4×4 matrix, four 3×3 determinants must be calculated, each of which involves three 2×2 determinants—a very tedious affair for hand calculation. Computer programs have been written to calculate determinants for any reasonably sized matrix, so we can turn this chore, as well as all the matrix calculations, over to the computer. Note that some computer programs are superior to others in minimizing rounding errors in matrix calculations. This can be important, particularly if the determinant of a matrix approaches zero.

12.3 SOLVING SIMULTANEOUS EQUATIONS WITH MATRIX ALGEBRA

Now that we have the fundamental matrix operations in hand, let's see how matrix algebra can be used to solve a set of simultaneous equations:

$$a_1 X + b_1 Y = c_1$$

$$a_2 X + b_2 Y = c_2$$

In matrix notation these two equations can be written as

$$\mathbf{AX} = \mathbf{c}$$

or,

$$\begin{bmatrix} a_1 & b_1 \\ a_2 & b_2 \end{bmatrix}_{2 \times 2} \begin{bmatrix} X \\ Y \end{bmatrix}_{2 \times 1} = \begin{bmatrix} c_1 \\ c_2 \end{bmatrix}_{2 \times 1}$$

where

$$\mathbf{A}_{2 \times 2} = \begin{bmatrix} a_1 & b_1 \\ a_2 & b_2 \end{bmatrix}, \quad \mathbf{X}_{2 \times 1} = \begin{bmatrix} X \\ Y \end{bmatrix}, \quad \text{and} \quad \mathbf{c} = \begin{bmatrix} c_1 \\ c_2 \end{bmatrix}$$

or, by multiplying the terms on the left-hand side:

$$\begin{bmatrix} a_1 X + b_1 Y \\ a_2 X + b_2 Y \end{bmatrix} = \begin{bmatrix} c_1 \\ c_2 \end{bmatrix}$$

Multiplying both sides of the matrix equation by $\mathbf{A}^{-1}$ gives

$$\mathbf{A}^{-1}\mathbf{A}\mathbf{X} = \mathbf{A}^{-1}\mathbf{c}$$

$$\mathbf{IX} = \mathbf{A}^{-1}\mathbf{c}$$

$$\mathbf{X} = \mathbf{A}^{-1}\mathbf{c}$$

The last equation is the same whether we are dealing with two or any number of simultaneous equations; that is, it is the solution for all systems of simultaneous linear equations.

Using a numerical example:

$$3X + 2Y = 6$$

$$2X - Y = 4$$

$$\mathbf{A} = \begin{bmatrix} 3 & 2 \\ 2 & -1 \end{bmatrix}, \quad \mathbf{X} = \begin{bmatrix} X \\ Y \end{bmatrix}, \quad \text{and} \quad \mathbf{c} = \begin{bmatrix} 6 \\ 4 \end{bmatrix}$$

$$|\mathbf{A}| = -3 - 4 = -7$$

$$\mathbf{A}^{-1} = \frac{1}{-7} \begin{bmatrix} -1 & -2 \\ -2 & 3 \end{bmatrix} = \begin{bmatrix} 1/7 & 2/7 \\ 2/7 & -3/7 \end{bmatrix}$$

$$\mathbf{X} = \mathbf{A}^{-1}\mathbf{c} = \begin{bmatrix} 1/7 & 2/7 \\ 2/7 & -3/7 \end{bmatrix}\begin{bmatrix} 6 \\ 4 \end{bmatrix} = \begin{bmatrix} 6/7 & +8/7 \\ 12/7 & -12/7 \end{bmatrix} = \begin{bmatrix} 14/7 \\ 0/7 \end{bmatrix} = \begin{bmatrix} 2 \\ 0 \end{bmatrix}$$

Or, $X = 2$ and $Y = 0$. These results can be checked by substituting them into the original equations.

As usual in solving systems of simultaneous equations, we must have as many different equations as there are unknowns. If one equation is merely a multiple of another, no new or different information is contained in that equation, and that equation is not different. In addition, the equations must not be contradictory, or the set of equations cannot be solved. If the value of X required to satisfy one equation does not satisfy all equations, the equations are said to be contradictory.

12.4 APPLICATION OF MATRICES TO CALIBRATION CURVES (LINEAR REGRESSION)

You will recall from Chapter 6 that the equation for a simple linear regression had the form

$$Y = a + bX + \varepsilon$$

and that in estimating the regression equation we were finding estimates A and B of a and b. For each of n observations of the population we have

$$Y_1 = a + bX_1 + \varepsilon_1$$

$$Y_2 = a + bX_2 + \varepsilon_2$$

$$Y_n = a + bX_n + \varepsilon_n$$

This is of course a set of simultaneous equations, which in matrix notation can be expressed as

$$\mathbf{y} = \mathbf{Xb} + \boldsymbol{\varepsilon}$$

where

$$\mathbf{y}_{n \times 1} = \begin{bmatrix} Y_1 \\ Y_2 \\ Y_n \end{bmatrix}, \quad \mathbf{b}_{2 \times 1} = \begin{bmatrix} a \\ b \end{bmatrix}, \quad \boldsymbol{\varepsilon}_{n \times 1} = \begin{bmatrix} 1 \\ 2 \\ n \end{bmatrix}, \quad \text{and} \quad \mathbf{X}_{n \times 2} = \begin{bmatrix} 1 & X_1 \\ 1 & X_2 \\ 1 & X_n \end{bmatrix}$$

The first column of 1's in the $\mathbf{X}_{n \times 2}$ matrix is required in order to pick up the term a in vector $\mathbf{b}$. The matrix solution, which is the same for every regression problem regardless of the number of independent variables, is given by

$$\mathbf{b} = (\mathbf{X'X})^{-1}\mathbf{X'y} \tag{12.1}$$

provided that the determinant of $(\mathbf{X'X})$ is not equal to zero so that its inverse $(\mathbf{X'X})^{-1}$ exists.

For the case of estimating a and b in the equation $Y = a + bX$, we have

$$(\mathbf{X'X}) = \begin{bmatrix} n & \sum X \\ \sum X & \sum X^2 \end{bmatrix} \tag{12.2}$$

and its determinant, $|\mathbf{X'X}| = n\sum X_i^2 - (\sum X_i)^2 = n\mathrm{SS}_x$. Thus,

$$(\mathbf{X'X})^{-1} = \begin{bmatrix} \dfrac{\sum X^2}{n\mathrm{SS}_x} & \dfrac{-\sum X}{n\mathrm{SS}_x} \\ \dfrac{-\sum X}{n\mathrm{SS}_x} & \dfrac{n}{n\mathrm{SS}_x} \end{bmatrix} \tag{12.3}$$

$$\mathbf{X'y} = \begin{bmatrix} \sum Y \\ \sum XY \end{bmatrix} \tag{12.4}$$

$$\mathbf{b} = (\mathbf{X'X})^{-1}\mathbf{X'y} = \begin{bmatrix} \dfrac{\sum X^2}{nSS_x} & \dfrac{-\sum X}{nSS_x} \\ \dfrac{-\sum X}{nSS_x} & \dfrac{n}{nSS_x} \end{bmatrix} \begin{bmatrix} \sum Y \\ \sum XY \end{bmatrix}$$

$$= \begin{bmatrix} \dfrac{\sum X^2 \sum Y - \sum X \sum XY}{nSS_x} \\ \dfrac{-\sum X \sum Y + n \sum XY}{nSS_x} \end{bmatrix} = \begin{bmatrix} \dfrac{\sum Y}{n} - \dfrac{SS_{xy} X}{SS_x n} \\ nSS_{xy}/nSS_x \end{bmatrix}$$

$$= \begin{bmatrix} \bar{Y} - b\bar{X} \\ SS_{xy}/SS_x \end{bmatrix} = \begin{bmatrix} A \\ B \end{bmatrix} \tag{12.5}$$

12.4.1 Estimating the Calibration Equation

EXAMPLE 12.1. Let us apply the matrix approach to Example 6.1, the calibration of a nephelometer. The data are replotted in Figure 12.1.

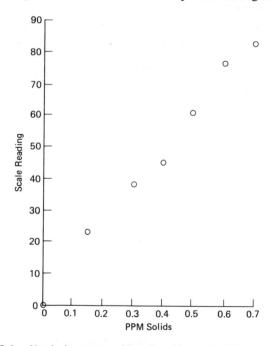

Figure 12.1. Nephelometer calibration, Example 6.1—data points.

The matrices are:

$$y = \begin{bmatrix} 0 \\ 23 \\ 38 \\ 45 \\ 61 \\ 76 \\ 82 \end{bmatrix}_{7 \times 1}, \quad b = \begin{bmatrix} A \\ B \end{bmatrix}_{2 \times 1}, \quad X = \begin{bmatrix} 1 & 0 \\ 1 & 0.15 \\ 1 & 0.30 \\ 1 & 0.40 \\ 1 & 0.50 \\ 1 & 0.60 \\ 1 & 0.70 \end{bmatrix}_{7 \times 2}$$

$$X' = \begin{bmatrix} 1 & 1 & 1 & 1 & 1 & 1 & 1 \\ 0 & 0.15 & 0.30 & 0.40 & 0.50 & 0.60 & 0.70 \end{bmatrix}$$

$$X'X = \begin{bmatrix} 1 & 1 & \cdots & 1 \\ 0 & 0.15 & & 0.70 \end{bmatrix} \begin{bmatrix} 1 & 0.00 \\ 1 & 0.15 \\ 1 & 0.30 \\ 1 & 0.40 \\ 1 & 0.50 \\ 1 & 0.60 \\ 1 & 0.70 \end{bmatrix} = \begin{bmatrix} 7 & 2.65 \\ 2.65 & 1.3725 \end{bmatrix}$$

$$X'y = \begin{bmatrix} 1 & 1 & \cdots & 1 \\ 0 & 0.15 & & 0.70 \end{bmatrix} \begin{bmatrix} 0 \\ 23 \\ 38 \\ 45 \\ 61 \\ 76 \\ 82 \end{bmatrix} = \begin{bmatrix} 325 \\ 166.35 \end{bmatrix}$$

$$X'X = 7(1.3725) - 2.65(2.65) = 9.6075 - 7.0225 = 2.585$$

$$(X'X)^{-1} = \frac{1}{2.585} \begin{bmatrix} 1.3725 & -2.65 \\ -2.65 & 7 \end{bmatrix}$$

$$= \begin{bmatrix} \dfrac{1.3725}{2.585} & \dfrac{-2.65}{2.585} \\[2ex] \dfrac{-2.65}{2.585} & \dfrac{7}{2.585} \end{bmatrix}$$

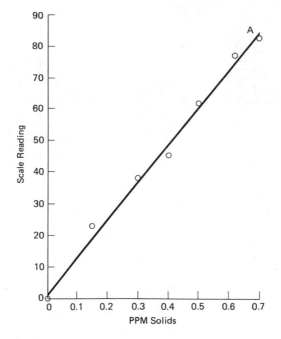

Figure 12.2.   Nephelometer calibration curve, Example 6.1.

$$\mathbf{b} = (\mathbf{X'X})^{-1}\mathbf{X'y} = \begin{bmatrix} \dfrac{1.3725}{2.585} & \dfrac{-2.65}{2.585} \\[2mm] \dfrac{-2.65}{2.585} & \dfrac{7}{2.585} \end{bmatrix} \begin{bmatrix} 325 \\ 166.35 \end{bmatrix}$$

$$= \begin{bmatrix} \dfrac{5.235}{2.585} \\[2mm] \dfrac{303.2}{2.585} \end{bmatrix} = \begin{bmatrix} 2.025145 \\ 117.29207 \end{bmatrix} = \begin{bmatrix} A \\ B \end{bmatrix}$$

Thus, $A = 2.025145$ and $B = 117.29207$, the same values we obtained using algebra in Section 6.2.1. The calibration is shown in Figure 12.2.

12.4.2   Estimating the Calibration Equation When the Curve Is Forced Through the Origin

In Section 6.3.1 we calculated the slope of the regression line when the regression curve was forced through the origin. Equation (6.11) gave the slope under this condition as

$$B = \sum XY/\sum X^2$$

We can calculate the slope from the matrix equations. The value for $\sum XY$ is given by the lower element of $\mathbf{X'y}$ (166.35), and the value for $\sum X^2$ is given by the lower right element of $\mathbf{X'X}$ (1.3725). These are the same values we obtained previously, and so the value of B is the same, $B = 121.2021858$. This gives us the same regression equation, $Y = 121.2022X$.

12.4.3 Coding *X* and *Y* Values for More Accurate Calculations

In Chapter 1 we saw that coding of data could be used to increase the accuracy of our calculations by reducing rounding errors. A special coding technique is recommended for matrix calculations, to minimize rounding errors and to simplify some of the calculations if they are performed on a hand calculator. This technique is called *correcting the variable for its mean* or *centering the data*, and is generally used in computer programs.

Correcting a variable for its mean consists of calculating the average of all its values, and then subtracting this average from each value of the variable. If we correct the variable X for its mean, the coded values are equal to $X_i - \bar{X}$, the linear equation becomes $Y = a' + b(X_i - \bar{X}) + \varepsilon$. If we code both X and Y, our linear equation becomes $Y_i - \bar{Y} = a' + b(X_i - \bar{X}) + \varepsilon$, and the matrices become:

$$\mathbf{X} = \begin{bmatrix} 1 & X_1 - \bar{X} \\ 1 & X_2 - \bar{X} \\ \vdots & \vdots \\ 1 & X_n - \bar{X} \end{bmatrix}, \quad \mathbf{b} = \begin{bmatrix} a' \\ b' \end{bmatrix}, \quad \mathbf{y} = \begin{bmatrix} Y_1 - \bar{Y} \\ Y_2 - \bar{Y} \\ \vdots \\ Y_n - \bar{Y} \end{bmatrix}$$

$$\mathbf{X'y} = \begin{bmatrix} \sum(Y_i - \bar{Y}) \\ \sum(Y_i - \bar{Y})(X_i - \bar{X}) \end{bmatrix}, \quad \mathbf{X'X} = \begin{bmatrix} n & \sum(X_i - \bar{X}) \\ \sum(X_i - \bar{X}) & \sum(X_i - \bar{X})^2 \end{bmatrix}$$

Since $\sum(Y_i - \bar{Y}) = 0$ for the corrected Y values, $\mathbf{X'y}$ becomes

$$\mathbf{X'y} = \begin{vmatrix} 0 \\ \sum(Y_i - \bar{Y})(X_i - \bar{X}) \end{vmatrix} \qquad (12.4A)$$

Since $\sum(X_i - \bar{X}) = 0$ for the corrected values, $\mathbf{X'X}$ becomes

$$\mathbf{X'X} = \begin{bmatrix} n & 0 \\ 0 & \sum(X_i - \bar{X})^2 \end{bmatrix} \qquad (12.2A)$$

And

$$(\mathbf{X'X})^{-1} = \begin{bmatrix} 1/n & 0 \\ 0 & 1/\sum (X_i - \bar{X})^2 \end{bmatrix} \tag{12.3A}$$

$$\mathbf{b} = (\mathbf{X'X})^{-1}\mathbf{X'y} = \begin{bmatrix} A' \\ B \end{bmatrix} \tag{12.5A}$$

Note that the value of B is unaffected by the coding, but we have a coded value A' for A. The value of A is readily calculated from the equation

$$A = \bar{Y} - B\bar{X}$$

where $\bar{Y}$ and $\bar{X}$ are the averages of the *uncoded* Y and X values. It should be obvious that the appearance of the zeros in the various matrices reduces the effort involved in performing the calculations and also assists in reducing rounding errors.

12.4.4 Application of Coding to the Nephelometer Calibration Example

EXAMPLE 12.2.   If we use the calibration data from Example 12.1 in Section 12.4.1 and code the values for X and Y, we obtain the following:

$$\bar{X} = 0.37857143, \qquad \bar{Y} = 46.42857143$$

$$\mathbf{y} = \begin{bmatrix} 0 - \bar{Y} \\ 23 - \bar{Y} \\ \vdots \\ 82 - \bar{Y} \end{bmatrix}, \qquad \mathbf{b} = \begin{bmatrix} a' \\ b \end{bmatrix}, \qquad \mathbf{X} = \begin{bmatrix} 1 & 0 - \bar{X} \\ 1 & 0.15 - \bar{X} \\ \vdots & \vdots \\ 1 & 0.70 - \bar{X} \end{bmatrix}$$

$$\mathbf{X'X} = \begin{bmatrix} 7 & 0 \\ 0 & 0.36928571 \end{bmatrix}$$

$$(\mathbf{X'X})^{-1} = \begin{bmatrix} 0.14285714 & 0 \\ 0 & 2.7079304 \end{bmatrix}$$

$$\mathbf{X'y} = \begin{bmatrix} -1.78 \times 10^{-15} \\ 43.314286 \end{bmatrix} = \begin{bmatrix} 0 \\ 43.31414286 \end{bmatrix}$$

$$\mathbf{b} = (\mathbf{X'X})^{-1}\mathbf{X'y} = \begin{bmatrix} -2.54 \times 10^{-16} \\ 117.29207 \end{bmatrix} = \begin{bmatrix} 0 \\ 117.29207 \end{bmatrix} = \begin{bmatrix} A' \\ B \end{bmatrix}$$

$$A = \overline{Y} - b\overline{X} = 46.42857143 - (117.29206983 \times 0.3785714)$$

$$= 2.0251451$$

$$B = 117.29207$$

Thus, we get the same estimates for A and B as we did using uncoded data.

12.5 CONFIDENCE INTERVALS

We can establish confidence intervals for Y, just as we did in Chapter 6. Recall the underlying assumptions for the regression and confidence intervals: (a) there is a perfect linear regression between X and the average Y for each value of X (the only error is due to the random errors in observing Y); (b) the scatter of Y values about its true value is uniform over the range studied (the variance is constant); and (c) each subpopulation of Y values is normal.

The first assumption of error being present only in Y (none in X, or at least much less error in X than Y) is frequently disregarded by statisticians working on actual problems. They frequently assign the variable with the greater error to Y, the other variable to X, and proceed to use the regression technique described in Chapter 6 and this chapter. They are careful to remember that their results may be subject to some error. The reason this assumption is violated is because of the lack of suitable techniques for handling cases with appreciable error in both variables.

The second assumption is illustrated in Figure 12.3.

When we assume that the variance of Y is constant, we are saying that the standard deviation σ_1 for Y_1 at X_1 is equal to the standard deviations at all other values of X and Y. Or, in Figure 12.3, $\sigma_1 = \sigma_2 = \sigma_3$.

The third assumption is also illustrated by Figure 12.3. When we assume normal distributions of the Y values for each subpopulation of Y, we are saying that the distributions of Y values at all levels of Y (for example Y_1, Y_2, and Y_3) are Gaussian in shape as opposed to being skewed.

In each of the following sections we will use the 95% confidence interval, simply because it is the one most commonly used. Other percentage intervals may be calculated by selecting the appropriate t value from the table of t-distribution values. The equations are those used in Chapter 6.

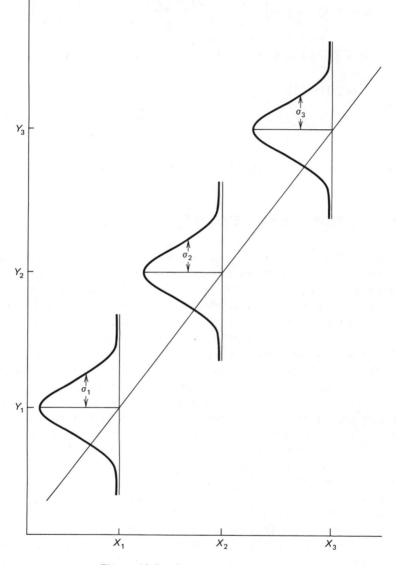

Figure 12.3. Constancy of variance.

12.5.1   Confidence Interval for *y*

The equation to calculate the 95% confidence interval that will include the true mean *y* for a specified X is:

$$y = A + BX \pm t_{0.05/2,\,n-2} \times s_{Y.X}\sqrt{\frac{1}{n} + \frac{(X - \bar{X})^2}{\sum X^2 - \frac{(\sum X)^2}{n}}} \qquad (6.5)$$

where

$$A = \text{intercept of regression line}$$

$$B = \text{slope of regression line}$$

$$s_{Y.X} = \sqrt{\frac{n-1}{n-2}(s_Y^2 - b^2 s_X^2)}$$

$$s_Y^2 = \frac{\sum Y^2 - \frac{(\sum Y)^2}{n}}{n-1}$$

$$s_X^2 = \frac{\sum X^2 - \frac{(\sum X)^2}{n}}{n-1}$$

The values for all the above terms can be obtained from our matrix calculations except for $t_{0.05/2,\,5}$, which of course is found in Table 5 of Appendix D, and $\sum Y^2$. The $\sum Y^2$ value is given by matrix $\mathbf{y'y}$, which we have not calculated because it is not used in estimating *a* and *b*. However, some computer regression programs include this matrix. If your program does not, the sum of the squares of the Y values is easily calculated with a hand calculator. The other terms are found in the following matrices:

n is the upper left corner element of $\mathbf{X'X}$
$\sum Y$ is the top element of $\mathbf{X'y}$
A is the upper element of $\mathbf{b}$
B is the lower element of $\mathbf{b}$
$\sum X^2$ is the lower right corner element of $\mathbf{X'X}$
$\sum X$ is the upper right (or lower left) corner element of $\mathbf{X'X}$
$\bar{X}$ is $\sum X/n$

For our nephelometer calibration example, we have the following values for the confidence interval calculation:

$$n = 7$$

$$\sum Y^2 = 20{,}219$$

$$\sum Y = 325$$

$$A = 2.025145$$

$$B = 117.29207$$

$$\sum X^2 = 1.3725$$

$$\sum X = 2.65$$

$$\bar{X} = 325/7 = 0.37875143$$

These values are the same as we obtained in Section 6.2 using simple algebra, and so the confidence interval given by Equation 6.2 will also be the same. This calculation was made in Section 6.2 and will not be repeated here.

12.5.2 Confidence Interval for an Individual Value of y

The equation for calculating the 95% confidence interval for an individual value of y for a specified value of X is identical to Equation (6.5) except for the additional unity term under the radical. Otherwise, the calculation is the same as in the preceding section.

12.5.3 Confidence Interval for the Intercept and Slope

Equations (6.3) and (6.4) are used to calculate the confidence intervals for the intercept and slope:

$$a = A \pm t_{0.05/2, n-2} \times s_{Y.X} \sqrt{\frac{1}{n} + \frac{\bar{X}^2}{\sum X^2 - \frac{(\sum X)^2}{n}}} \tag{6.3}$$

$$b = B \pm t_{0.05/2, n-2} \frac{s_{Y.X}}{\sqrt{\sum X^2 - \frac{(\sum X)^2}{n}}} \tag{6.4}$$

In Section 12.5.1 we saw how to obtain the values needed for these equations from the matrix calculations. Since the matrix values are the same as those we obtained in Section 6.2, the calculated intervals are also the same, and the calculations will not be repeated here.

12.6 CORRELATION COEFFICIENT AND COEFFICIENT OF DETERMINATION

In Chapter 6 we estimated the correlation coefficient r, a measure of the degree of association between two variables. We learned that the square of the correlation coefficient is called the coefficient of determination and that it measures the amount of variation in the dependent variable that is accounted for by the independent variable.

The equation we used to calculate the correlation coefficient was:

$$r = \frac{\sum XY - \frac{\sum X \sum Y}{n}}{\sqrt{\left(\sum X^2 - \frac{(\sum X)^2}{n}\right)\left(\sum Y^2 - \frac{(\sum Y)^2}{n}\right)}}; \quad df = n - 2 \quad (6.22)$$

We can use the results of our matrix calculations to obtain the values required by this equation. The only term we have not already obtained from our matrices is $\sum XY$, which is the lower element of $\mathbf{X'y}$.

Recall from Chapter 6 that use of the correlation coefficient is valid only in cases where the values of both X and Y are randomly selected. Thus, it would not be appropriate to calculate the correlation coefficient for the nephelometer calibration problem because the values of X were assigned rather than being randomly selected.

If we were to use the matrix technique to calculate the regression line for Example 6.2 and look at the matrix elements indicated above, we would find that these values are identical to those obtained in Chapter 6. Therefore, the calculation of the correlation coefficient would give the same value as obtained before and it will not be repeated here.

Since the coefficient of determination r^2 is the square of the correlation coefficient, we already have the matrix values to calculate it. Most computer regression programs provide the value of r^2. It is usually expressed as a percentage and is a measure of the proportion of variation in the dependent variable, Y, that is explained by the $X - Y$ relationship.

12.7 SUMMARY

We began this chapter with a brief description of basic matrix algebra operations. We used these operations to calculate linear regression equations for one independent variable, assuming there was no significant error in that variable. By using the data from an example from Chapter 6, we demonstrated that matrix algebra gave us the same regression equation as we obtained using simple algebra in Chapter 6. We were also able to obtain from the matrices the values needed to calculate establish confidence limits on the dependent variable y, the correlation coefficient, and the coefficient of determination.

In the next chapter we will test if our regression equation is appropriate for predicting the dependent variable.

12.8 PROBLEMS

You may want to try the matrix approach to regression on problems 2j, 4, and 5.

RESOURCES

Younger, M. S., *Handbook For Linear Regression*. New York, NY: Duxbury, 1979.
Draper, N. R., and Smith, H., *Applied Regression Analysis*, 2nd ed. New York, NY: John Wiley and Sons, 1981.

REFERENCES

1. SAS, SAS Institute, Inc., Publications Department, Box 8000, Carey, NC 17511.
    SPSS, SPSS Inc., 444 N. Michigan Ave., Suite 3000, Chicago, IL 60611.
    BMDP, Statistical Software Inc., 1440 Sepulveda Blud., Suite 316, Los Angeles, CA 90025.
    SPM, A-Priori Software, 1005 West Main, Vermillon, SD 57069.
    FLURP, LEDS Publishing Company, Inc., P. O. Box 12837, Research Triangle Park, NC 27709.
    MLR, Dynacomp, Inc., 1427 Monroe Ave., Rochester, NY 14618.
    CRISP, Crunch Software, 1541 Ninth Ave., San Francisco, CA 94122.
    STATPRO PC, Wadsworth Professional Software, Statler Office Building, 20 Park Plaza, Boston, MA 02116.
2. Hendrix, C. D., "What's that number mean?", *Chemtech*, October 1983, pp. 598–605.

Chapter 13
EVALUATION OF THE CALIBRATION EQUATION

OVERVIEW

In the preceding chapter we used matrix algebra to calculate the regression equation for the line that best expresses the linear relationship between X and Y. Before using this equation, we should examine it to see how appropriate it is. In this chapter we will see how analysis of variance can help us decide whether there is a linear relationship between X and Y, and how well the regression equation fits our data.

We will also check the validity of some of the assumptions we made in calculating the regression equation. In doing so we will make use of a technique called analysis of residuals.

13.0 EVALUATION OF THE CALIBRATION (LINEAR REGRESSION) EQUATION

Chapter 12 showed how to calculate the linear calibration equation using matrix algebra. This equation defines the line that best expresses the linear relationship between X and Y. However, the fact that we were able to calculate an equation and that its confidence interval for Y is satisfactory does not necessarily mean that the equation adequately describes the relationship of X and Y. So, before we use the regression equation, we ought to find out how good a job it will do for us.

The first question we want to answer is, "Does the regression equation really represent a linear relationship between X and Y?" It is possible that our particular sample of the population appears to show a linear relationship strictly by chance, while in reality the relationship is nonlinear or nonexistent.

If there really is a relationship, the next question is, "How well does the equation fit our data?" That is, how much scatter of the data points about the regression line is there? Analysis of variance can help answer these questions.

13.1 ANALYSIS OF VARIANCE

One way of determining if the regression equation represents a real relationship between Y and X is by use of analysis of variance. This approach is

TABLE 13.1.   ANOVA Table.

SOURCE OF VARIATION	SUM OF SQUARES	DEGREES OF FREEDOM	MEAN SQUARES
Regression	$(SS_R) = B(\sum(X - \bar{X})(Y - \bar{Y}))$	k	SS_R/k
Error	$(SS_E) = SS_T - SS_R$	$n - (k + 1)$	$SS_E/(n - (k + 1))$
Total	$(SS_T) = \sum(Y - \bar{Y})^2$	$n - 1$	

B = slope of regression line
k = number of independent variables
n = number of observations

TABLE 13.2.   ANOVA Table Using Matrix Notation.

SOURCE OF VARIATION	SUM OF SQUARES	DEGREES OF FREEDOM	MEAN SQUARES
Regression	$(SS_R) = \mathbf{b'X'y} - \dfrac{(\sum Y)^2}{n}$	k	SS_R/k
Error	$(SS_E) = SS_T - SS_R$	$n - (k + 1)$	$SS_E/(n - (k + 1))$
Total	$(SS_T) = \mathbf{y'y} - \dfrac{(\sum Y)^2}{n}$	$n - 1$	

particularly important when there are two or more independent variables. Table 13.1 shows the general form of the ANOVA table for one independent variable X and the dependent variable Y. You will note that it is very similar to the one we used in Chapter 7.

The mean square due to regression, SS_R/k, is that part of the total variability of Y due to the relationship of Y with X. The mean square due to error is the rest of the variability of Y: that unaccounted for by Y's relationship with X. It is equal to $s^2_{Y.X}$, which we calculated in Chapter 12; its square root, $s_{Y.X}$, is also known as the *standard error of estimate*.

The ANOVA table can be rewritten in terms of our matrix calculations as shown in Table 13.2.

The quantities given in the sum of squares column are obtainable from our matrix calculations. Matrix $\mathbf{b'}$ is the transpose of matrix $\mathbf{b}$. Matrix $\mathbf{X'y}$ was calculated in obtaining estimates of a and b in Section 12.4. The product of these two matrices is

$$\mathbf{b'X'y} = [A \quad B]\begin{bmatrix} \sum Y \\ \sum XY \end{bmatrix} = [A\sum Y + B\sum XY]$$

or, using the values from the nephelometer calibration example (Examples 6.1 and 12.1):

$$[2.025145 \quad 117.29206]\begin{bmatrix} 325 \\ 166.35 \end{bmatrix} = [658.1721 + 19{,}511.5758]$$

$$= 20{,}169.7079$$

Most computer regression programs include this calculation.

The $\sum Y$ is the upper element of $\mathbf{X'y}$ [Equation (12.4)], and n is the upper left element of $\mathbf{X'X}$ [Equation (12.3)]. The matrix $\mathbf{y'y}$ is equal to $\sum Y^2$ and is the product of the transpose of $\mathbf{y}$ and the $\mathbf{y}$-matrix:

$$\mathbf{y'y} = [Y_1 \; Y_2 \ldots Y_n]\begin{bmatrix} Y_1 \\ Y_2 \\ \vdots \\ Y_n \end{bmatrix} = [0\,23 \ldots 82]\begin{bmatrix} 0 \\ 23 \\ \vdots \\ 82 \end{bmatrix}$$

Using the nephelometer data:

$$\mathbf{y'y} = 0^2 + 23^2 + \cdots + 82^2 = 20{,}219$$

The $\mathbf{y'y}$ calculation is included in some computer programs.

Following the same logic we used in Chapter 7, if relationship of Y and X is real, the mean square due to regression will be significantly greater than that due to other sources (error). We can test two mean squares to see if they differ significantly by using the F test:

$$F = (SS_R/k)/(SS_E/(n - (k + 1)))$$

If the value of F exceeds the critical value of F for k and $n - (k + 1)$ degrees of freedom at the α significance level, we reject the null hypothesis that the variance due to regression is equal to the variance due to error. If the critical value is not exceeded, we accept the null hypothesis, and conclude that no relationship has been established between Y and X.

EXAMPLE 13.1.   Using the data from our nephelometer calibration example (Example 6.1 and 11.1), we have the following analysis of variance table:

ANOVA Table: Nephelometer Calibration.

SOURCE	SUM OF SQUARES		DF	MEAN SQUARES
Regression	$(SS_R) = 20169.7079 - \dfrac{325^2}{7}$		1	5080.4222
	$= 5080.4222$			
Error	$(SS_E) = SS_T - SS_R =$	49.2921	5	9.8584
Total	$(SS_T) = 20219.0 - \dfrac{325^2}{7}$		6	
	$= 5129.7143$			

$$F = 5080.4222/9.8584 = 515.34$$

$$F_{0.05,1,6} = 6.61$$

Thus, since the value of F exceeds the critical value, we reject the null hypothesis at $\alpha = 0.05$ and conclude that there is a linear relationship between the scale readings and ppm solids.

13.2   REGRESSION ANALYSIS WITH REPLICATED OBSERVATIONS

In Chapter 7 we saw that in the analysis of variance we needed replicate observations to be able to measure the significance of the error term. This is true here. In Table 13.1 the sum of squares for error is calculated by taking the difference between the total sum of squares and the sum of squares due to regression. Thus, the error sum of squares includes all variation not due to regression. If we have replicate observations, we can break the error term into two terms: error due to lack of fit and "pure error." In our nephelometer example, pure error would be the error inherent in making the scale readings at various concentrations of silica.

The lack of fit error is useful in deciding if our linear model, $y = a + bx + \varepsilon$, is appropriate, or if another model is needed to describe the relationship.

If we have replicate observations, the ANOVA table looks like Table 13.3. The sum of squares for pure error, SS_P, is obtained by first calculating the sum of squares for the set of replicate Y observations at each value of X and then summing the values. If we have j values of X, we will have j sets of Y values. For the first set of replicates of Y the contribution to the sum of squares is

TABLE 13.3.   ANOVA: Replicate Observations.

SOURCE	SUM OF SQUARES	DF	MEAN SQUARES
Regression	$(SS_R) = \mathbf{b'X'y} - \dfrac{(\sum Y)^2}{n}$	k	SS_R/k
Total error	$(SS_E) = SS_T - SS_R$	$n - (k + 1)$	$SS_T/(n - (k + 1))$
$\Big\{$ Lack of fit	$(SS_L) = SS_E - SS_P$	$\Big\{ \begin{array}{l} n - (k + 1) - \\ \sum(r_m - 1) \end{array}$	$\Big\{ \begin{array}{l} SS_L/(n - (k + 1) - \\ \sum(r_m - 1)) \end{array}$
$\Big\{$ Pure error	$(SS_P) = \sum\sum(Y_{mi} - \bar{Y_i})^2$	$\sum(r_m - 1)$	$SS_P/\sum(r_m - 1)$
Total	$(SS_T) = \mathbf{y'y} - \dfrac{(\sum Y)^2}{n}$	$n - 1$	

j = number of sets of replicated Y values, or number of X values
n = total number of Y values
r_m = number of replicates in set m of replicates
k = number of independent variables

$$\sum(Y_1 - \bar{Y_1})^2 = \sum Y_1^2 - \frac{(\sum Y_1)^2}{r_1}$$

with $r_1 - 1$ degrees of freedom, where r_1 is the number of replicates in the first set. Thus, for all j sets of replicates

$$SS_P = \left(\sum Y_1^2 - \frac{(\sum Y_1)^2}{r_1}\right) + \left(\sum Y_2^2 - \frac{(\sum Y_2)^2}{r_2}\right) + \cdots + \left(\sum Y_j^2 - \frac{(\sum Y_j)^2}{r_j}\right)$$

with $(r_1 - 1) + (r_2 - 1) + \cdots + (r_j - 1)$ degrees of freedom. This equation can be written more compactly as

$$SS_P = \sum_{m=1}^{j} \sum_{i=1}^{n_m} (Y_{mi} - \bar{Y_i})^2$$

with $\sum_{m=1}^{j} (r_m - 1)$ degrees of freedom.

Having obtained the corresponding mean squares in the usual manner, we can test the significance of the mean square for lack of fit by comparing it with the mean square for pure error:

$$F_{\text{l.o.f}} = MS_{\text{lack of fit}}/MS_{\text{pure error}}$$

If the value of F exceeds the critical value, we reject the null hypothesis, H_0: $\sigma^2_{\text{lack of fit}} = \sigma^2_{\text{pure error}}$. That is, we conclude the linear model does not fit our data. If the model is rejected, we need to look at our scatter plot of the data to see if we can discern what type of equation might be more appropriate, or what transformation might make our data fit the linear model. Of course, if the F value is less than the critical value, we accept the null hypothesis that the linear model has not been shown to be inappropriate for the data.

EXAMPLE 13.2. Calibration Curve with Replicate Observations. We shall use our nephelometer calibration example again, but this time we have the following duplicate measurements on each standard solution:

X, ppm SOLIDS	Y, SCALE READINGS		AVG. Y, SCALE READINGS
0.00	0,	0	0
0.15	27,	19	23
0.30	36,	40	38
0.40	42,	48	45
0.50	58,	64	61
0.60	78,	74	76
0.70	85,	79	82

(Note that the average of the replicates is exactly the same as in Example 6.1 when we had only one observation.) The data are plotted in Figure 13.1. Based on these amplified data, our matrices look like this:

$$
y = \begin{bmatrix} 0 \\ 0 \\ 27 \\ 19 \\ 36 \\ 40 \\ \vdots \\ 85 \\ 79 \end{bmatrix}, \quad b = \begin{bmatrix} A \\ B \end{bmatrix}, \quad X = \begin{bmatrix} 1 & 0 \\ 1 & 0 \\ 1 & 0.15 \\ 1 & 0.15 \\ 1 & 0.30 \\ 1 & 0.30 \\ \vdots & \vdots \\ 1 & 0.70 \\ 1 & 0.70 \end{bmatrix}
$$

$$
X' = \begin{bmatrix} 1 & 1 & 1 & 1 & \cdots & 1 & 1 \\ 0 & 0 & 0.15 & 0.15 & \cdots & 0.70 & 0.70 \end{bmatrix}
$$

$$
X'X = \begin{bmatrix} 1 & \cdots & 1 \\ 0 & \cdots & 0.70 \end{bmatrix} \begin{bmatrix} 1 & 0 \\ 1 & 0 \\ \vdots & \vdots \\ 1 & 0.70 \\ 1 & 0.70 \end{bmatrix} = \begin{bmatrix} 14 & 5.30 \\ 5.30 & 2.745 \end{bmatrix}
$$

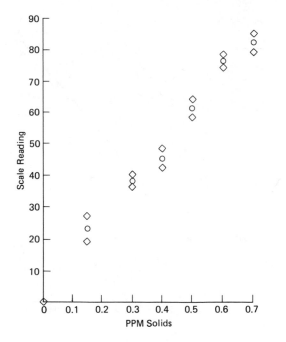

Figure 13.1.   Nephelometer calibration, Example 13.2—data points.
◇—Individual readings
○—Average readings

$$\mathbf{X'y} = \begin{bmatrix} 1 & \cdots & 1 \\ 0 & \cdots & 0.70 \end{bmatrix} \begin{bmatrix} 0 \\ 0 \\ \vdots \\ 85 \\ 79 \end{bmatrix} = \begin{bmatrix} 650 \\ 332.7 \end{bmatrix}$$

$$|\mathbf{X'X}| = 14(2.745) - 5.3(5.3) = 10.34$$

$$(\mathbf{X'X})^{-1} = \begin{bmatrix} \dfrac{2.745}{10.34} & \dfrac{-5.3}{10.34} \\ \dfrac{-5.3}{10.34} & \dfrac{14}{10.34} \end{bmatrix}$$

$$\mathbf{b} = (\mathbf{X'X})^{-1}\mathbf{X'y} = \begin{bmatrix} \dfrac{2.745}{10.34} & \dfrac{-5.3}{10.34} \\ \dfrac{-5.3}{10.34} & \dfrac{14}{10.34} \end{bmatrix} \begin{bmatrix} 630 \\ 332.7 \end{bmatrix} = \begin{bmatrix} 2.025145 \\ 117.29207 \end{bmatrix} = \begin{bmatrix} A \\ B \end{bmatrix}$$

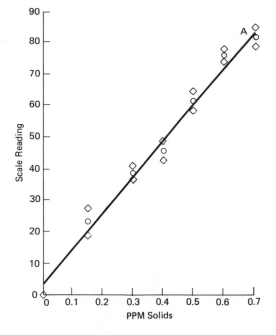

Figure 13.2.   Nephelometer calibration curve, Example 13.2.
◇—Individual readings
○—Average readings
A—Regression line of *Y* on *X*

These are the same values of A and B we previously obtained in Example 12.1 using single observations of Y (which are the average of the set of two observations in this example). Thus, we have the same regression line. The line, whose equation is $Y = 2.025 + 117.292X$, and the duplicate data points are shown in Figure 13.2.

The following values are needed for the ANOVA table:

$$\mathbf{b'X'y} = [2.025145 \quad 117.29206]\begin{bmatrix} 650 \\ 332.7 \end{bmatrix} = 40{,}339.4158$$

$$(\textstyle\sum Y)^2/n = 650^2/14 = 30{,}178.5714$$

$$\mathbf{y'y} = [0 \quad 0 \quad \cdots \quad 79]\begin{bmatrix} 0 \\ 0 \\ \vdots \\ 85 \\ 79 \end{bmatrix} = 0^2 + 0^2 + \cdots + 85^2 + 79^2 = 40{,}540$$

$$SS_R = 40{,}339.4158 - 30{,}178.5714 = 10{,}160.8444$$

$$SS_T = 40{,}540 - 30{,}178.5714 = 10{,}361.4286$$

$$SS_E = SS_T - SS_R = 10{,}361.4286 - 10{,}160.8444 = 200.5842$$

Sum of Squares for Pure Error:

$$SS_P = (0 - 0)^2 + (0 - 0)^2 \text{ (for 1st pair of } Y \text{ values)}$$

$$+ (27 - 23)^2 + (19 - 23)^2 \text{ (for 2nd pair)}$$

$$+ (36 - 38)^2 + (40 - 38)^2 \text{ (for 3rd pair)}$$

$$+ (42 - 45)^2 + (48 - 45)^2 \text{ (for 4th pair)}$$

$$+ (58 - 61)^2 + (64 - 61)^2 \text{ (for 5th pair)}$$

$$+ (78 - 76)^2 + (74 - 76)^2 \text{ (for 6th pair)}$$

$$+ (85 - 82)^2 + (79 - 82)^2 \text{ (for 7th pair)}$$

$$SS_P = 0 + 32 + 8 + 18 + 8 + 18 = 102$$

Degrees of freedom for $SS_P = \sum_{m=1}^{7} (2 - 1) = 7$.

Sum of Squares for Lack of Fit Error:

$$SS_L = SS_E - SS_P$$

$$= 200.5842 - 102.00 = 98.5842$$

We can now fill in the ANOVA table:

SOURCE OF VARIATION	SUM OF SQUARES		DEGREES OF FREEDOM	MEAN SQUARES
Regression	(SS_R)	10,160.8444	1	10,160.8444
Error	(SS_E)	200.5842	12	16.7153
⎰Lack of fit	⎰(SS_L)	⎰ 98.5842	⎰5	⎰19.7168
⎱Pure	⎱(SS_P)	⎱102.0000	⎱7	⎱14.5714
Total	(SS_T)	10,361.4286	13	

$$F_{\text{regression}} = 10{,}160.8444 / 16.7153 = 607.88$$

$$F_{0.05, 1, 12} = 4.75$$

$$F_{\text{lack of fit}} = 19.7168/14.5714 = 1.35$$

$$F_{0.05, 5, 7} = 3.97$$

Since the F value for regression exceeds the critical value at $\alpha = 0.05$, we conclude there is a linear relationship between Y and X. But the $F_{\text{lack of fit}}$ value does not exceed its critical value, and we conclude that the linear equation has not been shown to be inappropriate for the data.

13.3 TESTING OUR ASSUMPTIONS: ANALYSIS OF RESIDUALS

When we calculated the regression equation, we made some assumptions about errors: We assumed that they were independent, that their average would equal zero, that their variance or scatter would be constant over all values of the independent variable X, and that their distribution would be normal. If these assumptions have been seriously violated, the basis of our equation is faulty and we need to take corrective action to obtain a valid regression equation.

The approach we will use in checking on the validity of the assumptions makes use of *residuals*. A residual is merely the difference between an observed value of Y and the value of Y calculated from the regression equation. If our equation fits our data, the only difference between the observed Y and its value calculated from the equation would be that due to error. Thus a residual may be considered to be an observed error if the equation fits the data, and these residuals should have properties that tend to support the assumptions.

A graphical technique will be used to examine the residuals. It is easy to do and is generally effective in detecting violations of the assumptions. There are some statistical tests which attempt to provide numerical measures of the degree to which some of the assumptions are met, but for practical problems, plots of the residuals are easier to understand and are just as effective in revealing any violations of the assumptions that are serious enough to require corrective action.

There are various ways of plotting the residuals. They may be plotted against the values of the independent variable X (or each X if there is more than one independent variable in the regression). They may be plotted against the values of Y calculated from the regression equation. (They should not be plotted against the observed values of Y because these values are usually correlated with the residuals.) One may also plot the residuals against variables other than those included in the regression equation. In this latter case, if the pattern resembles Pattern A of Figure 13.3, the variable may be con-

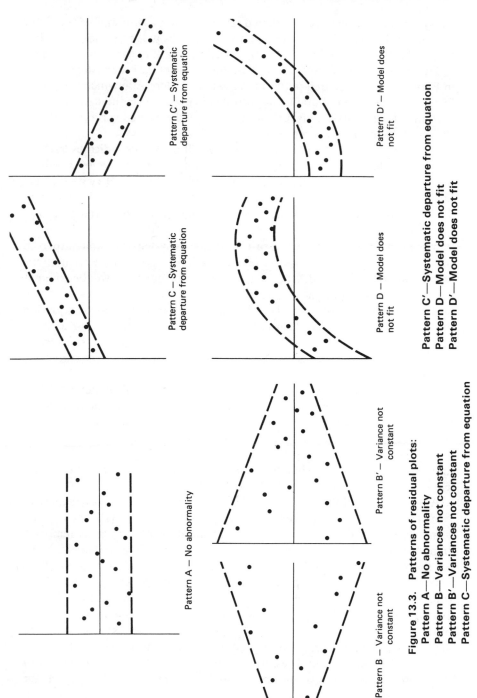

Figure 13.3. Patterns of residual plots:
Pattern A—No abnormality
Pattern B—Variances not constant
Pattern B'—Variances not constant
Pattern C—Systematic departure from equation
Pattern C'—Systematic departure from equation
Pattern D—Model does not fit
Pattern D'—Model does not fit

sidered as having no effect on the equation. Conversely, if any of the other patterns in Figure 13.3 are obtained, the variable is judged to have an effect and consideration should be given to including it in the regression equation.

The pattern of the plotted data will resemble one of the four patterns shown in Figure 13.3. The desired pattern is shown as Pattern A in which the points form a horizontal band about the zero residual axis. This indicates that the variance of the errors is constant for all values of the plotted variable and that the errors have a zero average value.

If the pattern obtained is similar to Pattern B or B', this indicates that the variance of the error (or scatter) is not constant over the range of X values, but instead tends to increase (Pattern B) or decrease (Pattern B') with increasing values of the plotted variable. This suggests that the values for observed Y should be transformed to achieve better uniformity of variance before recalculating the regression equation.

A pattern similar to Pattern C or C' indicates a systematic departure from the regression equation. This is usually the result of an error in the calculations which should be corrected. Of course the regression equation will be different as a result of correcting the errors.

A pattern similar to Pattern D or D' indicates that the regression equation does not fit the data. The inclusion of additional terms (like X^2 or a cross-product term if there are two or more independent variables) or a transformation of the observed Y values may be needed to improve the fit of the regression equation.

Table 13.4 shows the residuals for Example 13.2, the nephelometer calibration example. The values in the calculated Y column are obtained using the regression equation $Y = 2.025 + 117.292X$ and the listed X values. The residuals are the Y values minus the corresponding calculated Y values. The plot of these residuals versus the X values is shown in Figure 13.4. The points appear to lie in the desired horizontal band about the residual equal zero axis. Thus, there is no indication of violations of the assumptions.

A better way of plotting the residuals is to convert the residuals to *standardized residuals* by dividing each residual by the standard deviation, $s_{Y \cdot X}$. By using standardized residuals, any effect of the slope of the line is removed. In addition, because the Y values are probably normally distributed, almost all the standardized residuals will fall between -3 and $+3$ units which makes for easier, more compact plotting. Figure 13.5 shows the standardized residuals for the nephelometer calibration data. Again, the plot exhibits an even distribution within a horizontal band about the zero axis. The absence of a pattern like Patterns B through D of Figure 13.3 indicates uniform scatter, absence of calculation errors, and good fit of the equation to the data.

None of the standardized residual points exceeds ± 2 deviation units. For this reason the ± 3 limits are not shown in Figure 13.5. If a point on the

TABLE 13.4.   Table of Residuals
Nephelometer Calibration, Example 13.2.

X VALUE	Y VALUE	CALCULATED Y	RESIDUAL	STANDARDIZED RESIDUAL
0.00	0	2.02	−2.02	−0.50
0.00	0	2.02	−2.02	−0.50
0.15	19	19.62	−0.62	−0.15
0.15	27	19.62	7.38	1.81
0.30	36	37.21	−1.21	−0.30
0.30	40	37.21	2.79	0.68
0.40	42	48.94	−6.94	−1.70
0.40	48	48.94	−0.94	−0.73
0.50	58	60.71	−2.67	−0.65
0.50	64	60.71	3.33	0.81
0.60	78	72.40	5.60	1.37
0.60	74	72.40	1.60	0.39
0.70	85	84.13	0.87	0.21
0.70	79	84.13	−5.13	−1.25

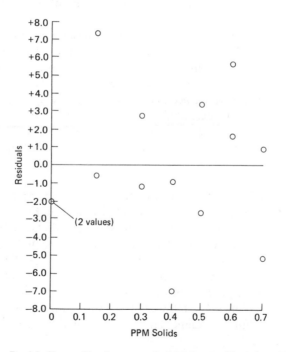

Figure 13.4.   Residuals vs. X values, nephelometer calibration, Example 13.2.

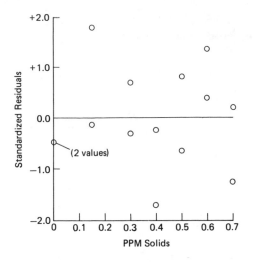

Figure 13.5. Standardized residuals vs. *X* values, nephelometer calibration, Example 13.2.

standardized residual plot exceeds ± 3 units, that point should be considered suspect as an outlier.

This does *not* mean that a point with a value of say $+3.5$ should arbitrarily be discarded! Rather, it means that the circumstances that resulted in that point's value should be examined for any explanation for its high value. It may have resulted from a transposition of digits, a misread observation, etc. Or there might be something peculiar to that value, such as the linear range of response having been exceeded or some experimental boundary having been reached. One should be very wary of discarding a value just because it is different; in general, it is better to retain such a value unless a specific reason (the statistical term is "assignable cause") can be found to explain the difference.

The plot of standardized residuals versus the *X* values can provide a rough check on whether the errors have a normal distribution. For a normal distribution about 68% of all standardized normal values will fall between -1 and $+1$ units, about 95% between -2 and $+2$, and more than 99% between -3 and $+3$. Thus, if we count the number of values falling within these ranges and compare the percentages with those just stated, we have a basis for detecting relatively large departures from the normal distribution. In Figure 13.5, 10 of the 14 points (71%) fall within ± 1 standardized residual units and all (100%) fall within ± 2 units. This is a reasonable agreement with the expected percentages.

Of course, this check works best with a relatively large number of data

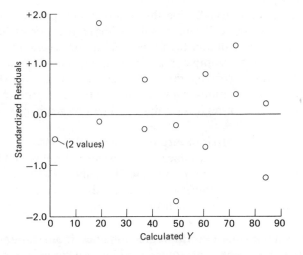

Figure 13.6. Standardized residuals vs. calculated Y values, nephelometer calibration, Example 13.2.

points. With only 14 points in the nephelometer calibration example, each point represents about 7%, so that it is difficult to compare the results with the above limits. With 20 or more points, this check for normality is more meaningful.

Figure 13.6 is a plot of the standardized residuals versus calculated Y for the nephelometer calibration data. Again, the pattern is similar to Pattern A of Figure 13.3. All points fall within -2 and $+2$ units and are evenly distributed about the standardized residual axis, indicating no abnormalities.

Had this pattern of standardized residuals versus calculated Y resembled any of the other patterns, the interpretation would be the same as previously given for the plot versus X except for Pattern C. In this case an error in analysis is still indicated, but the effect could also be caused by the erroneous omission of the intercept term a from the regression equation.

The better computer regression programs provide means for performing various plots of the data.

13.4 CAUTIONS IN THE USE OF REGRESSION LINES

Before we end our consideration of regression lines, it might be well to review some limitations in the correct use of regression equations and lines. These are applicable to all regression situations regardless of the number of variables.

In Chapter 6 we said that extrapolation of the regression line beyond the range of observations used to generate the line was risky. The least squares technique fits the best straight line through our data points. Unless we are very confident that the X-Y relationship is linear at lower or higher values than our data, we may obtain highly misleading or erroneous results if we extrapolate. A familiar example is calibration curves, which in general are linear over a certain working range, but usually begin to exhibit curvature at higher concentrations. Unwarranted extrapolation is probably the most common misuse of regression lines and equations; hence, the repeated warning.

In our study of the analysis of variance earlier in this book we distinguished between random and fixed variables. The concept in brief is that if a variable is random, it represents a random sample of a universe and our conclusions are thus applicable to the universe of that variable. Conversely, if a variable is not randomly selected, the conclusions are applicable only to the selected values of the variable.

We have a similar situation with regression lines. If our variable values are fixed, as in the case of the nephelometer calibration standards, our equation is strictly applicable only for those values used in the calibration. We generally assume that the equation is valid for values intermediate to those actually used in the experiment. In the case of a calibration curve, the underlying theory makes this a safe assumption. However, in other instances we could be on shaky ground unless the theoretical aspects of our work support the concept of a continuous linear relationship over our range of values. From a statistical point of view, we simply do not know whether the relationship is continuously linear.

If our experimental plan provides for the random selection of samples of our variable over the range of interest, the regression equation should be applicable to all values of the variable within that range. This was the case for the sulfuric acid color test problem in Chapter 6.

Another common misuse of regression equations is to conclude that if a significant relationship is found between two variables, then a cause-effect relationship has been established. If X does cause Y to change, then obviously Y and X will exhibit a significant relationship, but the reverse is not necessarily true. The fact that Y and X vary together may merely mean that a third variable affects X and Y. Cause and effect must be established by evidence other than just a significant linear regression equation or a significant correlation coefficient.

13.5 SUMMARY

In this chapter we saw how analysis of variance may be used to test the slope of the regression equation for significance. If replicate observations are available, analysis of variance can also show us how well the linear equation fits our data. We saw how examination of residuals can help us decide if the scatter of our data points is uniform, help us detect points that may be outliers, and provide us with a rough check on normality. Finally, we reviewed some of the common misuses of regression equations and lines.

13.6   PROBLEMS

The following problems make use of the techniques discussed in this chapter: Problems 2j, 4, and 5. The answers should be the same as those obtained using the equations in Chapter 6.

Appendix A
GLOSSARY OF SOME COMMON
STATISTICAL TERMS

Accuracy. The agreement between an experimentally determined value and the accepted reference value. In chemical work this term is frequently used to express freedom from bias, but in other fields it assumes a broader meaning as a joint index of precision and bias.[1]

Bias. A constant or systematic error as opposed to a random error. It manifests itself as a persistent plus or minus deviation of the method average from the accepted reference value.[1]

Chi-Square (χ^2) Test. A variance ratio test used to decide whether the observed variance is different from a known or established variance. This test is also used to determine if the observed number of occurrences of an event differs significantly from the expected number.

Coefficient of Determination. The square of the correlation coefficient. It is the proportion of the variation in the dependent variable which is accounted for by the independent variable, and is usually expressed as a percentage.

Coefficient of Variation (C.V.). or Relative Standard Deviation. A measure of relative precision; defined as the sample standard deviation divided by the sample average and multiplied by 100.

Confidence Level. This term [usually expressed as a percentage; e.g., 95% confidence level], is commonly used in establishing the probability of precision statements and means that there are [for example] 95 in 100 chances of being correct, and 5 in 100 chances of being wrong, in predicting that the expected precision (or expected value) will fall within the specified limits or range.[1]

Confidence Interval or **Confidence Limits.** These terms (usually expressed as a percentage; e.g., 95% confidence limit), refer to "that interval or range of values around an observed value which will in 95% of the cases include the expected value. The expected value is defined as the average of an infinite series of such determinations."[1]

Correlation Coefficient. A measure of the degree of correlation between two variables. Values of r may range from -1 to $+1$. A value of $+1$ denotes perfect functional relationship between the two variables, an increasing value of one being associated with an increasing value of the second. A value of -1 also denotes a perfect relationship, but in this case an increasing value of one variable is associated with a decreasing value of the second. When $r = 0$, there is no effect of one variable upon the other variable.

Degrees of Freedom (DF). Generally equal to the number of observations minus the number of constants calculated from it. Example: Variance is the average squared deviation about the mean of n observations. The variance can be calculated only after the mean has been calculated and this uses up one degree of freedom. No other constants are necessary to estimate the variance. Hence, the estimate of the variance has $n - 1$ degrees of freedom.

Distribution. The frequencies with which observations of given magnitudes occur in a sample.

Error. (1) Any deviation of an observed value from the true value. When expressed as a percentage of the value measured, it is called relative error.

(2) A second use of "error" applies not to data, but to decisions made regarding data. If we, on the basis of a statistical test, reject a true hypothesis, this is a Type I error. Example: We decide that two averages are significantly different when in fact they are equal. Conversely, if we accept a false hypothesis, this is a Type II error. Example: We decide that two averages are not significantly different when in fact they are different.

F Test. A variance ratio test used to decide whether two independent estimates of variance can reasonably be accepted as being two estimates of the variance of a single normally distributed universe.

Homogeneity of Variances. If set of estimates of a variance do not differ more than could be expected due to chance, they are said to be homogeneous.

Hypothesis. An assumption made concerning a parameter to provide a basis for a statistical test; usually expressed as a null hypothesis or as an alternative hypothesis. Example: Assume that the variance of data set 1 (σ_1^2) is the same as that for data set 2 (σ_2^2). The null hypothesis is expressed as: $H_0: \sigma_1^2 = \sigma_2^2$. The alternative hypothesis could take one of the following forms: $H_A: \sigma_1^2 \neq \sigma_2^2$, or $\sigma_1^2 > \sigma_2^2$, or $\sigma_1^2 < \sigma_2^2$.

Mean or Average Deviation. The average of the deviations of the individual measurements from the average of the set without regard to sign. The use of this term is not recommended as a measure of precision.[2]

Mean. The arithmetic average of a series of measurements.

Median. For samples with an odd number of items, the median is the middle item when the items are arranged in order of magnitude. For samples with an even number of items, the median is the arithmetic average of the two middle items when they are arranged in order of magnitude. The median is an estimate of the mean for symmetrical distributions.

Mode. The most frequent value in a frequency distribution.

Normal Distribution. A body of data or a universe whose values exhibit the frequency of the Gaussian curve.

Observation. An experimentally obtained value.

Outlier. A value in a set of observations which is so different from the rest that it is considered to be a member of another set or population.

Parameter. The unknown "true" value of the basic properties defining a population or distribution, such as the mean and the variance.

Pooling of Variances. A technique of combining estimates of a variance to achieve a better estimate of the variance. The individual estimates should exhibit homogeneity before they are pooled.

Population. Same as *universe*.

Precision. The degree of agreement of repeated measurements of the same property. There are various types of precision such as:

Duplicability. The agreement between duplicate or other multiple determinations performed by the same analyst at essentially the same time.

Repeatability. The precision of a method expressed as the agreement attainable between independent determinations performed by a single analyst using the same apparatus and techniques (on more than one day).[1]

Reproducibility. The precision of a method expressed as the agreement attainable between determinations performed in different laboratories.[1]

Note: There is no uniformity in the usage of the terms "repeatability" and "reproducibility." These definitions represent the recommendations of ASTM Committee E-15.[2]

Range. The absolute value of the algebraic difference between the highest and lowest values in a set of data.

Random Error. The chance variation encountered in all experimental work despite the closest possible control of all variables. It is characterized by the random occurrence of both positive and negative deviations from the mean value of the method, the algebraic average of which will approach zero in a long series of measurements.[1]

Statistic. An estimate of a parameter. Examples:

PARAMETER	STATISTIC
Average or mean, $\mu = \dfrac{\sum X}{N}$	$\bar{X} = \dfrac{\sum X}{n}$
Variance, $\sigma^2 = \dfrac{(X - \mu)^2}{N}$	$s^2 = \dfrac{\sum(X - \bar{X})^2}{n - 1}$
Standard deviation, $\sigma = \sqrt{\dfrac{\sum(X - \mu)^2}{N}}$	$s = \sqrt{\dfrac{\sum(X - \bar{X})^2}{n - 1}}$

Standard Deviation. A measure of the dispersion of a series of results around their average, expressed as the square root of the variance.

Standard Error. This term is sometimes used to represent $s/\sqrt{n}$ to express the precision of an average. Because of possible confusion with standard deviation, some professional organizations do not recommend its use.

t **Test (Student's *t*).** The ratio of a normally distributed variate with zero mean to its estimated standard deviation. This test is used to determine whether the mean of a set of values is consistent with their having been drawn from a universe having some specified mean, or whether the means of two sets of values are consistent with the two sets having been drawn from a single universe.

Variance. A measure of the dispersion of a series of results around their average. It is the sum of the squares of the individual deviations from the average of the results, divided by the number of results minus one.[1]

Universe or **Population.** Statistical reasoning employs the concept of a sample of observations drawn at random from a universe of all possible observations. When a number of determinations of the same quantity are made, the values obtained are regarded as a random sample of all the determinations which might have been made in infinite repetition of the test actually performed. A universe is generally characterized by one or more parameters, such as its mean and its standard deviation. A finite sample can give only estimates of these parameters.

REFERENCES

1. Reprinted, with permission from the *Annual Book of ASTM Standards*. E-180, Volume 15.05. Copyright, ASTM, 1916 Race Street, Philadelphia, PA 19103.
2. Standard Practice for Determining the Precision of ASTM Methods for Analysis and Testing of Industrial Chemicals, E-180, Volume 15.05, *Annual Book of Standards*, ASTM, 1916 Race Street, Philadelphia, PA 19103.

Appendix B
PROBLEMS

1. The following values were obtained for the normality of a solution of $KMnO_4$ when pure KI and As_2O_3 were used as primary standards. (a) Calculate the variance, standard deviation, and coefficient of variation for each set of data. (b) Calculate the 95% confidence limits for each average normality. (c) Calculate the 90% and 95% confidence limits for the standard deviation of each set of data. (d) Calculate the range for two determinations (95% confidence level) using the standard deviation of each set of data. (e) Is either method significantly more precise? (f) Do the average values obtained with each standard differ significantly? (g) Using the range of values, calculate the standard deviation for each set of data.

N USING KI	N USING As_2O_3
0.13110	0.13118
0.13126	0.13113
0.13120	0.13119
0.13113	0.13125
0.13129	0.13128
0.13108	

2. A plant laboratory wanted to compare a gas chromatographic method for assaying acetaldehyde with a wet chemical method (hydroxylamine hydrochloride–triethanolamine). The ten analyses by each method are tabulated below. (a) Test the wet chemical data for randomness. (b) Assuming that all analyses were made on one sample, calculate the variance, standard deviation, and coefficient of variation for each method. (c) Using the range of values, calculate the standard deviation for each method. (d) Calculate the 90% and 95% confidence limits for each standard deviation in part b. (e) Calculate the 95% confidence limits for the average of the 10 determinations made by each method. (f) For each method calculate the range for two results (95% confidence level). (g) Are the two methods equivalent in precision? (h) Assume that a different sample was used for each pair of measurements (analysis 1 by each method performed on sample 1, analysis 2 on sample 2, etc.). Do the two methods give equivalent average assays? (i) Assuming the ten samples were randomly selected, calculate the correlation coefficient. Is it significant at the 99% confidence level? (j) Calculate the equation for the least squares regression line to estimate values by the gas chromatographic method (Y) from values by the wet chemical method (X). (k) Estimate the 95% confidence limits for the slope of the regression line.

ANALYSIS	WET CHEMICAL METHOD	GAS CHROM. METHOD
1	98.18%	97.78%
2	97.92	97.79
3	98.10	97.81
4	98.41	97.84
5	97.92	97.78
6	97.79	97.70
7	98.16	97.83
8	98.55	97.86
9	97.84	97.74
10	98.03	97.85

3. The following values were obtained for the atomic weight of Cd. (a) Calculate the variance, standard deviation, and coefficient of variation of the data. (b) Calculate the 90% and 95% confidence limits for the standard deviation. (c) Calculate the 95% confidence limits for the average. (d) Calculate the range for two determinations at the 95% confidence level. (e) Does the experimental average value agree with the accepted value of 112.41?

$$112.23, 112.34, 112.30, 112.22, 112.32, 112.34$$

4. The following data were obtained from a study of the solubility of a new product as a function of temperature. (a) Plot the data and draw a freehand line representing the relationship between temperature and solubility. (b) Calculate the correlation coefficient. It is significant at the 99% confidence level? (c) Find the least squares estimate of the regression line of solubility versus temperature. (d) Calculate a point estimate of the solubility at 16C and its 95% confidence range.

TEMP., C X	SOLUBILITY, g/l Y
36	14.0
31	12.4
26	11.3
23	10.6
20	9.3
17	8.9
14	7.3
11	7.0
8	5.9
5	5.1

5. A set of iron standards were prepared to calibrate a spectrophotometer. Three absorbance readings were made on each standard. (a) Determine the correlation coefficient; is it significant at the 99% confidence level? (b) Determine the least squares calibration curve. (c) If the average of three absorbance readings on a

sample is 0.587, estimate the iron content of the sample and its 95% confidence interval. (d) What is the 95% confidence interval that will include the true average value of the sample?

ppm Fe	ABSORBANCE		
2.0	0.195	0.204	0.205
3.0	0.295	0.300	0.305
4.0	0.388	0.398	0.398
5.0	0.485	0.490	0.495
6.0	0.585	0.590	0.590
7.0	0.680	0.685	0.684
8.0	0.785	0.790	0.785
9.0	0.875	0.880	0.880
10.0	0.970	0.970	0.970

6. Each of four analysts carried out replicate sets of four determinations with the following results. (a) Calculate the standard deviation for each analyst. (b) Test the standard deviations for homogeneity, and pool if permitted. (c) Perform an analysis of variance to determine the precision of the method and the variation among the analysts.

	ANALYST:			
RUN	A	B	C	D
1	20.13%	20.14%	20.19%	20.19%
2	20.16	20.12	20.11	20.15
3	20.09	20.04	20.12	20.16
4	20.14	20.14	20.15	20.10

7. Five labs reported the following ppm Cr for triplicate analyses on a sample of water. (a) Calculate the standard deviation for each lab. (b) Test the standard deviations for homogeneity, and pool if permitted. (c) Perform an analysis of variance to answer these questions: Is the variance between labs significantly larger than that between replicate analyses within labs? What is the standard deviation for the average of three determinations between labs?

	LABS:				
REPLICATE	A	B	C	D	E
1	10.3	9.5	12.1	7.6	13.6
2	9.8	8.6	13.0	8.3	14.5
3	11.4	8.9	12.4	8.2	15.1

8. An investigation was carried out to determine if the percent Cl by a gravimetric method was affected by the quality of the $AgNO_3$ reagent used. Five bottles of

AgNO$_3$ from different suppliers were used with the following results. Is there a significant difference among the bottles of reagents?

	BOTTLE:				
RUN	A	B	C	D	E
1	4.40%	4.90%	5.55%	4.45%	5.15%
2	4.40	4.95	5.10	5.45	6.25
3	5.20	5.40	5.50	4.65	6.14
4	5.45		5.98	4.40	
5	5.80		5.60		
6	5.60		5.56		

9. Three drums of a new solvent were made during a test of a pilot unit. Information was needed on the variability of the water content and of the analyses as performed in a routine laboratory. One analyst was randomly selected from each shift. Each analyst analyzed a common sample from each drum using the same Karl Fischer method for water. The data generated are given below. Is there a significant difference among the analysts and/or among the drums? If so, which differ?

	ANALYST			
DRUM	A	B	C	D
1	1.35%	1.13%	1.06%	0.98%
2	1.40	1.23	1.26	1.22
3	1.49	1.46	1.40	1.35

10. A laboratory routinely determines diethylene glycol in ethylene glycol by gas chromatography. To determine the precision of this analysis three analysts and three chromotographs were picked at random. Each analyst ran the same sample in duplicate on each of the instruments. Write the ANOVA table, test for interaction, analyst effects and instrument effects at the 5% level of significance. Estimate the standard deviations for interaction variability, analyst variability, instrument variability, and the random error.

	CHROMATOGRAPH		
ANALYST	K	L	M
1	0.110%	0.101%	0.108%
	0.116	0.102	0.109
2	0.112	0.115	0.111
	0.111	0.106	0.109
3	0.114	p.107	0.113
	0.112	0.109	0.110

11. In the determination of chlorides in a laboratory there are 20 analysts and 12 photometers. It is desired to know if there are significant effects due to the analysts and instruments and if there is an analyst–photometer interaction. The data below (ppm Cl on a typical sample) were obtained using three analysts and three instruments, each selected at random. Each analyst made three determinations on each photometer. Calculate the standard deviation for each significant effect and for the method.

	PHOTOMETER:		
ANALYST	1	2	3
A	2.3	3.7	3.1
	3.4	2.8	3.2
	3.5	3.7	3.5
B	3.5	3.9	3.3
	2.6	3.9	3.4
	3.6	3.4	3.5
C	2.4	3.5	2.6
	2.7	3.2	2.6
	2.8	3.5	2.5

12. Four production runs of calcium sorbate have been made. The bagging line of each run was sampled at the beginning, the middle, and the end of each run. Each sample was analyzed in duplicate for calcium content. From the coded data perform an analysis of variance to determine the precision of the analytical method. Are the variances between runs and between samples significant? If so, calculate their standard deviations.

	SAMPLE		
PRODUCTION RUN	A	B	C
1	3.28%	3.52%	2.88%
	3.09	3.48	2.80
2	2.46	1.87	2.19
	2.44	1.92	2.19
3	2.77	3.74	2.55
	2.66	3.44	2.55
4	3.78	4.07	3.31
	3.87	4.12	3.31

13. Three methods for determining peroxide (polarographic, iodometric, and stannous chloride) were used to analyze a sample of a fatty acid ester. An undiluted aliquot of each material was analyzed in duplicate on each of three days (Monday, Thursday, and Friday) by each method. Perform an analysis of variance on the

data collected to determine if any of the factors (methods, days, and aliquots) are significant.

Method I   = polarographic   Days = M, T, F beside data
Method II = iodometric
Method III = SnCl$_2$

	ALIQUOT:		
METHOD	1	2	3
I	F4.51	M4.70	T4.28
II	M5.87	T5.86	F5.66
III	T6.92	F7.58	M7.46

14. Five batches of a 5% solution of CdSO$_4$ were analyzed several times. Using the data reported below, calculate the standard deviation for each batch of solution, test for homogeneity, and pool if permitted.

	BATCH:				
ANALYSIS NUMBER	1	2	3	4	5
a	4.90%	4.40%	4.45%	5.55%	5.15%
b	4.95	4.40	5.45	5.10	6.25
c	5.40	5.20	4.65	5.50	6.14
d		5.45	4.40	5.98	
e		5.80		5.60	
f		5.60		5.56	

15. The following acidity values were obtained when a series of samples were analyzed in duplicate. (a) Calculate the variance, standard deviation, and coefficient of variation on the paired data. (b) Calculate the 90% and 95% confidence limits on the standard deviation. (c) Calculate the 95% confidence limits on the average. (d) Calculate the range for two determinations (95% confidence limit). Code the data to simplify the calculations.

SAMPLE NUMBER	RUN 1	RUN 2
1	0.00110%	0.00116%
2	0.00112	0.00111
3	0.00114	0.00112
4	0.00101	0.00102
5	0.00115	0.00106
6	0.00107	0.00109
7	0.00108	0.00109
8	0.00111	0.00109
9	0.00113	0.00110

16. A sample of dodecanol was analyzed for hydroxyl number by five analysts. Each analyst made four determinations. (a) Calculate the standard deviation for each analyst. (b) Check the standard deviations for homogeneity, and pool if permitted. (c) Calculate the range for two results (95% confidence level). Code the data for ease of calculation.

DETERMINATION

ANALYST	1	2	3	4
A	292.0	294.6	291.2	293.4
B	292.1	288.0	287.2	287.2
C	290.3	291.1	291.6	289.2
D	297.1	296.9	298.6	301.4
E	291.2	289.9	289.5	290.6

17. A new method for determining hydroxyl was developed. To test the method over a range of values, a sample of ethylene glycol, nonylphenol, and pentaerythritol were analyzed ten times. (a) Calculate the variance, standard deviation, and coefficient of variation for each chemical. (b) Calculate the 90% and 95% confidence limits for each standard deviation. (c) Calculate the 95% confidence limits for each average determination. (d) Calculate the range for two results at the 95% confidence level using each estimate of the standard deviation. (e) Test the standard deviations and coefficients of variation for homogeneity, and pool if permitted.

RUN	ETHYLENE GLYCOL	NONYLPHENOL	PENTAERYTHRITOL
1	1767.0	248.8	1555.0
2	1767.9	243.8	1551.0
3	1798.0	261.8	1566.9
4	1818.1	250.1	1469.5
5	1783.0	248.0	1553.0
6	1716.1	245.0	1492.2
7	1782.0	246.7	1559.0
8	1782.7	249.3	1611.2
9	1805.4	246.9	1528.6
10	1776.2	244.3	1537.1

18. Joe Burret developed a new photometric endpoint detector for titrating acids. He claims the use of his detector gives the method a constant precision for acid levels between 0.1 and 99.9%. If this is true, the lab could save a lot of money by converting to this detector, and Joe should get a raise. The detector was tried on a series of acetic acid samples with the following results. (a) Calculate the variance, standard deviation, and coefficient of variation for each of the samples. (b) Calculate the 90% and 95% confidence limits for each standard deviation. (c) Calculate the range for two determinations (95% confidence level) based on each standard deviation. (d) Calculate the 95% confidence limits for each average. (e) Should Joe get a raise? (That is, is the precision constant over the range tested?) If so, what is the

pooled estimate of the precision? (Be sure to consider both standard deviation and coefficient of variation as measures of precision.)

SAMPLE	DETERMINATIONS				
0.10%	0.1500,	0.0992	0.0823,	0.1033,	0.0751
1.0%	0.9699,	1.0433,	0.9999,	0.9744,	0.9681
10.0%	10.05,	9.995,	9.991,	10.02,	10.07
100.0%	99.85,	99.88,	99.90,	99.86,	99.91

19. Four samples from the same lot of material had the following number of tests performed with the indicated values for standard deviation and coefficient of variation. Make a best estimate of the overall variability of the lot. What are the 95% confidence limits for this estimate?

$$n_1 = 7 \quad s_1 = 19.798 \quad \text{C.V.}_1 = 4.8990$$

$$n_2 = 10 \quad s_2 = 40.56 \quad \text{C.V.}_2 = 6.0828$$

$$n_3 = 13 \quad s_3 = 10.39 \quad \text{C.V.}_3 = 5.1962$$

$$n_4 = 22 \quad s_4 = 9.428 \quad \text{C.V.}_4 = 5.6568$$

20. Two analysts determined the percent unsaturates in a series of ten samples. If all ten samples were from the same well-mixed tank, (a) Calculate the variance, standard deviation, and coefficient of variation for each analyst; (b) Calculate the 90% and 95% confidence interval for each standard deviation value; (c) Calculate the range for two results (95% confidence level) for each analyst; (d) Compare the precision of the two analysts and pool if permitted; (e) Check analyst A's results for outliers.

BATCH	ANALYST A	ANALYST B
1	7.22%	9.15%
2	8.50	8.50
3	7.41	7.94
4	6.19	7.31
5	8.89	8.44
6	6.74	7.72
7	9.43	9.33
8	5.65	6.66
9	7.77	6.86
10	6.97	6.75

21. A sample of cellulose acetate was the subject of an interlaboratory study to determine the precision of a method for determining acetyl. Two analysts in each of

eight laboratories analyzed the sample in duplicate on each of three days. The data obtained (coded by subtracting 38.00 from the reported values[1]) is presented in the table below. Assume the analysts, laboratories, and days were selected at random. Determine the standard deviations associated with each effect: laboratories, analysts within laboratories, days within analysts, and replicates. Also calculate the standard deviation for the average of two runs obtained by two different analysts on different days in the same laboratory, and the standard deviation for the average of two runs obtained by two different laboratories.

LAB	ANALYST	DAY	RUN 1	RUN 2
1	1	1	1.01	1.22
		2	0.97	0.98
		3	0.86	1.00
	2	1	1.16	1.11
		2	1.13	1.06
		3	1.05	1.05
2	1	1	1.20	1.27
		2	1.16	1.01
		3	1.11	0.96
	2	1	1.31	1.36
		2	1.39	1.28
		3	1.13	1.11
3	1	1	1.26	1.39
		2	1.34	1.24
		3	1.13	1.11
	2	1	1.15	1.27
		2	1.24	1.21
		3	1.07	1.20
4	1	1	1.32	1.38
		2	1.37	1.42
		3	1.50	1.44
	2	1	1.39	1.31
		2	1.26	1.33
		3	1.29	1.34
5	1	1	0.94	1.08
		2	1.01	1.01
		3	1.07	1.03
	2	1	0.89	1.01
		2	0.92	0.97
		3	1.03	1.02

LAB	ANALYST	DAY	RUN 1	RUN 2
6	1	1	1.02	1.07
		2	1.22	1.16
		3	1.27	1.16
	2	1	1.05	1.03
		2	1.09	1.27
		3	1.16	1.11
7	1	1	0.77	0.84
		2	0.79	0.69
		3	0.69	0.53
	2	1	0.69	0.67
		2	0.84	0.80
		3	0.69	0.69
8	1	1	0.85	0.74
		2	0.61	0.66
		3	0.50	0.54
	2	1	0.66	0.59
		2	0.51	0.66
		3	0.40	0.62

22. Two samples of propylene glycol were subjected to an interlaboratory study of the o-ophenanthroline colorimetric method for iron. One analyst in each of the producer's four laboratories analyzed each sample in duplicate on each of two days. The data are shown below. Determine the standard deviations associated with the following effects: labs, days within labs, and replicates within days for each sample. Also calculate the standard deviation for two results, each the average of duplicate runs, obtained by the same analyst on two different days; and the standard deviation for two results, each the average of duplicate runs, obtained by two laboratories. If the results for the two samples are poolable, combine the estimates of precision to obtain an over-all estimate of each measure of precision.

LAB	DAY	RUN	SAMPLE 1	SAMPLE 2
A	1	1	0.115	0.450
		2	0.116	0.450
	2	1	0.104	0.451
		2	0.110	0.445
B	1	1	0.119	0.453
		2	0.118	0.460
	2	1	0.109	0.438
		2	0.109	0.446
C	1	1	0.106	0.491
		2	0.106	0.496

LAB	DAY	RUN	SAMPLE 1	SAMPLE 2
	2	1	0.106	0.472
		2	0.100	0.472
D	1	1	0.155	0.522
		2	0.148	0.525
	2	1	0.159	0.535
		2	0.156	0.531

23. In the study of a colorimetric determination of an impurity three variables were of interest: the reaction time at room temperature, the amount of 1.0N sulfuric acid added to the reaction mixture, and the concentration of the reagent solution:

Variable A = reaction time at 15, 30, and 60 minutes
Variable B = volume of 1.0N sulfuric acid at 5 and 15 ml
Variable C = reagent concentration at 5 and 10%

Duplicate measurements were made for each combination of the above levels of the variables with the results expressed in parts per million. The runs were made in a randomly selected order and recorded in the table below. From these data, perform an analysis of variance to determine which of the variables are significant. Also estimate the standard deviation of the analytical measurement process and that of each significant variable.

		Impurity, ppm			
		C, Reagent conc. 5%		C, Reagent conc. 10%	
A, Reaction time, min.	Run	B, ml acid		B, ml aciid	
		5	15	5	15
15	1	6.9	8.7	11.6	11.7
	2	7.8	8.7	12.1	12.9
	subtotal	14.7	17.4	23.7	24.6
30	1	9.3	9.7	12.0	13.5
	2	9.6	10.4	12.6	13.6
	subtotal	18.9	20.1	24.6	27.1
60	1	11.8	12.6	13.8	14.4
	2	12.2	12.9	14.1	15.1
	subtotal	24.0	25.5	27.9	29.5

24. A carbon tube furnace was being used in the atomic absorption determination of a relatively high boiling metal in a low boiling hydrocarbon. A typical sample was analyzed by this technique using various charring times at a constant temperature above the boiling point of the hydrocarbon, various atomizing temperatures, and various atomizing times. The results of the 16 runs are tabulated below. Which of the three variables are significant at the 95% confidence level? What is the standard deviation associated with each significant variable?

	ATOMIZING TIME, SEC.			
CHARRING TIME, SEC	10	15	20	25
20	A 28	C 50	D 33	B 28
30	B 20	D 30	A 30	C 38
40	C 35	A 40	B 24	D 35
50	D 22	B 35	C 36	A 34

Atomizing temperatures: $A = 2500$ C
$B = 2000$ C
$C = 2700$ C
$D = 2300$ C

25. As part of the development of a carbon tube–atomic absorption method for determining a metal in an organic matrix, a screening study was conducted to determine which of four variables were significant. Two levels of each variable were used, and the experiments were run in random order:

Variable A = Drying temperatures of 95 and 125 C
Variable B = Charring temperatures of 1400 and 1500 C
Variable C = Charring times of 30 and 60 seconds
Variable D = Atomizing times of 10 and 15 seconds

The detector's scale reading was recorded only once for each combination of variables, as given in the following table.

	B, Charring temperature							
	1,400 C				1,500 C			
	C, Charring time				C, Charring time			
	30 sec.		60 sec.		30 sec.		60 sec.	
	D, Atom. time		D, Atom. time		D, Atom. time		D, Atom. time	
	10 sec	15 sec	10 sec	15 sec	10 sec	15 sec	10 sec	15 sec
A, Drying temp. 95 C	(1) 4.51	d 4.70	c 5.35	cd 6.90	b 5.23	bd 6.05	bc 6.39	bcd 7.20
125 C	a 4.60	ad 4.65	ac 5.43	acd 6.72	ab 5.15	abd 6.21	abc 6.13	abcd 7.13

Perform an analysis of variance on the data to determine which variables and interactions are significant. Assume that all third and fourth order interactions are not significant and combine them to provide a measure of the error. Estimate the scale reading for the combination of the low level of drying temperature, the high levels of charring temperature and time, and the low level of atomizing time.

26. A laboratory uses two general methods for determining specific gravity at 20/20 C: a hydrometer method and a pycnometer method. Based on extensive experience with each method, the standard deviation for the hydrometer method is 0.0005 and for the pycnometer, 0.0002. The specific gravity of a shipment of n-hexanol was measured in triplicate using the hydrometer method: 0.8200, 0.8210, and 0.8195 for an average of 0.82107. A second shipment was analyzed by the pycnometer method: 0.8205, 0.8209, and 0.8207 for an average of 0.82070. Do the two shipments have the same specific gravity?

27. A customer purchased two tank cars of a residue amine product. The total nitrogen analyses are listed below. Do the two tank cars have equivalent total nitrogen contents?

% TOTAL NITROGEN

CAR 1	CAR 2
9.23	9.18
9.28	9.01
9.17	9.09
9.24	9.20
9.20	9.00
9.24	
9.19	
9.21	

REFERENCE

1. Wernimont, G., *Anal. Chem.*, 23, 1572–1576 (1951).

Appendix C
ANSWERS TO PROBLEMS

1. (a) KI data: $s^2 = 7.547 \times 10^{-9}$; $s = 8.687 \times 10^{-5}$;
C.V. $= 0.06622$; DF $= 5$
As_2O_3 data: $s^2 = 3.530 \times 10^{-9}$; $s = 5.941 \times 10^{-5}$;
C.V. $= 0.04528$; DF $= 4$

(b) KI data: $0.131177 \pm (2.571 \times 8.687 \times 10^{-5}/\sqrt{6})$, or
0.131086 to 0.131268
As_2O_3 data: $0.131206 \pm 5.9414 \times 10^{-5}/\sqrt{5})$, or
0.131132 to 0.13128

(c) 90% confidence intervals for standard deviations:
KI data: 5.8305×10^{-5} to 1.8114×10^{-4}
As_2O_3 data: 3.8553×10^{-5} to 1.4092×10^{-4}
95% confidence intervals for standard deviations:
KI data: 5.4295×10^{-5} to 2.1309×10^{-4}
As_2O_3 data: 3.5665×10^{-5} to 1.7080×10^{-4}

(d) Range for 2 determinations:
KI data: $8.687 \times 10^{-5} \times 2.77 = 2.406 \times 10^{-4}$
As_2O_3 data: $5.914 \times 10^{-5} \times 2.77 = 1.638 \times 10^{-4}$

(e) $F = 7.547 \times 10^{-9}/3.530 \times 10^{-9} = 2.14$
$F_{0.05/2,5,4} = 9.36$. Therefore, accept the null hypothesis of no difference in the precision for the two standards.

(f) $s_p = 7.5904 \times 10^{-5}$
$$t = \frac{0.131205 - 0.131177}{7.5904 \times 10^{-5}} \sqrt{\frac{6 \times 5}{6 + 5}} = 0.609, \; 9 \; DF$$
$t_{0.05/2,9} = 2.26$. Therefore, accept the null hypothesis of no difference between the two means.

(g) Standard deviation, using ranges:
KI data: $(0.13129 - 0.13108)/2.543 = 8.26 \times 10^{-5}$
As_2O_3 data: $(0.13128 - 0.13113)/2.324 = 6.45 \times 10^{-5}$

2. (a) Randomness on wet chemical data:
Median $= (98.03 + 98.10)/2 = 98.06$
$n_1 = n_2 = 5$; $R = 6$
$R_{Critical} = 2$ to 10. Since R lies within the critical limits, accept the null hypothesis that data are random.

(b) For wet chemical data:
$s^2 = 0.06011111$; $s = 0.24517567$; C.V. $= 0.2500\%$; DF $= 9$
For G. C. data:
$s^2 = 0.00257333$; $s = 0.05072803$; C.V. $= 0.05187\%$; DF $= 9$

(c) Standard deviation using range:
Wet chemical data: $(98.55 - 97.99)/3.078 = 0.2469$, 9 DF
G. C. data: $(97.85 - 97.70)/3.078 = 0.04873$, 9 DF

(d) 90% confidence intervals for standard deviations:
Wet chemical data: $0.17839 < s < 0.40307$
G. C. data: $0.03691 < s < 0.08340$
95% confidence intervals for standard deviations:
Wet chemical data: $0.16874 < s < 0.44140$
G. C. data: $0.03491 < s < 0.09262$

(e) 95% confidence limits for averages:
Wet chemical data: 97.915 to 98.265%
G. C. data: 97.762 to 97.834%

(f) Range for two results at 95% confidence level:
Wet chemical data: 0.68%; G. C. data: 0.14%

(g) $F = 0.245176^2/0.050728^2 = 23.36$
$F_{0.05/2,9,9} = 4.03$. Therefore, reject the null hypothesis of equal variances at $\alpha = 0.05$ and conclude that the variances differ significantly.

(h) t test using paired data:

$$s_d = 0.207728, 9 \text{ DF}; t = \frac{98.090 - 97.798}{0.207728}\sqrt{10} = 4.445$$

$t_{0.05/2,2,9} = 2.262$. Thus, the null hypothesis of equal means is rejected at $\alpha = 0.05$, and we conclude that the averages differ significantly.

(i) Correlation coefficient:
A plot of the data suggests a reasonable degree of correlation.

$$r = \frac{95,930.1461 - \dfrac{(980.90)(979.98)}{10}}{\sqrt{(96,217.0220 - 96,216.4810)(95,644.5112 - 95,644.48804)}}$$
$$= 0.0879/0.1119355 = 0.7853$$

$r_{0.01,8} = 0.765$. Thus, the null hypothesis of no correlation is rejected at $\alpha = 0.01$ and we conclude there is significant correlation between the results obtained by the two methods.

(j) Regression equation:
$\lambda = 0.0428096$ $SS_Y = 0.02316$
$SS_X = 0.5410$ $SS_{XY} = 0.0879$
$B = 0.2069$
$A = 97.798 - (0.2069 \times 98.09) = 77.503$
$Y = 77.503 + 0.2609X$

(k) 95% confidence limits on slope: 0.11650 to 0.36738

3. (a) $s^2 = 0.0028968$; $s = 0.05382$; C.V. $= 0.0479\%$; DF $= 5$

(b) 90% confidence interval: $0.03612 < s < 0.11223$
95% confidence interval: $0.03364 < s < 0.13202$

(c) 95% confidence interval for average: 112.292 ± 0.056

(d) Range for two results (95% confidence level): 0.149

(e) $t = \dfrac{112.41 - 112.292}{0.05382}\sqrt{6} = 5.37$, 5 DF

$t_{0.05/2, 2, 5} = 2.57$ and $t_{0.01/2, 2, 5} = 4.03$. Thus, even at $\alpha = 0.01$, the average experimental value differs significantly from the accepted value.

4. (a) The plot of the data suggests a probable linear association.
   (b) $r = 0.997$, 8 DF; $r_{0.01, 8} = 0.765$. Thus, the null hypothesis of no linear relationship is rejected at $\alpha = 0.01$, and we conclude there is a significant linear relationship.
   (c) $Y = 3.6780 + 0.28806X$
   (d) For 16 C, $Y = 8.29$ (point estimate)
       95% confidence interval for a single estimate: 7.70 to 8.88. ($s_{Y.X} = 0.244130$; DF $= 9$)

5. (a) $r = 0.99995$, 7 DF
       $r_{0.01, 7} = 0.798$. Therefore, the null hypothesis of no correlation is rejected at $\alpha = 0.01$ and we conclude there is significant correlation between the iron concentration and absorbance.
   (b) $Y = $ ppm Fe $= -0.0976 + 10.37\bar{X}$. ($\bar{X} = $ average of three absorbance measurements)
   (c) For an average absorbance of 0.587, ppm Fe $= 5.99$. $s_{Y.X} = 0.030315$ (Note: If an insufficient number of digits are used, $s_{Y.X}$ may appear to be the square root of a negative number. Ten significant places were used to obtain the indicated value.)
       95% confidence interval for a single value of $Y = 5.91$ to 6.07
   (d) 95% confidence interval for the average value of y to include the true value: 5.97 to 6.01

6. (a) Analyst A: $s = 0.029439$, 3 DF
       Analyst B: $s = 0.047610$, 3 DF
       Analyst C: $s = 0.035940$, 3 DF
       Analyst D: $s = 0.037417$, 3 DF
   (b) Cochran test: $n = 4$; $k = 4$; $g = 0.3891$
       $g_{0.05, 4, 4} = 0.6841$. Thus, the null hypothesis of equal variances is not rejected at $\alpha = 0.05$, and we conclude no significant differences have been detected among the 4 variances. The pooled standard deviation $= 0.038161$, 12 DF.
   (c) For the analysis of variance the data were coded by subtracting 20.00 from each observation.

$$T^2/16 = 0.26265625 \quad SS_c = 0.00856875$$
$$SS_t = 0.02604375 \quad SS_w = 0.017475$$

ANOVA Table.

SQUARE	SS	DF	MS	EMS
Bet. analysts	0.00856875	3	0.00285625	$\sigma^2 + 4\sigma_c^2$
Within analyst	0.017475	12	0.001456	σ^2
Total	0.02604375	15		

$$F = 0.00285625/0.001456 = 1.96$$

$F_{0.05/2, 3, 12} = 3.49$. Therefore, the null hypothesis of equal averages is not rejected at $\alpha = 0.05$, and we conclude that no significant difference has been found between the analysts. The precision of the method: $s = \sqrt{0.001456} = 0.03816$, 12 DF.

7. (a) Lab A: $s = 0.818535$, 2 DF
   Lab B: $s = 0.456258$, 2 DF
   Lab C: $s = 0.458258$, 2 DF
   Lab D: $s = 0.378594$, 2 DF
   Lab E: $s = 0.754983$, 2 DF

   (b) Cochran test: $n = 3$; $k = 5$; $g = 0.3715$

   $g_{0.05, 3, 5} = 0.6838$. Thus, the null hypothesis of equal variances is accepted at $\alpha = 0.05$ and we conclude that the standard deviations have not been shown to be significantly different. Pooling is therefore permitted. $s_p = 0.60056$, 10 DF

   (c) Analysis of variance:

$$T^2/N = 1{,}777.792667 \qquad SS_c = 80.390666$$
$$SS_t = 83.997333 \qquad SS_p = 3.606667$$

ANOVA Table.

SOURCE	SS	DF	MS	EMS
Bet. labs	80.390666	4	20.097666	$\sigma^2 + 3\sigma_c^2$
Within labs	3.606667	10	0.3606667	σ^2
Total	83.997333	14		

$$F = 20.097666/0.3606667 = 55.7$$

$F_{0.05, 4, 10} = 3.48$. Therefore, we reject the null hypothesis of equal variances at $\alpha = 0.05$ and conclude there is a significant difference between laboratories.

$$s_{\text{within lab}} = \sqrt{0.3606667} = 0.6006,\ 10\ \text{DF}$$

For the average of 3 determinations within a lab:

$$s = 0.6006/\sqrt{3} = 0.3468$$

$$s_{\text{between labs}} = \sqrt{(20.097666 - 0.360666)/3}$$

$$= 2.5650,\ 4\ \text{DF}$$

Total variance between averages of 3 determinations by different labs = $0.3468^2 + 2.5650^2 = 6.6995$ and the total standard deviation = $\sqrt{6.6995} = 2.588$

8. Analysis of variance:

$$T^2/N = 610.371564 \qquad SS_c = 2.799861$$
$$SS_t = 6.632036 \qquad SS_w = 3.832175$$

ANOVA Table.

SOURCE	SS	DF	MS	F
Between bottles	2.799861	4	0.699965	3.10*
Within bottles	3.832175	17	0.225422	
Total	6.632036	21		

$F_{0.05,4,17} = 2.96$. Since the critical value of F is exceeded, we reject the null hypothesis of equal variances at $\alpha = 0.05$ and conclude there is a significant difference between bottles.

The standard deviation of within bottles, s, may be considered a measure of the precision of the method:

$$s = \sqrt{0.225422} = 0.4748, \ 17 \ DF$$

9. Analysis of variance:

$$T^2/N = 19.584075 \quad SS_c = 0.086225$$
$$SS_r = 0.17405 \qquad SS_t = 0.282425$$
$$SS = 0.02215$$

ANOVA Table.

SOURCE	SS	DF	MS	EMS
Bet. colm. (analysts)	0.086225	3	0.028742	$\sigma^2 + 3\sigma_c^2$
Bet. rows (drums)	0.174050	2	0.087025	$\sigma^2 + \sigma_i^2 + 4\sigma_r^2$
Residual	0.022150	6	0.003692	$\sigma^2 + \sigma_i^2$
Total	0.282425	11		

Test row effect for significance:

$$F = 0.087025/0.003692 = 23.57$$

$F_{0.05,2,6} = 5.14$. Thus, we conclude there is a significant difference among drums at $\alpha = 0.05$.

Test column effect for significance:

For a valid test for the analyst effect, the components in the EMS column show that we must assume there is no interaction ($\sigma_i^2 = 0$). Because significant interaction between analysts and drums is unlikely, we proceed: $F = 0.028742/0.003692 = 7.78$

$F_{0.05, 3, 6} = 4.76$. Thus, we conclude there is a difference among analysts at $\alpha = 0.05$.

$$s_{\text{residual}} = 0.06075, \text{ 6 DF}$$
$$s_r = 0.1443, \text{ 2 DF}$$
$$s_c = 0.09138, \text{ 3 DF}$$

Duncan's separation of means procedure:

$$s_p \text{ for analysts} = 0.0675/\sqrt{3} = 0.03507$$
$$s_p \text{ for drums} = 0.06065/\sqrt{4} = 0.03038$$

For analysts:

D	C	B	A
1.183	1.240	1.273	1.413

For sample of:	2	3	4
Significant ranges:	3.46	3.58	3.64
Least significant ranges:	0.121	0.126	0.128
(at 5% level of significance)			

$A - D = 0.230$ vs. 0.128; thus, $A - D$ is significant
$A - C = 0.173$ vs. 0.126; thus, $A - C$ is significant
$A - B = 0.140$ vs. 0.121; thus, $A - B$ is significant
$B - D = 0.090$ vs. 0.126; thus, $B - D$ is not significant;
    denote by underscoring D, C, and B.
    Only analyst A differs significantly.

For drums: Using the same procedure as above, all 3 drums are significantly different.

Further study will be required to determine why analyst A's results are different and why the water content of the drums are different and appear to increase during the run, assuming the drums were numbered in chronological order.

10. Analysis of variance:

$$T^2/rcn = 0.2167013889 \quad SS_c = 0.0001027778$$
$$SS_r = 0.0000381111 \quad SS_s = 0.0002011111$$
$$SS_i = 0.0000602222 \quad SS_t = 0.0002716111$$
$$SS_w = 0.0000705000$$

ANOVA Table.

SOURCE	SS	DF	MS	EMS
Bet. colms (G. C.'s)	0.0001027778	2	0.0000513889	$\sigma^2 + 2\sigma_i^2 + 6\sigma_c^2$
Bet. rows (analysts)	0.0000381111	2	0.0000190556	$\sigma^2 + 2\sigma_i^2 + 6\sigma_r^2$
Colm. × row	0.0000602222	4	0.0000150556	$\sigma^2 + 2\sigma_i^2$
Subtotal	0.0002011111	8		
Within combination	0.0000705000	9	0.0000078333	σ^2
Total	0.0002716111	17		

$$F = 0.0000150556/0.0000078333 = 1.92$$

$F_{0.05,4,9} = 3.63$. Thus, the column-row interaction is not shown to be significant at $\alpha = 0.05$ and it is combined with the within combination term:

$$\frac{0.0000602222 + 0.0000705}{9 + 4} = 0.0000100556, 13 \text{ DF}$$

The new value for the within-combination mean square is used to test the significance of the row effects:

$$F = 0.0000190556/0.0000100556 = 1.90$$

$F_{0.05,2,13} = 3.81$. Thus, the row effect is not shown to be significant at $\alpha = 0.05$ (no significant analysts effect). The mean square for analysts may be combined with the within combination means square to provide a new estimate of error with which to test the significance of the mean square for columns:

$$\frac{0.0001307222 + 0.0000381111}{13 + 2} = 0.0000112556, 15 \text{ DF}$$

$$F = 0.0000513889/0.0000112556 = 4.57$$

$F_{0.05,2,15} = 3.68$. Thus, the column effect (G. C.'s) is significant at $\alpha = 0.05$.
Use the revised within-combination mean square as the best estimate of the random error:

$$s_w = \sqrt{0.0000112556} = 0.003355, 15 \text{ DF}$$

$$s_{GC} = \sqrt{0.000006689} = 0.002586, 2 \text{ DF}$$

The same conclusions would have been reached if the nonsignificant mean squares had not been combined with the within-combination mean square. By combining these estimates the standard deviation for error is based on 15 degrees of freedom instead of only 9 without the combination.

The chromatographs account for about 37% of the total variance with the remaining 63% being assigned to error. This suggests that if improvement in precision is needed, aspects of the method common to the chromatographs would be a good area to investigate.

11. Analysis of variance:

$$T^2/rcn = 274.563333 \qquad SS_t = 5.906667$$
$$SS_s = 3.446667 \qquad SS_r = 1.602223$$
$$SS_c = 1.446667 \qquad SS_i = 0.397777$$
$$SS_w = 2.460000$$

ANOVA Table.

SOURCE	SS	DF	MS	EMS
Bet. c (photomtr.)	1.446667	2	0.7233335	$\sigma^2 + 3\sigma_i^2 + 9\sigma_c^2$
Bet. r (analysts)	1.602223	2	0.8011115	$\sigma^2 + 3\sigma_i^2 + 9\sigma_r^2$
$c \times r$ interaction	0.397777	4	0.0994442	
Subtotal	3.446667	8		
Within combination	2.460000	18	0.1366667	σ^2
Total	5.906667	26		

Tests for significance of MS's:

$$F_{c \times r} = 0.0994442/0.1366667 = 0.73$$

$F_{0.05,4,18} = 2.93$. Thus, the interaction is not significant at $\alpha = 0.05$.

$$F_{\text{rows}} = 0.8011115/0.1298990 = 6.17$$

$F_{0.05,2,22} = 3.44$. Thus, the analysts effect is significant at $\alpha = 0.05$

$$F_{\text{colm}} = 0.723335/0.1298990 = 5.57$$

$F_{0.05,2,22} = 3.44$. Thus, the photometer effect is significant at $\alpha = 0.05$

In the above F tests for row and columns, the denominator is obtained by combining the SS's for the interaction and within combination sources and dividing by $18 + 4$ DF. This is possible because the interaction MS was not found to be significant. Standard deviations for significant effects:

$$s_w = \sqrt{0.1298990} = 0.3604, \ 22 \ \text{DF}$$

$$s_r = \sqrt{0.07457917} = 0.2731, 2 \text{ DF}$$

$$s_c = \sqrt{0.06593717} = 0.2568, 2 \text{ DF}$$

12. Analysis of variance:

$$T^2/24 = 217.7435 \qquad SS_c = 1.2111$$
$$SS_r = 7.5603 \qquad SS_s = 10.1905$$
$$SS_i = 1.4191 \qquad SS_t = 10.2704$$
$$SS_w = 0.0799$$

Samples are considered a fixed variable because they were not randomly selected.

ANOVA Table.

SOURCE	SS	DF	MS	F	$F_{0.05}$	MS
Bet. c (spls)	1.2111	2	0.6056	91.00*	3.89	$\sigma^2 + 8\sigma_c^2$
Bet. r (runs)	7.5603	3	2.5201	10.65*	4.76	$\sigma^2 + 2\sigma_r^2$
$c \times r$	1.4191	6	0.2365	35.55*	3.00	$\sigma^2 + 2\sigma_i^2$
Subtotal	10.1905	11				
Within comb.	0.0799	12	0.00666			σ^2
Total	10.2704	23				

Samples, runs, and interaction are all significant at $\alpha = 0.05$.
Standard deviations of sources:

$$s_w = \sqrt{0.00666} = 0.0816, 12 \text{ DF (unassigned error)}$$

$$s_i = \sqrt{0.11492} = 0.3390, 6 \text{ DF}$$

$$s_r = \sqrt{1.25672} = 1.1210, 3 \text{ DF}$$

$$s_c = \sqrt{0.0748675} = 0.2736, 2 \text{ DF}$$

Production runs account for over 86% of the total variance. The reason for the interaction term being significant is uncertain from the information at hand. Further work is required to discover the reason.

13. Analysis of variance, Latin square:

$$CF = 52.84^2/9 = 310.2295111$$

$$SS_c = \frac{931.1096}{3} - CF = 0.1403555556$$

$$SS_r = \frac{966.6338}{3} - CF = 11.98175556$$

$$SS_t = \frac{931.1870}{3} - CF = 0.1661555556$$

$$SS_{total} = 4.51^2 + 5.87^2 + 6.92^2 + \cdots + 7.46^2 - CF$$

$$= 322.5750 - CF = 12.3454889$$

$$SS = SS_{total} - SS_c - SS_r - SS_t = 0.0572222278$$

ANOVA Table.

SOURCE	SS	DF	MS	EMS
Bet. colm. (aliq.)	0.1403555556	2	0.070177778	$\sigma^2 + 3\sigma_c^2$
Bet. rows (method)	11.98175556	2	5.990877778	$\sigma^2 + 3\sigma_r^2$
Bet. treat. (days)	0.1661555556	2	0.083077778	$\sigma^2 + 3\sigma_t^2$
Residual (error)	0.0572222278	2	0.0286111139	σ^2
Total	12.3454889000	8		

Tests for significance:

$$F_{days} = 0.083077778/0.0286111139 = 2.90$$

$$F_{method} = 5.99087778/0.0286111139 = 209.4*$$

$$F_{aliquot} = 0.070177778/0.028111139 = 2.45$$

$F_{0.05, 2, 2} = 19.00$. Thus, only methods are significant at $\alpha = 0.05$; i.e., the three methods to do not give equivalent average results. Aliquots and days have not been shown to have significant effects.

14. Standard deviation for each batch:

1. $s = 0.275379$, 2 DF
2. $s = 0.606973$, 5 DF
3. $s = 0.487126$, 3 DF
4. $s = 0.280173$, 5 DF
5. $s = 0.605833$, 2 DF

Bartlett test:

$$N = 22 \qquad\qquad k = 5$$

$$A = 0.139542 \qquad DF_1 = 4$$

$$DF_2 = 308 \qquad\qquad b = 355.27$$

$$s_p^2 = 0.225422 \qquad\qquad M = 3.868319$$

$$F = 0.8476$$

$F_{0.05, 4, 308} = 2.40$. Thus, the variances have not been shown to differ significantly at $\alpha = 0.05$, and they may be pooled to give a standard deviation of 0.474786 with 17 DF.

15. (a) $s^2 = 7.8344 \times 10^{-10}$; $s = 2.799 \times 10^{-5}$;

$$C.V. = 2.55\%; 9\ DF$$

(b) 90% confidence limits of s:

$$2.037 \times 10^{-5} \text{ to } 4.602 \times 10^{-5}$$

95% confidence interval of s:

$$1.926 \times 10^{-5} \text{ to } 5.110 \times 10^{-5}$$

(c) 95% confidence limits of averages:

$$1.076 \times 10^{-3} \text{ to } 1.118 \times 10^{-3}$$

(d) Range for two determinations (95% confidence level): 0.00008%
16. (a) Analyst A, $s = 1.5055$, 3 DF
    Analyst B, $s = 2.3472$, 3 DF
    Analyst C, $s = 1.0472$, 3 DF
    Analyst D, $s = 2.0769$, 3 DF
    Analyst E, $s = 0.7528$, 3 DF
(b) Cochran test; $g = 0.4006$
    $g_{0.05, 4, 5} = 0.5981$. Thus, the standard deviations are not shown to be significantly different at $\alpha = 0.05$ and are poolable to give a standard deviation of 1.658, 15 DF.
(c) Range for two results at 95% confidence level: 4.59
17. (a) For ethylene glycol:

$$s^2 = 761.424889; \quad s = 27.5939;$$

$$C.V. = 1.5505\%, 9\ DF$$

For nonylphenol:

$$s^2 = 26.466778; \quad s = 5.1446;$$

$$C.V. = 2.0705\%, 9\ DF$$

For pentaerythritol:

$$s^2 = 1{,}556.365000; \quad s = 39.4508;$$

$$\text{C.V.} = 2.5578\%, \ 9 \ \text{DF}$$

(b)

	90% CI for s	95% CI for s
Ethylene glycol	20.07 to 45.36	18.99 to 50.38
Nonylphenol	3.74 to 8.46	3.54 to 9.39
Pentaerythritol	28.70 to 64.86	27.17 to 72.03

(c) 95% confidence limits for averages:

Ethylene glycol	1,759.92 to 1,799.96
Nonylphenol	249.79 to 252.15
Pentaerythritol	1,514.16 to 1,570.54

(d) Range for two values (95% confidence level):

Ethylene glycol	76.4
Nonylphenol	14.2
Pentaerythritol	109.3

(e) Cochran test on variances, s^2: $g = 0.6639$
$g_{0.05, 10, 3} = 0.6167$. Thus, the standard deviations are significantly different at $\alpha = 0.05$ and are not poolable.
Cochran test on C.V. values: $g = 0.4944$
$g_{0.05, 10, 3} = 0.6167$. Thus, the C.V. values have not been found to differ significantly at $\alpha = 0.05$, and may be pooled to give C.V.$_p = 2.100$, 27 DF.

18. (a)

SAMPLE	s^2	s	C.V.	DF
0.10%	0.0008563	0.02926	28.69%	4
1.0%	0.0010149	0.03186	3.21%	4
10.0%	0.0011827	0.03439	0.34%	4
100%	0.0006500	0.02550	0.03%	4

(b, c, d)

SAMPLE	90% CI of s	95% CI of s	2 values	95% CI of Avg.
0.10%	0.019–0.069	0.018–0.084	0.081	0.0656–0.1384
1.0%	0.021–0.076	0.019–0.092	0.088	0.9515–1.0307
10.0%	0.022–0.082	0.020–0.099	0.095	9.982–10.7
100%	0.016–0.060	0.015–0.073	0.071	99.85–99.91

(e) Cochran test on standard deviations: $g = 0.3193$
$g_{0.05, 5, 4} = 0.6287$. Thus, the standard deviations have not been shown to be significantly different and may be pooled to give $s_p = 0.03043$, 16 DF. (Joe should get his raise.)

19. The C.V.'s show reasonable agreement and may be pooled to give $\text{C.V.}_p = 5.5396$, 48 DF. The 95% confidence limits for C.V._p are 4.6203 and 6.9155. The χ^2 values at 48 DF were obtained by interpolation of the tabular values.

20. (a) Analyst A: $s^2 = 1.42313$; $s = 1.1930$; C.V. $= 15.95\%$; 9DF

Analyst B: $s^2 = 0.95236$; $s = 0.9759$; C.V. $= 12.41\%$; 9 DF

(b, c)	90% CI of s	95% CI of s	Range, two results
Analyst A	0.868–1.961	0.821–2.178	3.30
Analyst B	0.710–1.604	0.672–1.782	2.70

(d) $F = 1.42313/0.95236 = 1.494$
$F_{0.05/2, 9, 9} = 4.03$. Thus, the standard deviations have not been shown to be significantly different at $\alpha = 0.05$ and may be pooled: $s_p = 1.0899$, 18 DF.

(e) Check for outliers in Analyst A's data:
Lowest values:

$$R = \frac{5.65 - 6.19}{5.65 - 8.89} = 0.167$$

Highest value:

$$R = \frac{9.43 - 8.89}{9.43 - 6.19} = 0.167$$

$R_{95\%, 10} = 0.477$. Thus, neither the lowest nor the highest values appear to be outliers.

21. Analysis of variance:

$$SS_T = 1.01^2 + 1.22^2 + 0.97^2 + \cdots + 0.62^2 - \frac{99.47^2}{96}$$

$$= 109.300500 - 103.065425 = 6.235074$$

$$SS_L = \frac{12.60^2 + 14.29^2 + 14.61^2 + \cdots + 7.34^2}{12} - \frac{99.47^2}{96}$$

$$= 108.490242 - 103.065426 = 5.424816$$

$$SS_A = \left[\frac{6.04^2 + 6.56^2}{6} - \frac{12.60^2}{12} \right] + \left[\frac{6.71^2 + 7.58^2}{6} - \frac{14.29^2}{12} \right] + \cdots$$

$$+ \left[\frac{3.90^2 + 3.44^2}{6} - \frac{7.34^2}{12} \right] = 0.144907$$

$$SS_D = \left[\frac{2.23^2 + 1.95^2 + 1.86^2}{2} - \frac{6.04^2}{6} \right] + \cdots + \left[\frac{1.25^2 + 1.17^2 + 1.02^2}{2} - \frac{3.44^2}{6} \right]$$

$$= 0.442697$$

$$SS_R = \frac{(1.01 - 1.22)^2 + (0.97 - 0.98)^2 + \cdots + (0.40 - 0.62)^2}{2}$$

$$= 0.222650$$

ANOVA Table.

SOURCE	SS	DF	MS	EXPECTED MEAN SQUARE
Bet. labs	5.424816	7	0.774974	$\sigma_R^2 + 2\sigma_D^2 + 6\sigma_A^2 + 12\sigma_L^2$
Bet. analysts	0.144907	8	0.018113	$\sigma_R^2 + 2\sigma_D^2 + 6\sigma_A^2$
Bet. days	0.442697	32	0.012824	$\sigma_R^2 + 2\sigma_D^2$
Bet. rep.	0.222650	48	0.004639	σ_R^2
Total	6.235074	95		

Test of significance on mean squares:

$$F = 0.013834/0.004638 = 2.98$$

$F_{0.05, 32, 48} = 1.70$. Thus, the day effect is significant at $\alpha = 0.05$.

$$F = 0.018113/0.013834 = 1.31$$

$F_{0.05, 8, 32} = 2.24$. Thus, the analyst effect is not shown to be significant at $\alpha = 0.05$.

Since the day effect has not been proven to be significant, conclude that 0.018113 and 0.013834 are both estimates of the days effect and combine the SS's and DF's for analysts and days for a better estimate of the day's mean square:

$$\frac{0.144907 + 0.442697}{8 + 32} = 0.014690, \ 40 \ DF$$

This value replaces 0.013834 in the ANOVA table and the between-analysts line is deleted because it was not shown to be significant.

$$F = 0.774974/0.014690 = 52.75$$

$F_{0.05,7,40} = 2.25$. Thus, the labs effect is significant at $\alpha = 0.05$.

Standard deviation for replicates:

$$s_R = \sqrt{0.04639} = 0.0681, 48 \text{ DF}$$

Standard deviation for days:

$$s_D = \sqrt{\frac{0.014690 - 0.004639}{2}} = 0.0709, 40 \text{ DF}$$

Standard deviation for labs:

$$s_L = \sqrt{\frac{0.774974 - 0.014690}{12}} = 0.2517, 7 \text{ DF}$$

Standard deviation for average of two runs on different days within a laboratory:

$$s_W = \sqrt{\frac{0.0681^2}{2} + 0.0709^2} = 0.0857, 40 \text{ DF}$$

Standard deviation for average of two results by two laboratories:

$$s_B = \sqrt{\frac{0.0681^2}{2} + 0.0709^2 + 0.2517^2} = 0.2659, 7 \text{ DF}$$

22. Analysis of variance, Sample 1:

$$SS_T = 0.115^2 + 0.116^2 + \cdots + 0.156^2 - \frac{1.936^2}{16}$$

$$= 0.2406980 - 0.2342560 = 0.00644200$$

$$SS_L = \frac{0.445^2 + 0.445^2 + 0.418^2 + 0.618^2}{4} - \frac{1.936^2}{16}$$

$$= 0.24042450 - 0.2342560 = 0.00616850$$

$$SS_D = \left[\frac{0.231^2 + 0.214^2}{2} - \frac{0.445^2}{4} \right] + \cdots + \left[\frac{0.303^2 + 0.315^2}{2} - \frac{0.618^2}{4} \right]$$

$$= 0.0002075$$

$$SS_R = \frac{(0.115 - 0.116)^2 + (0.104 - 0.110)^2 + \cdots + (0.535 - 0.531)^2}{2} = 0.00006600$$

ANOVA Table—Sample 1.

SOURCE	SS	DF	MS	EMS
Between labs	0.0061685	3	0.00205617	$\sigma_R^2 + 2\sigma_D^2 + 4\sigma_L^2$
Between days	0.0002075	4	0.00005188	$\sigma_R^2 + 2\sigma_D^2$
Between reps.	0.0000660	8	0.00000825	σ_R^2
Total	0.0064420	15		

$$F = 0.00005188/0.00000825 = 9.29$$

$F_{0.05, 4, 8} = 3.84$. Thus, the days effect is significant at $\alpha = 0.05$.

$$F = 0.00205617/0.00005188 = 39.63$$

$F_{0.05, 3, 4} = 6.59$. Thus, the labs effect is significant at $\alpha = 0.05$.

Standard deviation for replicates:

$$s_R = \sqrt{0.00000825} = 0.00287, \; 8 \; \text{DF}$$

Standard deviation for days:

$$s_D = \sqrt{\frac{0.00005188 - 0.00000825}{2}} = 0.00467, \; 4 \; \text{DF}$$

Standard deviation for labs:

$$s_L = \sqrt{\frac{0.00205617 - 0.00005188}{4}} = 0.02238, \; 3 \; \text{DF}$$

Standard deviation, average of two runs on different days within one lab:

$$s_W = \sqrt{\frac{0.00000825}{2} + 0.000021815} = 0.00509, \; 4 \; \text{DF}$$

Standard deviation, average of two runs by two labs:

$$s_B = \sqrt{\frac{0.00000825}{2} + 0.000021815 + 0.0005010725} = 0.0230, 3 \text{ DF}$$

Analysis of variance, Sample 2:

$$SS_T = 0.450^2 + 0.450^2 + \cdots + 0.531^2 - \frac{7.637^2}{16}$$

$$= 3.6629550 - 3.64523556 = 0.01771944$$

$$SS_L = \frac{1.796^2 + 1.797^2 + 1.931^2 + 2.113^2}{4} - \frac{7.637^2}{16}$$

$$= 3.66208875 - 3.64523556 = 0.01685319$$

$$SS_D = \left[\frac{0.900^2 + 0.896^2}{2} - \frac{1.796^2}{4}\right] + \cdots + \left[\frac{1.047^2 + 1.066^2}{2} - \frac{2.113^2}{4}\right]$$

$$= 0.00076675$$

$$SS_R = \frac{(0.450 - 0.450)^2 + (0.451 - 0.445)^2 + \cdots + (0.535 - 0.531)^2}{2}$$

$$= 0.00009950$$

ANOVA Table—Sample 2.

SOURCE	SS	DF	MS	EMS
Between labs	0.01685319	3	0.00561773	$\sigma_R^2 + 2\sigma_D^2 + 4\sigma_L^2$
Between days	0.00076675	4	0.00019169	$\sigma_R^2 + 2\sigma_D^2$
Between reps.	0.00009950	8	0.00001244	σ_R^2
Total	.0.01771944	15		

$$F = 0.00019169/0.00001244 = 15.41$$

$F_{0.05, 4, 8} = 3.84$. Thus, the days effect is significant at $\alpha = 0.05$.

$$F = 0.00561773/0.00019169 = 29.31$$

$F_{0.05, 3, 4} = 6.59$. Thus, the labs effect is significant at $\alpha = 0.05$.

Standard deviation for replicates:

$$s_R = \sqrt{0.00001244} = 0.00353, 8 \text{ DF}$$

Standard deviation for days:

$$s_D = \sqrt{\frac{0.00019169 - 0.00001244}{2}} = 0.00947, 4 \text{ DF}$$

Standard deviation for labs:

$$s_L = \sqrt{\frac{0.00561773 - 0.00019169}{4}} = 0.03683, 3 \text{ DF}$$

Standard deviation, average of two runs on different days within one lab:

$$s_W = \sqrt{\frac{0.00001244}{2} + 0.000089625} = 0.00979, 4 \text{ DF}$$

Standard deviation, average of two runs by two labs:

$$s_B = \sqrt{\frac{0.00001244}{2} + 0.000089625 + 0.00135651} = 0.0381, 3 \text{ DF}$$

Comparison of results on Samples 1 and 2:

s_R: $F = 0.00001244/0.00000825 = 1.51$
$F_{0.05/2, 8, 8} = 4.43$. Thus, the variances for replicates on the samples have not been shown to differ significantly at $\alpha = 0.05$.

s_W: $F = 0.000095845/0.00002593 = 3.70$
$F_{0.05/2, 4, 4} = 9.60$. Thus, the variances for within labs on the samples have not been shown to differ significantly at $\alpha = 0.05$.

s_B: $F = 0.001452/0.00052701 = 2.76$
$F_{0.05/2, 3, 3} = 15.4$. Thus, the variances for 2 runs by 2 labs on the samples have not been shown to differ significantly at $\alpha = 0.05$.

Because the F tests show no significant differences between the two samples with respect to the variances for replicates, within labs, and between labs, we can pool these data to obtain a combined estimate of each precision. These values are likely to be closer to the true standard deviations than those based on just sample 1 or sample 2:

$$s_R = \sqrt{\frac{(0.00287^2)8 + (0.00353^2)8}{8 + 8}} = 0.003217, 16 \text{ DF}$$

$$s_W = \sqrt{\frac{(0.00509)^2 4 + (0.00979)^2 4}{4 + 4}} = 0.007802, 8 \text{ DF}$$

$$s_B = \sqrt{\frac{(0.0230)^2 3 + (0.0381)^2 3}{3 + 3}} = 0.031469, 3 \text{ DF}$$

Note that for s_R and s_W, the degrees of freedom for the pooled values equal the sum of those for each set. In the case of s_B, however, the pooled value still has only three degrees of freedom. Although we pooled the data obtained with two samples, we are still dealing with only four labs. If four labs had analyzed the first sample and four other labs had analyzed the second one, then we would have three plus three or six degrees of freedom for the pooled s_B.

23. Analysis of variance:

$$\text{CSS}_T = \sum X_i^2 = 3,332.840$$

$$\text{CF} = T^2/N = 278.0^2/24 = 3,220.166667$$

$$\text{SS}_T = \text{CSS}_T - \text{CF} = 112.673333$$

$$\text{SS}_R = \text{CSS}_T - \frac{\sum X_i^2}{n} = \text{CSS}_T - \frac{6.9^2 + 7.8^2 + \cdots + 15.1^2}{2}$$

$$= 3,332.840 - 3,330.70 - 2.140$$

$$\text{SS}_A = \frac{r_1^2 + r_2^2 + r_3^2}{8} - \text{CF} = 3,264.7825 - \text{CF} = 44.615833$$

$$\text{SS}_B = \frac{c_1^2 + c_2^2}{12} - \text{CF} = 3,224.673333 - \text{CF} = 4.506666$$

$$\text{SS}_{AB} = \frac{\sum X_i^2}{4} - \text{CF} - \text{SS}_A - \text{SS}_B = 3,269.3150 - \text{CF} - \text{SS}_A - \text{SS}_B = 0.25834$$

$$\text{SS}_C = \frac{c_1^2 + c_2^2}{12} - \text{CF} = 3,276.593333 - \text{CF} = 56.426666$$

$$\text{SS}_{AC} = \frac{\sum X_i^2}{4} - \text{CF} - \text{SS}_A - \text{SS}_C = 3,325.550 - \text{CF} - \text{SS}_A - \text{SS}_C = 4.340834$$

$$\text{SS}_{BC} = \frac{\sum X_i^2}{6} - \text{CF} - \text{SS}_B - \text{SS}_C = 3,281.106667 - \text{CF} - \text{SS}_B - \text{SS}_C$$

$$= 0.006668$$

$$\text{SS}_{ABC} = \text{SS}_T - \text{SS}_A - \text{SS}_B - \text{SS}_C - \text{SS}_{AB} - \text{SS}_{AC} - \text{SS}_{BC} - \text{SS}_R = 0.610832$$

Because all three variables are considered to be fixed, the expected mean squares for the fixed model are used in the ANOVA table:

ANOVA Table.

SOURCE	SS	DF	MS	EMS
A Reaction time	44.615833	2	22.307916*	$8\sigma_A^2 + \sigma^2$
B Acid volume	4.506666	1	4.506666*	$12\sigma_B^2 + \sigma^2$
C Reagent conc.	56.426666	1	56.426666*	$12\sigma_C^2 + \sigma^2$
AB	0.025834	2	0.012917	$4\sigma_{AB}^2 + \sigma^2$
BC	0.006668	1	0.006668	$6\sigma_{BC}^2 + \sigma^2$
AC	4.340834	2	2.170417*	$4\sigma_{AC}^2 + \sigma^2$
ABC	0.610832	2	0.305416	$2\sigma_{ABC}^2 + \sigma^2$
Replicates	2.140000	12	0.178333	σ^2
Total	112.673333	23		

Tests of significance of mean squares at $\alpha = 0.05$:

ABC: $F = 0.305416/0.178333 = 1.71$
$F_{0.05, 2, 12} = 3.88$. Thus ABC interaction has not been shown to be significant; combine SS's and DF's of ABC and replicates to get a new estimate of MS_R:
$MS_R = (0.610832 + 2.140000)/(12 + 2) = 0.196488$, 14 DF

AC: $F = 2.170417/0.196488 = 11.05$
$F_{0.05, 2, 14} = 3.74$. Thus, AC interaction is significant.

BC and AB: By inspection, the ratios of these MS's to $MS_R = 0.19648$ are less than unity. Therefore, these effects are not shown to be significant. Their SS's and DF's may be combined with those of ABC and replicates to provide a new MS_R values with 17 DF: 0.163726.

C: $F = 56.42666/0.163726 = 345.64$
$F_{0.05, 1, 17} = 4.45$. Thus, reagent concentration is significant.
B: $F = 4.506666/0.163726 = 27.53$
$F_{0.05, 1, 17} = 4.45$. Thus, acid volume is significant.
A: $F = 22.307916/0.163726 = 136.25$
$F_{0.05, 2, 17} = 3.59$. Thus reaction time is significant.

Standard deviations of significant sources:

$$s_{\text{Replicates}} = \sqrt{0.163726} = 0.4046, \text{ 17 DF}$$

$$s_{AC} = \sqrt{\frac{2.170417 - 0.163726}{4}} = \sqrt{0.501673} = 0.7983, \text{ 2 DF}$$

$$s_C = \sqrt{\frac{56.426666 - 0.163726}{12}} = \sqrt{4.688578} = 2.1653, \text{ 1 DF}$$

$$s_B = \sqrt{\frac{4.506666 - 0.163726}{12}} = \sqrt{0.361912} = 0.6016, \text{ 1 DF}$$

$$s_A = \sqrt{\frac{22.307916 - 0.163726}{8}} = \sqrt{2.768024} = 1.6637, \text{ 2 DF}$$

Reagent concentration (variable C) and reaction time (variable A) account for most of the variance in the data; about 55 and 33%, respectively. Their interaction, AC, accounts for another 6%. The volume of acid contributes only 4% and replicates, 2%. Additional studies could be made to optimize reaction time and reagent concentration.

24. Analysis of variance:

$$\sum A = 132; \sum B = 107; \sum C = 159; \sum D = 120$$

$$CF = 518^2/16 = 16,770.25$$

$$SS_c = \frac{105^2 + 155^2 + 123^2 + 135^2}{4} - CF = 17,101.0 - CF = 330.75$$

$$SS_r = \frac{139^2 + 118^2 + 134^2 + 127^2}{4} - CF = 16,832.5 - CF = 62.25$$

$$SS_t = \frac{132^2 + 107^2 + 159^2 + 120^2}{4} - CF = 17,138.5 - CF = 368.25$$

$$SS_{tt} = 23^2 + 20^2 + 35^2 + \cdots + 34^2 - CF = 17,588.0 - CF = 817.75$$

$$SS_e = SS_{tt} - SS_c - SS_r - SS_t = 56.50$$

ANOVA Table.

SOURCE	SS	DF	MS	EMS
Bet. colm. (atom. time)	330.75	3	110.2500	$\sigma^2 + 4\sigma_c^2$
Bet. row (char. time)	62.25	3	20.7500	$\sigma^2 + 4\sigma_r^2$
Bet. treat. (atom. temp.)	368.25	3	122.7500	$\sigma^2 + 4\sigma_t^2$
Residual	56.50	6	9.4167	σ^2
Total	817.75	15		

Tests of significance $(F_{0.05,3,6} = 4.76)$

$$F = \text{MS}_t/\text{MS}_e = 122.75/9.4167 = 13.04*$$

$$F = \text{MS}_r/\text{MS}_e = 20.75/9.4167 = 2.20$$

$$F = \text{MS}_c/\text{MS}_e = 110.25/9.4167 = 11.71*$$

Thus, atomization time and temperature are significant variables. Combine SS_r and SS_e for a new estimate of MS_e:

$$\text{MS}_e = (62.25 + 56.50)/(3 + 6) = 13.1944, 9 \text{ DF}$$

Standard deviations of significant sources:

$$s_e = \sqrt{13.1944} = 3.63, 9 \text{ DF}$$

$$s_t = \sqrt{\frac{122.75 - 13.1944}{4}} = 5.23, 3 \text{ DF}$$

$$s_c = \sqrt{\frac{110.25 - 13.1944}{4}} = 4.93, 3 \text{ DF}$$

25. Analysis of variance:

Calculation Table

I TREATMENT COMBINATION	II SCALE READING	III SUM	IV EFFECT (COL. III/8)	V SUM OF SQUARES: (COL. III)^2/16
(1)	4.51	92.35 = total		
a Drying temperature	4.60	−0.31	−0.03875	0.00600625
b Charring temperature	5.23	6.63	0.82875	2.74730625
ab	5.15	−0.19	−0.02375	0.00225625
c Charring time	5.35	10.15	1.26875	6.43890625
ac	5.43	−0.55	−0.06875	0.01890625
bc	6.39	−1.73	−0.21625	0.18705625
abc	6.13	−0.27	−0.03375	0.00455625
d Atomizing time	4.70	6.77	0.84625	2.86455625
ad	4.65	0.03	0.00375	0.00005625
bd	6.05	0.61	0.07625	0.02325625
abd	6.21	0.83	0.10375	0.04305625
cd	6.90	2.53	0.31625	0.40005625
acd	6.72	−0.17	−0.02125	0.00180625
bcd	7.20	−2.67	−0.33375	0.44555625
$abcd$	7.13	0.07	0.00875	0.00030625

ANOVA Table

SOURCE	DF	MEAN SQUARE	F RATIO	$(F_{0.05,1,5} = 6.61)$
A Drying temperature	1	0.00600625	0.061	$(F_{0.01,1,5} = 16.3)$
B Charring temperature	1	2.74730625	27.735*	
C Charring time	1	6.43890625	65.003*	
D Atomizing time	1	2.86455625	28.918*	
Interaction AB	1	0.00225625	0.023	
Interaction AC	1	0.01890625	0.191	
Interaction AD	1	0.00005625	0.001	
Interaction BC	1	0.18705625	1.888	
Interaction BD	1	0.02325625	0.235	
Interaction CD	1	0.40005625	4.039	
Error[a]	5	0.09905625		
Total	15			

[a] Error term composed of the 3rd and 4th order interactions with 1 DF, each:

ABC	0.00455625
ABD	0.04305625
ACD	0.00180625
BCD	0.44555625
ABCD	0.00030625
Error	0.49528112/5 = 0.09905625

Estimated scale reading for treatment bc:

Scale reading $= (92.35 - 0 + 6.63 - 0 + 10.15 - 0 + 0 - 0 - 6.77$

$$+ 0 - 0 + 0 - 0 + 0 - 0 + 0)/16$$

$$= 102.36/16$$

$$= 6.3975, \text{ or } 6.40$$

26. t test for independent averages and known variances:

$$t = \frac{0.82070 - 0.82017}{\sqrt{\dfrac{0.0005^2}{3} + \dfrac{0.0002^2}{3}}} = 1.70, \infty \text{ DF}$$

$t_{0.05/2,\infty} = 1.96$. Thus, the 2 averages have not been shown to differ significantly; the 2 shipments are concluded to have the same specific gravity.

27. t test for independent averages with variances unknown and unequal:

	CAR 1	CAR 2
n	8	5
$\bar{X}$	9.220	9.096
s^2	0.00120	0.00863

$$F = 0.00863/0.00120 = 7.19$$

$F_{0.05/2, 4, 7} = 5.52$. Thus, the variances not equivalent at $\alpha = 0.05$; use t-test for variances unknown and unequal.

$$t = \frac{9.220 - 9.096}{\sqrt{\dfrac{0.00120}{8} + \dfrac{0.00863}{5}}} = \frac{0.124}{0.0433128} = 2.86$$

$$DF = \left[\frac{0.001876^2}{\dfrac{0.0015^2}{9} + \dfrac{0.001726^2}{6}} \right] - 2 = 7.05 - 2 = 5.05,$$

$$= 5 \text{ (rounded value)}$$

$t_{0.05/2, 5} = 2.57$. Thus, reject the null hypothesis of equal means; conclude that the two tank cars differ significantly in total nitrogen content.

Appendix D

TABLE 1. Critical Values of the χ^2 Distribution.

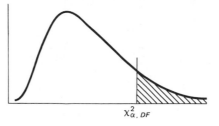

$$\chi^2_{\alpha,\, DF}$$

The entries in the table are the critical values for chi-square for which the shaded area is equal to α.

DF	α									
	0.995	0.990	0.975	0.950	0.900	0.100	0.050	0.025	0.010	0.005
1	0.0000393	0.000157	0.000982	0.00393	0.0158	2.71	3.84	5.02	6.64	7.88
2	0.0100	0.0201	0.0506	0.103	0.211	4.61	6.00	7.38	9.21	10.6
3	0.0717	0.115	0.216	0.352	0.584	6.25	7.82	9.35	11.4	12.9
4	0.207	0.297	0.484	0.711	1.0636	7.78	9.50	11.1	13.3	14.9
5	0.412	0.554	0.831	1.15	1.61	9.24	11.1	12.8	15.1	16.8
6	0.676	0.872	1.24	1.64	2.20	10.6	12.6	14.5	16.8	18.6
7	0.990	1.24	1.69	2.17	2.83	12.0	14.1	16.0	18.5	20.3
8	1.34	1.65	2.18	2.73	3.49	13.4	15.5	17.5	20.1	22.0
9	1.73	2.09	2.70	3.33	4.17	14.7	17.0	19.0	21.7	23.6
10	2.16	2.56	3.25	3.94	4.87	16.0	18.3	20.5	23.2	25.2
11	2.60	3.05	3.82	4.58	5.58	17.2	19.7	21.9	24.7	26.8
12	3.07	3.57	4.40	5.23	6.30	18.6	21.0	23.3	26.2	28.3
13	3.57	4.11	5.01	5.90	7.04	19.8	22.4	24.7	27.7	29.8
14	4.07	4.66	5.63	6.57	7.79	21.1	23.7	26.1	29.1	31.3
15	4.60	5.23	6.26	7.26	8.55	22.3	25.0	27.5	30.6	32.8
16	5.14	5.81	6.91	7.96	9.31	23.5	26.3	28.9	32.0	34.3
17	5.70	6.41	7.56	8.67	10.1	24.8	27.6	30.2	33.4	35.7
18	6.26	7.01	8.23	9.39	10.9	26.0	28.9	31.5	34.8	37.2
19	6.84	7.63	8.91	10.1	11.7	27.2	30.1	32.9	36.2	38.6
20	7.43	8.26	9.59	10.9	12.4	28.4	31.4	34.2	37.6	40.0
21	8.03	8.90	10.3	11.6	13.2	29.6	32.7	35.5	39.0	41.4
22	8.64	9.54	11.0	12.3	14.0	30.8	33.9	36.8	40.3	42.8
23	9.26	10.2	11.0	13.1	14.9	32.0	35.2	38.1	41.6	44.2
24	9.89	10.9	12.4	13.9	15.7	33.2	36.4	39.4	43.0	45.6
25	10.5	11.5	13.1	14.6	16.5	34.4	37.7	40.7	44.3	46.9
26	11.2	12.2	13.8	15.4	17.3	35.6	38.9	41.9	45.6	48.3
27	11.8	12.9	14.6	16.2	18.1	36.7	40.1	43.2	47.0	49.7
28	12.5	13.6	15.3	16.9	18.9	37.9	41.3	44.5	48.3	51.0
29	13.1	14.3	16.1	17.7	19.8	39.1	42.6	45.7	49.6	52.3
30	13.8	15.0	16.8	18.5	20.6	40.3	43.8	47.0	50.9	53.7
40	20.7	22.2	24.4	26.5	29.1	51.8	55.8	59.3	63.7	66.8
50	28.0	29.7	32.4	34.8	37.7	63.2	67.5	71.4	76.2	79.5
60	35.5	37.5	40.5	43.2	46.5	74.4	79.1	83.3	88.4	92.0
70	43.3	45.4	48.8	51.8	55.3	85.5	90.5	95.0	100.0	104.0
80	51.2	53.5	57.2	60.4	64.3	96.6	102.0	107.0	112.0	116.0
90	59.2	61.8	65.7	69.1	73.3	108.0	113.0	118.0	124.0	128.0
100	67.3	70.1	74.2	77.9	82.4	114.0	124.0	130.0	136.0	140.0

Adapted from E. S. Pearson and H. O. Hartley, *Biometrika Tables for Statisticians*, Vol. 1 (1962), pp. 130–131. Reprinted by permission of the Biometrika Trustees.

TABLE 2.   Critical Values of the F Distribution.

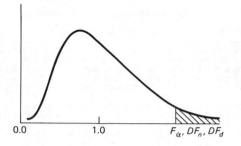

The entries in the table are critical values of F for which the area under the curve to the right is equal to α. Tables 2a, 2B, and 2C, in which α equals 0.05, 0.025, and 0.01, respectively, are from E. S. Pearson and H. O. Hartley, *Biometrika Tables for Statisticians*, Vol. 1 (1958), pp. 159–163. Reprinted by permission of the Biometrika Trustees.

TABLE 2A.   Critical Values of the F Distribution, $\alpha = 0.05$.

	Degrees of freedom for the numerator (n)																	
	1	2	3	4	5	6	7	8	9	10	11	12	13	14	15	16	17	18
1	161	200	216	225	230	234	237	239	241	242	243	244	245	245	246	246	247	247
2	18.5	19.0	19.2	19.2	19.3	19.3	19.4	19.4	19.4	19.4	19.4	19.4	19.4	19.4	19.4	19.4	19.4	19.4
3	10.1	9.55	9.28	9.12	9.01	8.94	8.89	8.85	8.81	8.79	8.76	8.74	8.73	8.71	8.70	8.69	8.68	8.67
4	7.71	6.94	6.59	6.39	6.26	6.16	6.09	6.04	6.00	5.96	5.94	5.91	5.89	5.87	5.86	5.84	5.83	5.82
5	6.61	5.79	5.41	5.19	5.05	4.95	4.88	4.82	4.77	4.74	4.70	4.68	4.66	4.64	4.62	4.60	4.59	4.58
6	5.99	5.14	4.76	4.53	4.39	4.28	4.21	4.15	4.10	4.06	4.03	4.00	3.98	3.96	3.94	3.92	3.91	3.90
7	5.59	4.74	4.35	4.12	3.97	3.87	3.79	3.73	3.68	3.64	3.60	3.57	3.55	3.53	3.51	3.49	3.48	3.47
8	5.32	4.46	4.07	3.84	3.69	3.58	3.50	3.44	3.39	3.35	3.31	3.28	3.26	3.24	3.22	3.20	3.19	3.17
9	5.12	4.26	3.86	3.63	3.48	3.37	3.29	3.23	3.18	3.14	3.10	3.07	3.05	3.03	3.01	2.99	2.97	2.96
10	4.96	4.10	3.71	3.48	3.33	3.22	3.14	3.07	3.02	2.98	2.94	2.91	2.89	2.86	2.85	2.83	2.81	2.80
11	4.84	3.98	3.59	3.36	3.20	3.09	3.01	2.95	2.90	2.85	2.82	2.79	2.76	2.74	2.72	2.70	2.69	2.67
12	4.75	3.89	3.49	3.26	3.11	3.00	2.91	2.85	2.80	2.75	2.72	2.69	2.66	2.64	2.62	2.60	2.58	2.57
13	4.67	3.81	3.41	3.18	3.03	2.92	2.83	2.77	2.71	2.67	2.63	2.60	2.58	2.55	2.53	2.51	2.50	2.48
14	4.60	3.74	3.34	3.11	2.96	2.85	2.76	2.70	2.65	2.60	2.57	2.53	2.51	2.48	2.46	2.44	2.43	2.41
15	4.54	3.68	3.29	3.06	2.90	2.79	2.71	2.64	2.59	2.54	2.51	2.48	2.45	2.42	2.40	2.38	2.37	2.35
16	4.49	3.63	3.24	3.01	2.85	2.74	2.66	2.59	2.54	2.49	2.46	2.42	2.40	2.37	2.35	2.33	2.32	2.30
17	4.45	3.59	3.20	2.96	2.81	2.70	2.61	2.55	2.49	2.45	2.41	2.38	2.35	2.33	2.31	2.29	2.27	2.26
18	4.41	3.55	3.16	2.93	2.77	2.66	2.58	2.51	2.46	2.41	2.37	2.34	2.31	2.29	2.27	2.25	2.23	2.22
19	4.38	3.52	3.13	2.90	2.74	2.63	2.54	2.48	2.42	2.38	2.34	2.31	2.28	2.26	2.23	2.21	2.20	2.18
20	4.35	3.49	3.10	2.87	2.71	2.60	2.51	2.45	2.39	2.35	2.31	2.28	2.25	2.22	2.20	2.18	2.17	2.15
21	4.32	3.47	3.07	2.84	2.68	2.57	2.49	2.42	2.37	2.32	2.28	2.25	2.22	2.20	2.18	2.16	2.14	2.12
22	4.30	3.44	3.05	2.82	2.66	2.55	2.46	2.40	2.34	2.30	2.26	2.23	2.20	2.17	2.15	2.13	2.11	2.10
23	4.28	3.42	3.03	2.80	2.64	2.53	2.44	2.37	2.32	2.27	2.23	2.20	2.18	2.15	2.13	2.11	2.09	2.07
24	4.26	3.40	3.01	2.78	2.62	2.51	2.42	2.36	2.30	2.25	2.21	2.18	2.15	2.13	2.11	2.09	2.07	2.05
25	4.24	3.39	2.99	2.76	2.60	2.49	2.40	2.34	2.28	2.24	2.20	2.16	2.14	2.11	2.09	2.07	2.05	2.04
26	4.23	3.37	2.98	2.74	2.59	2.47	2.39	2.32	2.27	2.22	2.18	2.15	2.12	2.09	2.07	2.05	2.03	2.02
27	4.21	3.35	2.96	2.73	2.57	2.46	2.37	2.31	2.25	2.20	2.17	2.13	2.10	2.08	2.06	2.04	2.02	2.00
28	4.20	3.34	2.95	2.71	2.56	2.45	2.36	2.29	2.24	2.19	2.15	2.12	2.09	2.06	2.04	2.02	2.00	1.99
29	4.18	3.33	2.93	2.70	2.55	2.43	2.35	2.28	2.22	2.18	2.14	2.10	2.08	2.05	2.03	2.01	1.99	1.97
30	4.17	3.32	2.92	2.69	2.53	2.42	2.33	2.27	2.21	2.16	2.13	2.09	2.06	2.04	2.01	1.99	1.98	1.96
32	4.15	3.29	2.90	2.67	2.51	2.40	2.31	2.24	2.19	2.14	2.10	2.07	2.04	2.01	1.99	1.97	1.95	1.94
34	4.13	3.28	2.88	2.65	2.49	2.38	2.29	2.23	2.17	2.12	2.08	2.05	2.02	1.99	1.97	1.95	1.93	1.92
36	4.11	3.26	2.87	2.63	2.48	2.36	2.28	2.21	2.15	2.11	2.07	2.03	2.00	1.98	1.95	1.93	1.92	1.90
38	4.10	3.24	2.85	2.62	2.46	2.35	2.26	2.19	2.14	2.09	2.05	2.02	1.99	1.96	1.94	1.92	1.90	1.88
40	4.08	3.23	2.84	2.61	2.45	2.34	2.25	2.18	2.12	2.08	2.04	2.00	1.97	1.95	1.92	1.90	1.89	1.87
42	4.07	3.22	2.83	2.59	2.44	2.32	2.24	2.17	2.11	2.06	2.03	1.99	1.96	1.93	1.91	1.89	1.87	1.86
44	4.06	3.21	2.82	2.58	2.43	2.31	2.23	2.16	2.10	2.05	2.01	1.98	1.95	1.92	1.90	1.88	1.86	1.84
46	4.05	3.20	2.81	2.57	2.42	2.30	2.22	2.15	2.09	2.04	2.00	1.97	1.94	1.91	1.89	1.87	1.85	1.83
48	4.04	3.19	2.80	2.57	2.41	2.29	2.21	2.14	2.08	2.03	1.99	1.96	1.93	1.90	1.88	1.86	1.84	1.82
50	4.03	3.18	2.79	2.56	2.40	2.29	2.20	2.13	2.07	2.03	1.99	1.95	1.92	1.89	1.87	1.85	1.83	1.81
55	4.02	3.16	2.77	2.54	2.38	2.27	2.18	2.11	2.06	2.01	1.97	1.93	1.90	1.88	1.85	1.83	1.81	1.79
60	4.00	3.15	2.76	2.53	2.37	2.25	2.17	2.10	2.04	1.99	1.95	1.92	1.89	1.86	1.84	1.82	1.80	1.78
65	3.99	3.14	2.75	2.51	2.36	2.24	2.15	2.08	2.03	1.98	1.94	1.90	1.87	1.85	1.82	1.80	1.78	1.76
70	3.98	3.13	2.74	2.50	2.35	2.23	2.14	2.07	2.02	1.97	1.93	1.89	1.86	1.84	1.81	1.79	1.77	1.75
80	3.96	3.11	2.72	2.49	2.33	2.21	2.13	2.06	2.00	1.95	1.91	1.88	1.84	1.82	1.79	1.77	1.75	1.73
90	3.95	3.10	2.71	2.47	2.32	2.20	2.11	2.04	1.99	1.94	1.90	1.86	1.83	1.80	1.78	1.76	1.74	1.72
100	3.94	3.09	2.70	2.46	2.31	2.19	2.10	2.03	1.97	1.93	1.89	1.85	1.82	1.79	1.77	1.75	1.73	1.71
125	3.92	3.07	2.68	2.44	2.29	2.17	2.08	2.01	1.96	1.91	1.87	1.83	1.80	1.77	1.75	1.72	1.70	1.69
150	3.90	3.06	2.66	2.43	2.27	2.16	2.07	2.00	1.94	1.89	1.85	1.82	1.79	1.76	1.73	1.71	1.69	1.67
200	3.89	3.04	2.65	2.42	2.26	2.14	2.06	1.98	1.93	1.88	1.84	1.80	1.77	1.74	1.72	1.69	1.67	1.66
300	3.87	3.03	2.63	2.40	2.24	2.13	2.04	1.97	1.91	1.86	1.82	1.78	1.75	1.72	1.70	1.68	1.66	1.64
500	3.86	3.01	2.62	2.39	2.23	2.12	2.03	1.96	1.90	1.85	1.81	1.77	1.74	1.71	1.69	1.66	1.64	1.62
1000	3.85	3.00	2.61	2.38	2.22	2.11	2.02	1.95	1.89	1.84	1.80	1.76	1.73	1.70	1.68	1.65	1.63	1.61
∞	3.84	3.00	2.60	2.37	2.21	2.10	2.01	1.94	1.88	1.83	1.79	1.75	1.72	1.69	1.67	1.64	1.62	1.60

Degrees of freedom for the denominator (m)

Example: $P\{F_{05;3,20} < 2.45\} = 95\%$.

$F_{.95;\nu_1,\nu_2} = 1/F_{.05;\nu_2,\nu_1}$.   Example: $F_{.95;3,20} = 1/F_{.05;20,3} = 1/3.15 = 0.317$.

Degrees of freedom for the numerator (n_1)

19	20	22	24	26	28	30	35	40	45	50	60	80	100	200	500	∞	Denominator
248	248	249	249	249	250	250	251	251	251	252	252	252	253	254	254	254	1
19.4	19.4	19.5	19.5	19.5	19.5	19.5	19.5	19.5	19.5	19.5	19.5	19.5	19.5	19.5	19.5	19.5	2
8.67	8.66	8.65	8.64	8.63	8.62	8.62	8.60	8.59	8.59	8.58	8.57	8.56	8.55	8.54	8.53	8.53	3
5.81	5.80	5.79	5.77	5.76	5.75	5.75	5.73	5.72	5.71	5.70	5.69	5.67	5.66	5.65	5.64	5.63	4
4.57	4.56	4.54	4.53	4.52	4.50	4.50	4.48	4.46	4.45	4.44	4.43	4.41	4.41	4.39	4.37	4.37	5
3.88	3.87	3.86	3.84	3.83	3.82	3.81	3.79	3.77	3.76	3.75	3.74	3.72	3.71	3.69	3.68	3.67	6
3.46	3.44	3.43	3.41	3.40	3.39	3.38	3.36	3.34	3.33	3.32	3.30	3.29	3.27	3.25	3.24	3.23	7
3.16	3.15	3.13	3.12	3.10	3.09	3.08	3.06	3.04	3.03	3.02	3.01	2.99	2.97	2.95	2.94	2.93	8
2.95	2.94	2.92	2.90	2.89	2.87	2.86	2.84	2.83	2.81	2.80	2.79	2.77	2.76	2.73	2.72	2.71	9
2.78	2.77	2.75	2.74	2.72	2.71	2.70	2.68	2.66	2.65	2.64	2.62	2.60	2.59	2.56	2.55	2.54	10
2.66	2.65	2.63	2.61	2.59	2.58	2.57	2.55	2.53	2.52	2.51	2.49	2.47	2.46	2.43	2.42	2.40	11
2.56	2.54	2.52	2.51	2.49	2.48	2.47	2.44	2.43	2.41	2.40	2.38	2.36	2.35	2.32	2.31	2.30	12
2.47	2.46	2.44	2.42	2.41	2.39	2.38	2.36	2.34	2.33	2.31	2.30	2.27	2.26	2.23	2.22	2.21	13
2.40	2.39	2.37	2.35	2.33	2.32	2.31	2.28	2.27	2.25	2.24	2.22	2.20	2.19	2.16	2.14	2.13	14
2.34	2.33	2.31	2.29	2.27	2.26	2.25	2.22	2.20	2.19	2.18	2.16	2.14	2.12	2.10	2.08	2.07	15
2.29	2.28	2.25	2.24	2.22	2.21	2.19	2.17	2.15	2.14	2.12	2.11	2.08	2.07	2.04	2.02	2.01	16
2.24	2.23	2.21	2.19	2.17	2.16	2.15	2.12	2.10	2.09	2.08	2.06	2.03	2.02	1.99	1.97	1.96	17
2.20	2.19	2.17	2.15	2.13	2.12	2.11	2.08	2.06	2.05	2.04	2.02	1.99	1.98	1.95	1.93	1.92	18
2.17	2.16	2.13	2.11	2.10	2.08	2.07	2.05	2.03	2.01	2.00	1.98	1.96	1.94	1.91	1.89	1.88	19
2.14	2.12	2.10	2.08	2.07	2.05	2.04	2.01	1.99	1.98	1.97	1.95	1.92	1.91	1.88	1.86	1.84	20
2.11	2.10	2.07	2.05	2.04	2.02	2.01	1.98	1.96	1.95	1.94	1.92	1.89	1.88	1.84	1.82	1.81	21
2.08	2.07	2.05	2.03	2.01	2.00	1.98	1.96	1.94	1.92	1.91	1.89	1.86	1.85	1.82	1.80	1.78	22
2.06	2.05	2.02	2.00	1.99	1.97	1.96	1.93	1.91	1.90	1.88	1.86	1.84	1.82	1.79	1.77	1.76	23
2.04	2.03	2.00	1.98	1.97	1.95	1.94	1.91	1.89	1.88	1.86	1.84	1.82	1.80	1.77	1.75	1.73	24
2.02	2.01	1.98	1.96	1.95	1.93	1.92	1.89	1.87	1.86	1.84	1.82	1.80	1.78	1.75	1.73	1.71	25
2.00	1.99	1.97	1.95	1.93	1.91	1.90	1.87	1.85	1.84	1.82	1.80	1.78	1.76	1.73	1.71	1.69	26
1.99	1.97	1.95	1.93	1.91	1.90	1.88	1.86	1.84	1.82	1.81	1.79	1.76	1.74	1.71	1.69	1.67	27
1.97	1.96	1.93	1.91	1.90	1.88	1.87	1.84	1.82	1.80	1.79	1.77	1.74	1.73	1.69	1.67	1.65	28
1.96	1.94	1.92	1.90	1.88	1.87	1.85	1.83	1.81	1.79	1.77	1.75	1.73	1.71	1.67	1.65	1.64	29
1.95	1.93	1.91	1.89	1.87	1.85	1.84	1.81	1.79	1.77	1.76	1.74	1.71	1.70	1.66	1.64	1.62	30
1.92	1.91	1.88	1.86	1.85	1.83	1.82	1.79	1.77	1.75	1.74	1.71	1.69	1.67	1.63	1.61	1.59	32
1.90	1.89	1.86	1.84	1.82	1.80	1.80	1.77	1.75	1.73	1.71	1.69	1.66	1.65	1.61	1.59	1.57	34
1.88	1.87	1.85	1.82	1.81	1.79	1.78	1.75	1.73	1.71	1.69	1.67	1.64	1.62	1.59	1.56	1.55	36
1.87	1.85	1.83	1.81	1.79	1.77	1.76	1.73	1.71	1.69	1.68	1.65	1.62	1.61	1.57	1.54	1.53	38
1.85	1.84	1.81	1.79	1.77	1.76	1.74	1.72	1.69	1.67	1.66	1.64	1.61	1.59	1.55	1.53	1.51	40
1.84	1.83	1.80	1.78	1.76	1.74	1.73	1.70	1.68	1.66	1.65	1.62	1.59	1.57	1.53	1.51	1.49	42
1.83	1.81	1.79	1.77	1.75	1.73	1.72	1.69	1.67	1.65	1.63	1.61	1.58	1.56	1.52	1.49	1.48	44
1.82	1.80	1.78	1.76	1.74	1.72	1.71	1.68	1.65	1.64	1.62	1.60	1.57	1.55	1.51	1.48	1.46	46
1.81	1.79	1.77	1.75	1.73	1.71	1.70	1.67	1.64	1.62	1.61	1.59	1.56	1.54	1.49	1.47	1.45	48
1.80	1.78	1.76	1.74	1.72	1.70	1.69	1.66	1.63	1.61	1.60	1.58	1.54	1.52	1.48	1.46	1.44	50
1.78	1.76	1.74	1.72	1.70	1.68	1.67	1.64	1.61	1.59	1.58	1.55	1.52	1.50	1.46	1.43	1.41	55
1.76	1.75	1.72	1.70	1.68	1.66	1.65	1.62	1.59	1.57	1.56	1.53	1.50	1.48	1.44	1.41	1.39	60
1.75	1.73	1.71	1.69	1.67	1.65	1.63	1.60	1.58	1.56	1.54	1.52	1.49	1.46	1.42	1.39	1.37	65
1.74	1.72	1.70	1.67	1.65	1.64	1.62	1.59	1.57	1.55	1.53	1.50	1.47	1.45	1.40	1.37	1.35	70
1.72	1.70	1.68	1.65	1.63	1.62	1.60	1.57	1.54	1.52	1.51	1.48	1.45	1.43	1.38	1.35	1.32	80
1.70	1.69	1.66	1.64	1.62	1.60	1.59	1.55	1.53	1.51	1.49	1.46	1.43	1.41	1.36	1.32	1.30	90
1.69	1.68	1.65	1.63	1.61	1.59	1.57	1.54	1.52	1.49	1.48	1.45	1.41	1.39	1.34	1.31	1.28	100
1.67	1.65	1.63	1.60	1.58	1.57	1.55	1.52	1.49	1.47	1.45	1.42	1.39	1.36	1.31	1.27	1.25	125
1.66	1.64	1.61	1.59	1.57	1.55	1.53	1.50	1.48	1.45	1.44	1.41	1.37	1.34	1.29	1.25	1.22	150
1.64	1.62	1.60	1.57	1.55	1.53	1.52	1.48	1.46	1.43	1.41	1.39	1.35	1.32	1.26	1.22	1.19	200
1.62	1.61	1.58	1.55	1.53	1.51	1.50	1.46	1.43	1.41	1.39	1.36	1.32	1.30	1.23	1.19	1.15	300
1.61	1.59	1.56	1.54	1.52	1.50	1.48	1.45	1.42	1.40	1.38	1.34	1.30	1.28	1.21	1.16	1.11	500
1.60	1.58	1.55	1.53	1.51	1.49	1.47	1.44	1.41	1.38	1.36	1.33	1.29	1.26	1.19	1.13	1.08	1000
1.59	1.57	1.54	1.52	1.50	1.48	1.46	1.42	1.39	1.37	1.35	1.32	1.27	1.24	1.17	1.11	1.00	∞

Degrees of freedom for the denominator (n_2)

Approximate formula for n_1 and n_2 larger than 30:

$$\log_{10} F_{.05;\nu_1,\nu_2} \simeq \frac{1.4287}{\sqrt{h-0.95}} - 0.681\left(\frac{1}{\nu_1}-\frac{1}{\nu_2}\right), \text{ where } \frac{1}{h}=\frac{1}{2}\left(\frac{1}{\nu_1}+\frac{1}{\nu_2}\right).$$

TABLE 2B.   Critical Values of the F Distribution, $\alpha = 0.025$.

					Degrees of freedom for the numerator (n)												
	1	2	3	4	5	6	7	8	9	10	11	12	13	14	15	16	17	18
1	648	800	864	900	922	937	948	957	963	969	973	977	980	983	985	987	989	990
2	38.5	39.0	39.2	39.2	39.3	39.3	39.4	39.4	39.4	39.4	39.4	39.4	39.4	39.4	39.4	39.4	39.4	39.4
3	17.4	16.0	15.4	15.1	14.9	14.7	14.6	14.5	14.5	14.4	14.4	14.3	14.3	14.3	14.3	14.2	14.2	14.2
4	12.2	10.6	9.98	9.60	9.36	9.20	9.07	8.98	8.90	8.84	8.79	8.75	8.72	8.69	8.66	8.64	8.62	8.60
5	10.0	8.43	7.76	7.39	7.15	6.98	6.85	6.76	6.68	6.62	6.57	6.52	6.49	6.46	6.43	6.41	6.39	6.37
6	8.81	7.26	6.60	6.23	5.99	5.82	5.70	5.60	5.52	5.46	5.41	5.37	5.33	5.30	5.27	5.25	5.23	5.21
7	8.07	6.54	5.89	5.52	5.29	5.12	4.99	4.90	4.82	4.76	4.71	4.67	4.63	4.60	4.57	4.54	4.52	4.50
8	7.57	6.06	5.42	5.05	4.82	4.65	4.53	4.43	4.36	4.30	4.24	4.20	4.16	4.13	4.10	4.08	4.05	4.03
9	7.21	5.71	5.08	4.72	4.48	4.32	4.20	4.10	4.03	3.96	3.91	3.87	3.83	3.80	3.77	3.74	3.72	3.70
10	6.94	5.46	4.83	4.47	4.24	4.07	3.95	3.85	3.78	3.72	3.66	3.62	3.58	3.55	3.52	3.50	3.47	3.45
11	6.72	5.26	4.63	4.28	4.04	3.88	3.76	3.66	3.59	3.53	3.47	3.43	3.39	3.36	3.33	3.30	3.28	3.26
12	6.55	5.10	4.47	4.12	3.89	3.73	3.61	3.51	3.44	3.37	3.32	3.28	3.24	3.21	3.18	3.15	3.13	3.11
13	6.41	4.97	4.35	4.00	3.77	3.60	3.48	3.39	3.31	3.25	3.20	3.15	3.12	3.08	3.05	3.03	3.00	2.98
14	6.30	4.86	4.24	3.89	3.66	3.50	3.38	3.29	3.21	3.15	3.09	3.05	3.01	2.98	2.95	2.92	2.90	2.88
15	6.20	4.76	4.15	3.80	3.58	3.41	3.29	3.20	3.12	3.06	3.01	2.96	2.92	2.89	2.86	2.84	2.81	2.79
16	6.12	4.69	4.08	3.73	3.50	3.34	3.22	3.12	3.05	2.99	2.93	2.89	2.85	2.82	2.79	2.76	2.74	2.72
17	6.04	4.62	4.01	3.66	3.44	3.28	3.16	3.06	2.98	2.92	2.87	2.82	2.79	2.75	2.72	2.70	2.67	2.65
18	5.98	4.56	3.95	3.61	3.38	3.22	3.10	3.01	2.93	2.87	2.81	2.77	2.73	2.70	2.67	2.64	2.62	2.60
19	5.92	4.51	3.90	3.56	3.33	3.17	3.05	2.96	2.88	2.82	2.76	2.72	2.68	2.65	2.62	2.59	2.57	2.55
20	5.87	4.46	3.86	3.51	3.29	3.13	3.01	2.91	2.84	2.77	2.72	2.68	2.64	2.60	2.57	2.55	2.52	2.50
21	5.83	4.42	3.82	3.48	3.25	3.09	2.97	2.87	2.80	2.73	2.68	2.64	2.60	2.56	2.53	2.51	2.48	2.46
22	5.79	4.38	3.78	3.44	3.22	3.05	2.93	2.84	2.76	2.70	2.65	2.60	2.56	2.53	2.50	2.47	2.45	2.43
23	5.75	4.35	3.75	3.41	3.18	3.02	2.90	2.81	2.73	2.67	2.62	2.57	2.53	2.50	2.47	2.44	2.42	2.39
24	5.72	4.32	3.72	3.38	3.15	2.99	2.87	2.78	2.70	2.64	2.59	2.54	2.50	2.47	2.44	2.41	2.39	2.36
25	5.69	4.29	3.69	3.35	3.13	2.97	2.85	2.75	2.68	2.61	2.56	2.51	2.48	2.44	2.41	2.38	2.36	2.34
26	5.66	4.27	3.67	3.33	3.10	2.94	2.82	2.73	2.65	2.59	2.54	2.49	2.45	2.42	2.39	2.36	2.34	2.31
27	5.63	4.24	3.65	3.31	3.08	2.92	2.80	2.71	2.63	2.57	2.51	2.47	2.43	2.39	2.36	2.34	2.31	2.29
28	5.61	4.22	3.63	3.29	3.06	2.90	2.78	2.69	2.61	2.55	2.49	2.45	2.41	2.37	2.34	2.32	2.29	2.27
29	5.59	4.20	3.61	3.27	3.04	2.88	2.76	2.67	2.59	2.53	2.48	2.43	2.39	2.36	2.32	2.30	2.27	2.25
30	5.57	4.18	3.59	3.25	3.03	2.87	2.75	2.65	2.57	2.51	2.46	2.41	2.37	2.34	2.31	2.28	2.26	2.23
32	5.53	4.15	3.56	3.22	3.00	2.84	2.72	2.62	2.54	2.48	2.43	2.38	2.34	2.31	2.28	2.25	2.22	2.20
34	5.50	4.12	3.53	3.19	2.97	2.81	2.69	2.59	2.52	2.45	2.40	2.35	2.31	2.28	2.25	2.22	2.19	2.17
36	5.47	4.09	3.51	3.17	2.94	2.79	2.66	2.57	2.49	2.43	2.37	2.33	2.29	2.25	2.22	2.20	2.17	2.15
38	5.45	4.07	3.48	3.15	2.92	2.76	2.64	2.55	2.47	2.41	2.35	2.31	2.27	2.23	2.20	2.17	2.15	2.13
40	5.42	4.05	3.46	3.13	2.90	2.74	2.62	2.53	2.45	2.39	2.33	2.29	2.25	2.21	2.18	2.15	2.13	2.11
42	5.40	4.03	3.45	3.11	2.89	2.73	2.61	2.51	2.44	2.37	2.32	2.27	2.23	2.20	2.16	2.14	2.11	2.09
44	5.39	4.02	3.43	3.09	2.87	2.71	2.59	2.50	2.42	2.36	2.30	2.26	2.21	2.18	2.15	2.12	2.10	2.07
46	5.37	4.00	3.42	3.08	2.86	2.70	2.58	2.48	2.41	2.34	2.29	2.24	2.20	2.17	2.13	2.11	2.08	2.06
48	5.35	3.99	3.40	3.07	2.84	2.69	2.57	2.47	2.39	2.33	2.27	2.23	2.19	2.15	2.12	2.09	2.07	2.05
50	5.34	3.98	3.39	3.06	2.83	2.67	2.55	2.46	2.38	2.32	2.26	2.22	2.18	2.14	2.11	2.08	2.06	2.03
55	5.31	3.95	3.36	3.03	2.81	2.65	2.53	2.43	2.36	2.29	2.24	2.19	2.15	2.11	2.08	2.05	2.03	2.01
60	5.29	3.93	3.34	3.01	2.79	2.63	2.51	2.41	2.33	2.27	2.22	2.17	2.13	2.09	2.06	2.03	2.01	1.98
65	5.27	3.91	3.32	2.99	2.77	2.61	2.49	2.39	2.32	2.25	2.20	2.15	2.11	2.07	2.04	2.01	1.99	1.97
70	5.25	3.89	3.31	2.98	2.75	2.60	2.48	2.38	2.30	2.24	2.18	2.14	2.10	2.06	2.03	2.00	1.97	1.95
80	5.22	3.86	3.28	2.95	2.73	2.57	2.45	2.36	2.28	2.21	2.16	2.11	2.07	2.03	2.00	1.97	1.95	1.93
90	5.20	3.84	3.27	2.93	2.71	2.55	2.43	2.34	2.26	2.19	2.14	2.09	2.05	2.02	1.98	1.95	1.93	1.91
100	5.18	3.83	3.25	2.92	2.70	2.54	2.42	2.32	2.24	2.18	2.12	2.08	2.04	2.00	1.97	1.94	1.91	1.89
125	5.15	3.80	3.22	2.89	2.67	2.51	2.39	2.30	2.22	2.15	2.10	2.05	2.01	1.97	1.94	1.91	1.89	1.86
150	5.13	3.78	3.20	2.87	2.65	2.49	2.37	2.28	2.20	2.13	2.08	2.03	1.99	1.95	1.92	1.89	1.87	1.84
200	5.10	3.76	3.18	2.85	2.63	2.47	2.35	2.26	2.18	2.11	2.06	2.01	1.97	1.93	1.90	1.87	1.84	1.82
300	5.08	3.74	3.16	2.83	2.61	2.45	2.33	2.23	2.16	2.09	2.04	1.99	1.95	1.91	1.88	1.85	1.82	1.80
500	5.05	3.72	3.14	2.81	2.59	2.43	2.31	2.22	2.14	2.07	2.02	1.97	1.93	1.89	1.86	1.83	1.80	1.78
1000	5.04	3.70	3.13	2.80	2.58	2.42	2.30	2.20	2.13	2.06	2.01	1.96	1.92	1.88	1.85	1.82	1.79	1.77
∞	5.02	3.69	3.12	2.79	2.57	2.41	2.29	2.19	2.11	2.05	1.99	1.94	1.90	1.87	1.83	1.80	1.78	1.75

Degrees of freedom for the denominator (m)

Example: $P\{F_{.025;8,20} < 2.91\} = 97.5\%$.

$F_{.975;\nu_1,\nu_2} = 1/F_{.025;\nu_2,\nu_1}$.   Example: $F_{.975;8,20} = 1/F_{.025;20,8} = 1/4.00 = 0.250$.

			Degrees of freedom for the numerator (n_1)														
19	20	22	24	26	28	30	35	40	45	50	60	80	100	200	500	∞	
992	993	995	997	999	1000	1001	1004	1006	1007	1008	1010	1012	1013	1016	1017	1018	1
39.4	39.4	39.5	39.5	39.5	39.5	39.5	39.5	39.5	39.5	39.5	39.5	39.5	39.5	39.5	39.5	39.5	2
14.2	14.2	14.1	14.1	14.1	14.1	14.1	14.1	14.0	14.0	14.0	14.0	14.0	14.0	13.9	13.9	13.9	3
8.58	8.56	8.53	8.51	8.49	8.48	8.46	8.44	8.41	8.39	8.38	8.36	8.33	8.32	8.29	8.27	8.26	4
6.35	6.33	6.30	6.28	6.26	6.24	6.23	6.20	6.18	6.16	6.14	6.12	6.10	6.08	6.05	6.03	6.02	5
5.19	5.17	5.14	5.12	5.10	5.08	5.07	5.04	5.01	4.99	4.98	4.96	4.93	4.92	4.88	4.86	4.85	6
4.48	4.47	4.44	4.42	4.39	4.38	4.36	4.33	4.31	4.29	4.28	4.25	4.23	4.21	4.18	4.16	4.14	7
4.02	4.00	3.97	3.95	3.93	3.91	3.89	3.86	3.84	3.82	3.81	3.78	3.76	3.74	3.70	3.68	3.67	8
3.68	3.67	3.64	3.61	3.59	3.58	3.56	3.53	3.51	3.49	3.47	3.45	3.42	3.40	3.37	3.35	3.33	9
3.44	3.42	3.39	3.37	3.34	3.33	3.31	3.28	3.26	3.24	3.22	3.20	3.17	3.15	3.12	3.09	3.08	10
3.24	3.23	3.20	3.17	3.15	3.13	3.12	3.09	3.06	3.04	3.03	3.00	2.97	2.96	2.92	2.90	2.88	11
3.09	3.07	3.04	3.02	3.00	2.98	2.96	2.93	2.91	2.89	2.87	2.85	2.82	2.80	2.76	2.74	2.72	12
2.96	2.95	2.92	2.89	2.87	2.85	2.84	2.80	2.78	2.76	2.74	2.72	2.69	2.67	2.63	2.61	2.60	13
2.86	2.84	2.81	2.79	2.77	2.75	2.73	2.70	2.67	2.65	2.64	2.61	2.58	2.56	2.53	2.50	2.49	14
2.77	2.76	2.73	2.70	2.68	2.66	2.64	2.61	2.58	2.56	2.55	2.52	2.49	2.47	2.44	2.41	2.40	15
2.70	2.68	2.65	2.63	2.60	2.58	2.57	2.53	2.51	2.49	2.47	2.45	2.42	2.40	2.36	2.33	2.32	16
2.63	2.62	2.59	2.56	2.54	2.52	2.50	2.47	2.44	2.42	2.41	2.38	2.35	2.33	2.29	2.26	2.25	17
2.58	2.56	2.53	2.50	2.48	2.46	2.44	2.41	2.38	2.36	2.35	2.32	2.29	2.27	2.23	2.20	2.19	18
2.53	2.51	2.48	2.45	2.43	2.41	2.39	2.36	2.33	2.31	2.30	2.27	2.24	2.22	2.18	2.15	2.13	19
2.48	2.46	2.43	2.41	2.39	2.37	2.35	2.31	2.29	2.27	2.25	2.22	2.19	2.17	2.13	2.10	2.09	20
2.44	2.42	2.39	2.37	2.34	2.33	2.31	2.27	2.25	2.23	2.21	2.18	2.15	2.13	2.09	2.06	2.04	21
2.41	2.39	2.36	2.33	2.31	2.29	2.27	2.24	2.21	2.19	2.17	2.14	2.11	2.09	2.05	2.02	2.00	22
2.37	2.36	2.33	2.30	2.28	2.26	2.24	2.20	2.18	2.15	2.14	2.11	2.08	2.06	2.01	1.99	1.97	23
2.35	2.33	2.30	2.27	2.25	2.23	2.21	2.17	2.15	2.12	2.11	2.08	2.05	2.02	1.98	1.95	1.94	24
2.32	2.30	2.27	2.24	2.22	2.20	2.18	2.15	2.12	2.10	2.08	2.05	2.02	2.00	1.95	1.92	1.91	25
2.29	2.28	2.24	2.22	2.19	2.17	2.16	2.12	2.09	2.07	2.05	2.03	1.99	1.97	1.92	1.90	1.88	26
2.27	2.25	2.22	2.19	2.17	2.15	2.13	2.10	2.07	2.05	2.03	2.00	1.97	1.94	1.90	1.87	1.85	27
2.25	2.23	2.20	2.17	2.15	2.13	2.11	2.08	2.05	2.03	2.01	1.98	1.94	1.92	1.88	1.85	1.83	28
2.23	2.21	2.18	2.15	2.13	2.11	2.09	2.06	2.03	2.01	1.99	1.96	1.92	1.90	1.86	1.83	1.81	29
2.21	2.20	2.16	2.14	2.11	2.09	2.07	2.04	2.01	1.99	1.97	1.94	1.90	1.88	1.84	1.81	1.79	30
2.18	2.16	2.13	2.10	2.08	2.06	2.04	2.00	1.98	1.95	1.93	1.91	1.87	1.85	1.80	1.77	1.75	32
2.15	2.13	2.10	2.07	2.05	2.03	2.01	1.97	1.95	1.92	1.90	1.88	1.84	1.82	1.77	1.74	1.72	34
2.13	2.11	2.08	2.05	2.03	2.00	1.99	1.95	1.92	1.90	1.88	1.85	1.81	1.79	1.74	1.71	1.69	36
2.11	2.09	2.05	2.03	2.00	1.98	1.96	1.93	1.90	1.87	1.85	1.82	1.79	1.76	1.71	1.68	1.66	38
2.09	2.07	2.03	2.01	1.98	1.96	1.94	1.90	1.88	1.85	1.83	1.80	1.76	1.74	1.69	1.66	1.64	40
2.07	2.05	2.02	1.99	1.96	1.94	1.92	1.89	1.86	1.83	1.81	1.78	1.74	1.72	1.67	1.64	1.62	42
2.05	2.03	2.00	1.97	1.95	1.93	1.91	1.87	1.84	1.82	1.80	1.77	1.73	1.70	1.65	1.62	1.60	44
2.04	2.02	1.99	1.96	1.93	1.91	1.89	1.85	1.82	1.80	1.78	1.75	1.71	1.69	1.63	1.60	1.58	46
2.02	2.01	1.97	1.94	1.92	1.90	1.88	1.84	1.81	1.79	1.77	1.73	1.69	1.67	1.62	1.58	1.56	48
2.01	1.99	1.96	1.93	1.91	1.88	1.87	1.83	1.80	1.77	1.75	1.72	1.68	1.66	1.60	1.57	1.55	50
1.99	1.97	1.93	1.90	1.88	1.86	1.84	1.80	1.77	1.74	1.72	1.69	1.65	1.62	1.57	1.54	1.51	55
1.96	1.94	1.91	1.88	1.86	1.83	1.82	1.78	1.74	1.72	1.70	1.67	1.62	1.60	1.54	1.51	1.48	60
1.95	1.93	1.89	1.86	1.84	1.82	1.80	1.76	1.72	1.70	1.68	1.65	1.60	1.58	1.52	1.48	1.46	65
1.93	1.91	1.88	1.85	1.82	1.80	1.78	1.74	1.71	1.68	1.66	1.63	1.58	1.56	1.50	1.46	1.44	70
1.90	1.88	1.85	1.82	1.79	1.77	1.75	1.71	1.68	1.65	1.63	1.60	1.55	1.53	1.47	1.43	1.40	80
1.88	1.86	1.83	1.80	1.77	1.75	1.73	1.69	1.66	1.63	1.61	1.58	1.53	1.50	1.44	1.40	1.37	90
1.87	1.85	1.81	1.78	1.76	1.74	1.71	1.67	1.64	1.61	1.59	1.56	1.51	1.48	1.42	1.38	1.35	100
1.84	1.82	1.79	1.75	1.73	1.71	1.68	1.64	1.61	1.58	1.56	1.52	1.48	1.45	1.38	1.34	1.30	125
1.82	1.80	1.77	1.74	1.71	1.69	1.67	1.62	1.59	1.56	1.54	1.50	1.45	1.42	1.35	1.31	1.27	150
1.80	1.78	1.74	1.71	1.68	1.66	1.64	1.60	1.56	1.53	1.51	1.47	1.42	1.39	1.32	1.27	1.23	200
1.77	1.75	1.72	1.69	1.66	1.64	1.62	1.57	1.54	1.51	1.48	1.45	1.39	1.36	1.28	1.23	1.18	300
1.76	1.74	1.70	1.67	1.64	1.62	1.60	1.55	1.51	1.49	1.46	1.42	1.37	1.34	1.25	1.19	1.14	500
1.74	1.72	1.69	1.65	1.63	1.60	1.58	1.54	1.50	1.47	1.44	1.41	1.35	1.32	1.23	1.16	1.09	1000
1.73	1.71	1.67	1.64	1.61	1.59	1.57	1.52	1.48	1.45	1.43	1.39	1.33	1.30	1.21	1.13	1.00	∞

Degrees of freedom for the denominator (n_2)

Approximate formula for n_1 and n_2 larger than 30: $\quad \log_{10} F_{.025;\nu_1,\nu_2} \simeq \dfrac{1.7023}{\sqrt{h - 1.14}} - 0.846\left(\dfrac{1}{n_1} - \dfrac{1}{n_2}\right)$, where $\dfrac{1}{h} = \dfrac{1}{2}\left(\dfrac{1}{n_1} + \dfrac{1}{n_2}\right)$.

TABLE 2C.   Critical Values of the F Distribution, $\alpha = 0.01$.

	Degrees of freedom for the numerator (ν_1)																	
	1	2	3	4	5	6	7	8	9	10	11	12	13	14	15	16	17	18
	Multiply the numbers of the first row $(\nu_1 = 1)$ by 10.																	
1	405	500	540	563	576	586	593	598	602	606	608	611	613	614	616	617	618	619
2	98.5	99.0	99.2	99.2	99.3	99.3	99.4	99.4	99.4	99.4	99.4	99.4	99.4	99.4	99.4	99.4	99.4	99.4
3	34.1	30.8	29.5	28.7	28.2	27.9	27.7	27.5	27.3	27.2	27.1	27.1	27.0	26.9	26.9	26.8	26.8	26.8
4	21.2	18.0	16.7	16.0	15.5	15.2	15.0	14.8	14.7	14.5	14.4	14.4	14.3	14.2	14.2	14.2	14.1	14.1
5	16.3	13.3	12.1	11.4	11.0	10.7	10.5	10.3	10.2	10.1	9.96	9.89	9.82	9.77	9.72	9.68	9.64	9.61
6	13.7	10.9	9.78	9.15	8.75	8.47	8.26	8.10	7.98	7.87	7.79	7.72	7.66	7.60	7.56	7.52	7.48	7.45
7	12.2	9.55	8.45	7.85	7.46	7.19	6.99	6.84	6.72	6.62	6.54	6.47	6.41	6.36	6.31	6.27	6.24	6.21
8	11.3	8.65	7.59	7.01	6.63	6.37	6.18	6.03	5.91	5.81	5.73	5.67	5.61	5.56	5.52	5.48	5.44	5.41
9	10.6	8.02	6.99	6.42	6.06	5.80	5.61	5.47	5.35	5.26	5.18	5.11	5.05	5.00	4.96	4.92	4.89	4.86
10	10.0	7.56	6.55	5.99	5.64	5.39	5.20	5.06	4.94	4.85	4.77	4.71	4.65	4.60	4.56	4.52	4.49	4.46
11	9.65	7.21	6.22	5.67	5.32	5.07	4.89	4.74	4.63	4.54	4.46	4.40	4.34	4.29	4.25	4.21	4.18	4.15
12	9.33	6.93	5.95	5.41	5.06	4.82	4.64	4.50	4.39	4.30	4.22	4.16	4.10	4.05	4.01	3.97	3.94	3.91
13	9.07	6.70	5.74	5.21	4.86	4.62	4.44	4.30	4.19	4.10	4.02	3.96	3.91	3.86	3.82	3.78	3.75	3.72
14	8.86	6.51	5.56	5.04	4.70	4.46	4.28	4.14	4.03	3.94	3.86	3.80	3.75	3.70	3.66	3.62	3.59	3.56
15	8.68	6.36	5.42	4.89	4.56	4.32	4.14	4.00	3.89	3.80	3.73	3.67	3.61	3.56	3.52	3.49	3.45	3.42
16	8.53	6.23	5.29	4.77	4.44	4.20	4.03	3.89	3.78	3.69	3.62	3.55	3.50	3.45	3.41	3.37	3.34	3.31
17	8.40	6.11	5.18	4.67	4.34	4.10	3.93	3.79	3.68	3.59	3.52	3.46	3.40	3.35	3.31	3.27	3.24	3.21
18	8.29	6.01	5.09	4.58	4.25	4.01	3.84	3.71	3.60	3.51	3.43	3.37	3.32	3.27	3.23	3.19	3.16	3.13
19	8.18	5.93	5.01	4.50	4.17	3.94	3.77	3.63	3.52	3.43	3.36	3.30	3.24	3.19	3.15	3.12	3.08	3.05
20	8.10	5.85	4.94	4.43	4.10	3.87	3.70	3.56	3.46	3.37	3.29	3.23	3.18	3.13	3.09	3.05	3.02	2.99
21	8.02	5.78	4.87	4.37	4.04	3.81	3.64	3.51	3.40	3.31	3.24	3.17	3.12	3.07	3.03	2.99	2.96	2.93
22	7.95	5.72	4.82	4.31	3.99	3.76	3.59	3.45	3.35	3.26	3.18	3.12	3.07	3.02	2.98	2.94	2.91	2.88
23	7.88	5.66	4.76	4.26	3.94	3.71	3.54	3.41	3.30	3.21	3.14	3.07	3.02	2.97	2.93	2.89	2.86	2.83
24	7.82	5.61	4.72	4.22	3.90	3.67	3.50	3.36	3.26	3.17	3.09	3.03	2.98	2.93	2.89	2.85	2.82	2.79
25	7.77	5.57	4.68	4.18	3.86	3.63	3.46	3.32	3.22	3.13	3.06	2.99	2.94	2.89	2.85	2.81	2.78	2.75
26	7.72	5.53	4.64	4.14	3.82	3.59	3.42	3.29	3.18	3.09	3.02	2.96	2.90	2.86	2.82	2.78	2.74	2.72
27	7.68	5.49	4.60	4.11	3.78	3.56	3.39	3.26	3.15	3.06	2.99	2.93	2.87	2.82	2.78	2.75	2.71	2.68
28	7.64	5.45	4.57	4.07	3.75	3.53	3.36	3.23	3.12	3.03	2.96	2.90	2.84	2.79	2.75	2.72	2.68	2.65
29	7.60	5.42	4.54	4.04	3.73	3.50	3.33	3.20	3.09	3.00	2.93	2.87	2.81	2.77	2.73	2.69	2.66	2.63
30	7.56	5.39	4.51	4.02	3.70	3.47	3.30	3.17	3.07	2.98	2.91	2.84	2.79	2.74	2.70	2.66	2.63	2.60
32	7.50	5.34	4.46	3.97	3.65	3.43	3.26	3.13	3.02	2.93	2.86	2.80	2.74	2.70	2.66	2.62	2.58	2.55
34	7.44	5.29	4.42	3.93	3.61	3.39	3.22	3.09	2.98	2.89	2.82	2.76	2.70	2.66	2.62	2.58	2.55	2.51
36	7.40	5.25	4.38	3.89	3.57	3.35	3.18	3.05	2.95	2.86	2.79	2.72	2.67	2.62	2.58	2.54	2.51	2.48
38	7.35	5.21	4.34	3.86	3.54	3.32	3.15	3.02	2.92	2.83	2.75	2.69	2.64	2.59	2.55	2.51	2.48	2.45
40	7.31	5.18	4.31	3.83	3.51	3.29	3.12	2.99	2.89	2.80	2.73	2.66	2.61	2.56	2.52	2.48	2.45	2.42
42	7.28	5.15	4.29	3.80	3.49	3.27	3.10	2.97	2.86	2.78	2.70	2.64	2.59	2.54	2.50	2.46	2.43	2.40
44	7.25	5.12	4.26	3.78	3.47	3.24	3.08	2.95	2.84	2.75	2.68	2.62	2.56	2.52	2.47	2.44	2.40	2.37
46	7.22	5.10	4.24	3.76	3.44	3.22	3.06	2.93	2.82	2.73	2.66	2.60	2.54	2.50	2.45	2.42	2.38	2.35
48	7.19	5.08	4.22	3.74	3.43	3.20	3.04	2.91	2.80	2.72	2.64	2.58	2.53	2.48	2.44	2.40	2.37	2.33
50	7.17	5.06	4.20	3.72	3.41	3.19	3.02	2.89	2.79	2.70	2.63	2.56	2.51	2.46	2.42	2.38	2.35	2.32
55	7.12	5.01	4.16	3.68	3.37	3.15	2.98	2.85	2.75	2.66	2.59	2.53	2.47	2.42	2.38	2.34	2.31	2.28
60	7.08	4.98	4.13	3.65	3.34	3.12	2.95	2.82	2.72	2.63	2.56	2.50	2.44	2.39	2.35	2.31	2.28	2.25
65	7.04	4.95	4.10	3.62	3.31	3.09	2.93	2.80	2.69	2.61	2.53	2.47	2.42	2.37	2.33	2.29	2.26	2.23
70	7.01	4.92	4.08	3.60	3.29	3.07	2.91	2.78	2.67	2.59	2.51	2.45	2.40	2.35	2.31	2.27	2.23	2.20
80	6.96	4.88	4.04	3.56	3.26	3.04	2.87	2.74	2.64	2.55	2.48	2.42	2.36	2.31	2.27	2.23	2.20	2.17
90	6.93	4.85	4.01	3.54	3.23	3.01	2.84	2.72	2.61	2.52	2.45	2.39	2.33	2.29	2.24	2.21	2.17	2.14
100	6.90	4.82	3.98	3.51	3.21	2.99	2.82	2.69	2.59	2.50	2.43	2.37	2.31	2.26	2.22	2.19	2.15	2.12
125	6.84	4.78	3.94	3.47	3.17	2.95	2.79	2.66	2.55	2.47	2.39	2.33	2.28	2.23	2.19	2.15	2.11	2.08
150	6.81	4.75	3.92	3.45	3.14	2.92	2.76	2.63	2.53	2.44	2.37	2.31	2.25	2.20	2.16	2.12	2.09	2.06
200	6.76	4.71	3.88	3.41	3.11	2.89	2.73	2.60	2.50	2.41	2.34	2.27	2.22	2.17	2.13	2.09	2.06	2.02
300	6.72	4.68	3.85	3.38	3.08	2.86	2.70	2.57	2.47	2.38	2.31	2.24	2.19	2.14	2.10	2.06	2.03	1.99
500	6.69	4.65	3.82	3.36	3.05	2.84	2.68	2.55	2.44	2.36	2.28	2.22	2.17	2.12	2.07	2.04	2.00	1.97
1000	6.66	4.63	3.80	3.34	3.04	2.82	2.66	2.53	2.43	2.34	2.27	2.20	2.15	2.10	2.06	2.02	1.98	1.95
∞	6.63	4.61	3.78	3.32	3.02	2.80	2.64	2.51	2.41	2.32	2.25	2.18	2.13	2.08	2.04	2.00	1.97	1.93

Degrees of freedom for the denominator (ν_2)

Example: $P\{F_{.01;3;20} < 3.56\} = 99\%$.

$F_{.99;\nu_1,\nu_2} = 1/F_{.01;\nu_2,\nu_1}$.   Example: $F_{.99;3;20} = 1/F_{.01;20;3} = 1/5.36 = 0.187$.

Degrees of freedom for the numerator (n_1)

Multiply the numbers of the first row ($n = 1$) by 10.

19	20	22	24	26	28	30	35	40	45	50	60	80	100	200	500	∞	
620	621	622	623	624	625	626	628	629	630	630	631	633	633	635	636	637	1
99.4	99.4	99.5	99.5	99.5	99.5	99.5	99.5	99.5	99.5	99.5	99.5	99.5	99.5	99.5	99.5	99.5	2
26.7	26.7	26.6	26.6	26.6	26.5	26.5	26.5	26.4	26.4	26.4	26.3	26.3	26.2	26.2	26.1	26.1	3
14.0	14.0	14.0	13.9	13.9	13.9	13.8	13.8	13.7	13.7	13.7	13.7	13.6	13.6	13.5	13.5	13.5	4
9.58	9.55	9.51	9.47	9.43	9.40	9.38	9.33	9.29	9.26	9.24	9.20	9.16	9.13	9.08	9.04	9.02	5
7.42	7.40	7.35	7.31	7.28	7.25	7.23	7.18	7.14	7.11	7.09	7.06	7.01	6.99	6.93	6.90	6.88	6
6.18	6.16	6.11	6.07	6.04	6.02	5.99	5.94	5.91	5.88	5.86	5.82	5.78	5.75	5.70	5.67	5.65	7
5.38	5.36	5.32	5.28	5.25	5.22	5.20	5.15	5.12	5.09	5.07	5.03	4.99	4.96	4.91	4.88	4.86	8
4.83	4.81	4.77	4.73	4.70	4.67	4.65	4.60	4.57	4.54	4.52	4.48	4.44	4.42	4.36	4.33	4.31	9
4.43	4.41	4.36	4.33	4.30	4.27	4.25	4.20	4.17	4.14	4.12	4.08	4.04	4.01	3.96	3.93	3.91	10
4.12	4.10	4.06	4.02	3.99	3.96	3.94	3.89	3.86	3.83	3.81	3.78	3.73	3.71	3.66	3.62	3.60	11
3.88	3.86	3.82	3.78	3.75	3.72	3.70	3.65	3.62	3.59	3.57	3.54	3.49	3.47	3.41	3.38	3.36	12
3.69	3.66	3.62	3.59	3.56	3.53	3.51	3.46	3.43	3.40	3.38	3.34	3.30	3.27	3.22	3.19	3.17	13
3.53	3.51	3.46	3.43	3.40	3.37	3.35	3.30	3.27	3.24	3.22	3.18	3.14	3.11	3.06	3.03	3.00	14
3.40	3.37	3.33	3.29	3.26	3.24	3.21	3.17	3.13	3.10	3.08	3.05	3.00	2.98	2.92	2.89	2.87	15
3.28	3.26	3.22	3.18	3.15	3.12	3.10	3.05	3.02	2.99	2.97	2.93	2.89	2.86	2.81	2.78	2.75	16
3.18	3.16	3.12	3.08	3.05	3.03	3.00	2.96	2.92	2.89	2.87	2.83	2.79	2.76	2.71	2.68	2.65	17
3.10	3.08	3.03	3.00	2.97	2.94	2.92	2.87	2.84	2.81	2.78	2.75	2.70	2.68	2.62	2.59	2.57	18
3.03	3.00	2.96	2.92	2.89	2.87	2.84	2.80	2.76	2.73	2.71	2.67	2.63	2.60	2.55	2.51	2.49	19
2.96	2.94	2.90	2.86	2.83	2.80	2.78	2.73	2.69	2.67	2.64	2.61	2.56	2.54	2.48	2.44	2.42	20
2.90	2.88	2.84	2.80	2.77	2.74	2.72	2.67	2.64	2.61	2.58	2.55	2.50	2.48	2.42	2.38	2.36	21
2.85	2.83	2.78	2.75	2.72	2.69	2.67	2.62	2.58	2.55	2.53	2.50	2.45	2.42	2.36	2.33	2.31	22
2.80	2.78	2.74	2.70	2.67	2.64	2.62	2.57	2.54	2.51	2.48	2.45	2.40	2.37	2.32	2.28	2.26	23
2.76	2.74	2.70	2.66	2.63	2.60	2.58	2.53	2.49	2.46	2.44	2.40	2.36	2.33	2.27	2.24	2.21	24
2.72	2.70	2.66	2.62	2.59	2.56	2.54	2.49	2.45	2.42	2.40	2.36	2.32	2.29	2.23	2.19	2.17	25
2.69	2.66	2.62	2.58	2.55	2.53	2.50	2.45	2.42	2.39	2.36	2.33	2.28	2.25	2.19	2.16	2.13	26
2.66	2.63	2.59	2.55	2.52	2.49	2.47	2.42	2.38	2.35	2.33	2.29	2.25	2.22	2.16	2.12	2.10	27
2.63	2.60	2.56	2.52	2.49	2.46	2.44	2.39	2.35	2.32	2.30	2.26	2.22	2.19	2.13	2.09	2.06	28
2.60	2.57	2.53	2.49	2.46	2.44	2.41	2.36	2.33	2.30	2.27	2.23	2.19	2.16	2.10	2.06	2.03	29
2.57	2.55	2.51	2.47	2.44	2.41	2.39	2.34	2.30	2.27	2.25	2.21	2.16	2.13	2.07	2.03	2.01	30
2.53	2.50	2.46	2.42	2.39	2.36	2.34	2.29	2.25	2.22	2.20	2.16	2.11	2.08	2.02	1.98	1.96	32
2.49	2.46	2.42	2.38	2.35	2.32	2.30	2.25	2.21	2.18	2.16	2.12	2.07	2.04	1.98	1.94	1.91	34
2.45	2.43	2.38	2.35	2.32	2.29	2.26	2.21	2.17	2.14	2.12	2.08	2.03	2.00	1.94	1.90	1.87	36
2.42	2.40	2.35	2.32	2.28	2.26	2.23	2.18	2.14	2.11	2.09	2.05	2.00	1.97	1.90	1.86	1.84	38
2.39	2.37	2.33	2.29	2.26	2.23	2.20	2.15	2.11	2.08	2.06	2.02	1.97	1.94	1.87	1.83	1.80	40
2.37	2.34	2.30	2.26	2.23	2.20	2.18	2.13	2.09	2.06	2.03	1.99	1.94	1.91	1.85	1.80	1.78	42
2.35	2.32	2.28	2.24	2.21	2.18	2.15	2.10	2.06	2.03	2.01	1.97	1.92	1.89	1.82	1.78	1.75	44
2.33	2.30	2.26	2.22	2.19	2.16	2.13	2.08	2.04	2.01	1.99	1.95	1.90	1.86	1.80	1.75	1.73	46
2.31	2.28	2.24	2.20	2.17	2.14	2.12	2.06	2.02	1.99	1.97	1.93	1.88	1.84	1.78	1.73	1.70	48
2.29	2.27	2.22	2.18	2.15	2.12	2.10	2.05	2.01	1.97	1.95	1.91	1.86	1.82	1.76	1.71	1.68	50
2.25	2.23	2.18	2.15	2.11	2.08	2.06	2.01	1.97	1.93	1.91	1.87	1.81	1.78	1.71	1.67	1.64	55
2.22	2.20	2.15	2.12	2.08	2.05	2.03	1.98	1.94	1.90	1.88	1.84	1.78	1.75	1.68	1.63	1.60	60
2.20	2.17	2.13	2.09	2.06	2.03	2.00	1.95	1.91	1.88	1.85	1.81	1.75	1.72	1.65	1.60	1.57	65
2.18	2.15	2.11	2.07	2.03	2.01	1.98	1.93	1.89	1.85	1.83	1.78	1.73	1.70	1.62	1.57	1.54	70
2.14	2.12	2.07	2.03	2.00	1.97	1.94	1.89	1.85	1.81	1.79	1.75	1.69	1.66	1.58	1.53	1.49	80
2.11	2.09	2.04	2.00	1.97	1.94	1.92	1.86	1.82	1.79	1.76	1.72	1.66	1.62	1.54	1.49	1.46	90
2.09	2.07	2.02	1.98	1.94	1.92	1.89	1.84	1.80	1.76	1.73	1.69	1.63	1.60	1.52	1.47	1.43	100
2.05	2.03	1.98	1.94	1.91	1.88	1.85	1.80	1.76	1.72	1.69	1.65	1.59	1.55	1.47	1.41	1.37	125
2.03	2.00	1.96	1.92	1.88	1.85	1.83	1.77	1.73	1.69	1.66	1.62	1.56	1.52	1.43	1.38	1.33	150
2.00	1.97	1.93	1.89	1.85	1.82	1.79	1.74	1.69	1.66	1.63	1.58	1.52	1.48	1.39	1.33	1.28	200
1.97	1.94	1.89	1.85	1.82	1.79	1.76	1.71	1.66	1.62	1.59	1.55	1.48	1.44	1.35	1.28	1.22	300
1.94	1.92	1.87	1.83	1.79	1.76	1.74	1.68	1.63	1.60	1.56	1.52	1.45	1.41	1.31	1.23	1.16	500
1.92	1.90	1.85	1.81	1.77	1.74	1.72	1.66	1.61	1.57	1.54	1.50	1.43	1.38	1.28	1.19	1.11	1000
1.90	1.88	1.83	1.79	1.76	1.72	1.70	1.64	1.59	1.55	1.52	1.47	1.40	1.36	1.25	1.15	1.00	∞

Degrees of freedom for the denominator (n)

Approximate formula for n_1 and n_2 larger than 30: $\quad \log_{10} F_{.01;\nu_1,\nu_2} \simeq \dfrac{2.0206}{\sqrt{h-1.40}} - 1.073\left(\dfrac{1}{\nu} - \dfrac{1}{n_2}\right)$, where $\dfrac{1}{h} = \dfrac{1}{2}\left(\dfrac{1}{n_1} + \dfrac{1}{n_2}\right)$.

TABLE 3A and 3B.   Critical Values of g.

Upper 1 Percentage Points of the Ratio of the Largest to the Sum of k Independent Estimates of Variance, Each of Which is Based on n Observations[1]

k \ n	2	3	4	5	6	7	8	9	10	11	17	37	145	∞
2	0.9999	0.9950	0.9794	0.9586	0.9373	0.9172	0.8988	0.8823	0.8674	0.8539	0.7949	0.7067	0.6062	0.5000
3	0.9933	0.9423	0.8831	0.8335	0.7933	0.7606	0.7335	0.7107	0.6912	0.6743	0.6059	0.5153	0.4230	0.3333
4	0.9676	0.8643	0.7814	0.7212	0.6761	0.6410	0.6129	0.5897	0.5702	0.5536	0.4884	0.4057	0.3251	0.2500
5	0.9279	0.7885	0.6957	0.6329	0.5875	0.5531	0.5259	0.5037	0.4854	0.4697	0.4094	0.3351	0.2644	0.2000
6	0.8828	0.7218	0.6258	0.5635	0.5195	0.4866	0.4608	0.4401	0.4229	0.4084	0.3529	0.2858	0.2229	0.1667
7	0.8376	0.6644	0.5685	0.5080	0.4659	0.4347	0.4105	0.3911	0.3751	0.3616	0.3105	0.2494	0.1929	0.1429
8	0.7945	0.6152	0.5209	0.4627	0.4226	0.3932	0.3704	0.3522	0.3373	0.3248	0.2779	0.2214	0.1700	0.1250
9	0.7544	0.5727	0.4810	0.4251	0.3870	0.3592	0.3378	0.3207	0.3067	0.2950	0.2514	0.1992	0.1521	0.1111
10	0.7175	0.5358	0.4469	0.3934	0.3572	0.3308	0.3106	0.2945	0.2813	0.2704	0.2297	0.1811	0.1376	0.1000
12	0.6528	0.4751	0.3919	0.3428	0.3099	0.2861	0.2680	0.2535	0.2419	0.2320	0.1961	0.1535	0.1157	0.0833
15	0.5747	0.4069	0.3317	0.2882	0.2593	0.2386	0.2228	0.2104	0.2002	0.1918	0.1612	0.1251	0.0934	0.0667
20	0.4799	0.3297	0.2654	0.2288	0.2048	0.1877	0.1748	0.1646	0.1567	0.1501	0.1248	0.0960	0.0709	0.0500
24	0.4247	0.2871	0.2295	0.1970	0.1759	0.1608	0.1495	0.1406	0.1338	0.1283	0.1060	0.0810	0.0595	0.0417
30	0.3632	0.2412	0.1913	0.1635	0.1454	0.1327	0.1232	0.1157	0.1100	0.1054	0.0867	0.0658	0.0480	0.0333
40	0.2940	0.1915	0.1508	0.1281	0.1135	0.1033	0.0957	0.0898	0.0853	0.0816	0.0668	0.0503	0.0363	0.0250
60	0.2151	0.1371	0.1069	0.0902	0.0796	0.0722	0.0668	0.0625	0.0594	0.0567	0.0461	0.0344	0.0245	0.0167
120	0.1225	0.0759	0.0585	0.0489	0.0429	0.0387	0.0357	0.0334	0.0316	0.0302	0.0242	0.0178	0.0125	0.0083
∞	0	0	0	0	0	0	0	0	0	0	0	0	0	0

Upper 5 Percentage Points of the Ratio of the Largest to the Sum of k Independent Estimates of Variance, Each of Which is Based on n Observations[1]

k \ n	2	3	4	5	6	7	8	9	10	11	17	37	145	∞
2	0.9985	0.9750	0.9392	0.9057	0.8772	0.8534	0.8332	0.8159	0.8010	0.7880	0.7341	0.6602	0.5813	0.5000
3	0.9669	0.8709	0.7977	0.7457	0.7071	0.6771	0.6530	0.6333	0.6167	0.6025	0.5466	0.4748	0.4031	0.3333
4	0.9065	0.7679	0.6841	0.6287	0.5895	0.5598	0.5365	0.5175	0.5017	0.4884	0.4366	0.3720	0.3093	0.2500
5	0.8412	0.6838	0.5981	0.5441	0.5065	0.4783	0.4564	0.4387	0.4241	0.4118	0.3645	0.3066	0.2513	0.2000
6	0.7808	0.6161	0.5321	0.4803	0.4447	0.4184	0.3980	0.3817	0.3682	0.3568	0.3135	0.2612	0.2119	0.1667
7	0.7271	0.5612	0.4800	0.4307	0.3974	0.3726	0.3535	0.3384	0.3259	0.3154	0.2756	0.2278	0.1833	0.1429
8	0.6798	0.5157	0.4377	0.3910	0.3595	0.3362	0.3185	0.3043	0.2926	0.2829	0.2462	0.2022	0.1616	0.1250
9	0.6385	0.4775	0.4027	0.3584	0.3286	0.3067	0.2901	0.2768	0.2659	0.2568	0.2226	0.1820	0.1446	0.1111
10	0.6020	0.4450	0.3733	0.3311	0.3029	0.2823	0.2666	0.2541	0.2439	0.2353	0.2032	0.1655	0.1308	0.1000
12	0.5410	0.3924	0.3264	0.2880	0.2624	0.2439	0.2299	0.2187	0.2098	0.2020	0.1737	0.1403	0.1100	0.0833
15	0.4709	0.3346	0.2758	0.2419	0.2195	0.2034	0.1911	0.1815	0.1736	0.1671	0.1429	0.1144	0.0889	0.0667
20	0.3894	0.2705	0.2205	0.1921	0.1735	0.1602	0.1501	0.1422	0.1357	0.1303	0.1108	0.0879	0.0675	0.0500
24	0.3434	0.2354	0.1907	0.1656	0.1493	0.1374	0.1286	0.1216	0.1160	0.1113	0.0942	0.0743	0.0567	0.0417
30	0.2929	0.1980	0.1593	0.1377	0.1237	0.1137	0.1061	0.1002	0.0958	0.0921	0.0771	0.0604	0.0457	0.0333
40	0.2370	0.1576	0.1259	0.1082	0.0968	0.0887	0.0827	0.0780	0.0745	0.0713	0.0595	0.0462	0.0347	0.0250
60	0.1737	0.1131	0.0895	0.0765	0.0682	0.0623	0.0583	0.0552	0.0520	0.0497	0.0411	0.0316	0.0234	0.0167
120	0.0998	0.0632	0.0495	0.0419	0.0371	0.0337	0.0312	0.0292	0.0279	0.0266	0.0218	0.0165	0.0120	0.0083
∞	0	0	0	0	0	0	0	0	0	0	0	0	0	0

[1] From *Techniques of Statistical Analysis*, by C. Eisenhart, M. W. Hastay, W. A. Willis. Copyright 1947. Used with the permission of McGraw-Hill Book Company.

TABLE 4A. Sample Size Required for Probability That s^2 Will Be Less Than $k\sigma^2$.

k	95%	97.5%	99%	99.5%	99.9%
3	3	5	7	8	11
2.5	5	7	10	12	17
2.0	9	12	18	21	31
1.5	27	39	56	69	100
1.25	97	139	197	243	352
1.10	565	807	1,142	1,404	2,026
1.05	2,211	3,151	4,448	5,462	7,872
1.01	54,310	77,180	108,760	133,444	192,050

Sample Size Required for Probability That s Will Be Less Than $k\sigma$

k	95%	97.5%	99%	99.5%	99.9%
3	—	—	2	2	3
2.5	—	2	3	3	4
2	2	3	4	4	7
1.5	6	9	12	15	22
1.25	22	32	45	56	81
1.10	134	193	274	338	488
1.05	538	769	1,089	1,338	1,931
1.01	13,509	19,207	27,078	33,224	47,830

From *Introduction to Statistics* by W. J. Dixon and F. J. Massey, copyright 1969. Used with permission of McGraw-Hill Book Company.

TABLE 5. Critical Values of Student's *t* Distribution

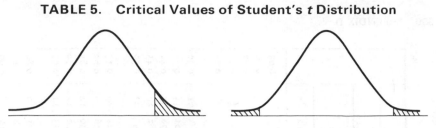

The shaded areas in the figures correspond to the column headings of the table.

	Single-sided test					Double-sided test			
	P					**P**			
DF	0·005	0·01	0·05	0·1	**DF**	0·005	0·01	0·05	0·1
1	63·7	31·8	6·31	3·08	1	127	63·7	12·7	6·31
2	9·92	6·96	2·92	1·89	2	14·1	9·92	4·30	2·92
3	5·84	4·54	2·35	1·64	3	7·45	5·84	3·18	2·35
4	4·60	3·75	2·13	1·53	4	5·60	4·60	2·78	2·13
5	4·03	3·36	2·01	1·48	5	4·77	4·03	2·57	2·01
6	3·71	3·14	1·94	1·44	6	4·32	3·71	2·45	1·94
7	3·50	3·00	1·89	1·42	7	4·03	3·50	2·36	1·89
8	3·36	2·90	1·86	1·40	8	3·83	3·36	2·31	1·86
9	3·25	2·82	1·83	1·38	9	3·69	3·25	2·26	1·83
10	3·17	2·76	1·81	1·37	10	3·58	3·17	2·23	1·81
11	3·11	2·72	1·80	1·36	11	3·50	3·11	2·20	1·80
12	3·05	2·68	1·78	1·36	12	3·43	3·05	2·18	1·78
13	3·01	2·65	1·77	1·35	13	3·37	3·01	2·16	1·77
14	2·98	2·62	1·76	1·34	14	3·33	2·98	2·14	1·76
15	2·95	2·60	1·75	1·34	15	3·29	2·95	2·13	1·75
16	2·92	2·58	1·75	1·34	16	3·25	2·92	2·12	1·75
17	2·90	2·57	1·74	1·33	17	3·22	2·90	2·11	1·74
18	2·88	2·55	1·73	1·33	18	3·20	2·88	2·10	1·73
19	2·86	2·54	1·73	1·33	19	3·17	2·86	2·09	1·73
20	2·85	2·53	1·72	1·32	20	3·15	2·85	2·09	1;72
21	2·83	2·52	1·72	1·32	21	3·14	2·83	2·08	1·72
22	2·82	2·51	1·72	1·32	22	3·12	2·82	2·07	1·72
23	2·81	2·50	1·71	1·32	23	3·10	2·81	2·07	1·71
24	2·80	2·49	1·71	1·32	24	3·09	2·80	2·06	1·71
25	2·79	2·48	1·71	1·32	25	3·08	2·79	2·06	1·71
26	2·78	2·48	1·71	1·32	26	3·07	2·78	2·06	1·71
27	2·77	2·47	1·70	1·31	27	3·06	2·77	2·05	1·70
28	2·76	2·47	1·70	1·31	28	3·05	2·76	2·05	1·70
29	2·76	2·46	1·70	1·31	29	3·04	2·76	2·05	1·70
30	2·75	2·46	1·70	1·31	30	3·03	2·75	2·04	1·70
40	2·70	2·42	1·68	1·30	40	2·97	2·70	2·02	1·68
60	2·66	2·39	1·67	1·30	60	2·91	2·66	2·00	1·67
120	2·62	2·36	1·66	1·29	120	2·86	2·62	1·98	1·66
∞	2·58	2·33	1·64	1·28	∞	2·81	2·58	1·96	1·64

TABLE 6.   Sample Size for t Test of Difference Between Two Means

The entries in this table show the number of observations needed in a t-test of the significance of the difference between two means in order to control the probabilities of the errors of the first and second kinds at α and β respectively.

Level of t-test

Level of t-test →	0·01					0·02					0·05					0·1				
Single-sided test (α =)	0·005					0·01					0·025					0·05				
Double-sided test (α =)	0·01					0·02					0·05					0·1				
Value of $D = \frac{\delta}{\sigma}$ ＼ β =	0·01	0·05	0·1	0·2	0·5	0·01	0·05	0·1	0·2	0·5	0·01	0·05	0·1	0·2	0·5	0·01	0·05	0·1	0·2	0·5
0·05																				
0·10																				
0·15																				
0·20																				137
0·25															124					88
0·30										123					87					61
0·35					110					90					64				102	45
0·40					85					70				100	50			108	78	35
0·45				118	68				101	55			105	79	39		108	86	62	28
0·50				96	55			106	82	45		106	86	64	32		88	70	51	23
0·55			101	79	46		106	88	68	38		87	71	53	27	112	73	58	42	19
0·60		101	85	67	39		90	74	58	32	104	74	60	45	23	89	61	49	36	16
0·65		87	73	57	34	104	77	64	49	27	88	63	51	39	20	76	52	42	30	14
0·70	100	75	63	50	29	90	66	55	43	24	76	55	44	34	17	66	45	36	26	12
0·75	88	66	55	44	26	79	58	48	38	21	67	48	39	29	15	57	40	32	23	11
0·80	77	58	49	39	23	70	51	43	34	19	59	42	34	26	14	50	35	28	21	10
0·85	69	51	43	35	21	62	46	38	31	17	52	37	31	23	12	45	31	25	18	9
0·90	62	46	39	32	19	55	41	34	28	15	47	34	27	21	11	40	28	22	16	8
0·95	55	42	35	29	17	50	37	31	24	14	42	30	25	19	10	36	25	20	15	7
1·00	50	38	32	26	15	45	33	28	22	13	38	27	23	17	9	33	23	18	14	7

1·1		6	12	15	19	27		8	14	19	23	32		11	19	23	28	38	
1·2		5	10	13	16	23		7	12	16	20	27		9	16	20	24	32	
1·3		5	9	11	14	20		6	11	14	17	23		8	14	17	21	28	
1·4		4	8	10	12	17		6	10	12	15	20		8	12	15	18	24	
1·5		4	7	9	11	15		5	9	11	13	18		7	11	14	16	21	
1·6		4	6	8	10	14		5	8	10	12	16		6	10	12	14	19	
1·7		3	6	7	9	12		4	7	9	11	14		6	9	11	13	17	
1·8			5	7	8	11		4	6	8	10	13		5	8	10	12	15	
1·9			5	6	7	10		4	6	7	9	12		5	8	9	11	14	
2·0			4	6	7	9		4	6	7	8	11		5	7	9	10	13	
2·1			4	5	6	8		3	5	6	8	10		5	7	8	9	12	
2·2			4	5	6	8			5	6	7	9		4	6	7	9	11	
2·3			4	5	5	7			5	6	7	9		4	6	7	8	10	
2·4			4	4	5	7			4	5	6	8		4	6	6	8	10	
2·5			3	4	5	6			4	5	6	8		4	5	6	7	9	
3·0				3	4	5			4	4	5	6		3	4	5	6	7	
3·5					3	4			3	4	4	5			4	4	5	6	
4·0						4				3	4	4			3	4	4	5	

Adapted from *Research*, 1, pp. 520–525 (1948) by permission of Butterworth Group, London, England.

TABLE 7.   Test for Outliers

	CRITICAL VALUES FOR R		
	SIGNIFICANCE LEVEL		
NUMBER OF VALUES IN SET	90%	95%	99%
3	0.886	0.941	0.988
4	0.679	0.765	0.889
5	0.557	0.642	0.780
6	0.482	0.560	0.698
7	0.434	0.507	0.637
8	0.479	0.554	0.683
9	0.441	0.512	0.635
10	0.409	0.477	0.597
11	0.517	0.576	0.679
12	0.490	0.546	0.642
13	0.467	0.521	0.615

Adapted from W. J. Dixon, "Processing Data for Outliers," *Biometrics*, Vol. 9, No. 1, 74–89, 1953, by permission of Biometric Society, Washington, D.C. 20005.

TABLE 8.   Critical Values of Correlation Coefficient, *r*

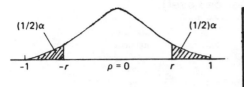

DF \ α	0.10	0.05	0.02	0.01
1	0.988	0.997	1.000	1.000
2	0.900	0.950	0.980	0.990
3	0.805	0.878	0.934	0.959
4	0.729	0.811	0.882	0.917
5	0.669	0.754	0.833	0.874
6	0.622	0.707	0.789	0.834
7	0.582	0.666	0.750	0.798
8	0.549	0.632	0.716	0.765
9	0.521	0.602	0.685	0.735
10	0.497	0.576	0.658	0.708
11	0.476	0.553	0.634	0.684
12	0.458	0.532	0.612	0.661
13	0.441	0.514	0.592	0.641
14	0.426	0.497	0.574	0.623
15	0.412	0.482	0.558	0.606
16	0.400	0.468	0.542	0.590
17	0.389	0.456	0.528	0.575
18	0.378	0.444	0.516	0.561
19	0.369	0.433	0.503	0.549
20	0.360	0.423	0.492	0.537
25	0.323	0.381	0.445	0.487
30	0.296	0.349	0.409	0.449
35	0.275	0.325	0.381	0.418
40	0.257	0.304	0.358	0.393
45	0.243	0.288	0.338	0.372
50	0.231	0.273	0.322	0.354
60	0.211	0.250	0.295	0.325
70	0.195	0.232	0.274	0.302
80	0.183	0.217	0.256	0.283
90	0.173	0.205	0.242	0.267
100	0.164	0.195	0.230	0.254

From E. S. Pearson and H. O. Hartley, *Biometrika Tables for Statisticians*, Vol. 1, p. 138 (1962). Reprinted by permission of the Biometrika Trustees.

TABLE 9. Factors for Calculating Range of Two Results (95% Confidence Level).

DEGREES OF FREEDOM	FACTOR	DEGREES OF FREEDOM	FACTOR	DEGREES OF FREEDOM	FACTOR
1	17.97	13	3.05	25	2.91
2	6.08	14	3.03	26	2.91
3	4.50	15	3.01	27	2.90
4	3.92	16	3.00	28	2.90
5	3.64	17	2.98	29	2.89
6	3.46	18	2.97	30	2.89
7	3.34	19	2.96	40	2.86
8	3.26	20	2.95	50	2.84
9	3.20	21	2.94	60	2.83
10	3.15	22	2.93	120	2.80
11	3.11	23	2.93	∞	2.77
12	3.08	24	2.92		

TABLE 10A. Duncan's Significant Ranges, 5% Level

Significant Studentized Ranges for a 5% Level New[1] Multiple Range Test

DF \ p	2	3	4	5	6	7	8	9	10	12	14	16	18	20	50	100
1	18.0	18.0	18.0	18.0	18.0	18.0	18.0	18.0	18.0	18.0	18.0	18.0	18.0	18.0	18.0	18.0
2	6.09	6.09	6.09	6.09	6.09	6.09	6.09	6.09	6.09	6.09	6.09	6.09	6.09	6.09	6.09	6.09
3	4.50	4.50	4.50	4.50	4.50	4.50	4.50	4.50	4.50	4.50	4.50	4.50	4.50	4.50	4.50	4.50
4	3.93	4.01	4.02	4.02	4.02	4.02	4.02	4.02	4.02	4.02	4.02	4.02	4.02	4.02	4.02	4.02
5	3.64	3.74	3.79	3.83	3.83	3.83	3.83	3.83	3.83	3.83	3.83	3.83	3.83	3.83	3.83	3.83
6	3.46	3.58	3.64	3.68	3.68	3.68	3.68	3.68	3.68	3.68	3.68	3.68	3.68	3.68	3.68	3.68
7	3.35	3.47	3.54	3.58	3.60	3.61	3.61	3.61	3.61	3.61	3.61	3.61	3.61	3.61	3.61	3.61
8	3.26	3.39	3.47	3.52	3.55	3.56	3.56	3.56	3.56	3.56	3.56	3.56	3.56	3.56	3.56	3.56
9	3.20	3.34	3.41	3.47	3.50	3.52	3.52	3.52	3.52	3.52	3.52	3.52	3.52	3.52	3.52	3.52
10	3.15	3.30	3.37	3.43	3.46	3.47	3.47	3.47	3.47	3.47	3.47	3.47	3.47	3.48	3.48	3.48
11	3.11	3.27	3.35	3.39	3.43	3.44	3.45	3.46	3.46	3.46	3.46	3.46	3.47	3.48	3.48	3.48
12	3.08	3.23	3.33	3.36	3.40	3.42	3.44	3.44	3.46	3.46	3.46	3.46	3.47	3.48	3.48	3.48
13	3.06	3.21	3.30	3.35	3.38	3.41	3.42	3.44	3.45	3.45	3.46	3.46	3.47	3.47	3.47	3.47
14	3.03	3.18	3.27	3.33	3.37	3.39	3.41	3.42	3.44	3.45	3.46	3.46	3.47	3.47	3.47	3.47
15	3.01	3.16	3.25	3.31	3.36	3.38	3.40	3.42	3.43	3.44	3.45	3.46	3.47	3.47	3.47	3.47
16	3.00	3.15	3.23	3.30	3.34	3.37	3.39	3.41	3.43	3.44	3.45	3.46	3.47	3.47	3.47	3.47
17	2.98	3.13	3.22	3.28	3.33	3.36	3.38	3.40	3.42	3.44	3.45	3.46	3.47	3.47	3.47	3.47
18	2.97	3.12	3.21	3.27	3.32	3.35	3.37	3.39	3.41	3.43	3.45	3.46	3.47	3.47	3.47	3.47
19	2.96	3.11	3.19	3.26	3.31	3.35	3.37	3.39	3.41	3.43	3.44	3.46	3.47	3.47	3.47	3.47
20	2.95	3.10	3.18	3.25	3.30	3.34	3.36	3.38	3.40	3.43	3.44	3.46	3.47	3.47	3.47	3.47
22	2.93	3.08	3.17	3.24	3.29	3.32	3.35	3.37	3.39	3.42	3.44	3.45	3.46	3.47	3.47	3.47
24	2.92	3.07	3.15	3.22	3.28	3.31	3.34	3.37	3.38	3.41	3.44	3.45	3.46	3.47	3.47	3.47
26	2.91	3.06	3.14	3.21	3.27	3.30	3.34	3.36	3.38	3.41	3.43	3.45	3.46	3.47	3.47	3.47
28	2.90	3.04	3.13	3.20	3.26	3.30	3.33	3.35	3.37	3.40	3.43	3.45	3.46	3.47	3.47	3.47
30	2.89	3.04	3.12	3.20	3.25	3.29	3.32	3.35	3.37	3.40	3.43	3.44	3.46	3.47	3.47	3.47
40	2.86	3.01	3.10	3.17	3.22	3.27	3.30	3.33	3.35	3.39	3.42	3.44	3.46	3.47	3.47	3.47
60	2.83	2.98	3.08	3.14	3.20	3.24	3.28	3.31	3.33	3.37	3.40	3.43	3.45	3.47	3.48	3.48
100	2.80	2.95	3.05	3.12	3.18	3.22	3.26	3.29	3.32	3.36	3.40	3.42	3.45	3.47	3.53	3.53
∞	2.77	2.92	3.02	3.09	3.15	3.19	3.23	3.26	3.29	3.34	3.38	3.41	3.44	3.47	3.61	3.67

[1] Using special protection levels based on degrees of freedom.

Reprinted from *Biometrics*, Vol. 11, No. 1 (1955), Tables II and III by permission of Biometric Society, Washington, D.C.

TABLE 10B. Duncan's Significant Ranges, 1% Level

Significant Ranges for a 1% Level New[1] Multiple Range Test

DF \ P	2	3	4	5	6	7	8	9	10	12	14	16	18	20	50	100
1	90.0	90.0	90.0	90.0	90.0	90.0	90.0	90.0	90.0	90.0	90.0	90.0	90.0	90.0	90.0	90.0
2	14.0	14.0	14.0	14.0	14.0	14.0	14.0	14.0	14.0	14.0	14.0	14.0	14.0	14.0	14.0	14.0
3	8.26	8.5	8.6	8.7	8.8	8.9	8.9	9.0	9.0	9.0	9.1	9.2	9.3	9.3	9.3	9.3
4	6.51	6.8	6.9	7.0	7.1	7.1	7.2	7.2	7.3	7.3	7.4	7.4	7.5	7.5	7.5	7.5
5	5.70	5.96	6.11	6.18	6.26	6.33	6.40	6.44	6.5	6.6	6.6	6.7	6.7	6.8	6.8	6.8
6	5.24	5.51	5.65	5.73	5.81	5.88	5.95	6.00	6.0	6.1	6.2	6.2	6.3	6.3	6.3	6.3
7	4.95	5.22	5.37	5.45	5.53	5.61	5.69	5.73	5.8	5.8	5.9	5.9	6.0	6.0	6.0	6.0
8	4.74	5.00	5.14	5.23	5.32	5.40	5.47	5.51	5.5	5.6	5.7	5.7	5.8	5.8	5.8	5.8
9	4.60	4.86	4.99	5.08	5.17	5.25	5.32	5.36	5.4	5.5	5.5	5.6	5.7	5.7	5.7	5.7
10	4.48	4.73	4.88	4.96	5.06	5.13	5.20	5.24	5.28	5.36	5.42	5.48	5.54	5.55	5.55	5.55
11	4.39	4.63	4.77	4.86	4.94	5.01	5.06	5.12	5.15	5.24	5.28	5.34	5.38	5.39	5.39	5.39
12	4.32	4.55	4.68	4.76	4.84	4.92	4.96	5.02	5.07	5.13	5.17	5.22	5.24	5.26	5.26	5.26
13	4.26	4.48	4.62	4.69	4.74	4.84	4.88	4.94	4.98	5.04	5.08	5.13	5.14	5.15	5.15	5.15
14	4.21	4.42	4.55	4.63	4.70	4.78	4.83	4.87	4.91	4.96	5.00	5.04	5.06	5.07	5.07	5.07
15	4.17	4.37	4.50	4.58	4.64	4.72	4.77	4.81	4.84	4.90	4.94	4.97	4.99	5.00	5.00	5.00
16	4.13	4.34	4.45	4.54	4.60	4.67	4.72	4.76	4.79	4.84	4.88	4.91	4.93	4.94	4.94	4.94
17	4.10	4.30	4.41	4.50	4.56	4.63	4.68	4.73	4.75	4.80	4.83	4.86	4.88	4.89	4.89	4.89
18	4.07	4.27	4.38	4.46	4.53	4.59	4.64	4.68	4.71	4.76	4.79	4.82	4.84	4.85	4.85	4.85
19	4.05	4.24	4.35	4.43	4.50	4.56	4.61	4.64	4.67	4.72	4.76	4.79	4.81	4.82	4.82	4.82
20	4.02	4.22	4.33	4.40	4.47	4.53	4.58	4.61	4.65	4.69	4.73	4.76	4.78	4.79	4.79	4.79
22	3.99	4.17	4.28	4.36	4.42	4.48	4.53	4.57	4.60	4.65	4.68	4.71	4.74	4.75	4.75	4.75
24	3.96	4.14	4.24	4.33	4.39	4.44	4.49	4.53	4.57	4.62	4.64	4.67	4.70	4.72	4.74	4.74
26	3.93	4.11	4.21	4.30	4.36	4.41	4.46	4.50	4.53	4.58	4.62	4.65	4.67	4.69	4.73	4.73
28	3.91	4.08	4.18	4.28	4.34	4.39	4.43	4.47	4.51	4.56	4.60	4.62	4.65	4.67	4.72	4.72
30	3.89	4.06	4.16	4.22	4.32	4.36	4.41	4.45	4.48	4.54	4.58	4.61	4.63	4.65	4.71	4.72
40	3.82	3.99	4.10	4.17	4.24	4.30	4.34	4.37	4.41	4.46	4.51	4.54	4.57	4.59	4.69	4.69
60	3.76	3.92	4.03	4.12	4.17	4.23	4.27	4.31	4.34	4.39	4.44	4.47	4.50	4.53	4.66	4.66
100	3.71	3.86	3.98	4.06	4.11	4.17	4.21	4.25	4.29	4.35	4.38	4.42	4.45	4.48	4.64	4.65
∞	3.64	3.80	3.90	3.98	4.04	4.09	4.14	4.17	4.20	4.26	4.31	4.34	4.38	4.41	4.60	4.68

[1] Using special protection levels based on degrees of freedom.
Reprinted from *Biometrics*, Vol. 11, No. 1 (1955), Tables II and III by permission of Biometric Society, Washington, D.C.

TABLE 11.   Runs Test, 5% Level

n_1	n_2	No. of runs		n_1	n_2	No. of runs	
2	2–11	—	—	10	16–18	8	19
2	12–20	2	—	10	19	8	20
3	3–5	—	—	10	20	9	20
3	6–14	2	—	11	11	7	17
3	15–20	3	—	11	12	7	18
4	4	—	—	11	13	7	19
4	5–6	2	9	11	14–15	8	19
4	7	2	—	11	16	8	20
4	8–15	3	—	11	17–18	9	20
4	16–20	4	—	11	19–20	9	21
5	5	2	10	12	12	7	19
5	6	3	10	12	13	8	19
5	7–8	3	11	12	14–15	8	20
5	9–10	3	—	12	16–18	9	21
5	11–17	4	—	12	19–20	10	22
5	18–20	5	—	13	13	8	20
6	6	3	11	13	14	9	20
6	7–8	3	12	13	15–16	9	21
6	9–12	4	13	13	17–18	10	22
6	13–18	5	—	13	19–20	10	23
6	19–20	6	—	14	14	9	21
7	7	3	13	14	15	9	22
7	8	4	13	14	16	10	22
7	9	4	14	14	17–18	10	23
7	10–12	5	14	14	19	11	23
7	13–14	5	15	14	20	11	24
7	15	6	15	15	15	10	22
7	16–20	6	—	15	16	10	23
8	8	4	14	15	17	11	23
8	9	5	14	15	18–19	11	24
8	10–11	5	15	15	20	12	25
8	12–15	6	16	16	16	11	23
8	16	6	17	16	17	11	24
8	17–20	7	17	16	18	11	25
9	9	5	15	16	19–20	12	25
9	10	5	16	17	17	11	25
9	11–12	6	16	17	18	12	25
9	13	6	17	17	19	12	26
9	14	7	17	17	20	13	26
9	15–17	7	18	18	18	12	26
9	18–20	8	18	18	19	13	26
10	10	6	16	18	20	13	27
10	11	6	17	19	19–20	13	27
10	12	7	17	20	20	14	28
10	13–15	7	18				

Adapted from F. Swed and C. Eisenhart, *Annals of Mathematical Statistics*, pp. 83–86, 1943, by permission of the Institute for Mathematical Statistics, Hayward, CA.

TABLE 12. Factors for Calculating Standard Deviation from Range.

NUMBER OF VALUE IN DATA SET	d_2
2	1.128
3	1.693
4	2.059
5	2.324
6	2.543
7	2.704
8	2.847
9	2.970
10	3.078
11	3.173
12	3.258
13	3.336
14	3.407
15	3.472

From Egon Pearson, *Biometrika*, Vol. 24, 416, Table A, 1932. By permission of Biometrika Trust, London, England.

TABLE 13. Main Effects and Interactions in up to a 2^4 Factorial Design

Effects

Treatment Combinations	T	A	B	AB	C	AC	BC	ABC	D	AD	BD	ABD	CD	ACD	BCD	ABCD
(1)	+	−	−	+	−	+	+	−	−	+	+	−	+	−	−	+
a	+	+	−	−	−	−	+	+	−	−	+	+	+	+	−	−
b	+	−	+	−	−	+	−	+	−	+	−	+	+	−	+	−
ab	+	+	+	+	−	−	−	−	−	−	−	−	+	+	+	+
c	+	−	−	+	+	−	−	+	−	+	+	−	−	+	+	−
ac	+	+	−	−	+	+	−	−	−	−	+	+	−	−	+	+
bc	+	−	+	−	+	−	+	−	−	+	−	+	−	+	−	+
abc	+	+	+	+	+	+	+	+	−	−	−	−	−	−	−	−
d	+	−	−	+	−	+	+	−	+	−	−	+	−	+	+	−
ad	+	+	−	−	−	−	+	+	+	+	−	−	−	−	+	+
bd	+	−	+	−	−	+	−	+	+	−	+	−	−	+	−	+
abd	+	+	+	+	−	−	−	−	+	+	+	+	−	−	−	−
cd	+	−	−	+	+	−	−	+	+	−	−	+	+	−	−	+
acd	+	+	−	−	+	+	−	−	+	+	−	−	+	+	−	−
bcd	+	−	+	−	+	−	+	−	+	−	+	−	+	−	+	−
abcd	+	+	+	+	+	+	+	+	+	+	+	+	+	+	+	+

2^2 2^3 2^4

INDEX

INDEX

Abbreviations, table of, 311–312
Accuracy, defined, 5, 245
Alternative hypothesis, 52, 69
Analysis of variance (ANOVA), 122–139,
        140–157, 158–179, 180–190,
        191–203
    factorial design, 180–190
    four independent variables, 180–190
    four-way classification, 180–190
    general analysis of a nested design,
        201–202
    interpretation of mean squares when
        interaction not significant, 156
    Latin square design, 174–179
    nested designs
        fixed effects model, 201–202
        mixed effects model, 201–202
        random effects model, 193–201
    nested experimental designs, 191–203
    one independent variable, 128–138
    one-way classification, 128–135
    one-way classification with unequal
        observations per average, 135–138
    three independent variables, 158–179
    three-way classification, 158–179
        fixed effects model, 165–169
        mixed effects model, 165–169
        random effects model, 169–174
    two independent variables, 140–157
    2^4 factorial design, 180–190
        with replicate observations, 186–190
    two-way classification, 140–157
        fixed effects model, 148–149
        interaction not significant, 156
        mixed effects model, 149–150
        n observations per combination,
            150–156
        no replicates, 144–146
        random effects model, 147–148
Answers to problems, 263–286
Average(s)
    comparison of two. See t test
    comparison of more than two. Duncan's
        procedure, 85–87. See also
        Analysis of variance

comparison with a theoretical value,
        70–72
    confidence interval, 83–84
    defined, 6–7
    deviation, defined, 246
    range of values expected, 84–85

Bartlett test, homogeneity of variances,
        63–65
Bias, defined, 5, 245

Calculations
    effect of significant figures in, 12–14
    number of significant figures to use,
        11–12
Calculators, use of, 9–10
Calibration curves, 89–107, 214–226
Calibration equation, 97–99, 216–218
    cautions in use of, 100, 241–242
    coding of X and Y values, 219–221
    confidence interval
        for intercept and slope, 99–100,
            224–225
        for X predicted from Y, 102
        for an individual, y, 101, 224
        for y, 100–101, 106, 223–224
    curve forced through origin, 104–107,
        218–219
    confidence interval
        for individual value of y, 106–107
        for slope, 104–105
        for x predicted from Y, 107
        for y, 106
    evaluation of using
        analysis of residuals, 236–241
        analysis of variance, 227–230
        analysis of variance, n replicates,
            230–236
        point estimate for average Y, 100
            when curve forced through origin,
                105–106
        test for significance of relationship,
            102–103,
            when curve forced through origin, 107
        test for zero intercept, 103
        test for zero slope, 102–103

Cause-and-effect relationship, 119, 242
Chi square
    critical values table, 287
    defined, 48, 245
Cochran test, homogeneity of variances,
        62–63
Coding of data, 15–17, 219–221
Coefficient of determination, 120, 225, 245
Coefficient of variation
    defined, 42, 245
    pooling of, 44–45
    when used, 42–43
Cofactor, 210
Comparison of more than two averages.
        See Analysis of variance;
        Duncan's procedure
Comparison of two averages. *See* t test
Comparison of two variances, F test, 56–59
Computer programs, 10–11
    list of examples, 18
Computers, use of, 10–11
Confidence interval (or limits), defined,
        8–9, 48, 245
Confidence level, defined, 245
Confidence range, defined, 8–9, 48
Correction factor, 126
Correlation coefficient, 118–120, 225, 245
    cautions in use of, 119, 225
Critical values, tables of
    for Chi square, 287
    for F, 289–295
    for g (Cochran test), 296–297
    for r (correlation coefficient), 303
    for R (test for outliers), 302
    for runs test, 307
    for t, 299
Crossed experimental design. *See* Experi-
        mental design, factorial.

Data
    coding of, 15–17, 219–221
    transformation of, 27–31, 93
Definitions
    glossary, 245–248
    matrix algebra terms, 205–207
    See also individual term
Degrees of freedom, defined, 41, 246
Dependent averages, 72–73
Design of experiments, 4–5
Determinant of a matrix, 209–210
Diagonal matrix, defined, 206
Dimension of a matrix, defined, 206

Distribution
    bell-shaped, 21
    binomial, 23
    Chi square, 48–50
        critical values table, 287
    F, 54–56
        critical values table, 289–295
    g, critical values table, 296–297
    Gaussian, 21
    lognormal, 28
    normal, 21
        test for, 23–24
    Poisson, 23
    skewed, 26–27
    t, 70–71
        critical values table, 299
Duncan's procedure, separation of means,
        85–87
Duplicability, defined, 247

Elements of a matrix, defined, 206
Equality of matrices, defined, 207
Error
    defined, 246
    random, defined, 247
    type I, 53, 68, 83, 246
    type II, 53, 68, 83, 246
Expected mean squares, 130, 146–147,
        166–168, 202
Experimental design. *See* Design of
        experiments
    crossed, *See* Experimental design,
        factorial
    factorial, 122–139, 140–157, 158–179,
        180–190
    hierarchical, 191–203
    nested, 191–203

F test, 56–59, 246
Factorial experimental design, 2^4, 180–190
Factors for standard deviation from range,
        308
Fixed effects, defined, 143

Gaussian distribution, 21
Geometric mean, defined, 30
Guide to selection of statistical tests,
        313–314

Hierarchical experimental design, 191–203
Homogeneity of variances. *See* F test;
        Bartlett test; Cochran test

defined, 246
Hypothesis
    alternative, 52, 68–69, 246
    null, 51–52, 68, 246
    testing, philosophy of, 51–54

Identity matrix, 207
Independent averages, 72–73
Interaction, defined, 141
Inverse of a matrix, 210–213

Least squares technique, 92
Level of significance, 49
Linear correlation coefficient. *See*
        correlation coefficient
Linear regression. *See* Linear relationships,
        two variables,
Linear relationships, two variables, 89–120,
        204–226, 227–243
    association relationship, 108–118
    calibration curves using matrix algebra,
        214–226, 227–243
    correlation coefficient, 118–120, 225
    functional relationship, 94–107
    using matrix algebra, 204–226, 227–243

Main effects and interactions table, up to 2^4
        factorial, 309
Matrix
    defined, 205
    multiplication, 207–209
Matrix algebra
    application to calibration curves,
        214–226
    coding values for greater accuracy,
        219–221
    operations, 207–214
    principles of, 205–214
    terms, defined, 205–207
Mean
    defined, 6–7, 246
    deviation, defined, 246
    square, 127
Median, defined, 7, 246
Mixed effects, defined, 144
Mode, defined, 7, 246

Nested experimental design, 191–203
Nonparametric tests, 20
Normal distribution, 21, 246
Null hypothesis, 51–52, 68, 246

Observation, defined, 247
Outliers
    defined, 247
    test for, 31–32

Paired data, 78–83
Parameter, defined, 3, 247
Philosophy of statistical testing, 51–54
Pooling of variances, 44–45, 247
Population, defined, 247–248
Precision, defined, 5, 247
Problems, 249–261

Random effects, defined, 143
Random error, defined, 247
Randomness, runs test for, 25–26
Range, defined, 247
Range of two results, 84–85
    factors for, 304
Regression (linear) equation for two variables
    assumptions, 95
        test of, 236–241
    calculation of
        for functional relationships, 97–98
        for association relationships, 111–112
    cautions in use of, 100
    coding of X and Y values, 219–221
    confidence interval
        for intercept and slope, 99–100
            224–225
        for X predicted from Y, 102
        for an individual y, 101, 224
        for y, 100–101, 223–224
    curve forced through origin, 104–107,
        218–219
        confidence interval
            for individual value of y, 106–107
            for slope, 104–105
            for x predicted from Y, 107
            for y, 108
    test for intercept equal zero, 103
    test for significance of relationship
            between variables, 102–103
        when curve forced through origin, 107
    test for zero slope, 102–103
Repeatability, defined, 247
Reproducibility, defined, 247
Residuals, defined, 236
Rounding, rules for, 14–15
Runs test for randomness, 25–26

Sample size
  for t test, 83, 300–301
  in estimating standard deviation and
      variance, 44, 298
Scalar
  defined, 206
  multiplication by, 207
Selection of statistical tests, guide to,
      313–314
Significant differences
  practical, 59–60
  statistical, 59–60
Significant figures, 11–12
  effect on results, 12–14
Significant ranges table, Duncan's procedure
      for separation of means, 305–306
Standard deviation
  calculation of from range, 41–42
      factors for, 308
  defined, 40, 248
  when to use, 42–43
Standard error, 248
  of estimate, 228
Statistic, defined, 3, 247
Statistical testing, philosophy of, 51–54
Statistical tests
  assumptions, 20, 236
  guide to selection of, 313–314
Statistics, defined, 1
Student's t test. *See* t test
Sum of squares, 126–127
Symbols, table of, 311–312
Symmetric matrix, defined, 207

t test
  defined, 248

discussion of, 67–83
  for paired data, 78–83
  for a theoretical value, 70–72
  for two dependent averages, 78–83
  for two independent averages
      with variances known, 73–74
      with variances unknown and equal,
          74–76
      with variances unknown and unequal,
          76–78
  sample size for, 83
Test of significance
  one-tailed, 52, 69–70
  two-tailed, 52, 69–70
Transformation of data, 27–31, 93
Transpose of a matrix, defined, 206
2^4 Factorial experimental design, 180–190

Universe, defined, 248

Variance
  comparison of two using F test, 56–59
  comparison with a reference value, 60–61
  confidence interval of, 47–50
  defined, 36, 248
  effect of skewed distribution on, 26–27
  equation for, 36–37
  homogeneity of. *See* F test; Bartlett
      test; Cochran test
  required sample size, 44
Variances
  comparison of more than two, 61–65
      Bartlett test, 63–65
      Cochran test, 62–63
  pooling of, 44–45, 247
Vector, defined, 206

Some Frequently Used Symbols and Abbreviations

α (Greek lower case alpha) level of significance; probability of type I error.

$\mathbf{a}$ vector a

A intercept in equation for regression line

$\mathbf{A}$ matrix $\mathbf{A}$

$|\mathbf{A}|$ determinant of matrix $\mathbf{A}$

$\mathbf{A}^{-1}$ inverse of matrix $\mathbf{A}$

β (Greek lower case beta) level of significance associated with type II error

B slope in equation for regression line

χ^2 (Greek upper case chi) read as chi-square; a statistic whose uses include the calculation of confidence intervals for variances

CI   confidence interval

C.V.   coefficient of variation

d difference between two observations

DF   degrees of freedom

F a statistic used to compare two variances

g Cochran test statistic used to compare more than two variances with equal degrees of freedom

H_A alternative hypothesis

H_0 null hypothesis

ln   natural logarithm

log   common logarithm (base 10)

μ (Greek lower case mu) population average or mean

n number of observations in a set of data

NS   used to identify a statistical test result which is not significant

ρ (Greek lower case rho) population linear correlation coefficient

r experimentally determined linear correlation coefficient

$\sum$ (Greek upper case sigma) summation sign

σ (Greek lower case sigma) population standard deviation

σ^2 population variance

s experimentally determined standard deviation

s^2 experimentally determined variance

s_P pooled standard deviation

$s_{Y \cdot X}$ standard deviation for regression of Y on X

SS   sum of squares

t Student's t statistic used in comparing two averages

T grand total of observations in a data set

T_c column total